THE GREAT BOOK OF
SEAFOOD
COOKING

Giuliana Bonomo

THE GREAT BOOK OF
SEAFOOD
COOKING

Photographs by Riccardo Marcialis

SIMON & SCHUSTER

LONDON·SYDNEY·NEW YORK·TOKYO·SINGAPORE·TORONTO

Cutlery, ceramics, china and table linen kindly supplied by Christofle, Frette, Koivú, Messulam and Sambonet.
The publishers wish to thank Dott. Renato Malandra and the Pescheria Venezia, Milan, Italy.

Translated by Sara Harris

This edition published 1992 by Simon & Schuster Ltd
West Garden Place
Kendal Street
London W2 2AQ

A Paramount Communications Company

A CIP catalogue for this book is available from the British Library

ISBN 0-671-71156-3

Typeset by Tradespools Ltd, Frome, Somerset
Printed and bound in Italy by Arnoldo Mondadori
Editore, Verona, Italy

·Contents·

All recipes serve 4, unless otherwise indicated.

Measures are given in imperial and metric. Use one or other system and do not combine the two in the same recipe.

·INTRODUCTION·

Fish, molluscs and crustaceans are the three basic foods grouped under the general heading of seafood and freshwater fish. Their variety is remarkable and many of us will inevitably have tasted only a very small proportion of them. This book includes both classic recipes and many new ways of cooking familiar fish. It also introduces a number of unusual ocean and freshwater fish to the cook who wishes to serve something delicious and different to family and guests. With a good fish market or fishmonger within reach you could easily sample a different type of fish, mollusc or crustacean every day of the year.

Despite this wide choice, sadly much depleted in some parts of the world through over-fishing and pollution, we eat much less per head each year than, for example, the French, who average 53 lb (24 kg) each, or the Japanese, who consume a staggering yearly average of no less than 80 lb (36 kg) per head.

Cost cannot be considered a valid reason for this comparatively low consumption: it is not difficult to find plenty of reasonably priced fresh fish, although a few fish varieties and molluscs and shellfish may be too expensive to serve as everyday food or for large family meals. Fish is a wonderful, healthy source of protein, minerals and vital trace elements, low in cholesterol and very digestible, but it has acquired an undeserved reputation for being complicated to prepare. Those who shop in supermarkets where fish is not often absolutely fresh may also gain a false impression from the tired, pre-packaged offerings in refrigerated display cabinets and from a succession of depressing slabs of deep-frozen, pre-breaded fish cutlets, ready to be fried and then drowned in tomato ketchup or over-sharp commercially prepared tartare sauce.

It takes just a little enthusiasm and very little effort to buy and prepare good seafood or freshwater fish, and the result may be a revelation to you. The aim of this book is to provide fresh inspiration for enthusiasts and to convert many more home cooks to the delights of fish cookery. For the latter our colour illustrations identifying the different types of fish will be of great help, as will the advice given at the beginning of each section on what to look for when checking on freshness and quality. The step-by-step illustrations will show you how to gut, clean and fillet fish and how to prepare shellfish or molluscs; the clear and simple instructions given with each recipe will guide you easily through the subsequent preparation and cooking processes.

The section on how much to allow for each person when buying fish (see page 40) will prevent over- or under-catering. Unless otherwise stated, all the recipes in this book serve four. There is plenty of information on: which herbs, spices and flavourings will go well with your chosen seafood or freshwater fish; how to make a court-bouillon for poaching or steaming; which sauces are suitable for poached, steamed, grilled or fried fish; in short, everything the cook needs to know.

We think you will enjoy cooking some traditional favourites among these recipes as well as some exciting new ones, whether the occasion is a simple meal at home, an adventurous experiment with something new or a sumptuous dish for a very special occasion.

·PREPARATION·

*F*ish, crustaceans and molluscs are very easy to prepare with the correct utensils, most of which you will already have in your kitchen. You can collect a few extra, specialist utensils gradually as you broaden your repertoire. An efficient knife sharpener (1) is indispensable. A selection of very sharp knives is also important: a good slicing knife (2); knives with fairly long, thin blades for filleting (3 and 4); a long-bladed peeling knife (5); a knife with an inwardly curved sharp edge (6) and the very useful gutting and descaling knife (7). A strong plastic chopping board (8) will retain fish smells less than a wood one and is more hygienic. Special fish scissors or good-quality kitchen scissors (9) are invaluable, while pincers (10) for holding and severing crustaceans are a very desirable but optional extra. A set of aluminium (or plastic) food trays (11) are handy for refrigerating fish and as receptacles for cleaned fish. Large tweezers with a scraping blade (12) will be useful, while the smaller tweezers (13) will enable you to extract any tiny bones in fillets with ease and precision. If you decide to serve oysters, then you will probably want to invest in these strong, triangular-bladed oyster knives (14 and 15). These and the similar clam knives make it easy to shuck the molluscs without risking injury to your hands, especially if you wear the protective chainmail half-glove (16) in case the knife slips.

REMOVING FINS

Hold the fish firmly by its belly, the right way up, and remove the dorsal fin, cutting from the tail end towards the head; turn the fish over and cut off the anal, ventral and pectoral fins, using the same method; trim the tail fin neatly.

DESCALING

Always work against the grain of the scales. Grip the tail of the fish tightly and run the descaler along the fish against the surface of the fish towards the head. The blunt edge (i.e. the back) of a heavy kitchen knife can be used instead. Do not press too hard or you may slit the skin.

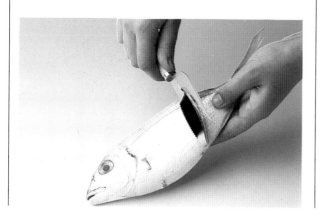

GUTTING

Large, round fish (i.e. round in cross section) such as bream are best gutted through the operculum or gill aperture on the left side of the fish, between the head and the gills; use special fish scissors if you have them or ordinary kitchen scissors to snip your way in on the belly side behind the head. This keeps the fish looking intact and presentable and is especially practical if the recipe calls for them to be stuffed. Introduce your index finger into the opening (1) and hook it round the intestines, drawing them out carefully.

Delve into the ventral cavity to remove any remaining organs, reddish or black material and any coagulated blood along the backbone; you can also make a little incision round the vent to remove any remains of the alimentary canal or its contents.

GUTTING

Smaller round fish are best cut from vent to gills with scissors and then thoroughly cleaned out.

When preparing flat fish, use your scissors to cut a slit on the belly side just behind the head and remove the guts from the fish's very small ventral cavity; snip away the gills and then remove the dark skin (and the white skin from the other side if necessary).

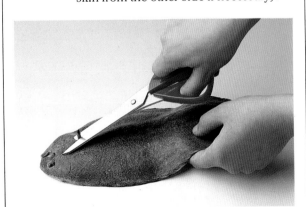

SKINNING

Only a few types of fish, such as sole, must always be skinned. For sole: slit the skin across the end of the fish just by the tail (1), using a fairly small, very sharp knife (with a blade about 6 in [15 cm] long), and slit the skin around the head. Snip off the dorsal and lateral fins using scissors. Start working the skin away from the flesh at the tail end (by pulling, or careful use of the knife). When you have enough to grasp, pull towards the head, while holding the fish tightly in your other hand, until all the skin has come away (2). The white skin on the other side of the fish is usually only removed if the fish is to be filleted; use the same method. If you have a very large fish, it is easier to pull the skin away working from head to tail.

□ SKINNING

When skinning an eel, rub coarse salt or bran all over the surface to remove the slime. Place the eel on the work surface and use a small, very sharp knife to slit the skin all the way round the fish, a few inches below the gills (1); work the skin away from the flesh (2) until you have enough to grasp with a rough, dry cloth. Grip the head tightly and pull the skin down towards the tail, peeling it downwards like a glove (3). With the eel held flat against the work surface, cut off the head at the point where you first slit the skin with a large cutting knife (4).

☐ FILLETING

This is one of the few stages of fish preparation which needs a little practice in order to do it well. If you need to fillet your fish for a special dish but feel too inexpert to do it neatly yourself, your fishmonger may be willing to fillet it for you while you watch.

The aim is to detach four fillets from each fish. After skinning and gutting the fish (sole is shown here) place it on the work surface, tail towards you. Use scissors to snip off the dorsal fin (1) and the ventral fin. With the head towards you, make an incision all the way down the backbone (2) and around the head.

Work the blade of the knife slowly and carefully underneath the flesh, working from the backbone towards the edge of the fish and pressing the knife against the bones which radiate from it, so that you leave as little flesh behind as possible. Your knife will be held almost flat as you work (3). Take care to keep each fillet as whole and neat as possible. Remove one fillet at a time, turning the fish over to remove the last two fillets (4).

☐ FILLETING

When filleting round fish (e.g. hake, trout, etc.) you should usually aim to end up with two fillets, one from each side. Descale the fish if necessary, gut, but do not skin. Lay the fish on its side, tail nearest to you, ventral cavity towards the left (if you are right-handed). Make a firm incision along the back of the fish, making sure you cut down to the backbone (1). Working from head to tail, cut the flesh carefully and completely away from the bones (2). Make an incision just below the head and just above the end of the tail to release the complete fillet (3).

Turn the fish over and repeat the operation. Use tweezers to remove any bones left in the fillets. Remove any traces of blood or discoloration from the fillets and then detach from the skin as shown in (4) below. Use your fingers to begin 'peeling' the skin away from the tail end of the fillet. Grasp this 'tail' end of the skin tightly and insert the knife, blade facing away from you, between the flesh and skin; slide it carefully away from you, the blade at a very acute angle, almost flat against the skin, pushing the flesh away from you.

☐ BONING

To bone a round fish and achieve a single, filleted piece, gut by means of a ventral incision from vent to gills (1). Clean the fish. Insert a sharp, pointed knife between the bones and flesh, working towards the backbone (2). Take care not to cut deeply into the flesh or the knife may cut right through the fish, puncturing the skin on the other side. With the scissors held at an angle to the head as shown in (3) below, snip off the head just short of the caudal fin and just behind the top of the head. Open the fish out flat (4) and gently pull away the backbone with the bones attached to it, working towards the tail.

LOBSTER, CRAYFISH

Although it may offend the tender-hearted, these should really be cooked live. The lobster has such a diffuse nervous system that a deep incision into the top of the head where a small cross-shaped depression can be discerned may not necessarily ensure an easier end, though it does immobilize your dinner for you. In order to ensure that the tail, containing the delicious white meat, remains straight when cooked you can follow the steps shown below, but this is an optional procedure. Cover your hands in thick rubber gloves for protection before placing the lobster, right side up, on a flat board large enough to accommodate it but not too large to fit into the cooking pot (1). Secure by tying strong pieces of kitchen string tightly at intervals around the board and lobster (2).

If dealing with a crayfish, ensure that the antennae or feelers are folded back and secured along the crustacean's sides (3). If preparing ordinary lobster with claws, fasten each claw closed with a strong rubber band before tying to the board just in front of the head.

If you are going to grill your lobster or crawfish, you can first immobilise it by piercing through the back of the head as described above, then lay it on its back and use a heavy, very sharp kitchen knife to split it in half from head to tail as shown in (4) below.

☐ DUBLIN BAY PRAWN (SCAMPI)

To peel raw Dublin Bay prawns, pull the head away from the tail (1). Holding the tail upside down in your left hand (if right-handed) use scissors to cut along each side of the underbelly of the crustacean (2) Peel off the shell and pull off the fan end of the tail (3).

Alternatively, pull off the end of the tail, then snip the underside of the first set of shell plating to the first 'hinge' (4); peel off this first ring and you can then push the flesh out of the remaining shell by inserting your thumb or finger in the narrower end (6).

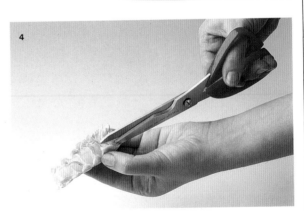

SHRIMPS, PRAWNS AND KING PRAWNS

To peel raw or cooked: pull the head off where the head armouring forms a natural division with the tail (1). You can then use scissors to remove the legs and cut lengthways down the underside (2). Pull the shell apart and remove the flesh (3) or you may prefer to snip and remove one ring of the shell plating at a time.

Shrimps or small prawns are more quickly peeled once the head is removed by simply pulling off the end of the tail and then inserting your thumbs into the underside among the legs (while the shrimp is upside down). By pushing apart the sides, the remaining shell should come away quickly and easily.

Use tweezers to remove the black vein (or intestinal tract) from the centre back of the peeled prawn (4) this is not essential if they are tiny.

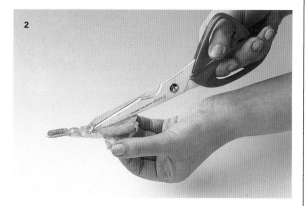

☐ MANTIS SHRIMP AND SIMILAR CRUSTACEANS

Mantis shrimp will usually reach you ready cooked in their shells (normally imported, deep-frozen) but should you have to peel these or similar delicacies, whether raw or cooked, start by snipping away the appendages on the underside with scissors (1). Then cut along the centre of the underside of the crustacean (2). Choose a suitably thin knife to insert between the flesh and the snipped underside near the head and, working towards the tail, gradually free the flesh from the underside of the shell (3). Repeat this operation, still holding the shellfish upside down, using the knife to free the flesh from the harder back shell plating (4), again working towards the tail. Cut off the head. These creatures often have flesh which is not very firm when raw; to make it easier to handle as you work, blanch in boiling water for 2 minutes before peeling.

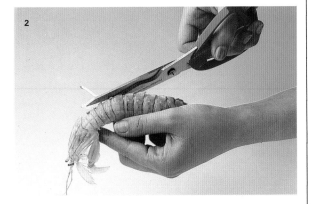

CRAB

Hold the crab upside down in the palm of your left hand; grasp the underside of the shell at the point where it joins the harder, upper shell near the mouth and pull away firmly (1). Many people choose to pull the underside away at the back of the crab; the method is the same. Remove and discard the feathery, greyish gills or lungs ('dead men's fingers') and the intestines, and save all the delicious yellowish brown soft meat and other contents of the shell.

Detach the legs and cut with special pincers (2) or very strong scissors so that the white flesh can be removed. You will need to use the other section of these crab pincers to break open the claws. (Nutcrackers or even a hammer will do as well.)

DUNGENESS CRAB

Stuff pieces of bread firmly into any apertures or breaks in the shell, claws etc. (1) before cooking these crabs or they will be watery. Tie the crab up neatly with strong string (2) before boiling in water (optional). When cooked, shell as for crab (see left), remembering to remove and discard the gills and stomach sac.

CUTTLEFISH, SQUID

Most of these cephalopod molluscs are prepared in the same way. The step-by-step illustrations show how to prepare cuttlefish. Rub off the dark, very thin skin with your fingers (1) under running cold water. Remove the one bony part from within the sac (it will come away easily); the flat, white bone or cuttle is shown in (2) below. The squid has a transparent, cartilaginous quill.

Use your fingers to push out the hard beak (horny mouth parts) hidden in the centre of the tentacles (3) and snip these away; cut out the eyes.

Hold the main sac in your left hand firmly and pull all the tentacles together with your other hand; the innards will come away with them (4). Be careful not to break the ink sac at this point when cleaning cuttlefish. Unless you want to colour your dish black (which some recipes call for) discard it. Wash the main sac and tentacles thoroughly.

Tiny, tender molluscs such as small curled octopus are not skinned but their innards, mouth parts and eyes are removed.

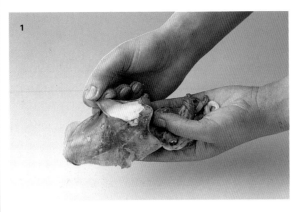

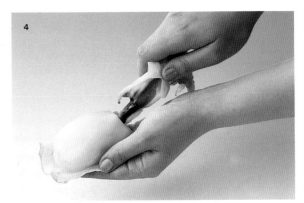

☐ OCTOPUS

Turn the sac inside out, gaining access by means of the opening between the tentacles and body, then remove and discard the innards (1). Turn the sac the right way out and prepare as for cuttlefish (see opposite), removing and discarding the beak (horny mouth parts) and eyes.

Rub the skin away from the sac and tentacles (2).

☐ GASTROPODS

These small, snail-like shellfish such as whelks should be boiled in plenty of water; remove the hard covering at the entrance to the shell (the operculum) with a sharp, preferably hooked knife (1). Use a skewer or long, thin tweezers to remove the mollusc from its shell.

OYSTERS

Hold the oyster with the hinge part of the shell in the palm of your hand. Protect yourself with a cloth. Push the blade of a special oyster knife or thick, strong short-bladed knife between the shells (actually the two valves of the shell) near the hinge. Run the knife around until you can cut the muscle that holds the valves together (1). Open the oyster, taking care not to spill the juice or liquor surrounding the oyster. Carefully cut the oyster free where it is attached to the inside of the shell (2).

MUSSELS

Scrub well (1) and remove any traces of filaments or 'beards' (2). Discard those which do not close when handled. Insert a sharp knife carefully at the pointed end (3) to sever the muscle. Mussels are usually cooked briefly until they open. Discard any which do not open when cooked.

☐ CLAMS AND COCKLES

Work very carefully, preferably with protective gloves or similar covering over your hands or hold the clam firmly with the hinge part of the shell towards your palm. Insert the knife blade between the valves (1). Use gentle leverage to sever the muscle at the hinge and free the clam from the shells, top and bottom (2).

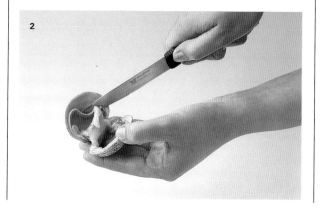

☐ SCALLOPS

Open as for oysters (see opposite page). The tender white or ivory-coloured circular piece of flesh (actually the hinge muscle) and the bright orange curved roe are delicious. The sandy sac and any dark coloured parts should be discarded.

☐ CLEANING

When you have prepared your fish, crustaceans or molluscs they must be thoroughly cleaned and washed before cooking. A whole (gutted) fish should be held under running cold water, mouth gaping open and filled several times with water; drain well and pat dry with a clean cloth. Mussels should be scrubbed very thoroughly under running cold water with a stiff brush; this will help rid them of any filaments, seaweed and sand. Mussels, clams and cockles often have sand enclosed inside their shells so benefit from soaking for an hour or more in very cold, heavily salted water.

·COOKING·

There are numerous ways of cooking fish, each calling for the correct utensils, but with a little resourcefulness you can adapt your existing equipment to provide perfectly good substitutions. For poaching you will need a fish kettle (1). Square fish kettles are also available. Oval baking or gratin dishes (2) are invaluable for baking fillets in the oven while an earthenware casserole dish with a lid (3) is ideal for gentle, slow braising. When cooking fish in a paper case (en papillote) you will need greaseproof paper or foil (4).

For frying, use a heavy or cast iron frying pan (5), for sautéing a tin-lined copper sauteuse (6) or any frying pan with good conductivity and for deep-frying, a deep, heavy pan with frying basket (7) or, safer, an electric deep-fryer. Steamers, made of bamboo (8) or stainless steel, or at least stainless steel steamer inserts (9) are an inexpensive necessity, while the grill holder (10) or folding grid which hinges shut to enclose small fish is a useful, but optional, extra. The perforated slice (11), palette knife (12) and broad slice (13) are probably already in your kitchen.

COURT-BOUILLON

Poached fish sounds a very simple (even rather dull) dish to prepare. In fact it is delicious, providing you use the right materials. First is the cooking liquid, the *court-bouillon*. The fish should be added to the lukewarm cooking liquid, which is then gradually brought to the boil and gently poached until just done. Small whole fish or portions of fish to be eaten cold can be just brought to the boil, the heat turned off, then left to cool in the *court-bouillon*. Larger fish to be served cold should be poached as required, and also allowed to cool in the liquid. When cold, transfer carefully to a serving dish.

The water or the *court-bouillon* must be lightly salted (about ¹/₂ oz [15–20 g] salt to every 1³/₄ pints [1 litre] liquid), flavoured with pieces of celery, carrot and parsley stalks as well as a little dry white wine or cider vinegar. Boil for 30 minutes to 1 hour then allow to cool considerably. Wrap the fish in foil if you are using an ordinary saucepan, or on the special grid or perforated tray in a fish kettle. Place over gentle, even heat. (If you are using a fish kettle, you will need to place it over two burners.)

Take care not to overcook fish. Cooking times vary: 20–25 minutes for freshwater fish weighing around 2¹/₄ lb (1 kg) to about 30 minutes for saltwater fish of this weight. For each additional 1 lb (500 g) in weight, allow an extra 10–12 minutes for freshwater fish and 15 minutes for saltwater fish. As a general guide, the fish is ready when the flesh turns opaque and the eye has turned white. Fish with a pronounced flavour are best suited to this treatment, e.g. saltwater fish such as sea bass, hake, cod and halibut. Freshwater varieties such as trout, carp, pike, salmon and perch also work well cooked in this way.

Allow similar times for cooking large

crustaceans (lobsters etc.). Small crustaceans should be added to a warm *court-bouillon* and removed as soon as the liquid has come to the boil. Squid are usually poached for 10 minutes or longer, depending on their size, in water to which cider vinegar or dry white wine has been added.

☐ 'POCHADE'

By this process fillets and very small whole fish are cooked in very shallow boiling *court-bouillon* and remain moist. Make a small quantity of *court-bouillon* with the usual water, celery, carrot, herbs of your choice that are suitable for fish and a little dry white wine. Place the fish in a buttered flameproof dish and add just enough *court-bouillon* to come barely half way up the fish or fillets. Bring quickly to the boil, then simmer over a very low heat or bake in a moderate oven, adding a little more liquid at frequent intervals as the *court-bouillon* evaporates. The remaining *court-bouillon* and the cooking juices can be used as the basis of a sauce.

☐ STEAMING

Bamboo steamers and stainless steel slotted inserts are cheap and very efficient ways of steaming. Although the *court-bouillon* is kept at a much faster boil than in poaching, steaming takes longer.

Fish can also be steamed in a fish kettle, with the perforated rack or grid turned upside down and using a smaller quantity of *court-bouillon* (the liquid must never come into direct contact with the fish).

'*AU BLEU*'

Particularly well suited for freshwater fish (such as trout and pike), imparting an attractive, faintly bluish hue to the skin.

Make a *court-bouillon*, acidulating the liquid with plenty of white wine or tarragon vinegar. Sprinkle plenty of vinegar all over the skin of the fish before lowering into the warm *court-bouillon* and bringing slowly up to a simmer. Use only the very freshest fish for this method of cooking; handle as little as possible and do not rinse prior to cooking: it is the surface slime on the skin that turns the fish blue.

'*À LA MEUNIÈRE*'

The fish is lightly coated with flour before cooking, hence the name, which means 'in the miller's wife style'. Prepare and clean small fish or fillets and dust all over with seasoned flour, shaking gently to remove excess. Heat a little oil and butter in a pan large enough to take the fish laid out flat and fry for about 5 minutes on each side. The butter, lightly browned, lemon juice and parsley are then sprinkled over the fish before serving.

□ BAKING

Marinate the prepared and cleaned fish for an hour or two in an ovenproof dish with some oil and herbs, turning now and then. Transfer the fish directly into the oven, preheated to 400°F (200°C) mark 6 for medium to large fish, and 350°F (180°C) mark 4 for small fish. Take care that they do not stick to the bottom of the dish during cooking. Sprinkle the surface of the fish with breadcrumbs if wished. Season with a little salt and pepper halfway through the cooking time. Moisten at frequent intervals with a little dry white wine or lemon juice. A 2¼-lb (1-kg) fish will take about 30–40 minutes. Fish that tend to dry out should be covered loosely with foil.

□ BRAISING

A good method for cooking whole fish and substantial slices or steaks from large fish. Arrange a layer of finely sliced onion rings, a few pieces of celery and a few mushroom stalks in the bottom of an earthenware casserole. Add a little oil, 2 bay leaves, parsley and thyme. Place the fish on this bed; add sufficient dry white wine or cold, strained *court-bouillon* to just cover the vegetable and bacon layer. Season with salt and pepper. Bring to the boil over direct heat, cover and cook in the oven, preheated to 400°F (200°C) mark 6 until done.

☐ FRYING

The art of frying, as the French chef Escoffier claimed, is easily mastered. To ensure successful results, however, certain basic rules have to be remembered.

Iron or non-stick pans are the best for shallow-frying. Electric deep-fryers, with thermostat, are safest for deep-frying. Use plenty of good olive or vegetable oil. (Fish and seafood deep-fried in olive oil tend not to stick to each other and will colour evenly all over.) When deep-frying small fish and large pieces the oil should be kept at 350°F (180°C) mark 4; for fillets and very small fish, the temperature should be 400°F (200°C) mark 6. Do not try to deep-fry whole large fish: these should be filleted.

Try dipping the prepared fish or fish pieces into herb-flavoured milk; pat gently with kitchen paper to remove excess moisture before rolling in flour; shake off excess. Using a slotted or wire ladle, lower carefully into the very hot oil. When done, remove with the ladle, allowing excess oil to drain off, then place on kitchen paper on a warm plate.

Alternatively, you can dip the fish pieces in a flour and water batter to which beaten egg white has been added for lightness. When fried, the batter should be crisp, light and golden brown, enclosing the tender, moist fish. Do not keep your deep-fried fish waiting for any length of time, or the batter coating will lose its crispness and become indigestible.

Small crustaceans and molluscs (such as prawns, oysters, mussels and baby octopus) are fried whole, while squid should be cut into thin rings. Squid and other cephalopods should be fried for the briefest possible time or they will lose their delicate flavour (see recipes under specific headings).

Marinate shelled bivalves (mussels,

clams, oysters, etc.) in oil, lemon juice and parsley; drain well and roll in very fine fresh or dried (not toasted or coloured) breadcrumbs before deep-frying briefly in very hot oil. Alternatively, pat lightly with kitchen paper after draining off the marinade and dip in batter; fry quickly.

Never leave hot oil unattended during frying, and remember to remove it from the source of heat as soon as you have finished.

□ GRILLING

Prepare and clean the fish; if grilling a medium to large scaly fish, do not remove the scales as they provide a protective coating for the fish during the prolonged time it will be under the grill. The skin can be peeled off, scales and all, just before serving.

Wash the fish and wipe dry; sprinkle with a little oil. Grease the grill pan or its grid or holder. Sprinkle the surface of the fish lightly with fine fresh or dried breadcrumbs if wished, to help form a crisp coating while grilling. Sprinkle with oil at frequent intervals to keep the fish moist. You may choose to marinate the fish in oil and herbs for an hour or two; drain before grilling. When barbecuing, use plenty of non-resinous wood or charcoal; make sure it is glowing hot before you start cooking. Fish steaks (e.g. tuna or swordfish) to be grilled should be only ³/₄ in (2 cm) thick or less or they will be dry and hard on the outside before they are cooked through. For the same reason, avoid cooking the slices too close to the source of heat.

Whole, oily fish (such as eel, mackerel and sardines) should be grilled quickly and briefly, enclosed in a folding double wire holder (shown above right and below and on page 24) so they can be turned by simply turning the holder and will remain intact.

Very small or very large fish are not really suitable for grilling, although the latter can be scored with deep diagonal criss-crossed cuts, regularly spaced and close together on each side to help the heat penetrate more deeply.

As mentioned above, leaving the scales in place permits longer, slower grilling; peel them off, with the skin, when the fish is cooked. Turn the fish as infrequently as possible, while ensuring it is cooked through, or it will start to look a little messy. Crustaceans should be split lengthwise in half,

placed cut side uppermost, sprinkled with a little salt, pepper and any other flavourings you choose and cooked under a very hot grill: allow 15 minutes' cooking time for each 14 oz–1 lb (400–500 g) weight. Molluscs (such as mussels, oysters, etc.) can be threaded on to skewers, brushed with oil and grilled under a medium heat for a few minutes, turning the skewers once or twice.

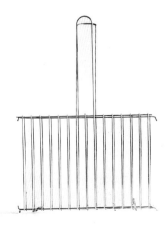

☐ 'EN PAPILLOTE'

The fish, together with seasonings or herbs, is enclosed securely in the chosen packaging, usually foil, (leaving plenty of air space inside), and is placed on a baking tray or similar dish in the oven, preheated to 350°F (180°C) mark 4. Cook for 10–15 minutes for a fish weighing approximately 8 oz (250 g).

☐ BREADCRUMBS

This protective coating is used for fillets or fish pieces. Dust with flour and shake off excess. Dip in a mixture made of lightly beaten eggs, salt, pepper and a very little olive oil (this adds crispness when fried), then coat well with breadcrumbs. Fry in hot oil, preferably in an iron or non-stick pan, for about 5 minutes on each side.

□ SALT

Sprinkle a layer of coarse salt 1 in (3 cm) deep in the bottom of a fish brick or an oval unglazed earthenware pot; place cleaned well-dried fish in this and add more salt, packing this around the fish until it is completely buried. Cover with the lid and bake at 400°F (200°C) mark 6, allowing slightly longer cooking times than those given for fish baked in the normal way. The salt sets into a hard casing during cooking, trapping all the flavours and juices of the fish, without making it at all salty (provided the fish is gutted as shown on page 9 and thoroughly dried before cooking).

□ CASSEROLING

Make a sauce with chopped, peeled tomatoes (tinned tomatoes can be used), drained and simmered with a little olive oil and finely chopped garlic. Add the prepared seafood: baby octopus, squid and cuttlefish go particularly well, but pieces of firm-fleshed fish can also be used, or prawns, shrimps, etc. Add some dry white wine, cover, and simmer gently for about 30 minutes. Season to taste and sprinkle with freshly chopped parsley just before serving.

'À L'AMÉRICAINE'

This method involves lightly sautéing pieces of raw lobster, whole (peeled) Dublin Bay prawns, and similar varieties of crustaceans in a little olive oil until cooked; the oil is then drained off, leaving just enough in which to fry some chopped garlic, parsley and thyme. Stir; add a little brandy, heat, and then flame. Add blanched, skinned, seeded and chopped tomatoes (tinned or fresh) and a half-and-half mixture of *court-bouillon* (see page 39) and dry white wine. Simmer for up to 15 minutes, season to taste with salt and pepper, adding a little chopped tarragon if desired.

MEDITERRANEAN STYLE

This method of cooking molluscs (known as 'in zimino') involves first frying finely chopped garlic, onion, parsley and celery in olive oil; add Swiss chard or spinach and turn once or twice until wilted. Add whole, small molluscs (clams, etc.) or larger molluscs (such as squid) sliced into rings. Cover tightly and cook over extremely low heat for 30–40 minutes (longer for squid).

□ 'AU GRATIN'

A wonderful way of presenting bivalves (mussels, clams, etc.). Clean and prepare the shells before placing the unopened bivalves (see page 22) in a large frying pan containing a very little water over a high heat; discard all those that fail to open and discard one half of each bivalve. Place the molluscs on their remaining half shells in a single layer in a large shallow oven dish and cover with a topping (e.g. finely chopped shallots or spring onions, parsley, garlic mixed with fine fresh or dry breadcrumbs, butter, salt and pepper). Add grated cheese if liked. Always cook in a very hot oven or under the grill until lightly browned on top.

□ SIMMERED SHELLFISH

Suitable for bivalve molluscs (especially scallops). Clean and prepare the molluscs (see pages 22–23), opening the shells with a knife as shown or by heating for a few seconds in a large frying pan. The shells are discarded. Sauté briefly in a little olive oil with very finely chopped or grated shallots or onion and mixed herbs of your choice. Moisten with dry white wine and fish stock (*fumet*, see page 39). Season lightly with salt and pepper. Do not over-cook; 5–6 minutes over a very low heat is ample.

·HERBS AND SPICES·

A judicious use of herbs and spices will enhance the delicate flavours of fish and seafood.

The classic herbs associated with fish cookery are parsley, bay leaf and thyme which together make up a bouquet garni; basil and sage are effective in small quantities while dill is particularly good with salmon. A little tarragon will add a very pronounced, delicious flavour to certain sauces.

Spices used include paprika, curry and turmeric, all three imparting colour as well as taste to the fish, horseradish, saffron (which gives a wonderful colour to food), nutmeg, mace (which is the dried outer covering of the nutmeg), cayenne, and many types of 'pepper'.

Bay leaf: evergreen shrub with highly aromatic leaves, used fresh or dried, to add flavour to marinades and stock.

Dill: the subtle aniseed flavour of this herb is lost if it is overcooked; it goes very well with salmon.

Basil: a full-flavoured and scented herb; enhances many types of fish (especially red mullet) and crustaceans.

Tarragon: try to get real French tarragon for the best flavour. Use sparingly. Excellent with sole.

Parsley: use with any type of fish. Buy the flat-leaved parsley for a change when you can find it, for its sweeter, fuller taste. Essential in marinades and fish stock.

Sage: a few fresh leaves or a tiny pinch of dried sage go well with baked or grilled fish.

Rosemary: the leaves of this shrub also go well with oven-baked or broiled fish.

Turmeric: the bright golden yellow colour of this spice makes it valuable for enhancing the appearance of fish and crustaceans. Its flavour is slightly bitter.

Curry powder: use only a mild curry powder or you will swamp the flavour of the fish or seafood. Many fish recipes from the Far East make selective use of the individual spices used to make up curry powder.

Mace: the dried husk of the nutmeg, coloured a soft apricot yellow. Sold in pieces or ground. Use sparingly to add a warm, spicy touch.

Nutmeg: always buy whole nutmegs (hard, slightly oval, dark brown dried fruits of the nutmeg tree) and grate a little on a fine grater as and when you need it.

Paprika: dried, ground red peppers. Add towards the end of cooking: it can become bitter if cooked too long.

Pepper: the fruits of the pepper start off as green, turn red, and then brown. Green peppercorns are sold in tins and jars as are red peppercorns: they should be used very sparingly. For the very aromatic black peppercorns the pepper fruits are gathered when still red, before they are fully ripe, and dried. White peppercorns come from fully ripened fruit, dried and skinned.

Saffron: dried stamens of the crocus flower which give a beautiful soft orange gold colour to food and a warm, subtle, faintly bitter taste. Excellent in fish soups and dishes made with molluscs.

·CLASSIC SAUCES, BUTTERS· AND STOCKS

*M*any of the sauces and accompaniments given here are suitably delicate in flavour to complement poached or steamed fish; some, however, are quite piquant to provide a pronounced contrast. Mayonnaise is the most classic of all cold sauces, a blend of egg yolks and oil, transformed by the addition of a few extra ingredients to make such sauces as rémoulade and aïoli; all are excellent with cold poached or hot grilled fish. Herb- or spice-flavoured butters go well with grilled fish. Sauces based on blending butter with egg yolks (hollandaise *and* béarnaise) *demanding careful preparation, are also classic favourites, for serving with fish which has been very lightly poached, steamed or baked in a paper case.*

Both court-bouillon *(for which we give two recipes) and a good fish stock* (fumet) *are simple and cheap to prepare; the latter is made from trimmings, bones, etc., and is indispensable for many types of sauces.*

MAYONNAISE

2 egg yolks, 7 fl oz (200 ml) olive or sunflower oil, ¹/₂ lemon, salt

Have all your ingredients at room temperature before you start. Place the egg yolks in a bowl, stir them briefly with a wooden spoon, add a pinch of salt and a few drops of lemon juice. Keep beating continuously in the same direction as you add the oil a few drops at a time until the mixture becomes thick, paler and greatly increased in volume. Stir in 1 tsp lemon juice.

You can save time and energy by making mayonnaise in the liquidizer. To one whole egg and one extra yolk in the liquidizer bowl, add a pinch of salt, 1 tsp lemon juice and 3–4 tbsp oil. Turn on the liquidizer at low speed and slowly add the olive oil in a very thin stream through the

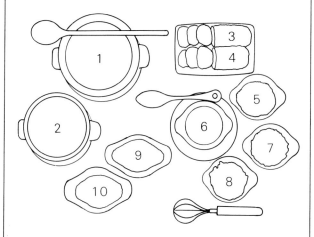

1 Fumet
2 Court-bouillon
3 Curry butter
4 Colbert butter
5 Tartare sauce
6 Béarnaise sauce
7 Rémoulade sauce
8 Mayonnaise
9 Hollandaise sauce
10 Aïoli

hole in the liquidizer lid. Process until the mayonnaise has thickened and emulsified.

HOLLANDAISE SAUCE

2 egg yolks

5 oz (150 g) unsalted butter

1 tsp lemon juice

salt and white peppercorns

Place the egg yolks in a small, non-metallic saucepan or the top of a double boiler (ceramic, enamel or non-stick). Add 1 tsp cold water, a pinch of salt, and place over very gently simmering water. Beat with a whisk until the egg yolks are creamy. Do not overheat.

Have the butter at room temperature, cut into small pieces, and immediately start beating these into the egg yolks one at a time. Ensure that each piece of butter is completely blended into the egg mixture before adding the next. Keep beating well as you add the butter and the sauce will soon increase in lightness and volume. If you allow it to overheat it will curdle. When fairly thick and creamy, stir in the lemon juice and a little freshly ground white pepper. Draw aside from the heat and serve.

BÉARNAISE SAUCE

2 shallots

7 fl oz (200 ml) white wine vinegar

1 sprig fresh tarragon

3 egg yolks

5 oz (150 g) unsalted butter

salt

Peel and finely chop the shallots and place in a small saucepan with the vinegar and a few tarragon leaves. Reduce the vinegar over a moderate heat for about 20 minutes, or until all but

1–1½ tbsp has evaporated. Place the egg yolks in the top of a double boiler (see previous recipe) or into a bowl over barely simmering water. Stir in the strained reduced vinegar, add a pinch of salt and beat until creamy. Have the butter cut into very small pieces (see previous recipe) and beat one at a time into the egg yolk and vinegar mixture, only adding a fresh piece once the previous one has been well beaten in. The sauce will gradually thicken and expand. Do not overheat or it will curdle. Draw aside from the heat, stir in 1 tbsp chopped tarragon, and serve as soon as possible.

TARTARE SAUCE

2 eggs
7 fl oz (200 ml) olive or sunflower oil
½ lemon
1½ tbsp chopped chives
1½ tbsp finely chopped parsley
salt

Hard-boil the eggs (10 minutes), cool under running cold water, then shell. Place the yolks in a bowl and crush with a fork. Add the oil a few drops at a time, stirring continuously with a wooden spoon, until the sauce becomes creamy. Stir in a pinch of salt, the lemon juice, chives and parsley.

AÏOLI

3–4 cloves garlic
2 egg yolks
10 fl oz (300 ml) olive or sunflower oil
2 tsp lemon juice
coarse sea salt

Pound the peeled garlic cloves with 1 tsp of the coarse sea salt using a pestle and mortar. Work in the egg yolks and continue working with the pestle until pale and smooth. Add scant 3½ fl oz (100 ml)

of the oil a few drops at a time, allowing it to dribble down the inside of the mortar; keep working the pestle in a clockwise direction.

When the sauce begins to thicken, gradually add the lemon juice, stirring continuously, and 2½ tbsp hot water. Continue stirring as you add the remaining oil.

RÉMOULADE SAUCE

1 quantity mayonnaise (see page 37)
1 tsp mustard (powder or ready-made Dijon)
1½ tbsp chopped parsley
1 tbsp chopped capers
2 chopped cocktail gherkins
½ small mild onion or 1 shallot, finely chopped

Work the mustard into the mayonnaise. Add the very finely chopped parsley, capers, gherkins and onion (or shallot). Stir well.

COLBERT BUTTER

2 tbsp finely chopped parsley
2 tbsp lemon juice
4 oz (120 g) unsalted butter
1 tsp meat extract
salt and pepper

Mix the parsley and lemon in a small bowl; have the butter softened at room temperature and beat into the lemon and parsley a small piece at a time. Beat until pale and fluffy. Stir in the meat extract, followed by a pinch of salt and a little freshly ground white pepper. Shape into a long cylinder, wrap in foil and chill in the refrigerator until needed. Serve small pats of this butter with grilled fish.

CURRY BUTTER

4 oz (120 g) butter

1 shallot or spring onion

1 tsp mild curry powder

salt and pepper

Have the butter at room temperature. Peel the shallot or spring onion and chop very finely; simmer it in the vinegar with a seasoning of salt and pepper until the vinegar has totally evaporated. Leave to cool before stirring in the curry powder. Beat gradually into the butter, and chill until needed.

FISH STOCK (FUMET)

$2^{1}/_{4}$ lb (1 kg) fresh fish trimmings (heads, bones, skin)

1 onion

1 carrot

1 leek

1 celery stalk

1 bouquet garni

18 fl oz (500 ml) dry white wine

salt and black or white peppercorns

Place the fish trimmings in a large saucepan with the sliced vegetables and approx. $3^{1}/_{2}$ pints (2 litres) water. Add a generous pinch of salt and bring slowly to the boil, skimming off the scum which rises to the surface. Cover and simmer for 15 minutes. Add the white wine and a few peppercorns; simmer for a further 15 minutes. Strain.

COURT-BOUILLON WITH WINE

1 large onion

1 carrot

1 celery stalk

1 leek

1 small bunch parsley

1 bay leaf

18 fl oz (500 ml) dry white wine

salt and peppercorns

Wash and trim the vegetables; slice into a large saucepan or directly into the fish kettle. Add the well-washed parsley, the bay leaf, approx. $3^{1}/_{2}$ pints (2 litres) water and a generous pinch of salt. Bring to the boil; turn down the heat and boil gently for 15 minutes. Add the wine and a few peppercorns. Simmer for a further 15 minutes, then leave to cool.

COURT-BOUILLON WITH VINEGAR

2 onions

1 celery stalk

2 leeks

1 carrot

1 small bunch parsley

1 sprig thyme

1 bay leaf

7 fl oz (200 ml) white wine vinegar

salt and peppercorns

Place all the prepared, cleaned and sliced vegetables in a large saucepan, add the herbs, approx. $3^{1}/_{2}$ pints (2 litres) water and a generous pinch of salt. Bring to the boil; simmer for 15 minutes, then add the vinegar and a few peppercorns. Simmer for a further 15 minutes. Strain.

39

Below is a guide to how much raw fish, crustaceans and molluscs to buy. Weights given are one person's serving.

Fish
Weights are for raw untrimmed fish before gutting, where whole, and for raw shucked molluscs:

Whole small fish (e.g. trout, mullet, hake, perch, etc.)	8 oz (200–250 g)
Fillets of flat fish (e.g. sole, lemon sole, etc.)	4–6 oz (130–180 g)
Steaks (slices cut from large fish, e.g. cod, salmon)	6–7 oz (180–200 g)

Crustaceans and molluscs

Lobster (in shell)	10–14 oz (300–400 g)
Dublin Bay prawns (unshelled)	10 oz (300 g)
Dublin Bay prawns (shelled)	3 oz (80 g)
Crab (in the shell)	14 oz–1 lb (400–500 g)
Oysters	6–12
Scallops	2–3
Mussels, clams	14 oz (400 g)
Cuttlefish, octopus	7 oz (200 g)
Baby squid, baby cuttlefish	6 oz (180 g)

Wastage
When buying fish or shellfish it is important to bear in mind the proportion of edible flesh to those parts you will throw away.

Here is a selection to illustrate how much you will need to discard:
Anchovies and sardines: 30%; Eel: 35%; Grey mullet: 50%; Dentex: 25%; Pike: 45%; Cod: 25%; Hake: 25%; Gilt-head bream: 40%; Monkfish: 65%; Rays and skate: 65%; Turbot: 45%; John Dory: 60%; Sea bream: 45%; Mackerel: 20%; Sole: 55%; Sea bass: 45%; Red mullet: 20%; Trout: 45%.

·OCEAN FISH - SMALL FISH·

BREAM WITH CUCUMBER

p. 49

*Time: 40 minutes
+ 3–4 hours marinating time
Difficulty: Very easy
Cold appetizer*

SARDINES WITH PINE NUTS

p. 49

*Time: 50 minutes
+ 48 hours marinating time
Difficulty: Very easy
Cold appetizer*

RED MULLET ON GARLIC TOAST

p. 49

*Time: 50 minutes
+ 30 minutes standing time
Difficulty: Very easy
Cold appetizer*

MOULDED FISH MOUSSE

p. 50

*Time: 30 minutes
+ cooling time
Difficulty: Very easy
Cold appetizer*

GRATIN OF SOLE AND SCALLOPS

p. 50

*Time: 45 minutes
Difficulty: Very easy
Hot appetizer*

SEA BASS AND LEEK MOUSSE

p. 51

*Time: 1 hour 10 minutes
Difficulty: Easy
Cold appetizer*

MARINATED BREAM WITH GINGER SAUCE

p. 51

*Time: 40 minutes
+ 4 hours marinating time
Difficulty: Easy
Cold appetizer*

SMELTS LEVANTINE STYLE

p. 51

*Time: 1 hour
+ 12 hours standing time
Difficulty: Very easy
Cold appetizer*

SPICED HAKE INDIAN STYLE

p. 52

*Time: 45 minutes
Difficulty: Easy
Cold appetizer*

HERRING SALAD

p. 52

*Time: 30 minutes
Difficulty: Very easy
Cold appetizer*

FISHERMAN'S FLAN

p. 53

*Time: 1 hour
Difficulty: Easy
First course*

FISH SOUP WITH PAPRIKA

p. 53

*Time: 1 hour 30 minutes
Difficulty: Easy
First course*

PASTA WITH SEA BASS AND HERBS

p. 54

*Time: 30 minutes
Difficulty: Easy
First course*

Sole and spinach rings

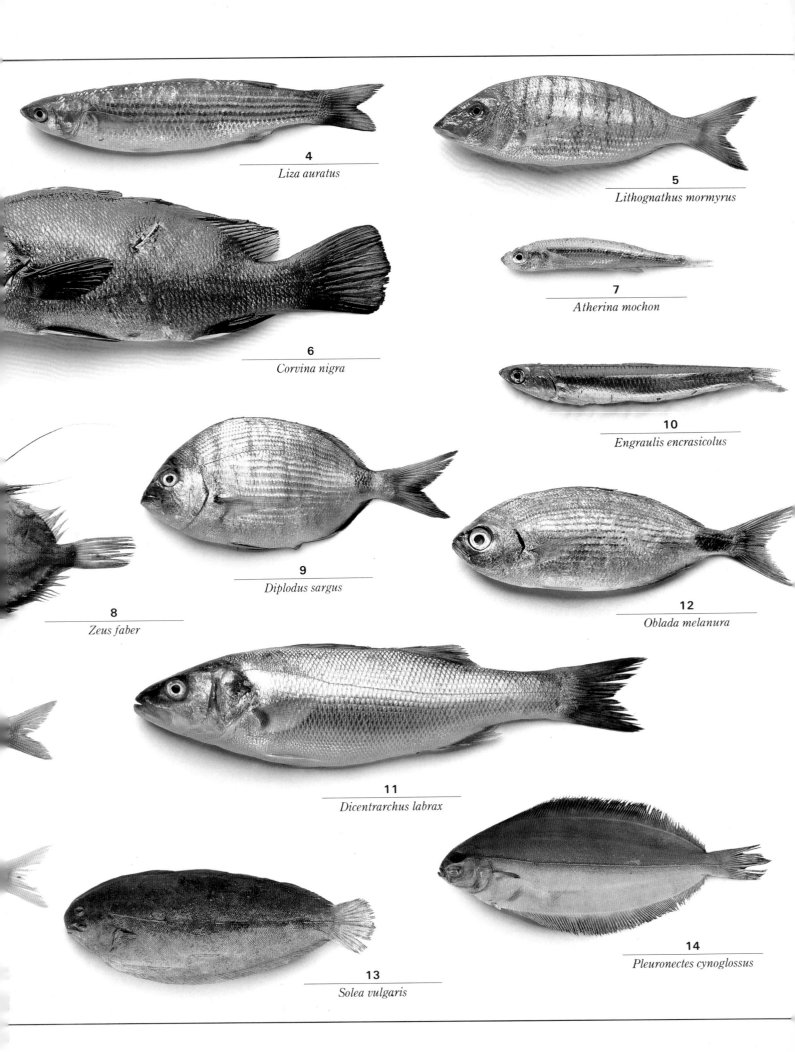

4
Liza auratus

5
Lithognathus mormyrus

6
Corvina nigra

7
Atherina mochon

10
Engraulis encrasicolus

9
Diplodus sargus

8
Zeus faber

12
Oblada melanura

11
Dicentrarchus labrax

13
Solea vulgaris

14
Pleuronectes cynoglossus

1

English: Tub gurnard, Tubfish
French: Grondin galinette
Italian: Capone gallinella
Spanish: Bejel

2

English: Red mullet
French: Rouget de roche
German: Gestreifte
Italian: Triglia di scoglio
Spanish: Moll de roca

3

English: Red mullet
French: Rouget barbet
German: Rothbart
Italian: Triglia di fango
Spanish: Imbriaco

4

English: Grey mullet
French: Mulet doré
Italian: Cefalo
Spanish: Galupe

5

English: Striped bream
French: Marbré
Italian: Mormora
Spanish: Herrera

6

French: Corb
Italian: Corvina
Spanish: Corvallo

7

English: Smelt
French: Prêtre
Italian: Latterino
Spanish: Pejerrey

8

English: John Dory
French: Saint-Pierre
Italian: Pesce San Pietro
Spanish: Pez de San Pedro

9

French: Sar commun
Italian: Sarago maggiore
Spanish: Sargo

10

English: Anchovy
French: Anchois
German: Sardelle
Italian: Acciuga
Spanish: Anchoa

11

English: Bass
French: Bar
German: Meer
Italian: Spigola
Spanish: Lubina

12

English: Saddled bream
French: Oblade
Italian: Occhiata
Spanish: Oblada

13

Dutch: Tong
English: Sole
French: Sole
German: Seezunge
Italian: Sogliola
Spanish: Lenguado

14

English: Lemon sole
French: Sole limande
German: Rotzunge
Italian: Sogliola limanda
Spanish: Limanda

15

English: Scorpionfish
French: Rascasse rouge
Italian: Scorfano rosso
Spanish: Cabracho

16

English: Bluemouth
French: Rascasse de fond
German: Drachenkopf
Italian: Scorfano di fondale
Spanish: Gallineta

17

French: Vive araignée
Italian: Tracina ragno
Spanish: Araña

18

English: Bogue
French: Bogue
Italian: Boga
Spanish: Boga

19

English: Hake
French: Colin
German: Hechtdorsch
Italian: Nasello
Spanish: Merluza

20

English: Dentex
French: Denté
German: Zahnbrasse
Italian: Dentice
Spanish: Dentón

21

English: Mackerel
French: Maquereau
German: Makrele
Italian: Sgombro
Spanish: Caballa

22

English: Herring
French: Hareng
German: Hering
Italian: Aringa
Spanish: Arenque

23

English: Gilt-head bream
French: Daurade
German: Goldbrassen
Italian: Orata
Spanish: Dorada

24

English: Sardine
French: Sardine
German: Sardine
Italian: Sardina
Spanish: Sardina

25

English: Sprat
French: Sprat
German: Breitling
Italian: Papalina/Spratto
Spanish: Espadín

26

English: Three-bearded rockling
French: Mostelle
Italian: Motella
Spanish: Bertorella

27

English: Sea bream
French: Pagre
Italian: Pagro comune
Spanish: Pargo

28

English: Pandora
French: Pageot rouge
Italian: Pagello/Fragolino
Spanish: Breca

29

English: Garfish
French: Aiguille
Italian: Aguglia
Spanish: Aguja

30

English: Plaice
French: Carrelet
German: Scholle
Italian: Passera
Spanish: Platija

31

English: Salema
French: Saupe
Italian: Salpa
Spanish: Salema

32

French: Ombrine
Italian: Ombrina
Spanish: Verrugato

1

Trigla lucerna

2

Mullus surmuletus

3

Mullus barbatus

Moulded fish mousse

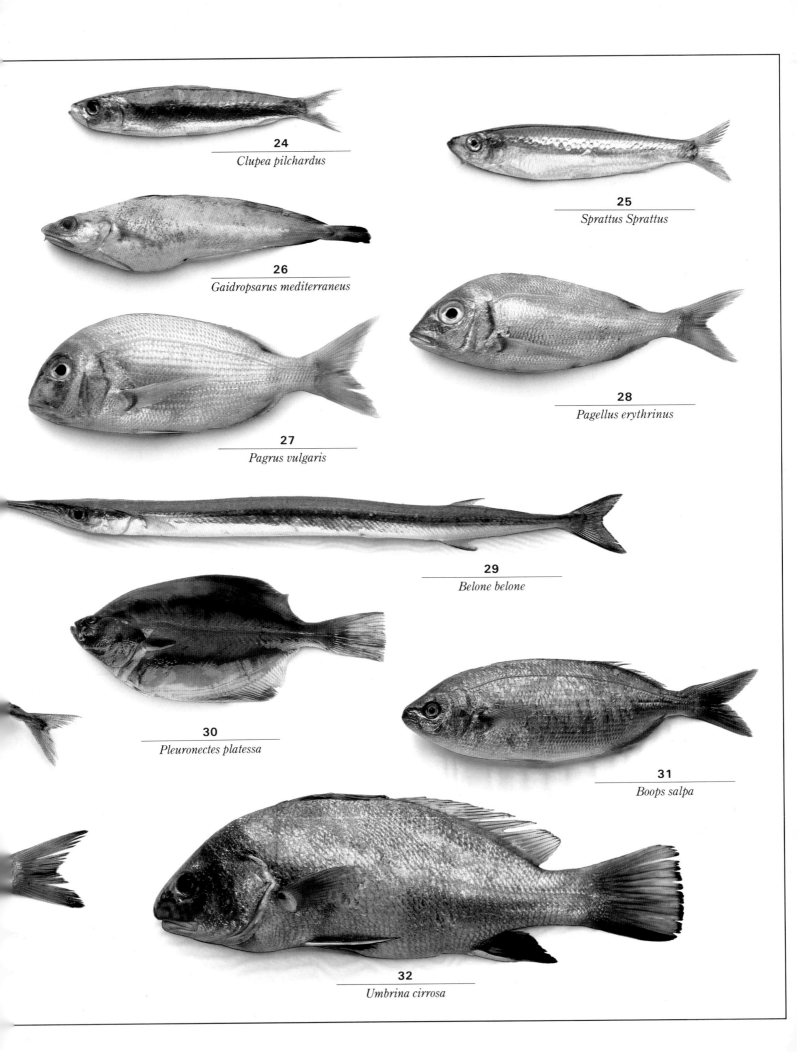

24
Clupea pilchardus

25
Sprattus Sprattus

26
Gaidropsarus mediterraneus

28
Pagellus erythrinus

27
Pagrus vulgaris

29
Belone belone

30
Pleuronectes platessa

31
Boops salpa

32
Umbrina cirrosa

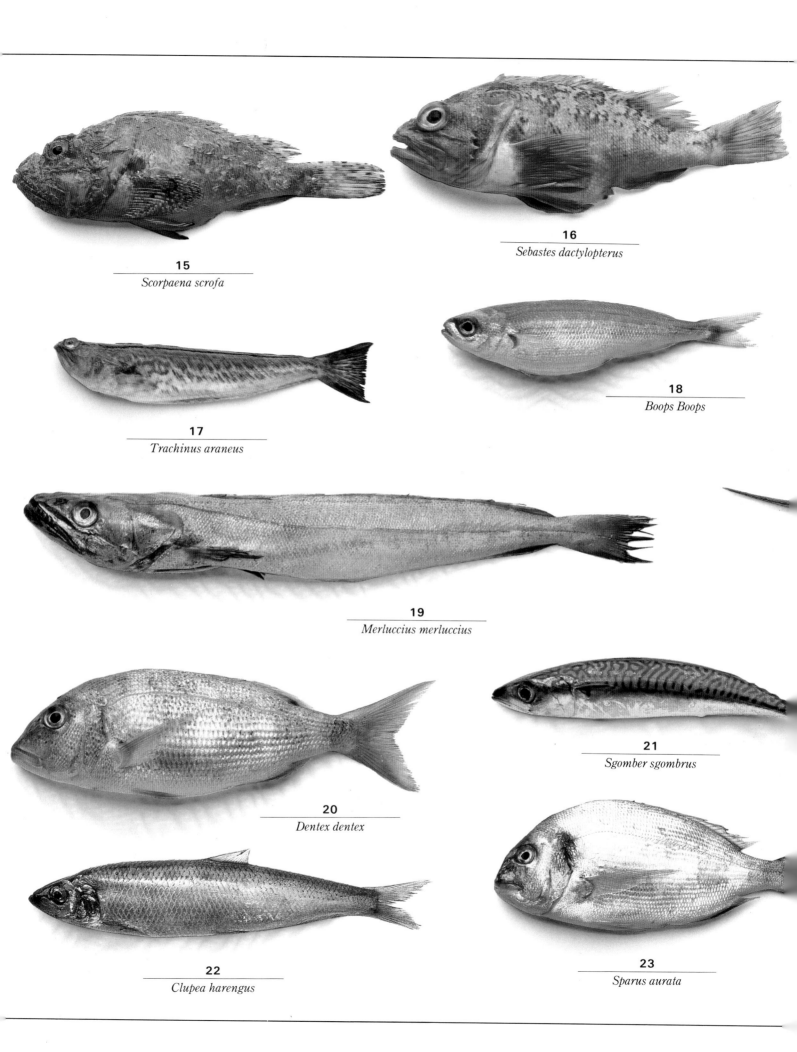

15
Scorpaena scrofa

16
Sebastes dactylopterus

17
Trachinus araneus

18
Boops Boops

19
Merluccius merluccius

20
Dentex dentex

21
Sgomber sgombrus

22
Clupea harengus

23
Sparus aurata

BAKED WHITING WITH GARLIC AND ROSEMARY

p. 82

*Time: 40 minutes
+ 30 minutes marinating time
Difficulty: Very easy
Main course*

WHITING WITH MIXED HERB SAUCE

p. 82

*Time: 50 minutes
Difficulty: Easy
Main course*

BRAISED WHITING WITH SORREL SAUCE

p. 83

*Time: 1 hour
Difficulty: Very easy
Main course*

WHITING WITH PEAS

p. 83

*Time: 1 hour
Difficulty: Very easy
Main course*

SARDINE BAKE

p. 84

*Time: 1 hour
Difficulty: Easy
Main course*

BAKED STUFFED SARDINES

p. 84

*Time: 1 hour
Difficulty: Easy
Main course*

SARDINES WITH ALMOND AND SULTANA STUFFING

p. 84

*Time: 1 hour 15 minutes
Difficulty: Very easy
Main course*

DEEP-FRIED SANDWICHED SARDINES

p. 85

*Time: 1 hour
Difficulty: Easy
Main course*

SAVOURY SARDINES

p. 85

*Time: 1 hour
Difficulty: Very easy
Main course*

SCORPIONFISH WITH ANCHOVY SAUCE

p. 85

*Time: 40 minutes
Difficulty: Very easy
Main course*

FRIED FLOUNDER WITH COLD SAVOURY SAUCE

p. 86

*Time: 1 hour
Difficulty: Easy
Main course*

Sardine bake

FLOUNDER WITH MUSHROOM SAUCE

p. 86

*Time: 1 hour
Difficulty: Easy
Main course*

FLOUNDER IN WINE AND CREAM SAUCE

p. 87

*Time: 1 hour
Difficulty: Fairly easy
Main course*

EEL WITH SOUR CREAM AND PAPRIKA

p. 87

*Time: 1 hour
Difficulty: Very easy
Main course*

EEL BAKED IN WINE

p. 88

*Time: 40 minutes
Difficulty: Very easy
Main course*

PROVENÇAL BRAISED EEL

p. 88

*Time: 1 hour 10 minutes
Difficulty: Easy
Main course*

EEL BAKED WITH MUSSELS AND CLAMS

p. 88

*Time: 1 hour
Difficulty: Easy
Main course*

DENTEX ORIENTAL STYLE

p. 89

*Time: 1 hour
+ 3 hours marinating time
Difficulty: Easy
Main course*

DENTEX PIZZAIOLA

p. 89

*Time: 1 hour
+ 30 minutes standing time
Difficulty: Easy
Main course*

BAKED DENTEX WITH LEMON STUFFING

p. 90

*Time: 45 minutes
Difficulty: Very easy
Main course*

PIQUANT GREY MULLET

p. 90

*Time: 45 minutes
Difficulty: Very easy
Main course*

GREY MULLET FLAMBÉ

p. 90

*Time: 40 minutes
Difficulty: Very easy
Main course*

BAKED GREY MULLET WITH HERBS

p. 91

*Time: 45 minutes
Difficulty: Very easy
Main course*

GREY MULLET SPANISH STYLE

p. 91

*Time: 1 hour 15 minutes
Difficulty: Very easy
Main course*

HERRING FILLETS WITH SAUERKRAUT

p. 92

*Time: 3 hours
Difficulty: Easy
Main course*

HERRINGS WITH DILL

p. 92

*Time: 30 minutes
+ overnight marinating time
Difficulty: Easy
Main course*

HERRINGS NORMANDY STYLE

p. 93

*Time: 1 hour 20 minutes
+ 2 hours standing time
Difficulty: Easy
Main course*

BAKED ANCHOVIES WITH CHEESE STUFFING

p. 93

*Time: 1 hour 15 minutes
Difficulty: Very easy
Main course*

FRENCH ANCHOVIES WITH PEPPERS

p. 93

*Time: 1 hour
Difficulty: Very easy
Main course*

ANCHOVY PIE

p. 94

*Time: 1 hour 30 minutes
Difficulty: Very easy
Main course*

ANCHOVIES WITH AUBERGINE SAUCE

p. 94

*Time: 1 hour 15 minutes
Difficulty: Very easy
Main course*

BOGUE WITH SULTANAS

p. 95

*Time: 1 hour
Difficulty: Very easy
Main course*

BAKED FISH BROCHETTES

p. 95

*Time: 50 minutes
Difficulty: Very easy
Main course*

MEAGRE IN MILK SAUCE

p. 95

*Time: 1 hour
Difficulty: Easy
Main course*

SWEET AND SOUR BREAM

p. 96

*Time: 45 minutes
Difficulty: Easy
Main course*

BREAM WITH CUCUMBER

1 gilt-head bream weighing 2¹/₄ lb (1 kg)

3 limes

1 small (or ¹/₂ large) cucumber

3¹/₂ fl oz (100 ml) single cream

2 fl oz (50 ml) natural yoghurt

1 tsp English mustard

1 tbsp chopped parsley

salt

Gut (see page 10) and fillet (see pages 12–13) the bream. Flatten the fillets slightly by pressing with the blade of a heavy kitchen knife, then slice crosswise into very thin strips. Place in a bowl and sprinkle with the juice of 2 limes. Cover and chill in the refrigerator for 3–4 hours.

Slice the unpeeled, washed and dried cucumber into a colander; sprinkle with coarse salt and leave to stand for 1 hour to draw off excess water. Rinse in cold water and dry. Mix together the cream, yoghurt, mustard and parsley. Drain the fish, mix gently with the cucumber slices and half of the creamy dressing; transfer to a chilled serving dish and decorate with the remaining lime, cut into wedges. Hand round the remaining dressing separately.

SARDINES WITH PINE NUTS

1³/₄ lb (800 g) fresh sardines (or 2–3 tins)

plain flour

oil for frying

2 large onions

³/₄ pint (400 ml) cider vinegar

2 oz (50 g) pine nuts

salt

Gut the sardines by carefully pulling off their heads: the innards will usually come out attached to the head. Wash and dry well, coat lightly with flour and deep-fry briefly in very hot oil in several batches to ensure the temperature of the oil remains constant. Spread out on kitchen paper and sprinkle with a little salt. Peel the onions, slice into thin rounds, and shallow- or deep-fry in fresh oil until crisp and golden brown; drain well. Spread out on kitchen paper. Arrange half the sardines in a single layer in a wide, shallow serving dish; sprinkle with a third (¹/₄ pint/130 ml) of the vinegar. Cover with a layer of half the fried onions, topped by half the pine nuts, sprinkling with the same amount of vinegar. Repeat this layering process, using the rest of the sardines, followed by the onions and pine nuts. Sprinkle with the remaining vinegar. Leave to stand in a cool place for 48 hours before serving.

Note: If fresh sardines are unavailable, use tinned and omit cooking instructions.

RED MULLET ON GARLIC TOAST

1¹/₂–1³/₄ lb (750 g) red mullet

1 onion

7 fl oz (200 ml) dry white wine

4 thick slices coarse bread

1 clove garlic

olive oil

4 tomatoes

juice of 1 lemon

2 tbsp chopped parsley

salt and pepper

Clean and prepare the fish (see page 9). Peel the onion, chop finely and spread out in the bottom of a well-oiled ovenproof dish; place the fish on top. Sprinkle the wine all over the fish, season with salt and pepper and cover with foil. Bake in the oven, preheated to 350°F (180°C) mark 4 for 15–20 minutes.

Meanwhile, cut the garlic clove in half and rub the cut surface over the slices of bread to flavour;

sprinkle sparingly with good olive oil. Place in the oven briefly to crisp and brown slightly. Set aside. When the fish is done, allow to cool a little, reserving the cooking liquor. Flake the mullet flesh off the bone, breaking it into fairly small pieces. Place in a bowl. Blanch, peel and seed the tomatoes, cut into strips and add to the fish. Strain the cooking liquor and mix 3 tbsp of this with the lemon juice, 3 tbsp oil, the finely chopped parsley, a pinch of salt and plenty of freshly ground pepper. Beat with a fork or small whisk to blend thoroughly. Pour over the fish and tomato mixture; stir briefly and carefully. Leave to stand in a cool place for 30 minutes, then, just before serving, pile on to the garlic toast slices, using a slotted spoon. Sprinkle with a little of the juices left in the bowl if wished.

MOULDED FISH MOUSSE

8 oz (250 g) white fish fillets
2 oz (50 g) butter
2 oz (50 g) plain flour
scant $^3/_4$ pint (400 ml) fish stock (fumet) (see page 39)
1 sachet gelatine powder
3$^1/_2$ fl oz (100 ml) double cream
salt and white peppercorns

Make this recipe with any flavoursome white fish or with a half-and-half mixture of fresh tuna (poached as below) and tinned tuna.

Melt the butter in a saucepan, stir in the flour and cook gently for a minute or two. Poach the fish fillets for 5 minutes in the fish stock, remove, and set aside; add half the hot stock gradually to the flour and butter roux while beating continuously. Continue cooking the sauce, stirring, for 10 minutes; set aside to cool slightly. Reduce the cooked fish fillets to a fairly smooth purée in the processor, adding 2–3 tbsp of the remaining stock to make this easier. Dissolve the gelatine completely in the rest of the hot (not boiling) stock; allow to cool. Stir the fish into the sauce, followed by the liquid containing the gelatine. Beat

the cream lightly and fold gently but thoroughly into the fish mixture, seasoning to taste with freshly ground white pepper and a little salt if necessary.

Rinse out the inside of a fluted mould or ring mould with cold water and fill to the brim with the mixture, tapping the base on the work surface to eliminate any air bubbles. Smooth the surface level. Chill for several hours or overnight; turn out on to a serving plate and decorate as wished.

GRATIN OF SOLE AND SCALLOPS

4 large scallops in their shells
4 fillets of Dover sole
1 mild onion or 2 shallots
2 oz (50 g) butter
3$^1/_2$ fl oz (100 ml) dry white wine
2 tbsp finely chopped parsley
1 small clove garlic (optional)
1$^1/_2$ oz (40 g) freshly grated Parmesan cheese
3 tbsp fine breadcrumbs
salt and pepper

Wash the scallop shells well; place in a single layer in a large frying pan and heat for a few moments until they open. Discard the flat half of the shell. Wash the deeper halves and grease them, using just under half the butter. Clean and trim the molluscs (see page 23). Use a very sharp knife to cut the white of the scallop into 3 or 4 slices. Slice the sole or flounder fillets into small, bite-sized pieces.

Chop the onion very finely, sauté until just tender in the remaining butter in a large, shallow frying pan; add the fish pieces and sauté gently. Add the scallop slices and the whole orange roes or coral of the scallops, the parsley and the garlic (peeled and chopped finely) if used. Sauté for a few seconds, season with a little salt and pepper, sprinkle with the wine and cook until the wine has evaporated. Draw aside from the heat and divide equally between the four greased half shells; mix the cheese and breadcrumbs together and sprinkle over the surface as a topping. Place in the oven, preheated to 450°F (230°C) mark 8, for 10 minutes or place under the grill to brown lightly on top.

SEA BASS AND LEEK MOUSSE

14 oz–1 lb (400 g) fillets of sea bass
4 oz (100 g) trimmed white part of leeks
2 oz (50 g) butter
7 fl oz (200 ml) single cream
1 egg white
1 shallot or spring onion
3¹/₂ fl oz (100 ml) fish stock (fumet) (see page 39)
3¹/₂ fl oz (100 ml) dry white wine
salt and pepper

Wash the fish fillets and pat dry. Slice the leek into very thin rings and sweat in 1 oz (20 g) butter until softened; allow to cool a little. Reduce the fillets to a smooth paste with the leeks in the food processor; turn this purée into a bowl, stir in half the cream, half the egg white and season with salt and pepper. Blend thoroughly. Use half the remaining butter to grease a round mould or pudding bowl which will just accommodate the mixture, smooth the top level with a palette knife and cover loosely with foil. Stand the bowl or mould in a dish of hot water (in a bain-marie) in the oven, preheated to 400°F (200°C) mark 6 for 40 minutes. When cooked, remove the mould from the oven and leave until completely cold.

Finely chop the shallot or spring onion, place in a saucepan with the fish stock and the wine, and boil hard until the liquid has reduced by half. Reduce the heat, add the remaining cream and simmer gently for 3 minutes. Season with salt and pepper.

Just before serving turn the fish mould out on to a plate; pour the sauce over the top and serve at once.

MARINATED BREAM WITH GINGER SAUCE

1 bream weighing 2¹/₄–2¹/₂ lb (1 kg)
7 fl oz (200 ml) fresh lime juice
7 fl oz (200 ml) lemon juice
1 tbsp finely chopped parsley
1 tsp finely chopped fresh ginger
¹/₂ clove garlic, crushed
2 fl oz (50 ml) oil
salt and pepper

Prepare and clean the fish (see pages 9–12) and detach the fillets, cutting each of these into 2 or 3 pieces; make sure that no bones have been left in the fillets. Place in a glass or china dish with the lime and lemon juice and parsley. Cover and chill in the refrigerator for at least 4 hours, turning at fairly frequent intervals: the fillets will react to the acidity in the lemon juice and turn opaque, as if they had been cooked.

One hour before serving, drain off and discard all the juice; mix the fish gently with the ginger, garlic, oil, a pinch of salt and plenty of freshly ground white pepper, then transfer to a serving bowl. Chill until time to serve.

SMELTS LEVANTINE STYLE

1 lb (500 g) smelts
2–3 tbsp milk
plain flour
approx. 8 fl oz (250 ml) oil
10 oz (300 g) onions
1 carrot
1 celery heart
1 sage leaf, 10 rosemary leaves, ¹/₂ bay leaf, 1 clove garlic, all very finely chopped together

4 fl oz (125 ml) white wine vinegar
5 fl oz (150 ml) dry white wine
1 vegetable stock cube
1 small bunch parsley
salt and white peppercorns

Clean the smelts (there is no need to gut), rinse well under running cold water and dry very thoroughly; moisten with the milk and then coat lightly with flour. Heat 7 fl oz (200 ml) oil and fry a few of the smelts at a time so that the oil remains very hot, draining them well and placing on kitchen paper. Sprinkle with a little salt and set aside.

Thinly slice the onions, carrot and celery and fry in fresh oil; add 3 peppercorns and the chopped herbs. When the onion is just soft, add the wine, followed by the vinegar, the crumbled stock cube and 3½ fl oz (100 ml) cold water. Bring to the boil and simmer for 15 minutes. Place the fried fish in a deep serving dish and pour the boiling hot liquid over them, allow to cool completely, cover and leave to stand in a cool place (the refrigerator is too cold) for 12 hours or overnight. Sprinkle with coarsely chopped parsley just before serving.

SPICED HAKE INDIAN STYLE

4 hake steaks weighing 5 oz (150 g) each
9 oz (250 g) onions
3 green peppers
2 chilli peppers
1 small piece fresh ginger
1 clove garlic
5 tbsp oil
1 tsp turmeric
1 tbsp whole coriander seeds
2 bay leaves

4 fl oz (125 ml) cup wine vinegar
salt

Peel the onions and cut into very thin rings. Slice the green peppers equally thinly. Chop the chilli peppers finely with the peeled ginger and garlic (discard the chilli seeds if a less peppery taste is preferred).

Heat the oil in a frying pan and fry the onions gently; add the chilli, ginger and garlic and heat for 10 minutes. Add the turmeric, coriander and bay leaves and cook for a further 3 minutes.

Sprinkle the vinegar over the contents of the pan and when very hot, add the fish steaks. Cook for 10 minutes, turning once with a fish slice.

Leave to cool, then chill in the refrigerator for 24 hours. Serve cold, garnished with lemon slices.

HERRING SALAD

8 salted herring fillets
2 mild red onions
2 large tomatoes
1 red pepper
1 green pepper
1 tsp strong English mustard powder
pinch sugar
cayenne pepper
pinch garlic powder
4 tbsp oil
4 tbsp vinegar
1 small bunch chives
salt

Rinse the herring fillets thoroughly under running cold water to remove excess salt; drain on kitchen paper. Cut into bite-sized pieces and place in a salad bowl.

Peel the onions and slice into very thin rings; wash the tomatoes and cut across into rounds, removing the seeds; add the onion and tomato rings to the fish. Grill the peppers briefly, turning every few seconds, to loosen the skin. Peel, slice in half, and discard the seeds, stalk and pale inner membrane. Slice thinly into rings or strips and add to the salad bowl.

Mix together the mustard, sugar and a pinch each of cayenne pepper and garlic powder. Gradually add the oil and vinegar, beating as you do so to blend well; add salt to taste. Pour the dressing over the herring salad, mix gently and garnish with chopped chives.

FISHERMAN'S FLAN

8 oz (250 g) frozen puff pastry
1 bream weighing 1 lb (450 g)
2 oz (50 g) butter
fine fresh or dried breadcrumbs
1 onion
2 leeks
3¹/₂ fl oz (100 ml) dry white wine
1 tbsp tomato purée
2 eggs
2 oz (50 g) freshly grated Parmesan cheese
3¹/₂ fl oz (100 ml) single cream
salt and pepper

Thaw the frozen pastry at room temperature. Clean, fillet and skin the fish (see pages 9–12). Cut the fish into small pieces.

Peel the onions and slice with the thoroughly washed leeks into very thin rings; sweat them together in 1 oz (30 g) of the butter for 10–15 minutes.

Add the fish and fry gently for a minute or two. Blend together the wine and tomato purée

and add to the pan. Season with a little salt and pepper and continue cooking for 5 minutes. Leave to cool.

Grease a ceramic flan dish with the remaining butter and sprinkle with the breadcrumbs; roll out the thawed puff pastry and use to line the dish. Prick the surface of the pastry with a fork, cover with foil, and weigh down with dried beans. Bake blind for 10 minutes at 350°F (180°C) mark 4.

While the pastry is cooking, blend the fish mixture with the lightly beaten eggs, a little salt, the cheese and cream. Remove the beans and foil from the pastry case and fill with the fish mixture, smoothing level; replace in the oven, increase the heat to 400°F (200°C) mark 6, and cook for about 15 minutes. Serve hot.

FISH SOUP WITH PAPRIKA

2¹/₄ lb (1 kg) John Dory
2 onions
2 tbsp oil
1 oz (25 g) butter
¹/₂ tsp paprika
4 medium-sized waxy potatoes
1 large red pepper
8 slices coarse white bread
salt

Clean, fillet and skin the fish (see pages 9–10). Cut into bite-sized pieces.

Peel and chop the onion finely; fry until just tender in the oil and butter in a large, heavy-bottomed saucepan.

Add 2¹/₂ pints (1¹/₄ litres) hot water, the fish pieces, salt and paprika; bring to the boil, reduce the heat, cover and simmer for 40 minutes. Peel the potatoes, cut into fairly small pieces, and add to the soup with the red pepper, cut into very fine strips. Continue cooking for about 20 minutes, or

53

until the potatoes are tender. Toast the bread slices in the oven until crisp and serve with the soup.

PASTA WITH SEA BASS AND HERBS

1 sea bass weighing 1¼ lb (300 g)
10 oz (600 g) macaroni or similar pasta shapes
14 oz (400 g) tinned tomatoes
1 carrot
1 onion
1 celery stalk
1 clove garlic
1 sprig parsley
1 sprig fresh basil (or pinch dried basil)
3½ fl oz (100 ml) dry white wine
4 tbsp oil
salt and pepper

Any well-flavoured white fish which remains firm when cooked can be used for this recipe. Clean, gut, fillet and skin the fish (see pages 9–12) and cut the fillets into fairly large pieces.

Wash and prepare the vegetables and herbs; chop them all very finely and fry gently in the oil in a large frying pan. When tender, add the fish pieces, cook slowly for a few minutes, then remove and set aside. Add the drained and chopped tomatoes to the pan; season with salt and pepper and boil until slightly thickened. Add the wine and continue boiling until the liquid is considerably reduced. Turn down the heat. Add the pasta to plenty of fast boiling salted water. When the pasta has only a few minutes left to cook, return the fish pieces to the tomato sauce in the frying pan and cook for a further 5 minutes. Serve the pasta *al dente* (tender, but retaining some bite), topped with the fish sauce.

PASTA WITH SARDINES AND FENNEL

2 tbsp sultanas
³/₄ lb (350 g) fresh sardines (or 2 tins)
2 bulbs fennel
1 large onion
4 fl oz (125 ml) oil
2 tbsp tomato purée
1 oz (25 g) pine nuts
6 tinned anchovy fillets
12 oz (350 g) short macaroni or pasta shells
salt and pepper

Soak the sultanas in warm water for 15 minutes. Meanwhile, pull the heads off the sardines, removing the innards with them; open up the sardines by slitting down their bellies if necessary to remove the backbone. Boil the fennel until tender in 7 pints (4 litres) salted water; drain, reserving this flavoured water to cook the pasta, and chop. Peel and chop the onion finely; boil in 8 fl oz (250 ml) water in a fairly large saucepan until the water has almost completely evaporated; add all but 3 tbsp of the oil, the tomato purée, pine nuts and the drained sultanas. Cover and simmer for 15 minutes.

Reduce the heat, add the sardines, the fennel and salt and pepper. Simmer for 10 minutes. Crush the anchovies into the remaining oil in a small saucepan over a low heat. Add to the fish mixture.

Cook the pasta fast in the reserved fennel-flavoured water until *al dente* (just tender but retaining some bite); drain and serve immediately with the fish and fennel sauce.

Note: If fresh sardines are unavailable, substitute tinned and omit the preparation instructions given in the recipe.

LIVORNO FISH SOUP

4 red mullet

2¼–2½ lb (1 kg) mixed seafood (e.g. bream, octopus, Dublin Bay prawns, squid, etc.)

4 fl oz (125 ml) oil

2 cloves garlic

1 chilli pepper

1 onion

4 fl oz (125 ml) dry red wine

4 fl oz (125 ml) sieved tinned tomatoes

½ sachet saffron powder

1 small bunch parsley

4 thick slices coarse white bread

salt and pepper

This is a traditional Italian recipe, made with red mullet. You can vary your choice of seafood. Trim and clean the red mullet (see page 9), place on a plate, sprinkle with 3–4 tbsp oil, season with salt and pepper and leave in a cool place. Clean and prepare all the other seafood (see page 9) and cut into small, bite-sized pieces. Pour the remaining oil into a large saucepan and fry the garlic clove gently in it, with the chilli pepper and finely chopped onion. Add all the fish except the red mullet and cook gently, turning once or twice, for 5–10 minutes. Add the red wine and cook until it has evaporated. Season with salt and pepper, add half the sieved tomato, the saffron, finely chopped parsley and 4 fl oz (125 ml) hot water. Cover and simmer for 20 minutes.

While this is cooking, select a saucepan just large enough to take the red mullet in one layer and in it fry the other whole, peeled garlic clove in ¼ cup oil until faintly coloured. Remove the garlic and discard, then add the remaining strained tomato to the flavoured oil with a little salt and pepper, followed by the red mullet. Cover and cook gently for 15–20 minutes.

When both batches of fish are ready, add the red mullet to the assorted seafood, sprinkle with chopped parsley and serve hot. Toast the bread slices in the oven and hand round separately.

SPAGHETTI WITH ANCHOVY SAUCE

3 fresh anchovies

3 salted anchovies

1 onion

1 clove garlic

1 small bunch parsley

1 small sprig rosemary

10 fresh basil leaves (or pinch dried basil)

1 tsp oregano

4 fl oz (125 ml) olive oil

1 small red pepper

10 oz (400 g) spaghetti

salt

Prepare and fillet the fresh anchovies; chop roughly and set aside. Chop the onion and garlic finely with the parsley, rosemary and basil. Sauté this mixture gently in the oil, then add the oregano and the finely chopped red pepper. Continue cooking over a gentle heat for 5 minutes. Keep warm.

Rinse the salted anchovies under running cold water to wash off excess salt; remove most of their bones. Crush with 1–2 tsp olive oil in a saucepan, add the chopped fresh anchovies, and cook very gently for 7–8 minutes.

Cook the spaghetti in plenty of boiling salted water until tender but with a little bite to them; drain well and add to the saucepan containing the herbs. Stir over a low heat for a minute.

Serve in warmed individual plates or bowls, topping each serving with some of the anchovy sauce.

VERMICELLI WITH ANCHOVY AND AUBERGINE SAUCE

4 fresh anchovies

2 salted anchovies
4 fl oz (125 ml) oil
2 cloves garlic
1 medium-sized aubergine
3 large ripe tomatoes
1 yellow pepper
2 oz (50 g) black olives, stoned
1 tbsp capers
4–5 fresh basil leaves (or pinch dried)
14 oz (400 g) vermicelli
salt and pepper

Gut, wash and fillet the fresh anchovies. Rinse the salted anchovies under running cold water, and bone. (Use 4 drained tinned anchovy fillets instead of salted if necessary.)

Sauté the whole peeled garlic cloves in the oil, remove and discard; add the salted (or tinned) anchovies and work into the oil until they break up. Add the fresh anchovies, finely chopped, and the diced aubergine. Cook, stirring carefully, then add the peeled, seeded and chopped tomatoes (use tinned if wished). Simmer for 5 minutes. Add the pepper cut into thin strips, the coarsely chopped olives, capers and basil. Season with freshly ground pepper and a very little salt if wished. Simmer for 20 minutes. Cook the pasta until *al dente* (tender, but retaining some bite) in plenty of salted water; drain and serve with the piping hot fish and aubergine mixture.

Note: Spaghetti may replace the vermicelli if wished.

SEAFOOD SPAGHETTI

1 scorpionfish weighing approx. 1¼ lb (600 g) (or use monkfish or lobster)
1 lb (500 g) clams
2 cloves garlic
4 tbsp oil
1 chilli pepper

4 fl oz (125 ml) dry white wine
pinch oregano
14 oz (400 g) tinned tomatoes, drained
1 small bunch parsley
12 oz (350 g) spaghetti
salt

Clean, gut and fillet the scorpionfish (or your chosen alternative); remove the skin (see pages 9–10) and cut the flesh into bite-sized pieces. If using fresh clams, wash well, place in a pan over a high heat for a few seconds to open, take them out of their shells, and strain the liquor from the shells through a fine cloth placed in a sieve. (Tinned shelled clams may be used if preferred. An 8-oz [245-g] tin will be ample; drain and save the juice.)

Sauté the whole peeled garlic clove and the chilli pepper in the oil in a saucepan, add the clams and fry for 2 minutes; add the fish pieces and sauté for 3–4 minutes. Add the white wine and about 4–6 fl oz (120–175 ml) of the juice from the clams. Sprinkle on the oregano. Simmer for a minute or two; remove the clams and fish pieces using a slotted spoon and keep hot. Coarsely chop the tomatoes and add to the saucepan. Add a little salt and boil to reduce and thicken the sauce.

Boil the pasta until tender but not soft in plenty of salted water. Return the clams and fish to the thickened sauce with the finely chopped parsley; if you decide to use cooked lobster instead of fish, cut it into fairly small pieces and add it at this point. Simmer for 2 minutes while you drain the pasta thoroughly. Combine the two gently and serve at once.

SCORPIONFISH SOUP WITH GARLIC BREAD

2¼ lb (1 kg) scorpionfish or monkfish
2 tbsp oil

3 cloves garlic

2 large ripe tomatoes

7 fl oz (200 ml) dry white wine

pinch crumbled dried chilli pepper

4 thick slices coarse white bread or French bread

1 small bunch parsley

salt

Prepare your chosen fish as necessary (see page 9) and keep whole. Sauté the whole, peeled garlic cloves in the oil until they begin to colour, then remove and discard them. Skin and seed the tomatoes (use tinned tomatoes if wished), chop, and add to the flavoured oil. Cook for 5–10 minutes before adding the fish. Turn two or three times while cooking, using a wooden spoon to avoid breaking the skin; add the white wine and continue cooking until it has reduced by half. Season with a pinch each of salt and chilli pepper, add 3½ pints (2 litres) hot water, bring to boiling point then simmer gently for about 30 minutes. Remove the fish carefully from the saucepan, using large slotted spoons or a ladle; flake off all the flesh, discarding the head, tail, fins, bones, etc. and return the flesh to the soup, increasing the heat for a few minutes.

Cut the remaining garlic clove in half and rub the cut surfaces over the bread slices; place one slice each in the bottom of 4 warmed soup bowls and ladle the soup on top. Sprinkle with chopped parsley and serve.

CREAM OF SCORPIONFISH SOUP

2¾ lb (1.2 kg) scorpionfish or monkfish

1 carrot

1 celery stalk

1 onion

2 or 3 peppercorns

salt

Prepare your chosen fish (see page 9), wash and drain. Bring 5¼ pints (3 litres) water to the boil in a very large saucepan with the peeled, thinly sliced carrot and onion, thinly sliced celery and peppercorns. Boil for 20 minutes; draw aside from the heat, add the fish and bring slowly back to the boil; simmer for 50 minutes, uncovered, by which time the liquid should have reduced to half its original volume.

Put through a food mill three times, using a smaller gauge disc each time you purée the mixture; lastly, strain through a fine-gauge *chinois* sieve. Add salt to taste and reheat but do not allow to boil.

Serve in small individual bowls or consommé cups, with croûtons.

SEAFOOD SOUP

1¾ lb (800 g) assorted fish (e.g. red mullet, fresh tuna, grey mullet, baby squid, cuttlefish)

7–8 fl oz (200–225 ml) olive oil

1 onion

2 tbsp chopped parsley

2 bay leaves

pinch ground cinnamon

1 clove garlic

2 leeks

2 celery stalks

1 tbsp wine vinegar

salt and pepper

Trim, gut and fillet all the fish; wash, dry and cut into fairly small, even-sized pieces. Reserve the heads, tails and bones for the stock, washing the heads thoroughly.

Sauté the thinly sliced onion very gently in 6 fl oz (175 ml) of the oil and add the parsley, bay leaves, cinnamon, salt and freshly ground pepper. When the onion is very soft, start adding the fish, beginning with the squid and cook for a few minutes before adding the rest. Sauté gently for

15–20 minutes; turn off the heat and leave to stand. Sweat the garlic and the roughly chopped leeks and celery in the remaining oil; pour in the vinegar and allow to evaporate. Add the fish heads, tails and bones, stirring gently, then pour in 1¾–2 pints (1 litre) cold water. Boil for 30 minutes, then strain through a fine sieve. Remove and discard the bay leaves from the pan containing the cooked fish; pour in the fish stock and bring to a very gentle boil, adding more water if necessary and more salt and pepper if needed.

Serve with crisp oven-toasted slices of French bread.

BOURRIDE

2³/₄–3 lb (approx. 1.2 kg) assorted fish (e.g. sea bass, monkfish, whiting, mackerel, grey mullet)
4 cloves garlic
4 egg yolks
10 fl oz (300 ml) olive oil
1¹/₂ tbsp lemon juice
10 fl oz (300 ml) dry white wine
1 leek
1 onion
1 sprig thyme
1 bay leaf
1 small piece fennel
1 carrot
rind (with no pith) of 1 orange
8 thick slices coarse white or French bread
salt and black peppercorns

This is a traditional Provençal recipe. Make 1 quantity *aïoli* (see page 38 for method) using 2 of the egg yolks (at room temperature) and all the oil and lemon juice as listed above. Cover with cling film and keep cool.

Clean, fillet and prepare all the fish (see page 9) and cut into fairly small pieces. Slice the leek, onion and carrot. Pour 1¾ pints (1 litre) water into a fish kettle or large saucepan, and add the white wine, leek, onion, carrot, thyme, bay leaf, fennel and orange peel, a little salt and 4–5 peppercorns. Cover and bring to the boil. Place the fish pieces on the fish kettle grid (or in a frying basket if using a saucepan for poaching) and lower into the liquid; cover and immediately reduce the heat, then simmer gently for 10 minutes. Remove the fish pieces, draining well, and keep warm in a covered serving dish. Strain the liquid.

Toast the bread slices in the oven until crisp, and keep warm. Set 6 tbsp of the *aïoli* aside in a small bowl; transfer the remainder to a large, heavy-bottomed saucepan and stir in the remaining 2 egg yolks with a wooden spoon. Place the saucepan on a heat diffuser on the hob or just to the side of a very gentle heat and use the wooden spoon to blend the fish stock a little at a time into the egg mixture. When all the stock has been added, heat the soup gradually over a very gentle heat while stirring: the egg mixture will thicken the soup slightly. Do not allow to boil or it will curdle.

Ladle the soup into warmed soup bowls and add 1 or 2 slices of toasted bread. Serve the fish pieces as a second course, handing round the remaining *aïoli* to accompany it.

HAKE SPECIAL

4 hake weighing approx. 8 oz (250 g) each
2 oz (50 g) dried ceps (boletus edulis)
1 lb (500 g) waxy potatoes
1 celery stalk
1 carrot
1 onion
3 sprigs chervil
2 fl oz (50 ml) oil
1 oz (25 g) butter
8 anchovy fillets (tinned)
1¹/₂ tbsp capers
salt and pepper

Prepare the hake (see page 9), trimming, gutting and cutting off their heads if wished. (They can be filleted while being left 'whole' as shown on page 14, if wished.) Wash and dry. Soak the dried mushrooms in a cup of warm water to soften. Boil the potatoes in salted water until tender but not soft; drain and peel. Clean and finely chop the celery, carrot and onion with the chervil. Rinse the mushrooms, squeeze out excess moisture and chop coarsely.

Heat the oil in a large, heavy-bottomed saucepan or casserole; fry the chopped vegetable mixture very gently. Add salt and pepper. Sweat for 20 minutes, moistening with a little hot water when necessary. Place the fish on top in a single layer, cover and cook for 15 minutes. Melt the butter. Slice the potatoes and lay them in a single layer on a large warmed serving platter; place the hake carefully on top. Heat the butter left in the pan until it begins to turn golden brown and then mix with the very finely chopped anchovies and capers. Pour over the hake and serve very hot.

SPICED RED MULLET

8 red mullet weighing 4 oz (120 g) each
plain flour
7 fl oz (200 ml) oil
7 fl oz (200 ml) dry white wine
1³/₄ lb (800 g) ripe tomatoes
1 clove garlic
pinch dried thyme
curry powder
1 lemon
salt and pepper

Trim, gut, wash, descale and dry the fish; dust lightly with flour. Fry in very hot oil over a high heat for 5 minutes on each side. Grease a fairly shallow ovenproof dish with butter, place the drained, fried fish in it in a single layer, pour in the wine and leave to stand.

Wash the tomatoes; cut into quarters without

skinning them, cook gently for 1 hour in a covered dish in the oven with the garlic, 3 tbsp oil, a pinch of thyme and a little curry powder to taste, salt and freshly ground pepper. Pour this sauce over the fish and bake in the oven at 425°F (220°C) mark 7 for 10–15 minutes. Serve decorated with lemon wedges.

BAKED FISH PASTA

12 oz (350 g) sprats
1 clove garlic
1 small bunch parsley
10 basil leaves (or pinch dried basil)
3¹/₂ fl oz (100 ml) oil
14 oz (400 g) tinned tomatoes, drained
14 oz (400 g) pasta shapes (e.g. quills or macaroni)
4 oz (120 g) stoned black olives
2 tbsp capers
2 oz (50 g) fine dried breadcrumbs
salt

Prepare the sprats, removing their heads, tails, innards and backbone (see page 14). Wash and dry well with kitchen paper and set aside. Chop the garlic, parsley and basil finely together; place in a saucepan with the oil and tomatoes; cook gently for 10 minutes. Chop the sprats into fairly small pieces and add to the tomato mixture. Simmer for 4–5 minutes.

Boil the pasta in plenty of salted water until tender; drain well and stir in the tomato mixture. Chop the olives and capers and add, mixing well. Transfer to a wide, fairly shallow oven-to-table dish. Cover the surface with a generous sprinkling of breadcrumbs and place in the oven, preheated to 400°F (200°C) mark 6 until lightly browned.

SEAFOOD PARCELS

1 gilt-head bream weighing 1³/₄–2 lb (800–900 g)

8 oz (220 g) prawns
1 lb (500 g) mussels
1 onion
2 cloves garlic
1 small bunch parsley
4 fl oz (120 ml) olive oil
juice of 1 lemon
salt and pepper

Prepare the fish, gutting through the gill aperture (see page 9); wash and dry. Prepare the mussels (see page 22) and heat briefly in a large saucepan over a high heat to open; remove the molluscs from their shells.

Chop the onion finely with the garlic and parsley. Grease a sheet of foil large enough to wrap the fish with half the oil; sprinkle with 1 generous tbsp of the chopped mixture; distribute the mussels and peeled prawns on top. Place the bream on this bed, sprinkle with salt and freshly ground pepper, the remaining chopped herb mixture, the strained lemon juice and the remaining oil. Fold the foil to enclose the fish, leaving an air space inside but no gaps through which steam can escape; place in the oven, preheated to 350°F (180°C) mark 4, for about 20 minutes.

GREY MULLET SOUP FRIULI STYLE

2¼ lb (1 kg) grey mullet
4 fl oz (100 ml) olive oil
3 cloves garlic
4 fl oz (120 ml) white wine vinegar
salt and pepper

Prepare and fillet the fish (see page 9), cutting it into fairly small slices. Sauté the garlic cloves slowly in the oil in a large, heavy-bottomed saucepan; when they turn pale golden brown, remove and discard them. Add the fish to the flavoured oil and fry for a few minutes, turning once with a fish slice.

Sprinkle with the vinegar, turn up the heat and allow the vinegar to evaporate. Add sufficient water to completely cover the fish; season with salt and freshly ground pepper; simmer gently for 20 minutes.

In the Friuli region of Italy, this substantial soup is traditionally served with piping hot polenta.

FISH SOUFFLÉ

approx. 8 oz (200 g) poached or baked fish fillets
2 oz (50 g) butter
2 oz (50 g) plain flour
18 fl oz (500 ml) milk
4 eggs
50 g (2 oz) freshly grated Parmesan cheese
salt and pepper

You can use almost any fish (or cooked fish leftovers) for this soufflé. Make sure there are no bones, scales or skin and flake the fish finely with a fork. Melt 2 tbsp of the butter in a saucepan; stir in the flour and cook gently until this roux has coloured slightly. Heat the milk to scalding point gradually and beat it into the roux; continue beating to prevent any lumps forming until you have a smooth sauce. Season with salt and pepper; cook for 10 minutes, stirring continuously. Draw aside from the heat.

Stir in the fish followed by the egg yolks, beating each one in well before adding the next. Stir in the cheese. Beat the egg whites with a pinch of salt until stiff but not dry; fold gently but thoroughly into the fish mixture with a mixing spatula.

Grease a soufflé dish with the remaining butter and turn the mixture into it (choose a size which the mixture will three-quarters fill). Tap the bottom of the dish lightly on the work surface to make the mixture settle evenly. Place in a preheated oven at 400°F (200°C) mark 6 for 40 minutes. Serve at once.

UZUKURI

1 sea bass weighing 1³/₄ lb (800 g)

1 large radish or 2-in (1-cm) piece Daikon root

1 chilli pepper

1 spring onion

5 tbsp lemon juice

5 tbsp dashi *(see method)*

2 fl oz (50 ml) light soy sauce

Choose only extremely fresh sea bass for this recipe. Trim, gut, fillet and skin the fish (see pages 9–12). Peel and grate the radish or Daikon root and mix with the very finely chopped chilli pepper. Cut the fillets into thin strips, slicing obliquely with the knife held at an angle of about 45° to the chopping board. Arrange on a serving plate and sprinkle with finely sliced spring onion and the radish mixture. Mix the lemon juice, *dashi* (instant Japanese broth, mixed and allowed to cool) and soy sauce, and hand round separately for each person to pour over a serving of fish.

SUSHI

12 oz (300 g) very fresh filleted assorted fish (e.g. sea bass, sole, salmon, fresh tuna)

4 large prawns

3 tbsp white wine vinegar

1 tbsp sugar

1 tbsp saké

14 oz (400 g) boiled short-grain rice

finely sliced vinegar-pickled ginger root

light soy sauce

ground ginger

Peel the cooked prawns, cut lengthwise in half and remove the black vein. Slice the raw fish thinly, cutting diagonally across the fillets and with the knife held at an acute angle. Mix the vinegar with the sugar and saké in a bowl and mix this with the cold boiled rice (use short-grain rice, which holds its shape well when moulded). Rinse your hands in cold water and shape the rice into oval rissoles about 2¹/₂ in (6 cm) long. Place these on a serving plate and top each with a thin slice of pickled ginger and a prawn or a slice of fish. Put the plate in the centre of the table, surrounded by little bowls of soy sauce flavoured with a few drops of ground ginger mixed with a little water.

FISH SALAD

1 lb (500 g) mixed fish (e.g. sea bass, hake or cod, grey mullet, dentex)

1 bay leaf

3 eggs

10 green olives, stoned

2 oz (50 g) French beans

2 tbsp frozen small peas

2 oz (50 g) gherkins or dill pickles

1 lettuce heart

1¹/₂–2 tbsp capers

8 fl oz (225 ml) mayonnaise

salt

Prepare the fish (see page 9), wash and poach in lightly salted water with the bay leaf for about 20 minutes. Drain; remove any remaining bones, skin, etc. and cut into bite-sized pieces. Cool.

Hard-boil the eggs, cool under running cold water, then shell and cut into quarters. Trim the beans and boil until tender; drain and cut into 1-in (2–3-cm) lengths. Boil the peas until just tender, drain and cool. Cut the gherkins lengthwise in half. Arrange half the lettuce leaves in a salad bowl; place the fish fillets on top with the olives, gherkins, beans, peas and capers; top with the mayonnaise. Shred the remaining lettuce leaves and sprinkle on top of the mayonnaise. Garnish with the hard-boiled egg wedges and chill until just before serving.

STEAMED SEA BASS

1 sea bass or striped bass weighing approx. 2¼ lb (1 kg)

8 fl oz (225 ml) court-bouillon (see page 39)

12 new potatoes

3 tbsp butter

1 oz (25 g) plain flour

1 egg yolk

1½ lemons

3 tbsp single cream

few sprigs parsley

salt and pepper

Trim, gut, descale and wash the fish thoroughly (see page 10). Dry with kitchen paper.

Pour the *court-bouillon* into the fish kettle (see page 25), put the rack in upside down (handles downwards), and place the fish on top; ensure that the fish is well above the level of the liquid. Cover, bring to the boil, then steam for 14 minutes. Check whether the fish is done by inserting a sharp pointed knife down to the backbone: the flesh should be absolutely white with no trace of pink.

Steam the potatoes and keep warm with the fish, covered with foil. Melt the butter in a saucepan, stir in the flour and cook for a few minutes until the roux starts to colour. Beat in 6 tbsp of the hot, strained *court-bouillon* and cook for a few minutes, stirring continuously. Season with salt and freshly ground white pepper to taste. Beat the egg yolk and lemon juice together in a small bowl, stir in the cream and the finely chopped parsley. Beat into the hot sauce and serve with the steamed fish and potatoes.

SEA BASS WITH BRANDY, CREAM AND GREEN PEPPERCORNS

1¼–1½ lb (600 g) fillets of sea bass

3 shallots or large spring onions

2 fl oz (50 ml) olive or sunflower oil

1 oz (25 g) butter

2 fl oz (50 ml) brandy

1 tbsp bottled green peppercorns, drained

5 fl oz (150 ml) double cream

salt

Rinse the fish fillets in cold water and pat thoroughly dry with kitchen paper. Peel and finely chop the shallots or spring onions and fry very gently in the oil and butter in a casserole dish until transparent but do not allow to colour. Add the fish fillets to the casserole and fry for a few minutes; turn once, using a fish slice to avoid breaking up the fillets. Pour the brandy over the fish; allow to heat until almost boiling and then set alight. When the flames have died down completely, spoon the cream over the fish and sprinkle with the peppercorns. Transfer the casserole dish (uncovered) to the oven, preheated to 475°F (240°C) mark 9, for 5 minutes. Transfer the fish to a heated serving dish. Strain all the cooking liquid and juices left in the casserole into a small saucepan, add salt to taste, and stir very briefly over a moderate heat before pouring over the fish.

MARINATED SEA BASS

4 sea bass steaks weighing 8 oz (200 g) each

plain flour

4 tbsp oil

9 fl oz (250 ml) white wine vinegar

9 fl oz (250 ml) dry white wine

1 onion

generous pinch saffron powder

pinch cinnamon

1 whole clove

1 small sprig rosemary

1 bay leaf

1 lemon

salt and peppercorns

Wash the fish and dry thoroughly. Coat lightly with flour and fry in the oil over a high heat for 2–3 minutes, turning once. Reduce the heat and cook for 5–10 minutes or until done; set aside.

Pour the vinegar and wine into a saucepan, add half the onion (sliced), the saffron, cinnamon, a pinch of crushed or chopped clove, the rosemary, bay leaf, salt and a few peppercorns. Boil for 15 minutes; leave to cool.

Transfer the fish into a glass or ceramic dish; pour the marinade and the juice of half the lemon over it. Cover with a tight-fitting lid or foil and leave to stand for at least 12 hours in a cool place, turning the fish carefully two or three times.

Use a slotted fish slice to remove and drain the fish, transfer to a serving dish and garnish with the remaining half lemon cut into wedges, and the rest of the onion, sliced into thin rings.

SEA BASS WITH CAVIAR CREAM SAUCE

4 small sea bass weighing approx. 8 oz (250 g) each

1¹/₂ oz (40 g) butter

14 fl oz (400 ml) dry sparkling wine or dry white wine

2 eggs

7 fl oz (200 ml) olive oil

1 lemon

7 fl oz (200 ml) whipping cream

4 tbsp black lumpfish roe (Danish 'caviar')

salt and pepper

Trim, gut, wash and dry the fish (see page 9). Dot small pieces of the butter all over the bottom of a casserole dish just large enough to accommodate all 4 fish in a single layer, heads to tails; pour in the wine and season with salt and pepper. Heat until the liquid boils, then cover, place in the

oven, preheated to 350°F (180°C) mark 4, and bake for 8–10 minutes. Drain off the liquid into a small saucepan and set aside. Replace the lid on the dish containing the fish and return to the oven, turning the heat off as you do so.

Prepare the sauce: beat the egg yolks with a pinch of salt and a few drops of lemon juice; beat in the oil, adding a few drops at a time. The sauce will thicken and increase in volume; when it has done so, beat in a little more lemon juice.

Reduce the reserved cooking liquid over a high heat; when all but 3 tbsp has evaporated, allow to cool for a minute or two and then beat into the egg and lemon sauce. Fold in the lightly beaten cream and then the caviar, taking care not to crush it. Allow the sauce to cool. Serve the fish hot, handing round the cold sauce separately.

BAKED SEA BASS WITH PRAWN SAUCE

1 sea bass weighing 2³/₄ lb (1.2 kg)

1³/₄ pints (1 litre) fish stock (fumet) (see page 39)

8 oz (200 g) peeled small prawns or shrimps

3¹/₂ oz (100 g) butter

1¹/₂ oz (40 g) plain flour

3¹/₂ fl oz (100 ml) single cream

¹/₂ lemon

salt and pepper

Make the *fumet* (see page 39) and strain it. Prepare the fish for cooking (see page 9), wash well and dry; season with salt and pepper and place in a casserole with about 11 fl oz (325 ml) of the fish stock. Cover tightly with a lid or foil and place in the oven, preheated to 350°F (180°C) mark 4, for 40 minutes, basting the fish at frequent intervals. Drain off all the juices, and reserve, when the fish is done; keep the fish warm in the oven, turned down very low with the door slightly ajar.

Blend 2 oz (50 g) of the prawns or shrimps with 3¹/₂ fl oz (100 ml) fish stock in the blender. Melt the butter in a saucepan, stir in the flour and cook for 2 minutes over a very low heat while stirring. Stir in

63

about 4 fl oz (120 ml) of the cooking juices and liquid drained from the fish; gradually add 10 fl oz (300 ml) of the fish stock, stirring all the time. Cook gently for 7–8 minutes; add the liquidized prawns, the cream and the remaining, whole, shellfish. Season with salt and pepper to taste. Cook for a further 3–4 minutes; add the lemon juice, stir well and cook for a final minute.

Remove the skin from the fish. Serve with some of the sauce and hand round the rest separately in a sauceboat.

BRAISED SEA BASS WITH CHAMPAGNE AND MUSHROOMS

1 sea bass weighing approx. 2¹/₄ lb (1 kg)
2 oz (50 g) dried ceps (boletus edulis)
1 onion
1 shallot
1 clove garlic
1 sprig marjoram
1 celery stalk
1 carrot
3¹/₂ fl oz (100 ml) oil
4 anchovy fillets
plain flour
3¹/₂ fl oz (100 ml) champagne or sparkling dry white wine
3 tbsp tomato purée
3¹/₂ fl oz (100 ml) single cream
salt and pepper

Clean and gut the sea bass (see page 9). Soak the dried mushrooms in warm water for 1 hour to soften and plump up. Finely chop the onion, shallot, garlic, marjoram, celery and carrot. Heat the oil gently in an oval casserole; crush the anchovy fillets into the oil and stir until they have dissolved. Add the chopped vegetable mixture and sweat, covered, until tender, stirring occasionally. Season with freshly ground pepper. Squeeze excess moisture out of the mushrooms, chop coarsely and add to the casserole. Cook gently for about 10 minutes. Coat the fish lightly with flour and shake off excess. Place in the casserole and cook until lightly browned on each side, turning once. Mix the tomato purée with the wine and pour over the fish; add salt and more pepper if necessary. Cover and cook gently for 20 minutes, turning only once, half way through cooking.

When the fish is cooked, transfer to a heated serving platter. Put all the juices and ingredients left in the pan into the blender and purée with the cream. Heat in a small saucepan; do not allow to boil. Pour this sauce over the fish or hand round separately in a sauceboat.

POACHED SEA BASS WITH AVOCADO SAUCE

1 sea bass weighing approx. 2¹/₄ lb (1 kg)
court-bouillon *(see page 25)*
2 avocados
juice of 1 lemon
1 small onion or shallot
1¹/₂ tbsp oil
salt and cayenne pepper

Clean and gut the fish (see page 9). Lower into the lukewarm or cold *court-bouillon* and bring slowly to boiling point; immediately reduce the heat so that the liquid barely simmers; cook for 15–20 minutes. Remove from the heat and leave the fish to cool completely in the *court-bouillon*. Make the sauce: cut the avocados lengthwise in half, remove the stone, and scoop out all the flesh, mixing immediately with half the lemon juice to prevent discoloration. Place in the blender with the chopped onion and the remaining lemon juice, the oil and a pinch each of salt and cayenne pepper. Process until very smooth.

Spoon the avocado sauce into a shallow serving dish and place the skinned fish on top. Serve cold.

WHISKY SOUR HAKE

1¹/₂ lb (700 g) fillets of hake or cod
1 onion
2 cloves garlic
10 basil leaves
2 lemons
3¹/₂ fl oz (100 ml) oil
7 fl oz (200 ml) whisky
1¹/₂ tsp plain flour
salt and pepper

Wash the fish fillets and dry well. Finely chop the onion, garlic and basil. Mix with the grated rind of ¹/₂ lemon.

Pour the oil into a wide, shallow casserole dish; arrange the fillets in a single layer, season with salt and pepper, and sprinkle with the chopped ingredients. Fry for a few minutes, turning once only with a fish slice. Pour the whisky all over the fish and continue cooking over a moderate heat for 7–8 minutes.

Remove the fillets and transfer to a heated serving plate; stir the flour into the juice from the remaining lemons, blend well and add to the whisky-flavoured juices in the casserole. Cook over a slightly higher heat, stirring constantly, until fairly thick and smooth. Pour over the hake fillets and serve.

SUMMER HAKE

2 hake weighing 1 lb (500 g) each
3 tbsp soy sauce
2 fl oz (50 ml) sweet sherry
2 star anise
4¹/₂ fl oz (115 ml) sunflower oil
4 spring onions
1 tsp sugar
salt

Prepare the fish, trimming, gutting (see page 9), washing and drying it. Slice into steaks about ³/₄ in (1 cm) thick; place in a shallow dish. Mix 2 tbsp of the soy sauce with the sherry, star anise and salt, and sprinkle over the fish slices; leave to stand for 10 minutes, turning two or three times.

Slice the spring onions and sweat gently in 3 tbsp of the oil and 3 tbsp water. Add a pinch of salt, the remaining soy sauce and the sugar. Sweat over a very low heat for a further 5–10 minutes; sieve. Pour 4 tbsp of the oil into a frying pan and fry the well drained fish slices over a fairly high heat for 5–6 minutes each side. When golden brown and crisp on the outside, transfer to a shallow dish. Spoon a little of the sauce over each slice and leave to cool. Serve cold.

HAKE AND OLIVE FRICADELLES

6 oz (175 g) fresh white breadcrumbs
milk
14 oz (400 g) fillets of hake or cod
2 oz (50 g) butter
1 small bunch parsley
5 basil leaves
2 tbsp freshly grated Parmesan cheese
1 egg
24 stuffed green olives
olive oil for deep-frying
salt and pepper
4–6 oz (120–175 g) fine dry breadcrumbs

Soak the fresh white breadcrumbs in a little milk, squeeze out excess moisture. Wash and dry the fillets. Heat the butter in a frying pan until light brown; add the fillets and cook over a very low heat for 10 minutes; season. Draw aside from the heat; place in the food processor with the fresh breadcrumbs and reduce to a smooth, thick purée. Transfer to a bowl; add the finely chopped parsley and basil, the Parmesan cheese and lightly beaten egg and blend well, adding more fresh breadcrumbs (fine and not presoaked in milk) if the mixture is not very firm. Shape into firm, compact, oval olive-shaped patties or fricadelles, enclosing an olive in the centre of each; roll in fine dry breadcrumbs and deep-fry in plenty of very hot olive oil.

HAKE IN PARSLEY SAUCE

4 hake weighing 8 oz (250 g) each
plain flour
3¹/₂ oz (100 g) butter
3 cloves garlic
1 small bunch parsley
7 fl oz (200 ml) single cream
salt and pepper

Trim, gut and skin the hake (see page 9). Wash and dry well. Coat lightly with flour. Melt half the butter in a frying pan. Fry the fish gently until pale golden brown, turning once. Transfer carefully to an ovenproof dish and keep warm. Add the peeled and thinly sliced garlic to the butter and juices left in the pan and fry gently. Add the finely chopped parsley and 1 tbsp butter worked with 1¹/₂ tsp flour into a *beurre manié*. Stir over a gentle heat, until the juices thicken. Add the remaining butter and the cream. Season with salt and pepper. Pour the sauce over the hake. Cover with a sheet of foil and place in the oven for 15 minutes at 225°F (110°C) mark ¹/₄.

STEAMED HAKE WITH HAM AND MUSHROOMS

2 hake weighing 1 lb (500 g) each
1 tbsp sesame oil
2 tbsp light soy sauce
5 oz (150 g) thinly sliced ham
7 oz (200 g) button mushrooms
2 spring onions
salt and pepper

Prepare the fish (see page 9), and fillet; wash and dry well. Place the fillets in a shallow dish and sprinkle with the sesame oil mixed with the soy sauce and a generous pinch of salt; leave to marinate for 15 minutes, then cover with a layer of the ham, shredded into very thin strips, and the finely sliced mushrooms. Leave to stand for a further 10 minutes.

Trim the outermost skin and the roots from the spring onions and cut lengthwise into strips (green leafy part included); use to cover the bottom of an ovenproof dish which will fit easily in your steamer; use a fish slice to transfer the fish with its topping carefully on top of the spring onions; pour any remaining marinade over the fish. Season with salt and pepper. Place the dish or plate, covered with foil, in the steamer or over a saucepan of boiling water, and cook for 20–25 minutes. Remove the foil and serve.

HAKE ALSACE STYLE

4 slices hake weighing 8 oz (250 g) each
1 thick slice smoked bacon weighing 4 oz (100 g)
12 oz (300 g) onions
1³/₄ lb (800 g) small new potatoes
4 tbsp oil
18 fl oz (500 ml) milk
18 fl oz (500 ml) single cream
salt and pepper

Dice the bacon and finely chop the onion; sauté both in 3 tbsp oil over a fairly high heat. Slice the potatoes into very thin rounds; grease a casserole dish with 1 tbsp oil and use half the sliced potatoes to cover the bottom. Cover with half the bacon and onion mixture; place the fish steaks on top.

Surround the fish with the remaining potatoes and bacon and onion. Season with salt and freshly ground pepper; sprinkle the milk and cream all over the surface. Bake at 350°F (180°C) mark 4 for 1 hour or until the potatoes are very tender and lightly browned. Serve at once.

BAKED BREAM

4 bream weighing 8 oz (250 g) each
4 fl oz (125 ml) dry white wine
juice of 1 lemon
1 oz (25 g) butter
3 tbsp breadcrumbs
1 tbsp capers
1 clove garlic
1 tsp oregano
18 fl oz (500 ml) oil
salt and pepper

Prepare the fish for cooking (see page 9), trimming, gutting through the gill aperture, washing and drying well. Place in an ovenproof dish large enough to accommodate them in a single layer. Season with salt and pepper; pour the wine and strained lemon juice all over them and leave to stand for 30 minutes.

Heat the butter in a pan and lightly brown the breadcrumbs in it; sprinkle over the fish, followed by the well drained, squeezed and chopped capers, chopped garlic, oregano and oil. Place in the oven, preheated to 350°F (180°C) mark 4, and bake for 30 minutes or until done, spooning the cooking juices over the fish at frequent intervals to moisten.

SASHIMI

1 sea bass or red snapper weighing approx. 2¼ lb (1 kg)
1 lemon
1 small bunch parsley
1 1-in (3-cm) piece fresh ginger
soy sauce
steamed rice (gohan)
Japanese pickles

Use only the freshest fish for this recipe. Gut the fish and fillet (see pages 9–12). Cut the fillets diagonally into wafer-thin slices, holding the knife at an oblique angle; transfer to a serving plate, preferably square or rectangular, arranging the slices so that they overlap. Slice the lemon into rounds; cut these in two and use these half slices to garnish the fish, or arrange in a pattern in one corner of the plate. Do likewise with sprigs of parsley and the peeled and very finely sliced ginger. Serve the rice in a bowl, and the soy sauce in little bowls for each person to dip pieces of fish. Place a selection of Japanese pickles in small bowls.

FILLETS OF SOLE WITH MUSHROOM AND PRAWN SAUCE

1¼ lb (600 g) fillets of Dover sole or lemon sole
3 shallots
1½ oz (30 g) butter
5 oz (150 g) button mushrooms
5 oz (150 g) peeled prawns
3 egg yolks
1 pint (600 ml) single cream
18 fl oz (500 ml) fish stock (fumet) (see page 39)
salt

67

Wash and dry the fillets thoroughly. Chop the shallots finely and sweat in 2 tbsp of the butter for 5–10 minutes before adding the finely chopped mushrooms and the coarsely chopped prawns. Cover and cook over a very gentle heat for 10 minutes; draw aside from the heat. Lightly beat the egg yolks into the cream with a pinch of salt and stir into the mushroom and prawn mixture.

Grease a shallow ovenproof dish with the remaining butter; arrange the fillets in it in a single layer, sprinkle with a small pinch of salt and cover with the egg and cream mixture and the *fumet*. Cook in the oven, preheated to 400°F (200°C) mark 6, for about 15 minutes.

SOLE À LA MEUNIÈRE

8 fillets of Dover sole

plain flour

3$\frac{1}{2}$ oz (90 g) butter

1 small bunch parsley

juice of 2 lemons

salt and pepper

Wash the fillets of sole and dry thoroughly. Coat lightly with flour, shaking off excess. Heat 1 oz (20 g) of the butter in a large frying pan and as soon as it starts to foam, add the fish fillets and cook, turning once, until pale golden brown on both sides. Sprinkle with a little salt, plenty of finely chopped parsley and the lemon juice. Cook gently for 7 minutes.

Transfer the fish to a heated serving plate. Add the remaining butter to the juices in the pan and continue cooking until it is golden brown (*noisette*). Pour over the fish and serve.

SOLE IN MADEIRA SAUCE

8 fillets of Dover sole or lemon sole

2 oz (50 g) butter

plain flour

9 fl oz (250 ml) single cream

nutmeg

7 fl oz (200 ml) Madeira

3$\frac{1}{2}$ oz (100 g) foie gras

salt and pepper

Wash the fish fillets. Dry well. Heat 1 oz (20 g) of the butter in a small saucepan and when it starts to foam, add 2 tbsp flour; mix well, then gradually stir in the cream. Continue cooking for 5 minutes, stirring continuously. Draw aside from the heat, season with salt, pepper and a pinch of freshly grated nutmeg. Add the Madeira and return to a very gentle heat for 5 minutes. Lightly coat the fish fillets with flour and fry in the remaining butter until golden brown on both sides. Place a slice of *foie gras* on each fillet. Completely cover with the sauce and simmer for 5 minutes. Serve at once while still very hot.

Note: If Madeira is unavailable, substitute medium sherry.

SPICED SOLE DELHI STYLE

4 Dover sole or lemon sole weighing approx. 9–10 oz (250–300 g) each

1 tsp coriander seeds

1 tbsp cumin seeds

2 cloves garlic

1 onion

1 oz fresh ginger

1 tsp turmeric

1 spring onion

1 chilli pepper

1 tbsp fresh coriander leaves

4 tbsp oil

salt

Trim, gut and skin the soles or flounders on both sides (see page 10). Score the fish deeply, down to the backbone, in diagonal lines and repeat in the opposite direction to achieve a lattice effect; do likewise on the other side.

Pound the coriander seeds with the cumin seeds (or use ground spices) and mix with the chopped garlic, grated onion, finely grated fresh ginger and the turmeric. Add the salt and a little water to form a thin paste.

Mix half this mixture with the finely chopped spring onion, chilli pepper and coriander leaves and work carefully into the deep incisions on both sides of the fish. Spread the other half of the mixture all over both sides of the fish and leave to stand for 1½ hours.

Heat the oil in one or two large frying pans (the fish are large and should lie flat when cooking) and fry on both sides until a deep golden brown. Serve at once.

DEEP-FRIED FILLETS OF SOLE

8 fillets of Dover sole or lemon sole

5 oz (150 g) plain flour

1 egg

3½ fl oz (100 ml) beer

olive oil for deep-frying

salt and pepper

Sift the flour into a bowl, make a well in the centre, place the egg yolk, 1 tbsp oil, a pinch of salt and a little white pepper in it and gradually work in the flour. When smooth and free of any lumps, fold in the stiffly beaten egg white. Add just enough beer to make a fairly thick coating batter.

Wash the fillets and dry very thoroughly. Heat the oil to the correct temperature in the deep-fryer; dip the fillets in the batter to coat completely and fry, cooking 1 or 2 at a time, until the batter is crisp and golden brown. Drain well on kitchen paper and keep hot while you fry the remaining fillets. Serve as quickly as possible, decorated with lemon wedges.

SOLE WITH SHELLFISH AND CHAMPAGNE

4 fillets of Dover sole or lemon sole

2 oz (50 g) butter

3½ fl oz (100 ml) champagne

4 scallops

4 peeled Dublin Bay prawns

3½ oz (100 g) button mushrooms

7 fl oz (200 ml) double cream

4 tsp red lumpfish roe ('Danish caviar')

salt and white peppercorns

Wash the fillets and dry them well. Heat the butter in a large frying pan and fry the fish for 1 minute on each side; transfer to a warm dish. Open the scallops, wash, clean, trim (see page 23) and thinly slice the raw white meat. (Use thawed frozen scallops if preferred.) Cut the Dublin Bay prawns into fairly small pieces. Wash, dry and thinly slice the mushrooms; add them to the cooking juices and butter left in the pan, frying briskly for 5 minutes; lower the heat and continue cooking for a further 5 minutes. Add the sliced scallops and prawns, followed by the champagne and continue cooking for 5 minutes more. Season with salt and freshly ground white pepper; add the cream and simmer very gently to reduce and thicken the sauce slightly. Return the fish fillets to the pan and when thoroughly heated through, serve with a generous coating of sauce and 1 tsp lumpfish roe on top of each.

SOLE AND SPINACH RINGS

4 large fillets of Dover sole or lemon sole

4 small carrots

8 oz (200 g) frozen chopped spinach, partially thawed

69

2 oz (50 g) butter

10 oz (300 g) broccoli

4 ripe tomatoes

1 onion

salt and pepper

Boil the peeled carrots in salted water for 20 minutes or until tender. Cook the spinach over a fairly low heat with 1½ oz (40 g) butter, stirring until it has lost all excess moisture. Cut the broccoli into florets and boil in salted water for 5 minutes. Rinse briefly in cold water, cover and keep hot on a plate over warm water. Blanch and peel the tomatoes, discard the seeds and chop the flesh roughly; peel the onion and chop; sauté the tomatoes and onion with ½ oz (15 g) butter in a non-stick pan for 10 minutes. Season with salt and pepper and liquidize until smooth. Keep this sauce hot.

Season the fish fillets lightly with salt and pepper; spread a layer of spinach on top of each one and roll up tightly, enclosing a carrot in the centre; secure with cocktail sticks or kitchen string, wrap in lightly oiled foil and steam over fast boiling water for 5–6 minutes.

Remove the foil and cocktail sticks or string carefully. Slice the rolls into rings; ladle some of the tomato sauce on to warmed individual plates, place a few slices of sole on the sauce and arrange some broccoli florets on each plate.

SOLE WITH LEMON SAUCE

4 Dover sole or lemon sole weighing approx. 8 oz (250 g) each

4 egg yolks

5 fl oz (150 ml) milk

1 tbsp plain flour

2½ oz (70 g) butter

1 lemon

1 tbsp chopped parsley

salt

Trim and prepare the sole (see page 10), wash, dry and fry in 1½ oz (40 g) of the butter until golden brown on each side; sprinkle with a little salt when cooked then transfer to a heated serving plate to keep warm.

Add the remaining butter to the juices and butter in the pan; stir in the flour and gradually blend in the milk, heated to scalding point. Continue cooking until the sauce is smooth and creamy. Draw aside from the heat. Beat the egg yolks with the lemon juice and finely chopped parsley. Stir into the sauce in the pan; cook over a very low heat for a few seconds (do not allow to boil) and pour all over the fish. Serve at once.

Note: A garnish of lemon slices and watercress looks very attractive with this dish.

LEMON SOLE WITH MUSTARD CREAM SAUCE

8 fillets of lemon sole

4 gherkins

1 oz (25 g) butter

4 tbsp double cream

2 tbsp mild French mustard (e.g. Dijon)

salt and pepper

Use all the butter to grease a very large, shallow ovenproof dish or casserole dish; place the lemon sole fillets in a single layer in the dish and bake in the oven (preheated to 425°F (220°C) mark 7) for 12 minutes. Remove from the oven and drain off the liquid released by the fish.

Mix the mustard with the cream and chopped gherkins in a bowl; add a little salt and pepper. Spread this mixture on top of the fish fillets and return the dish to the oven for a further 10 minutes. Serve at once.

Note: Any good flatfish can be used for this recipe.

LEMON SOLE WITH ORANGE SAUCE

8 fillets of lemon sole

plain flour

2¹/₂ oz (70 g) butter

5 oranges

3¹/₂ fl oz (100 ml) dry white wine

1 tsp Worcestershire sauce

3 tbsp brandy

salt and pepper

Wash and dry the fillets; coat lightly with flour, shaking off excess. Heat the butter in a large frying pan; peel two oranges (cut away the skin and membrane, exposing the flesh), slice and add to the pan. Sauté for a few minutes on each side, remove, draining well, and keep warm. Place the fillets in the pan, cook until lightly coloured on both sides, turning once very carefully; season with salt and pepper. Sprinkle the wine over the fish, increase the heat and allow the wine to evaporate. Add the juice of the remaining oranges and the Worcestershire sauce. Allow to reduce and thicken a little.

Return the sautéed orange slices to the pan, sprinkle with the brandy, heat and flame. When the flames have died down, transfer the fish and orange slices to a heated serving dish; pour the juices from the pan over the fish and serve at once.

BREAM BURGUNDY STYLE

1 gilt-head bream weighing approx. 2¹/₄ lb (1 kg)

2 tbsp olive oil

2 onions

5 oz (150 g) button mushrooms

4 oz (100 g) smoked bacon

8 fl oz (225 ml) Burgundy

1 tsp plain flour

2 tbsp fish stock (fumet) *(see page 39) or water*

1 small bunch parsley

1 oz (25 g) butter

salt and pepper

Prepare the fish (see page 10), gutting it through the gill aperture. Heat the oil in a large frying pan, add the very thinly sliced onions, and sweat gently until soft and transparent. Wash, dry and slice the mushrooms. Remove the onions from the pan, draining as much oil as possible back into the pan, and spread out over the bottom of a large, fairly shallow casserole; sauté the mushrooms in the oil over a high heat for a few seconds; reduce the heat and fry gently for 10 minutes.

Cut the bacon into very thin strips and blanch for 3 minutes in boiling water. Arrange the fish on top of the onions in the casserole and surround with the mushrooms and bacon. Season with salt and pepper; sprinkle the wine all over the fish and place in the oven, preheated to 375°F (190°C) mark 5, to bake for 20 minutes. After 10 minutes' cooking, cover with a sheet of foil.

Transfer the fish carefully from the casserole to a warmed serving platter and keep warm. Purée all the juices and other ingredients left behind in the dish, together with the flour mixed with the cold fish stock or water, in a blender until very smooth; bring the resulting sauce to the boil in a small saucepan; remove from the heat and stir in the finely chopped parsley. Beat in the butter one small piece at a time, allowing each piece to melt completely before adding the next. Pour the sauce over the fish and serve.

BREAM WITH TOMATOES

4 bream weighing approx. 8 oz (250 g) each

4 large ripe tomatoes

1 small onion or shallot

71

1 clove garlic
3¹/₂ fl oz (100 ml) dry white wine
8 fl oz (225 ml) fish stock (fumet) (see page 39)
pinch cayenne pepper
1¹/₂ tbsp finely chopped parsley
juice of ¹/₂ lemon
salt

Blanch and peel the tomatoes, remove all the seeds and chop. Place the tomatoes, finely chopped onion and garlic, wine, fish stock, cayenne pepper and a generous pinch of salt in a very large, shallow pan or casserole dish, large enough to take all the fish in a single layer.

Sauté the contents of the pan or dish for 2–3 minutes. Place the prepared, washed and dried bream (see page 9) on top, arranging them head to tail. Add a little more fish stock (preheated if necessary). Cover and cook gently on the hob for about 20 minutes, or cover and bake in the oven at 400°F (200°C) mark 6. When done, sprinkle with the lemon juice and chopped parsley. Serve straight from the pan or casserole dish.

BAKED BREAM WITH ORANGES AND MUSHROOMS

1 gilt-head bream weighing 2¹/₄–2¹/₂ lb (1 kg)
3 oz (60 g) button mushrooms
juice of ¹/₂ lemon
3 oranges
12 fl oz (450 ml) white wine
2 oz (50 g) fine breadcrumbs
2 oz (50 g) butter
salt and pepper

Rinse the mushrooms briefly under running cold water; dry thoroughly and then slice them; sprinkle with the lemon juice to prevent discoloration.

Wash the oranges well, dry them and slice into thin circles without peeling them, saving any juice produced as they are cut.

Use 1 oz (25 g) of the butter to grease the inside of a wide, fairly shallow ovenproof dish. Place the washed and prepared fish in the centre of the dish. Arrange the orange slices (overlapping if necessary) so that they surround the fish, adding any juice produced by slicing. Pour the white wine over the fish; sprinkle with the breadcrumbs and finish with a layer of the sliced mushrooms. Dot the surface with the remaining butter. Season with salt and freshly ground white or black pepper.

Place in the oven, preheated to 350°F (180°C) mark 4, for about 25 minutes or until done. Serve very hot, straight from the dish.

BREAM WITH ALMOND STUFFING

1 gilt-head bream weighing approx. 2¹/₄ lb (1 kg)
10 oz (300 g) mushrooms
1 oz (25 g) butter
3 shallots
2 tbsp blanched, skinned almonds
2 onions
3 tomatoes
2 lemons
3¹/₂ fl oz (100 ml) dry white wine
pinch thyme
2 tbsp olive oil
salt and pepper

Prepare the bream (see page 9); fillet it, following the instructions for round fish (see page 13). Wash well and dry.

Wipe the mushrooms with a damp cloth and roughly chop one third of them. Heat the butter in a frying pan and fry the finely chopped shallots and chopped mushrooms together over a low heat for 4 minutes. Add the coarsely chopped almonds and continue cooking for 2 minutes.

Season the inside of the fish with salt and pepper, fill with the sautéed mixture, close the fish over the stuffing, and secure with cocktail sticks. Place in a casserole dish. Chop the remaining mushrooms, slice the onions into very thin rings and the tomatoes into thicker slices; slice one lemon. Arrange all these round the fish.

Sprinkle the juice of the remaining lemon over the fish, followed by the white wine. Season with salt, pepper and thyme; drizzle the oil all over the contents of the dish and bake for 40 minutes at 350°F (180°C) mark 4, spooning the juices over the fish at intervals.

RED MULLET WITH LETTUCE SAUCE

4 cos lettuces

12 red mullet weighing approx. 3 oz (80 g) each

plain flour

oil

7 fl oz (200 ml) double cream

3 oz (80 g) butter

salt and pepper

Use the outer, greener lettuce leaves, washing them well and cutting out the paler stems and ribs. Blanch in boiling salted water for 3 minutes. Drain, squeeze out excess moisture and purée in a blender. Trim, gut, descale and fillet the fish (see page 9). Sprinkle a pinch of flour, salt and pepper inside each fish. Close up the fish and place in a single layer in an oiled casserole dish. Bake in the oven, preheated to 425°F (220°C) mark 7, for 4 minutes without turning. Simmer the cream in a small saucepan to reduce and thicken slightly; turn down the heat to moderate, add the puréed lettuce and a little salt. Add the butter a small piece at a time, beating with a balloon whisk to

blend in each piece before adding the next. Add a little pepper before pouring this sauce over the centre of four warmed plates. Place 3 fish in the middle of each plate and serve immediately.

RED MULLET WITH MUSTARD SAUCE

4 red mullet weighing 10 oz (300 g) each

1 onion

1 clove garlic

1¹/₂ oz (40 g) butter

1 tbsp mild French mustard (e.g. Dijon)

7 fl oz (200 ml) single cream

¹/₂ lemon

salt and pepper

Chop the onion and garlic finely; sweat in the butter in a large saucepan for 10–15 minutes. Spread out over the bottom of a casserole dish large enough to take all the fish in one layer. Prepare the red mullet for cooking, wash and dry, then place them in the casserole dish. Mix the mustard with the cream, add plenty of salt and freshly ground pepper and a few drops of lemon juice. Stir well. Pour the sauce over the fish and bake at 400°F (200°C) mark 6 for about 30 minutes. Spoon the creamy sauce over the fish frequently during cooking. Serve from the casserole.

BAKED RED MULLET WITH BACON AND FENNEL

8 red mullet weighing about 4 oz (100 g) each

73

3 tbsp olive oil
juice of 1 lemon
1 tsp fennel seeds
3 tbsp finely chopped parsley
1 thick slice cured bacon weighing 5 oz (150 g)
salt and pepper

Prepare the fish, wash and dry well. Mix the lemon juice with 1½ tbsp oil, the crushed (or ground) fennel seeds, parsley, salt and freshly ground pepper. Cut the bacon into small dice.

Spread out 4 large sheets of foil. Place 1½ tsp of the mixture inside each fish, press closed, and place 2 fish in the centre of each sheet of foil, head to tail. Sprinkle plenty of diced bacon on top of each fish, together with 1 tbsp oil and wrap in the foil, sealing tightly but leaving an air space inside. Cook in a preheated oven at 400°F (200°C) mark 6 for 20 minutes; serve in the foil cases, each person unwrapping their own parcel at the table.

RED MULLET EN PAPILLOTE

8 red mullet weighing approx. 3½ oz (100 g) each
plain flour
4 oz (120 g) butter
5 fl oz (150 ml) dry white wine
4 oz (100 g) button mushrooms
4 oz (100 g) ham
3 tbsp chopped parsley
3 tbsp chopped shallot
2 cloves garlic
finely grated rind of 1 lemon
salt and pepper

Prepare the fish, remembering to descale; wash and dry. Coat lightly with flour and fry in 3 oz (80 g) of the butter over a fairly high heat for 2–3 minutes

each side; pour in the wine, increase the heat and cook until the liquid has evaporated.

Chop the mushrooms and place in a bowl with the diced ham, parsley, chopped shallot and garlic, 1 tbsp grated lemon rind and a pinch of salt and freshly ground pepper.

Spread out 4 large sheets of foil. Place 2 fish in the centre of each sheet head to tail, sprinkle the fish with equal amounts of the mushroom and ham mixture and dot with the remaining butter. Close up the foil parcels securely, leaving an air space inside, and bake in a preheated oven at 350°F (180°C) mark 4 for 25–30 minutes. Place the parcels on individual plates, to be unwrapped at table, or transfer the contents carefully to a heated serving platter (in the latter case the fish can all be cooked together in one large parcel, if wished).

MACKEREL WITH LEMON AND BLACK OLIVES

4 mackerel weighing 8 oz (250 g) each
4 lemons
2 oz (50 g) butter
4 oz (100 g) black olives, stoned
1½ tbsp chopped parsley
salt and pepper

Trim the fish (removing heads and tails), gut, fillet and skin (see pages 9–12). Place in a casserole packed close together in a single layer. Sprinkle with the strained juice of the lemons, season with salt and plenty of freshly ground pepper, cover with cling film and leave to marinate in the refrigerator for 12 to 18 hours. Turn once or twice during this time.

Shortly before cooking, remove from the refrigerator, take off the covering and allow the fish to return to room temperature; dot with small pieces of butter. Place in the oven, preheated to 400°F (200°C) mark 6, and bake for 12 minutes. Add the olives and return to the oven for a further 6 minutes. Sprinkle with the parsley and serve.

MACKEREL IN SUMMER SAUCE

8 small mackerel weighing 4 oz (100 g) each

9 fl oz (250 ml) dry white wine

1 small bunch parsley

4 baby onions or spring onions

1¹/₂ tbsp white wine vinegar

3 tbsp oil

2 onions

2 tbsp plain flour

salt and pepper

Prepare the mackerel for cooking (see page 9). Wash thoroughly and dry. Mix the white wine with the finely chopped parsley; peel the baby onions or spring onions and make a deep cross cut at the stalk end; stir in the vinegar, salt and plenty of freshly ground pepper. Place the fish in a deep, non-metallic dish or casserole, pour the marinade all over them, add the baby onions or spring onions and leave to stand for 4–5 hours. Peel the onions and slice into very thin rings; sweat gently in the oil in a deep, wide frying pan or saucepan until they just begin to colour. Take up the mackerel from the marinade (reserve this) and pat dry with kitchen paper. Coat lightly with flour and fry with the onions for 5–10 minutes, turning two or three times. Add the marinade, which should completely cover the fish; if not, add a little water.

Simmer for about 30 minutes by which time the liquid should have reduced to half its original volume. Allow to cool completely before serving.

GRILLED MACKEREL WITH APPLES

4 mackerel weighing 8 oz (250 g) each

cider vinegar

2¹/₄ lb (1 kg) green apples

5 tbsp oil

1 oz (25 g) butter

1 lemon

salt and pepper

Trim off the fins, tail and head and gut (see page 9). Rinse the fish in the vinegar and dry with kitchen paper. Season with salt and freshly ground pepper. Grill for about 15 minutes, sprinkling with a little oil now and then and turning once (use a folding holder or rack if you have one as this makes it very easy to turn the fish without damaging them).

Peel, quarter, core and slice the apples fairly thickly. (Choose a variety which remains firm when cooked.) Fry in the oil and butter in a large frying pan. Remove and drain briefly on kitchen paper.

Serve the fish on a warmed platter; surround with the hot apple slices, sprinkling these with the lemon juice and freshly ground pepper.

MACKEREL WITH CHEESE AND MUSSEL STUFFING

4 mackerel weighing approx. 8 oz (250 g) each

20 mussels

5 tbsp olive oil

3 cloves garlic

1 egg

1¹/₂ tbsp fine soft breadcrumbs

3 tbsp freshly grated Parmesan cheese

2 tbsp finely chopped parsley

juice of 1 lemon

3 tbsp dry white wine (optional)

salt and pepper

Trim, gut and fillet the mackerel (see page 12). Wash and dry. Scrub the mussels thoroughly, removing all beards and barnacles. Discard any that do not shut when tapped sharply. Spread out in a frying pan over high heat with a lid on for a few seconds to open. (Discard any mussels that fail to open.) Remove the mussels from their shells and chop coarsely.

Mix 4 tbsp of the oil with the juice of 2 garlic cloves (use a garlic crusher). Grease a very shallow ovenproof casserole dish with the remaining 1 tbsp oil, spread the mackerel fillets out flat in it, season with salt and pepper and sprinkle the garlic-flavoured oil all over the fish. Grill under a high heat for 12 minutes.

Beat the egg in a bowl; add the breadcrumbs, cheese, parsley, the finely chopped remaining garlic clove, the lemon juice and chopped mussels with 3 tbsp of their strained liquor (if any) or dry white wine. Add salt and freshly ground pepper; spread this mixture over the fish.

Replace under the grill for 5 minutes; serve immediately.

MACKEREL AEGEAN STYLE

4 mackerel weighing 8 oz (250 g) each
1 lb fresh or tinned tomatoes
4 tbsp oil
2 cloves garlic
1 sprig thyme
10 coriander seeds
7 fl oz (200 ml) dry white wine
1 lemon
5 oz (150 g) black olives, stoned
salt and pepper

Blanch and peel the tomatoes; discard the seeds and chop (if tinned, drain and remove the seeds before chopping). Fry the peeled, halved garlic cloves in the oil; add the tomatoes, thyme, coriander seeds, salt and freshly ground black pepper. Simmer for 15 minutes; add the wine and the juice of half the lemon. Prepare the mackerel

for cooking (see page 9), wash and dry. Place in a casserole dish, cover with the tomato sauce and bake in the oven, preheated to 400°F (200°C) mark 6, for 20 minutes.

Remove from the oven and leave to cool. Sprinkle with the olives and chill until just before serving. Slice the remaining half lemon into quarter slices and use to garnish the dish.

OMBRINE WITH SEAFOOD STUFFING

1 ombrine or sea bass weighing approx. 2¼ lb (1 kg)
1 lb (500 g) mussels
few sprigs parsley
½ clove garlic
1 small sprig rosemary
3 oz (80 g) stale white bread (no crust)
2 oz (50 g) grated Gruyère cheese
olive oil
5 fl oz (150 ml) dry white wine
salt and pepper

Trim the fins and tail, leaving on the head and gutting the fish through the gill aperture (see page 9). Wash out the ventral cavity very thoroughly. Scrub the mussels thoroughly removing all beards and barnacles. Discard any that do not shut when tapped sharply. Open the mussels in a frying pan over a high heat. Discard any that fail to open. Remove the molluscs from their shells and place in a bowl.

Chop the parsley, garlic and rosemary leaves very finely and mix with the mussels. Soak the bread in water briefly, squeeze out excess moisture and add to the mussels, together with the grated Gruyère, salt and plenty of freshly ground pepper. Mix all these ingredients very thoroughly and use to stuff the ventral cavity of the fish; secure with cocktail sticks or very small steel skewers. Place the fish in a shallow, lightly oiled non-stick or ordinary ovenproof dish, brush the surface of the fish with a little oil, season with salt and pepper, and bake in a preheated oven at 350°F (180°C) mark 4 for about 35 minutes.

When the fish has been in the oven for 10 minutes, pour the wine over it; continue baking, spooning the juices which collect in the bottom of the dish over the fish from time to time as it cooks.

OMBRINE PROVENÇAL

| *1 ombrine or sea bass weighing approx. 2¹/₄ lb (1 kg)* |
| *7 tbsp olive oil* |
| *1 onion* |
| *2 cloves garlic* |
| *4 drained tinned anchovy fillets* |
| *3¹/₂ fl oz (100 ml) dry white wine* |
| *7 fl oz (200 ml) fish stock* (fumet) *(see page 39)* |
| *1 oz (20 g) plain flour* |
| *1 oz (20 g) butter* |
| *2 tbsp lemon juice* |
| *salt and pepper* |

Prepare and gut the fish (see page 9), wash, dry and season lightly inside and out with salt and freshly ground pepper.

Grease an ovenproof dish liberally with 4 tbsp of the oil and spread the thinly sliced onion rings, crushed garlic and the anchovies, crushed to a smooth paste, over the bottom. Place the fish on this layer, pour the wine and fish stock over it and bake at 375°F (190°C) mark 5 for 25 minutes or until done. Transfer the fish to a warmed serving platter.

Cook the flour until lightly coloured in the remaining oil in a small saucepan; gradually beat in the strained liquid left over from cooking the fish, adding a little at a time; bring to the boil then cook, stirring continuously, for 5 minutes over a low heat; beat in the butter a small piece at a time, using a balloon whisk and alternating with the

lemon juice. Coat the fish with some of this sauce and hand round the remainder separately in a sauceboat.

OMBRINE EN PAPILLOTE

| *1 ombrine or sea bass weighing approx. 2¹/₄ lb (1 kg)* |
| *1 clove garlic* |
| *1 lemon* |
| *1 tsp fennel seeds* |
| *1 small bunch parsley* |
| *4 tbsp oil* |
| *salt and pepper* |

Prepare the fish (see page 9), remembering to remove the scales; wash and dry and place on non-stick baking paper or heavy-duty greaseproof paper.

Cut the garlic into very thin slivers and place these under and on top of the fish; slice the lemon into thin rounds and lay these over the fish. Season with salt and freshly ground pepper and sprinkle with the fennel seeds and chopped parsley. Drizzle the oil all over the fish and parcel up securely, leaving a generous air space inside. Cook in the oven, preheated to 425°F (220°C) mark 7, for about 25 minutes. Unwrap the fish parcels at the table.

BAKED OMBRINE WITH BACON AND HERBS

| *1 ombrine or sea bass weighing 1³/₄–2 lb (1 kg)* |
| *1 sprig rosemary* |
| *4–6 fresh sage leaves* |
| *3¹/₂ oz (100 g) very thinly sliced cured bacon* |
| *3¹/₂ fl oz (100 ml) olive oil* |

77

2 cloves garlic
1 onion
1 sprig fresh marjoram
2 oz (50 g) freshly grated Parmesan cheese
3¹/₂ fl oz (100 ml) dry white wine
salt and pepper

Prepare the fish for cooking, gutting through the gill aperture (see page 9). Stuff the ventral cavity with the chopped sage and rosemary leaves, and season inside and out with salt and freshly ground pepper. Wrap the bacon around the fish and secure with cocktail sticks or small steel skewers.

Heat half the oil in an oval casserole dish; sweat the finely chopped garlic, onion and marjoram then add the fish, sprinkling with the remaining oil. Cover with the grated cheese and bake in a preheated oven at 400°F (200°C) mark 6 for 30 minutes or until the fish is done. Sprinkle the fish with the white wine at intervals while it cooks to moisten.

Remove the skewers and the bacon; place the fish on a heated serving platter with the reheated cooking liquid poured over it.

OMBRINE WITH BRANDY

1 ombrine or sea bass weighing approx. 2¹/₄ lb (1 kg)
olive oil
2 oz (50 g) cup breadcrumbs
2 lemons
1 oz (25 g) butter
3¹/₂ fl oz (100 ml) cup brandy
1 small bunch marjoram
1 small bunch chervil
salt and pepper

Trim the fins from the fish (see page 9), descale and gut. Wash and dry well; brush lightly with oil and roll in the breadcrumbs to coat. Grease a casserole dish with the butter, slice the lemon thinly into rounds and spread over the bottom of the casserole. Place the fish on top of the lemon slices, sprinkle with salt and pepper and cook in a preheated oven at 400°F (200°C) mark 6 for 30 minutes.

Half way through the cooking time, sprinkle the fish with brandy and turn carefully. When the fish is done, sprinkle with finely chopped marjoram and chervil and serve.

BAKED FILLETS OF JOHN DORY

1³/₄ lb (800 g) fillets of John Dory
1 onion
1 small bunch parsley
14 oz (400 g) fresh or tinned tomatoes
olive oil
3¹/₂ fl oz (100 ml) dry white wine
¹/₂ lemon
pinch oregano
salt and pepper

Wash and dry the fillets. Peel and finely chop the onion. Chop the parsley; blanch, peel, deseed and chop the tomatoes. Mix these ingredients together and spread over the bottom of a casserole dish. Place the fish fillets on top; sprinkle with 1–2 tbsp oil and the wine. Season with salt and pepper and bake at 350°F (180°C) mark 4 for 20 minutes.

Remove the casserole from the oven and transfer the fish to a warmed serving dish. Purée the remaining contents of the casserole in a blender, pour into a small saucepan and add the lemon juice and oregano; boil over a high heat to reduce and thicken. Add salt and pepper to taste and pour over the fish. Serve at once.

JOHN DORY WITH LEEKS AND WHITE WINE

2 John Dory, each weighing approx. 1¹/₄ lb (600 g)

4 leeks

2 spring onions or shallots

3 oz (80 g) butter

7 fl oz (200 ml) dry white wine

1 tbsp plain flour

salt and pepper

Wash the fish, trim and fillet (see pages 9–12). Trim and thoroughly clean the leeks; chop the white parts (discard the green parts) and the spring onions into thin rounds.

Melt 2 oz (50 g) butter in a frying pan and gently fry the leeks and spring onions for a few minutes. Add the fish fillets and cook, turning once. Season with salt and pepper and sprinkle with the wine.

Simmer until the wine has almost completely evaporated, remove from heat and transfer the fish to a warmed serving dish. Work the remaining butter with the flour into a *beurre manié* and add this paste to the juices left in the pan. Stir continuously until thickened. (As the butter in the *beurre manié* melts, the flour is released and will thicken the juices.) Pour over the fish and serve.

BAKED JOHN DORY WITH FENNEL AND BREADCRUMBS

1 John Dory weighing approx. 2¹/₄ lb (1 kg)

4 medium-sized waxy potatoes

2 fl oz (50 ml) oil

4 oz (120 g) fennel or 1 sprig fresh fennel leaves

4 large ripe tomatoes

1 small bunch parsley

4 cloves garlic

2 tbsp breadcrumbs

pinch dried thyme

12 black olives

salt and pepper

Peel the potatoes, and slice as thinly as possible. Grease a fairly shallow rectangular casserole dish with 3 tbsp oil, and line with the potato slices.

Prepare the fish, cutting off the fins, trimming the tail, and gutting (see page 9). Wash and dry; season the ventral cavity with salt, pepper and the finely chopped fennel or fennel leaves. Place on the layer of potatoes. Cut the tomatoes across in half, remove their seeds, sprinkle with salt and arrange around the fish.

Chop the parsley with the garlic and mix with the breadcrumbs; sprinkle this mixture all over the fish. Drizzle 2 fl oz (50 ml) olive oil all over the surface. Finish with a pinch of dried thyme and bake in the oven at 375°F (190°C) mark 5 for 45 minutes.

When done, take out of the oven, decorate with the black olives and serve.

BAKED JOHN DORY WITH CHEESE

1³/₄ lb (800 g) fillets of John Dory

butter

3 tbsp oil

2 oz (50 g) freshly grated Parmesan cheese

1 small bunch parsley

1 clove garlic

2 fl oz (50 ml) milk

salt and pepper

Grease a wide, shallow ovenproof dish with butter. Arrange the fillets in a single layer in the dish (cut the fillets horizontally in half if necessary). Season with salt and pepper.

Mix the oil and cheese in a bowl, stir in the finely chopped parsley and garlic and enough milk to form a thick paste. Spread this evenly over the fish fillets.

Cover the dish with foil and bake in a preheated oven at 400°F (200°C) mark 6 for about 15 minutes. Remove the foil and grill for 2–3 minutes until the top turns pale golden brown. Serve very hot, straight from the casserole dish.

GARFISH BRAISED IN RED WINE

2 garfish weighing approx. 1 lb (500 g) each
1 small bunch parsley
2 cloves garlic
1 small onion
5 tbsp oil
plain flour
1 lemon
3¹/₂ fl oz (100 ml) dry red wine
salt and pepper

Gut the fish (see page 9), discarding the roes, which are toxic, cut off the heads, and cut into large, even-sized slices. Wash and dry well. Chop the parsley, garlic and onion; pour the oil into a pan large enough to accommodate the fish pieces in a single layer and sweat the chopped mixture over a very low heat.

Coat the fish pieces with flour, shaking off any excess; add to the pan and fry lightly, turning once with a fish slice. Sprinkle with the lemon juice and the wine; season with salt and freshly ground white pepper. Simmer, uncovered, for about 20 minutes over a low heat. The fish should be moist but not sloppy: increase the heat if necessary to reduce any remaining liquid. Serve very hot.

Note: The backbone of the garfish turns bright green in cooking; this is harmless.

GARFISH RINGS

2¹/₄–2¹/₂ lb (1 kg) small garfish
plain flour
olive oil
salt and pepper

Trim and gut the fish (see page 9) but do not cut off the heads. Wash and dry. Push their sharp 'beaks' through the soft, lower part of their belly towards the tail, so that they form rings. Dust lightly with flour and sprinkle a very little oil over them. Preheat the grill until it is very hot and grill 2 fish at a time, turning carefully. Start cooking each batch on a high heat, then reduce the heat and continue grilling more gently for 10–15 minutes. Keep the cooked fish warm while grilling the rest.

Note: See note given in previous recipe.

BREAM AU GRATIN

1 bream weighing approx. 2¹/₂ lb (1 kg)
4 tbsp oil
1 onion
1 lemon
1 clove garlic
1 tsp mustard
7 fl oz (200 ml) dry white wine
2 oz (50 g) butter
9 fl oz (250 ml) béchamel sauce (see method)
4 tbsp freshly grated Parmesan cheese
2 tbsp breadcrumbs
salt and pepper

Pour the oil into a bowl; add the finely chopped onion, the lemon juice, the peeled and thinly sliced garlic, white wine, a pinch of salt and plenty of freshly ground pepper. Beat well with a fork.

Trim and gut the fish (see page 9), wash and dry well. Place in a deep oval dish, pour the marinade all over it and leave to stand for 2 hours, turning 2 or 3 times.

Make the béchamel sauce: put 8 fl oz (250 ml) milk into a small saucepan, add 1 peeled, sliced shallot (or small onion), 1 chopped carrot, ½ celery stalk, chopped, 1 bay leaf and a few peppercorns. Bring to the boil, remove from the heat, and leave to infuse for 15–20 minutes. Strain the milk and discard the flavourings. Melt 1 oz (25 g) butter in a clean saucepan, stir in 4 tbsp plain flour and cook the resulting roux for a few minutes. Gradually add the flavoured milk and bring to the boil, stirring constantly. Cook for a further minute or two until thickened.

Drain the fish well; heat 2–3 tbsp butter until it foams, add the fish and fry briefly, turning once. Sprinkle with a little salt, moisten with half the marinade, cover and simmer for 25 minutes, adding more marinade if necessary. Draw aside from the heat; remove the head and skin. Detach the fillets and place in a shallow ovenproof dish which has been greased with butter; completely cover the fillets with béchamel sauce, sprinkle with the mixed cheese and breadcrumbs and bake in the oven, preheated to 425°F (220°C) mark 7, for 15 minutes, or place under the grill until browned on top.

BARBECUED BREAM WITH FENNEL AND BRANDY

1 bream weighing 2¼–2½ lb (1 kg)
1 medium-sized bulb fennel (with feathery leaves if available)
2 lemons
1 tbsp olive oil
1 tbsp fennel seeds
2 fl oz (50 ml) brandy
salt and pepper

Trim the fish and gut through the gill aperture (see page 9), wash and dry. Chop the fennel bulb coarsely into a bowl, add the strained juice of 1 lemon, the oil, and a generous pinch each of salt and freshly ground pepper. Slice the remaining lemon and stuff the ventral cavity with these slices, together with some fresh fennel leaves if available. Place the fish in a deep, oval dish and pour the marinade over it. Leave to stand in a cool place for 1 hour.

Barbecue the fish for 20–30 minutes, turning once half way through and basting with the marinade. Sprinkle the fennel seeds on to a warmed plate, place the fish on top, heat the brandy, set light to it and immediately pour all over the fish. Serve when the flames have died down.

BREAM STEAKS WITH HERBS AND TOMATOES

1 bream weighing 2¼–2½ lb (1 kg)
3½ fl oz (100 ml) olive oil
few fresh basil leaves
1 small bunch parsley
1 small bunch chervil
2 fresh bay leaves
10 oz (300 g) tinned tomatoes
plain flour
1 clove garlic
4 anchovy fillets
pinch dried oregano
salt and pepper

Prepare the fish, gut it by slitting the belly (see page 9), cut off the head and slice into 4 steaks (save the tail for stock, etc.). Place in a dish, sprinkle with half the oil and the finely chopped basil parsley and chervil. Cover and marinate for 30 minutes, turning frequently.

Drain the tomatoes, remove their seeds and cut

81

into strips. Drain the marinade from the fish, brush lightly to remove any clinging herbs, coat lightly with flour and fry in the remaining oil on both sides until golden brown (10–12 minutes). Remove with a slotted fish slice and keep hot. Fry the peeled garlic in the oil remaining in the pan; crush the anchovy fillets into the oil to make a thin paste; add the tomatoes, a small pinch of salt and plenty of freshly ground pepper. Boil, uncovered, until reduced and thickened; discard the garlic clove. Pour over the fish steaks and sprinkle with oregano. Serve at once.

BRAISED BREAM WITH CHILLI

1 sea bream weighing 2^1/$_4$–2^1/$_2$ lb (1 kg)
plain flour
3^1/$_2$ fl oz (100 ml) oil
2 cloves garlic
1 chilli pepper
3^1/$_2$ fl oz (100 ml) dry white wine
juice of 1 lemon
small bunch parsley
salt

Prepare the fish (see page 9), gut, cut off the head and tail and slice into steaks; coat lightly with flour. Sauté the peeled garlic clove and the chilli pepper in the oil in a large pan; when the garlic turns pale golden brown, crush with a fork to release its juices, then remove and discard together with the chilli pepper. Add the fish steaks to the flavoured oil and fry until golden brown on both sides. Sprinkle with the white wine and lemon juice; add the finely chopped parsley and a little salt.

Cover and continue cooking over a low heat for 10–15 minutes, turning half way through cooking. Use a slotted fish slice to transfer the fish to a warmed serving plate; reduce the juices left in the pan boiling briefly over a higher heat and pour over the fish.

BAKED WHITING WITH GARLIC AND ROSEMARY

4 whiting weighing 8 oz (250 g) each
4 cloves garlic
1 sprig rosemary
3^1/$_2$ fl oz (100 ml) olive oil
1 cup breadcrumbs
salt and pepper

Clean the fish (see page 9), wash and dry well. Place a peeled garlic clove and a few rosemary leaves in the ventral cavity of each fish. Place in a deep dish and pour the oil over them. Leave to marinate for 30 minutes, turning once or twice.

Mix the breadcrumbs with a generous pinch of salt, plenty of freshly ground pepper and a few rosemary leaves. Drain the oil from the fish and use 3–4 tbsp of it to sprinkle over the bottom of an ovenproof dish. Roll the fish in the breadcrumbs and place in the dish; bake for about 20 minutes at 400°F (200°C) mark 6, sprinkling with the remaining oil at frequent intervals. Serve at once.

WHITING WITH MIXED HERB SAUCE

4 whiting weighing 8 oz (250 g) each
4 tbsp plain flour
3^1/$_2$ fl oz (100 ml) oil
3^1/$_2$ fl oz (100 ml) chicken stock
1 small bunch chervil
1 small bunch parsley
1 sprig tarragon
few chives
1 clove garlic

2 shallots
1 tbsp tomato purée
salt and pepper

Prepare the fish (see page 9); wash and dry thoroughly, roll in seasoned flour, shaking off excess, and fry for 2 minutes on each side in 4 tbsp hot oil.

Heat the stock with 2 tbsp oil; stir in the finely chopped chives, garlic and shallot; add salt and pepper and boil for 3 minutes. Stir the tomato purée into the sauce until blended; turn off the heat.

Arrange the fish in a single layer in an ovenproof dish; sprinkle with the hot stock and cook in the oven, preheated to 400°F (200°C) mark 6, for 20 minutes. Serve straight from the ovenproof dish.

BRAISED WHITING WITH SORREL SAUCE

1 large middle cut of whiting or cod weighing approx. 1³/4 lb (800 g)
15 sorrel leaves
3 sprigs mint
5 sprigs parsley
1 sprig thyme
juice of 1 lemon
1 oz (30 g) butter
3¹/2 fl oz (100 ml) single cream
salt and pepper

Rinse the sorrel and all the herbs; remove the mint, parsley and thyme leaves from their stalks.

Sweat the sorrel leaves in the butter in a non-metallic or fireproof earthenware casserole dish. Place the fish, in one piece, over the sorrel and

press the herb leaves so that they adhere all over the surface of the fish. Mix 9 fl oz (250 ml) water with the lemon juice and pour it around the sides of the fish. Season with salt and pepper, heat to boiling point, reduce the heat, then cover and simmer for 25 minutes.

Remove the fish from the casserole; skin it and place it on a warmed serving dish. Purée the remaining contents of the casserole in a blender, including the herbs; mix with the cream and heat without allowing to boil; pour the resulting sauce over and around the fish and serve.

Note: Serve with glazed carrots and steamed broccoli.

WHITING WITH PEAS

1 whiting weighing 2¹/4–2¹/2 lb (1 kg)
1 onion
1 clove garlic
1 small bunch basil or pinch dried basil
3¹/2 fl oz (100 ml) olive oil
12 oz (350 g) frozen peas
3¹/2 fl oz (100 ml) dry white wine
1 tbsp tomato purée
salt and pepper

Prepare the fish for cooking (see page 9), wash and dry. Chop the onion, garlic and basil leaves finely. Heat the oil in a fish kettle or wide frying pan and sweat the chopped mixture over a low heat; add the fish; fry gently, turning carefully once.

Pour the wine all over the fish; cook until it has evaporated. Cook the peas in boiling salted water as directed on the packet; drain and add to the fish, followed by the tomato purée diluted with 3¹/2 fl oz (100 ml) water. Cover and cook gently for 15 minutes.

Transfer the fish to a warmed serving platter, pour over the juices left in the pan and serve.

SARDINE BAKE

1¹/₂ lb (700 g) fresh sardines

15 sage leaves, chopped or pinch dried sage

1¹/₂ tbsp chopped parsley

2 tbsp chopped fresh basil or pinch dried basil

1 tsp chopped rosemary leaves

1 bay leaf

olive oil

4 oz (100 g) breadcrumbs

salt

Trim off the sardines' heads and tail fins, slit open to remove the innards and fillet carefully (see page 14) to avoid breaking them up; rinse and dry thoroughly. Mix all the finely chopped herbs and the chopped or crumbled bay leaf with the breadcrumbs.

Grease a deep, straight-sided ovenproof dish with a little oil; cover the bottom with a layer of one third of the sardines, sprinkle with one third of the chopped mixture, and sprinkle with a little of the oil; repeat this layering process twice more, using up the remaining two thirds of the ingredients. Place in a preheated oven at 350°F (180°C) mark 4 and cook for 30 minutes. Serve straight from the cooking dish.

Note: If fresh sardines are unavailable, substitute tinned.

BAKED STUFFED SARDINES

2¹/₂ lb (1 kg) fresh sardines (or 5 tins)

5 oz (150 g) fine fresh breadcrumbs (from slightly stale white bread)

6 tbsp olive oil

1¹/₂ tbsp sultanas

1¹/₂ tbsp pine nuts

2 tbsp finely chopped parsley

3 oz (80 g) salted anchovies

bay leaves

juice of 1 lemon

1¹/₂ tbsp sugar

salt and pepper

This is a traditional Sicilian recipe, with a pleasant sweet-and-sour taste. If using fresh sardines, prepare as directed in the preceding recipe, taking care that the filleted fish are neat in shape.

Soak the sultanas in warm water to soften, then squeeze out excess moisture before using. Fry the breadcrumbs in 3 tbsp oil until golden; place two thirds of them in a bowl and add the drained sultanas, the pine nuts, parsley and rinsed, filleted, finely chopped anchovies. Mix thoroughly. Open each sardine out flat (see illustration 4 on page 14) and place a small amount of mixture on it, near the 'head' end; roll up working from head to tail and pack these rolls firmly in a single layer in a shallow ovenproof dish, separating one from the other by inserting bay leaves between them. Sprinkle with the remaining breadcrumbs, followed by the mixed lemon juice and sugar; drizzle the remaining oil over the surface. Bake in the oven, preheated to 350°F (180°C) mark 4, for 15–20 minutes.

SARDINES WITH ALMOND AND SULTANA STUFFING

16 fresh sardines

3 oz (80 g) fresh white bread (no crusts)

milk

6–7 tbsp olive oil

pinch oregano

2 tbsp blanched and peeled almonds

2 tbsp sultanas

2–3 bay leaves

salt and pepper

Prepare the sardines (for method see Sardine Bake recipe on page 84).

Soak the bread briefly in the milk, and squeeze out excess moisture. Soak the sultanas in warm water for 15 minutes, drain and squeeze out excess moisture. Mix the bread thoroughly with 4 tbsp of the oil, oregano, finely chopped almonds and the sultanas. Season with salt and pepper. Stuff the sardines with this mixture, arrange in a single layer in a wide, fairly deep casserole dish, sprinkle with 2–3 tbsp oil and bake at 400°F (200°C) mark 6 for 25–30 minutes.

Note: If fresh sardines are unavailable, substitute fresh anchovies or any similar oily fish.

DEEP-FRIED SANDWICHED SARDINES

$1^3/_4$ lb (800 g) large fresh sardines or silversides
2 oz (50 g) tinned anchovy fillets
$1^1/_2$ tbsp finely chopped parsley
1 tbsp finely chopped capers
1 tsp English mustard powder
pinch dried thyme
oil for deep-frying
plain flour
2 large eggs
4 oz (100 g) fine dried breadcrumbs
1 lemon
salt and pepper

Prepare the sardines as directed in the recipe for Sardine Bake on page 84 and then open the fillets out flat.

Chop the well-drained anchovies very finely and mix with the parsley and capers; transfer to a bowl, stir in the mustard and finely crumbled thyme, 1 tbsp olive oil, salt and freshly ground pepper. Spreading a little of the herb mixture on to one sardine (laid out flat, inside uppermost), top with another sardine to make a sandwich with the skin sides on the outside. Press together. Dust lightly with flour; dip in the lightly beaten eggs and coat with breadcrumbs. These are best deep-fried in very hot oil two at a time; if shallow-fried, turn once carefully. Place on kitchen paper and keep hot until all are cooked. Serve as quickly as possible, with lemon wedges.

SAVOURY SARDINES

$1^3/_4$ lb (800 g) fresh sardines (or 4 tins)
15 bay leaves
4 tbsp olive oil
1 cup breadcrumbs
$3^1/_2$ fl oz (100 ml) white wine vinegar
salt and pepper

Prepare the sardines as directed for Sardine Bake on page 84. Open out flat, wash and dry, then fold closed again and pack tightly, side by side, backs uppermost in a fairly shallow ovenproof dish. Cover with a layer of bay leaves; sprinkle first with the oil and then the breadcrumbs. Season with salt and freshly ground pepper. Sprinkle all the vinegar over the surface and bake for about 30 minutes at 400°F (200°C) mark 6.

When done, the top should be golden brown and crisp. Serve straight from the ovenproof dish.

Note: If fresh sardines are unavailable, substitute tins and omit the preparation instructions.

SCORPIONFISH WITH ANCHOVY SAUCE

1 scorpionfish weighing $2^1/_4$–$2^1/_2$ lb (1 kg)
$3^1/_2$ fl oz (100 ml) olive oil
10 anchovy fillets
7 fl oz (200 ml) dry white wine
salt and pepper

Trim the fins off very carefully if preparing the scorpionfish yourself (see page 9), and wear heavy gloves if possible to avoid being pricked by the painful sharp points which can cause inflammation. Heat half the oil in a heavy-bottomed casserole dish which will take the whole fish on its side. Fry the fish gently, browning on both sides. Season with plenty of freshly ground pepper and a very small pinch of salt.

Place the casserole dish in the oven, preheated to 400°F (200°C) mark 6, and cook for 15 minutes or until done. Heat the remaining oil over a low heat; work the anchovy fillets into it, crushing with a fork until broken up. Add the wine and reduce over a high heat. Pour the sauce over the fish when it has been cooking for 15 minutes and cook for a further 15 minutes, turning once with great care.

FRIED FLOUNDER WITH COLD SAVOURY SAUCE

4 flounders weighing 10 oz (300 g) each
2 bay leaves
2 oz (50 g) butter
plain flour
2 tbsp finely chopped parsley
2 pickled onions, drained and finely chopped
1 tbsp capers, finely chopped
1 tbsp anchovy essence
1 oz (25 g) tinned tuna
3 oz (80 g) white bread (no crusts)
vinegar
1 hard-boiled egg, very finely chopped
juice of 1 lemon
3¹/₂ fl oz (100 ml) olive oil
green olives
salt and pepper

Trim, gut and prepare the flounder (see page 9), rinse well and poach for 10 minutes in salted water with the bay leaves. Leave to cool in the liquid. Meanwhile, prepare the sauce: mix the very finely chopped parsley, onions and capers in a bowl with the rinsed, filleted and finely chopped anchovy and the well drained tuna. Soak the white bread in the vinegar, squeeze out excess and add to the bowl, with the hard-boiled egg and some freshly ground pepper. Gradually work in the oil and the lemon juice.

Drain the fish from the cooking liquid and detach the fillets; pat these dry, coat with flour and fry in the butter in a large frying pan until golden brown on both sides.

Arrange the fillets on a warmed serving plate, radiating out from the centre like the spokes of a wheel; top each fillet with some of the mixture and garnish with the olives.

FLOUNDER WITH MUSHROOM SAUCE

4 flounders weighing approx. 8 oz (250 g) each
breadcrumbs
3 oz (80 g) butter
3 tbsp olive oil
1 tbsp finely chopped shallot
1 small sage leaf
5 rosemary leaves
2 basil leaves
1 small bunch parsley
2 oz (50 g) button mushrooms
2 fl oz (50 ml) dry white wine
3 tbsp tomato purée
dried thyme
dried marjoram
salt and pepper

Gut the fish, trim off the lateral fins and remove the dark skin only (see page 10); wash and dry. Coat lightly with breadcrumbs and fry, one at a time if necessary, for 5–6 minutes on each side in a large frying pan with 1 oz (30 g) butter and the oil. Season with salt and pepper, transfer to a warmed serving plate and keep warm.

Mix the chopped shallot with the finely chopped sage, rosemary, basil and some of the parsley. Sauté gently in 1 oz (30 g) butter; add the cleaned, chopped mushrooms and cook slowly for 5 minutes. Season with salt and pepper. Add the wine and heat through before stirring in the tomato purée; add a pinch each of the thyme and marjoram; continue cooking while stirring until reduced and slightly thickened.

Pour the sauce over the fish; decorate with the remaining parsley and serve.

FLOUNDER IN WINE AND CREAM SAUCE

8 fillets of flounder
3¹/₂ oz (100 g) butter
3 small onions or shallots
1 carrot
1 small bunch parsley
7 fl oz (200 ml) dry white wine
7 fl oz (200 ml) single cream
salt and pepper

Wash the fillets and dry thoroughly. Chop one onion, the carrot and the parsley very finely. Sauté gently in 2 oz (50 g) of the butter; transfer to a lightly greased casserole dish and spread out to cover the bottom of the dish; season with salt and pepper.

Roll up the fish fillets and fasten with cocktail sticks or small steel skewers; place these in a single layer on top of the sautéed mixture. Sprinkle with a small pinch of salt and some freshly ground pepper. Peel the remaining onions and slice wafer-thin; scatter on top of the fish. Dilute the wine with 3¹/₂ fl oz (100 ml) boiling water and pour over. Cover with foil and bake in the oven, preheated to 400°F (200°C) mark 6, for 15 minutes.

Remove from the oven, uncover and transfer the fillets very carefully with a slotted fish slice to a warmed, ovenproof serving platter. Keep warm.

Purée all the juices and other ingredients left in the casserole in a blender; pour into a small saucepan, add the cream and simmer, stirring continuously, until reduced by half. Draw aside from the heat; with a balloon whisk, beat in the remaining butter (cut into small pieces) a piece at a time. Adjust the seasoning, and pour the wine sauce over the fish. Place the serving dish in the oven for a few minutes to heat through, if necessary.

EEL WITH SOUR CREAM AND PAPRIKA

1 eel weighing 2¹/₄–2¹/₂ lb (1 kg)
4 tbsp oil
1 tbsp melted butter
3 large onions
2 cloves garlic
10 oz (300 g) ripe tomatoes
4 tbsp plain flour
1 tbsp tomato purée
7 fl oz (200 ml) dry white wine
2¹/₂ tsp paprika
3 tbsp sour cream
salt

Gut the eel (see page 9), skin (see page 11) and cut off the head; cut into four sections, discarding the very end of the tail. Heat 2 tbsp of the oil in a heavy saucepan with the melted butter and sweat the very finely chopped onions and garlic, covered, over a very low heat for 15–20 minutes, adding 2 tbsp water to prevent them crisping.

Add the peeled, seeded and coarsely chopped tomatoes (tinned tomatoes can be used instead of fresh); mix 1 tbsp of the flour with the wine and tomato purée, and add to the pan. Stir in half the paprika and a little salt, cover and simmer very slowly for 20 minutes.

Mix the remaining flour and paprika on a plate, roll the pieces of eel in this and fry for 5 minutes, turning once or twice in the remaining oil. Salt these pieces lightly and transfer to the sauce. Simmer for a further 10 minutes. Place the eel pieces on a warmed serving plate. Stir the sour cream into the paprika sauce, heat almost to boiling point and pour over the eel. Serve at once.

EEL BAKED IN WINE

1 eel weighing 2¹/₄–2¹/₂ lb (1 kg)
4 tbsp pine nuts
6 tinned anchovy fillets, drained
1 onion
3 tbsp olive oil
3 tbsp finely chopped parsley
7 fl oz (200 ml) dry white wine
salt and pepper

Prepare the eel as directed on pages 9–11, gut and cut into portions of even thickness. Pound the pine nuts and anchovies together, preferably using a pestle and mortar, to form a smooth paste.

Peel and slice the onion very thinly, fry in the oil with the chopped parsley in a flameproof casserole dish; work in the anchovy and pine nut mixture when the onion is soft. Add the eel pieces; fry briskly for 5–6 minutes on each side, season with salt and pepper. Pour the wine over the eel pieces and transfer the casserole, uncovered, to the oven, preheated to 350°F (180°C) mark 4, to cook for 10–15 minutes, by which time the wine should have considerably reduced.

PROVENÇAL BRAISED EEL

1 eel weighing 2¹/₄–2¹/₂ lb (1 kg)
2 carrots
2 onions
2 fl oz (50 ml) olive oil
nutmeg
1 tbsp fresh fennel leaves
3¹/₂ fl oz (100 ml) dry white wine
1 tbsp breadcrumbs
1 tbsp finely chopped parsley
salt and pepper

Clean, gut and skin the eel. Leave whole but remove the head (see pages 9–11).

Peel and thinly slice the carrots; peel the onions and slice wafer-thin; cover the bottom of a heavy flameproof casserole dish with these and sprinkle the oil over them; sweat the vegetables gently for 5 minutes.

Place the eel on top of the vegetables; sprinkle with a generous pinch of freshly grated nutmeg and the fennel leaves (some are usually left attached when fennel is sold in the shops) and pour in the white wine.

Bring to the boil, lower the heat, and cook slowly for about 45 minutes, turning the eel after 25 minutes. Just before serving, sprinkle with the mixed breadcrumbs and parsley.

EEL BAKED WITH MUSSELS AND CLAMS

1 eel weighing 2¹/₄–2¹/₂ lb (1 kg)
1 lb (500 g) mussels
1 lb (500 g) clams
2 fl oz (50 ml) olive oil
1 onion
2 cloves garlic
1 small bunch parsley
1 sprig fresh basil

14 oz (900 g) tomatoes

10 fl oz (300 ml) dry white wine

salt and pepper

Prepare the eel (see pages 9–11): gut, skin and remove the head. Slice into portions of even thickness.

Scrub the mussels and clams under running cold water (see pages 22–23, bottom right) before spreading out in a large pan, moistening with a little white wine and opening over a high heat. Remove their shells and strain the juices they release and the wine through a fine cloth. (If fresh mussels and clams are unavailable, use well thawed, frozen shucked mussels and approx. 1 10-oz (300-g) tin shucked clams, reserving all the juice in the tin.)

Lightly oil a casserole dish, and place the eel steaks in it, preferably in a single layer. Finely chop the onion, garlic, parsley and basil leaves and sprinkle half over the eel; cover with the mussels and clams. Add frozen and tinned seafood at this point. Top with a layer of the drained tomatoes and add the liquor from the mussels and clams, the white wine, a pinch of salt and freshly ground pepper. Drizzle a very small amount of olive oil over the surface and cook for about 30 minutes in the oven, preheated to 400°F (200°C) mark 6. Serve straight from the casserole.

DENTEX ORIENTAL STYLE

1 dentex weighing 2¼–2½ lb (1 kg)

3 tbsp lemon juice

1 tbsp soy sauce

2 bay leaves

2 apples

2 oz (50 g) butter

1 tbsp plain flour

1 tbsp mild curry powder

salt and pepper

Gut and fillet the fish, removing the skin from the fillets (see pages 9–12). Place the fillets on a plate, sprinkle with the lemon juice and soy sauce and leave to marinate for 3 hours, turning two or three times.

Drain the marinade from the fish, place in a shallow casserole dish, add 14 fl oz (400 ml) water, a little salt, freshly ground pepper and the bay leaves. Poach gently for 10–12 minutes.

Peel and core the apples, slice into rings and sauté in 1 oz (25 g) of the butter for 5 minutes. Keep hot. Melt the remaining butter, and blend in the flour. Stir in 4 fl oz (120 ml) of the hot cooking liquid from the fish; cook gently, stirring continuously, for 5 minutes. Add the curry powder, salt and pepper. Drain the remaining cooking liquid from the fish fillets, transfer to a warmed serving plate and cover with the sauce; surround with the apple rings.

DENTEX PIZZAIOLA

1 dentex weighing 2¼–2½ lb (1 kg)

juice of 1 lemon

1 clove garlic

5 tinned anchovy fillets

1 small bunch parsley

1 tbsp capers

5 tbsp olive oil

3½ fl oz (100 ml) dry white wine

9 oz (250 g) tinned tomatoes

5 oz (150 g) black olives, stoned

2 tbsp toasted almonds

pinch oregano

salt and pepper

Remove all the scales and gut the fish (see page 9); wash and dry well. Sprinkle inside and out with salt, the lemon juice and freshly ground pepper and leave on a plate for 30 minutes.

Chop the garlic, anchovies, parsley and capers finely together; fry the chopped mixture gently in the oil in a large pan. Add half the wine, and the drained, roughly chopped tomatoes. Cook over a high heat for a few minutes; add the coarsely chopped olives, the almonds (cut into long thin pieces) and cook for 10 minutes more. Use plenty of olive oil to grease a casserole dish, preferably oval, into which the whole fish will fit neatly, drain the lemon juice from the fish and place in the casserole. Add the tomato mixture and sprinkle with oregano. Cover and place in a preheated oven (400°F (200°C) mark 6) to cook for 20 minutes. Serve very hot.

Note: Serve with garlic bread and a crisp green salad.

BAKED DENTEX WITH LEMON STUFFING

2 dentex weighing 1 lb (500 g) each

5 small slices white bread

5 tbsp dry white wine

1¹/₂ tbsp finely chopped parsley

3 tbsp lemon juice

5 tbsp olive oil

salt

Descale and gut the fish through the gill aperture (see page 9), wash and dry well inside and out. Cut the crusts off the bread and crumble into a bowl; work in the white wine, parsley, lemon juice, 1 tbsp of the oil and a pinch of salt. Blend. Use this mixture to stuff the fish. Grease a shallow baking dish with plenty of oil; arrange the fish in it, side by side, head to tail. Sprinkle with the remaining oil and a little salt. Preheat the oven to 400°F (200°C) mark 6 and bake the fish for 15–20 minutes or until done, basting several times with the cooking juices.

PIQUANT GREY MULLET

4 small grey mullet weighing 8 oz (250 g) each

3¹/₂ fl oz (100 ml) olive oil

juice of 1 lemon

10 basil leaves

4 sage leaves

few sprigs parsley

2 bay leaves

¹/₂ or 1 chilli pepper

3 tinned anchovy fillets

1 tbsp white wine vinegar

3¹/₂ fl oz (100 ml) dry white wine

salt and pepper

Trim, descale, gut and wash the fish. Dry well. Place in an ovenproof dish and season with salt and pepper. Use a fork or small balloon whisk to beat the oil into the lemon juice in a bowl; finely chop all the herbs, chilli pepper and drained anchovies; stir into the bowl. Pour this mixture all over the fish. Add the white wine and bake for 15 minutes in a preheated oven at 350°F (180°C) mark 4.

GREY MULLET FLAMBÉ

1 grey mullet weighing 2¹/₄–2¹/₂ lb (1 kg)

4 tbsp oil

3 tbsp very finely chopped mixture of bay leaf, dill, parsley and chervil

4 tbsp brandy

salt and pepper

Prepare the fish for cooking (see page 9 and previous recipe). Wash and dry well.

90

Brush all over with oil and place under the grill. Season with freshly ground pepper; grill fairly slowly for 15 minutes on each side; brush with a little more oil if necessary. Sprinkle half the herb mixture over the bottom of a heatproof serving dish large enough to contain the whole fish; place the cooked fish in the dish on top of the herbs and sprinkle with the remaining mixture. Gently heat the brandy in a small saucepan, pour it over the fish and flame. Serve as soon as the flames have died down.

BAKED GREY MULLET WITH HERBS

4 small grey mullet weighing 8 oz (250 g) each
1 sprig basil
1 sprig parsley
2 mint leaves
2 cloves garlic
4 tinned anchovy fillets
2 oz (50 g) breadcrumbs
2 oz (50 g) freshly grated Parmesan cheese
3¹/₂ fl oz (100 ml) olive oil
juice of 1 lemon
7 fl oz (200 ml) dry white wine
salt and pepper

Prepare the fish, trimming, descaling and gutting them.

Wash the herbs and chop very finely with the peeled garlic; chop the anchovies separately then mix with the herbs in a bowl. Add the breadcrumbs, cheese, lemon juice, salt, plenty of freshly ground pepper and half the oil; blend well.

Use half the remaining oil to grease an ovenproof dish large enough to contain all the fish in a single layer; place the fish in it and sprinkle with the remaining oil. Sprinkle with the herb, cheese and bread mixture; trickle the wine into the dish down one side to avoid disturbing the topping. Add a little salt if wished and bake in a preheated oven at 400°F (200°C) mark 6 for about 18 minutes or until done.

GREY MULLET SPANISH STYLE

1 grey mullet weighing 2¹/₄–2¹/₂ lb (1 kg)
1 lb mixed red, yellow and green peppers
1 bulb fennel
2 mild red onions
14 oz (400 g) tinned tomatoes
3¹/₂ fl oz (100 ml) olive oil
14 fl oz (400 ml) white wine
salt and pepper

Prepare the fish for cooking (see page 9). Slice the peppers open, remove the stalks and seeds and cut into thin strips. Slice the fennel very thinly. Peel the onions and cut into thin rings.

Choose an oval ovenproof dish in which the fish will fit flat and grease with oil; cover the bottom with a layer of the onion rings and season with a little salt and pepper; place a layer of the drained, roughly chopped tomatoes on top; follow with the layer of the fennel slices, then all the peppers, packed down quite firmly. Season each layer to taste.

Place the fish on this bed; season with a little more salt and pepper. Sprinkle all over with the remaining oil, then add half the white wine. Bake, uncovered, in a preheated oven, at 400°F (200°C) mark 6 for 15 minutes; add the remaining wine and continue cooking for a further 20 minutes, basting the fish frequently with the cooking juices and turning it once, very carefully.

Note: Saffron rice makes an excellent and colourful accompaniment to this dish.

91

HERRING FILLETS WITH SAUERKRAUT

1 lb (500 g) smoked herring fillets

1 lb (500 g) hake or cod fillets

1³/₄ lb (800 g) plain Sauerkraut (available tinned)

2 onions

1¹/₂ oz (40 g) butter

2 tbsp lard

1 tbsp oil

1 tsp juniper berries

1 bottle sweet white wine (e.g. Muscatel)

10 fl oz (300 ml) milk

3 shallots

3 fl oz (100 ml) white wine vinegar

5 fl oz (150 ml) double cream

2 egg yolks

salt and pepper

Rinse the Sauerkraut in a sieve under running cold water and drain well. Peel and chop the onions finely and fry in the butter, lard and oil; when they begin to colour, add the Sauerkraut, stirring well, followed by 18 fl oz (500 ml) of the wine, the juniper berries and a little salt. Cover and cook gently over a very low heat for 2¹/₄ hours. About half an hour before you wish to serve the dish, pour the milk into a saucepan with 3¹/₂ fl oz (100 ml) water. Heat to boiling point, add the herring fillets, and immediately turn off the heat. Leave the fillets in the liquid for 30 minutes. Drain and keep warm. Bring the liquid back to the boil; add the hake or cod fillets and poach gently for 4 minutes. Drain well and keep warm.

While the herring fillets are standing in the cooking liquid, chop the shallots finely and place in a small saucepan with the vinegar and 7 fl oz (200 ml) of the wine. Boil until the liquid has reduced to less than half its original volume. Beat the cream and fold in the lightly beaten egg yolks; remove the wine mixture from the heat and stir in the cream and egg mixture. Season with salt and

pepper; return to a very low heat (do not allow to boil) and stir continuously until slightly thickened.

Arrange the Sauerkraut in the centre of a hot serving platter, pour the sauce over it, and surround or top with the fish fillets, alternating herring with hake or cod. Serve at once, with boiled potatoes.

HERRINGS WITH DILL

8 salted herring fillets

3¹/₂ fl oz (100 ml) dry white wine

1 apple

1 small onion

2 sprigs dill

1 lemon

7 fl oz (200 ml) plain yoghurt

2 tbsp single cream

pinch sugar

salt

Rinse the herrings well to remove excess salt. Pour the wine into a bowl, add the peeled, cored and diced apple, the thinly sliced onion, 1 sprig dill and 2 small pieces lemon rind (with no pith). Stir well. Spread the herring fillets out in a fairly deep dish; cover completely with the wine marinade and leave to stand overnight.

Shortly before serving the herrings, drain them well and spread out on a serving plate. Use a slotted spoon to remove the diced apple from the marinade; sieve or liquidize it. Mix the yoghurt with the cream, sugar, apple purée, 1 tbsp lemon juice and a little salt. Pour this dressing over the herring fillets and sprinkle with the remaining dill leaves.

Note: Serve with rye bread, boiled potatoes and a green salad.

HERRINGS NORMANDY STYLE

12 herrings
2 onions
2 shallots
1 carrot
1 small bunch parsley
1 tsp mixed herbs
7 fl oz (200 ml) dry cider
2 fl oz (50 ml) cider vinegar
oil
7 oz (200 g) curd cheese
2 fl oz (50 ml) plain yoghurt
1 tsp Dijon mustard or English mustard powder
few chives
salt

Finely chop the onions, shallots, carrots and parsley; place in a non-metallic saucepan with the mixed herbs, cider and vinegar. Simmer for 10 minutes; leave to cool.

Clean and prepare the herrings; slash the skin with thin deep cuts. Place in a deep, non-metallic dish, pour the marinade over them and leave to stand for 2 hours in a cool place.

Drain the fish and pat dry. Boil the marinade until it has reduced by half and leave to cool again. Brush the fish with oil and grill or barbecue for 5 minutes on each side, brushing with a little more oil from time to time. Strain the marinade and mix with the curd cheese, yoghurt, mustard, salt and pepper in a blender. Pour this sauce into a bowl and hand round with the grilled herrings.

BAKED ANCHOVIES WITH CHEESE STUFFING

1¹/₂ lb (700 g) fresh anchovies
2 salted anchovies
1 clove garlic
1 small bunch parsley
2 oz (50 g) breadcrumbs
2 oz (50 g) grated Parmesan cheese
olive oil
salt and pepper

Rinse the salted anchovies, trim and fillet; chop these fillets together with the peeled garlic and parsley. Place in a bowl and add the breadcrumbs and cheese, 2 tbsp oil, salt and freshly ground pepper. Mix thoroughly, then leave to stand for 20 minutes.

Trim the anchovies, removing heads and tails, slit right down their bellies, remove the innards and the backbone (take care not to break the fish up) and open them out flat. Place a little of the cheese stuffing on each opened fillet, at the wider, head end; roll up towards the tail and secure each one with one or two cocktail sticks or small steel skewers.

Choose an ovenproof dish, preferably round, into which the anchovy rolls will just fit in a single layer; grease generously with oil and arrange the anchovy rolls in a spiral or concentric circular pattern. Drizzle a little more oil over the fish and bake for 20 minutes at 400°F (200°C) mark 6.

Note: If Parmesan is unavailable, any good hard cheese suitable for grating can be used.

FRESH ANCHOVIES WITH PEPPERS

1¹/₄ lb (600 g) fresh anchovies
2 onions
2 cloves garlic
4 green peppers
3¹/₂ fl oz (100 ml) olive oil

1 chilli pepper
7 fl oz (200 ml) dry white wine
3½ fl oz (100 ml) white wine vinegar or tarragon vinegar
1 small bunch parsley
salt

Prepare the anchovies as instructed in the previous recipe (Baked Anchovies with Cheese Stuffing). Spread out on a very large platter and sprinkle sparingly with salt. Chop the onions and garlic very finely and coarsely chop the peppers. Sauté these together in a large frying pan in the oil until the peppers are fairly tender; add the chopped chilli pepper and the fish. Cook gently for 10 minutes, turning the fish only once very carefully. Moisten with the wine and vinegar at frequent intervals. Add a little more salt if necessary (taste first) and then cook over a higher heat for up to 10 minutes or until the wine and vinegar have evaporated.

Sprinkle with plenty of finely chopped parsley and serve.

Note: Serve with pasta spirals and a tomato and cucumber salad.

ANCHOVY PIE

1½ lb (700 g) fresh anchovies
1¾ lb (800 g) waxy potatoes
1 large bunch parsley
1 lb (500 g) tinned tomatoes
olive oil
generous pinch oregano
salt and pepper

Prepare the anchovies as directed in the recipe for Baked Anchovies with Cheese Stuffing on page 93. Rinse and dry well.

Peel the potatoes and slice just under ¼ in (½ cm) thick. Chop the parsley finely. Drain the tomatoes and chop coarsely.

Lightly grease a wide casserole dish with a little oil. Layer the ingredients, starting with a layer of potatoes, followed by an anchovy layer then tomatoes. Continue, sprinkling each layer with salt, freshly ground pepper and oregano, until all the ingredients are used up. Finish with a tomato layer.

Sprinkle a very little oil over the surface and bake at 350°F (180°C) mark 4 for 1 hour. Serve straight from the casserole dish.

ANCHOVIES WITH AUBERGINE SAUCE

2¼–2½ lb (1 kg) fresh anchovies
2 fl oz (50 ml) olive oil
1 onion
1 clove garlic
1 small bunch parsley
10 thyme leaves or pinch dried thyme
3 small aubergines
7 fl oz (200 ml) dry white wine
4 large ripe tomatoes
½ lemon
salt and pepper

Gut, wash and dry the anchovies. Season sparingly with salt and pepper inside their cavities. Cook under a very hot grill for 5 minutes each side, sprinkling with oil whenever necessary. Transfer to a plate and allow to cool. Chop the onion, garlic, parsley and thyme very finely and fry in a large pan with 2 tbsp oil. Add the peeled aubergine cut into very small dice. Cover and cook for 5 minutes; add the wine and increase the heat. Cook uncovered until half the liquid has evaporated.

Add the peeled, seeded and chopped tomatoes, the lemon juice, salt and freshly ground pepper. Cook over a moderate heat until the aubergine dice have turned into a purée. Leave to cool and serve with the anchovies.

Bogue with Sultanas

1 bogue or bream weighing 2¹/₄–2¹/₂ lb (1 kg)

7 fl oz (200 ml) dry white wine

1 onion

2 cloves garlic

1 carrot

1 celery stalk

4 oz (100 g) sultanas

1¹/₂ oz (40 g) butter

¹/₂ tbsp plain flour

peppercorns

salt

Trim, descale and gut the fish (see page 9). Place in a non-metallic pan in which it can be laid flat (an oval enamelled cast iron casserole is suitable) and pour in the wine. Add the finely sliced onion, garlic, carrot and celery, a generous pinch of salt and a few peppercorns. Cover, bring to the boil and immediately reduce the heat; simmer gently for about 30 minutes.

Soak the sultanas in warm water to soften and plump them up. When the fish is cooked, remove carefully from the pan and place on a warmed serving platter. Strain the liquid and ingredients left behind in the pan into a small saucepan; add the drained sultanas and, after working the flour into half the butter to make a *beurre manié*, add this to the liquid.

Bring slowly to the boil, stirring continuously. As the butter melts and releases the flour, it will help to thicken the sauce. Boil hard to reduce and thicken further. Draw aside from the heat and beat in the remaining butter (do not melt beforehand) with a balloon whisk. Add a little more salt if needed; pour the sauce over the fish and serve very hot.

Note: Serve with new potatoes, steamed courgettes and carrots.

Baked Fish Brochettes

4 salema or bream weighing 8 oz (250 g) each

4 tinned anchovy fillets

2 lemons

1 small bunch parsley

1 clove garlic

4 sage leaves

olive oil

breadcrumbs

salt and pepper

Descale the fish carefully; trim, gut and rinse well under running cold water; pat dry.

Chop the parsley finely with the peeled garlic. Into the ventral cavity of each fish place 1 anchovy fillet, 1 peeled lemon segment (remove the segments from their thin membranous inner skins) and a quarter of the chopped mixture. Thread the fish belly to belly and head to tail (so that they dovetail neatly) on to two skewers, placing a sage leaf over each.

Grease an ovenproof dish large enough to contain the fish in a single layer and sprinkle the bottom with salt. Place the fish in the dish, sprinkle with a little oil, salt and pepper. Place in a preheated oven, at 400°F (200°C) mark 6, and bake for about 15 minutes. Turn the fish, still on their skewers, half way through cooking and sprinkle breadcrumbs over the top once they have been turned. Transfer to a warmed serving dish and garnish with lemon wedges. Serve immediately.

Meagre in Milk Sauce

1³/₄ lb (800 g) fillets of meagre or sea bass

4–5 tbsp olive oil

plain flour
3 shallots, finely chopped
1 clove garlic
2 fl oz (50 ml) dry white wine
1 chicken stock cube
1 tbsp tomato purée
3¹/₂ fl oz milk
2 tbsp pine nuts
salt and pepper

Rinse the fillets and dry well. Coat with flour, shaking off excess and fry in 4 tbsp hot oil until golden brown on both sides. Season with salt and pepper. Remove from the oil, using a slotted fish slice, and keep hot in an ovenproof dish.

Peel the onions and slice wafer-thin, chop the garlic finely and fry both in the oil left in the pan (adding a little more oil if necessary). Add the wine and the chicken stock cube crumbled into it; cook until it has evaporated; stir in the tomato purée, followed by the cold milk, adding a little at a time. Stir well, add salt to taste and simmer for 5 minutes. Purée in a blender with the pine nuts.

Pour all over the fish; cover with foil and place in a preheated oven, at 400°F (200°C) mark 6, for 20 minutes. Remove the foil and serve.

SWEET AND SOUR BREAM

2 bream weighing 1 lb (500 g) each
4 tbsp sunflower oil
2 chilli peppers
3¹/₂ fl oz (100 ml) white wine
3 baby onions or spring onions
4 tbsp light soy sauce
1 tsp sugar
1 tbsp vinegar
salt

Trim, gut (preferably through the gill aperture for this recipe) and prepare the fish; wash and dry. Heat the oil in a non-stick pan and when very hot add the fish; fry for 4–5 minutes on each side.

Add the chilli peppers, fry for 1 minute, then add the wine. Keep cooking over a high heat until the liquid has reduced by half; add the finely sliced onions and the soy sauce. Cover, lower the heat a little, and cook for 5 minutes. Turn the fish carefully, cover again, and cook for a further 3 minutes over a low heat.

Add the sugar, vinegar and a pinch of salt; increase the heat a little, cover and cook for 1 minute. Using a wooden spoon, lightly shift the fish and onions in the pan to make sure they are not catching at all while cooking for a final 2 minutes. Serve at once.

Skate Salad

p. 105

*Time: 40 minutes
+ 12–15 hours marinating time
Difficulty: Very easy
Cold appetizer*

Cold Fish Pie

p. 105

*Time: 1 hour 40 minutes
Difficulty: Fairly easy
Cold appetizer*

Avocado with Haddock Purée

p. 105

*Time: 40 minutes
+ 2 hours marinating time
Difficulty: Easy
Cold appetizer*

Salt Cod Mousse

p. 106

*Time: 45 minutes
+ setting time
Difficulty: Very easy
Cold appetizer*

Fish Salad with Grapefruit and Walnuts

p. 106

*Time: 50 minutes
Difficulty: Very easy
Cold appetizer*

Savoury Tuna Rolls

p. 107

*Time: 40 minutes
Difficulty: Very easy
Cold appetizer*

Fish Cocktail

p. 107

*Time: 1 hour
Difficulty: Easy
Cold appetizer*

Portuguese Salt Cod Soup

p. 107

*Time: 2 hours 15 minutes
Difficulty: Very easy
First course*

Fish and Mushroom Soup

p. 108

*Time: 1 hour
Difficulty: Easy
First course*

Fish Ravioli with Tomato and Chive Sauce

p. 108

*Time: 1 hour 30 minutes
Difficulty: Fairly easy
First course*

Tagliatelle with Tuna

p. 109

*Time: 50 minutes
Difficulty: Easy
First course*

Spaghetti with Tuna and Pesto

p. 109

*Time: 45 minutes
Difficulty: Very easy
First course*

Brill in shrimp sauce

1
Thunnus thynnus

2
Euthynnus alletteratus

3
Rhombus laevis

4
Rhombus maximus

5
Gadus morrhua

6
Mustelus Mustelus

1

Dutch: Tonijn
English: Tuna
French: Thon, Thon rouge
German: Thunfisch
Italian: Tonno comune
Spanish: Atun

2

English: Little tuna
French: Boniton, Thonine
German: Bonitol
Italian: Tonnetto
Spanish: Tonyina, Bacoreta

3

Dutch: Griet
English: Brill
French: Barbue
German: Glattbutt
Italian: Rombo liscio
Spanish: Barbadar

4

Dutch: Tarbot
English: Turbot
French: Turbot
German: Steinbutt
Italian: Rombo chiodato
Spanish: Rodaballo

5

Dutch: Kabeljauw
English: Cod
French: Cabillaud, Morue
German: Kabeljau
Italian: Merluzzo comune
Spanish: Merluza

6

Dutch: Toonhaai, gladde haai
English: Smooth hound
French: Émissole lisse
German: Glatthai
Italian: Palombo
Spanish: Musola

7

Dutch: Kleine gevlekte
  hondshaai
English: Lesser spotted dogfish
French: Petite roussette
German: Kleingefleckter
  Katzenhai
Italian: Gattuccio
Spanish: Pintarroja, gato
  marino

8

Dutch: Zwaardvis
English: Swordfish
French: Espadon
German: Schwertfisch
Italian: Pesce spada
Spanish: Pez espada

9

English: Moray eel
French: Murène
Italian: Murena
Spanish: Morena

10

Dutch: Zeeduivel
English: Monkfish
French: Baudroie, Lotte,
  Diable de mer
German: Seeteufel
Italian: Rana pescatrice
Spanish: Rape

11

Dutch: Zeepaling
English: Conger eel
French: Anguille de mer,
  Congre
German: Meeraal
Italian: Grongo
Spanish: Congrio

12

Dutch: Schelvis
English: Haddock
French: Aiglefin
German: Schellfish
Italian: Eglefino
Spanish: Merluza

13

English: Grouper
French: Mérou
Italian: Cernia
Spanish: Mero

14

English: Amberjack
French: Sériole
Italian: Ricciola
Spanish: Pez de limón

15

English: Scabbard fish
French: Sabre
Italian: Pesce sciabola
Spanish: Pez cinto

16

English: White skate
French: Raie blanche
Italian: Razza
Spanish: Raja blanca

Baked hake with peas and olives

SALT COD WITH PEPPERS

p. 120

Time: 3 hours
Difficulty: Very easy
Main course

DEEP-FRIED SALT COD

p. 120

Time: 1 hour
+ 2 hours standing time
Difficulty: Fairly easy
Main course

STOCKFISH BERGEN STYLE

p. 121

Time: 1 hour 25 minutes
+ pastry resting time
Difficulty: Easy
Main course

WHITING PIE

p. 121

Time: 1 hour 15 minutes
Difficulty: Fairly easy
Main course

AMERICAN FISH MOULD

p. 121

Time: 1 hour 15 minutes
Difficulty: Easy
Main course

SPICED FISH STEAKS

p. 122

Time: 30 minutes
Difficulty: Very easy
Main course

FISH STEAKS WITH BASIL AND OLIVES

p. 122

Time: 1 hour
Difficulty: Very easy
Main course

Fish ravioli with tomato and chive sauce

SMOOTH HOUND WITH MUSHROOMS

p. 123

Time: 50 minutes
Difficulty: Very easy
Main course

FISH STEAKS WITH ANCHOVIES

p. 123

Time: 40 minutes
Difficulty: Very easy
Main course

SWORDFISH STEAKS IN TOMATO AND BLACK OLIVE SAUCE

p. 123

Time: 45 minutes
Difficulty: Very easy
Main course

GOURMET'S SWORDFISH STEAKS

p. 124

Time: 45 minutes
Difficulty: Very easy
Main course

LEMON AND GARLIC SWORDFISH STEAKS

p. 124

Time: 20 minutes
+ 1 hour marinating time
Difficulty: Very easy
Main course

SWORDFISH STEAKS AU GRATIN

p. 124

Time: 45 minutes
Difficulty: Very easy
Main course

STUFFED SWORDFISH ROLLS

p. 125

Time: 45 minutes
Difficulty: Easy
Main course

SWORDFISH SICILIAN STYLE

p. 125

Time: 1 hour
Difficulty: Very easy
Main course

MONKFISH IN SAFFRON SAUCE

p. 126

Time: 30 minutes
Difficulty: Very easy
Main course

MONKFISH AND VEGETABLE PIE

p. 126

Time: 1 hour
Difficulty: Very easy
Main course

Monkfish in saffron sauce

103

8

Xiphias gladius

14

Seriola dumerili

15

Lepidopus caudatus

11

Conger Conger

16

Raja marginata

7
Scyliorhinus canicula

9
Muraena helena

10
Lophius piscatorius

12
Gadus aeglefinus

13
Epinephelus caninus

SKATE SALAD

1³/₄ lb (800 g) wings of skate

14 fl oz (400 ml) dry white wine

juice of 4 lemons

2 cloves garlic

2 spring onions

2 lb (1 kg) small peas

6 tbsp single cream

3 tbsp tomato ketchup

salt and cayenne pepper

Boil the wine until it has reduced to 7 fl oz (200 ml). Wash and dry the fish and cut into thin strips; place in a bowl and pour the lemon juice and cooled white wine over it. Crush the garlic, finely chop the spring onions, and add these to the bowl; season with salt and pepper, stir and leave the fish to marinate for 12–15 hours in the refrigerator.

Cook the peas in boiling salted water for about 5 minutes. Drain and leave to cool. A few minutes before serving, drain the marinade from the fish pieces, place in a salad bowl with the peas and mix. Stir the tomato ketchup into the cream, add a little salt and cayenne pepper and stir in 3 tbsp of the marinade. Pour the dressing over the salad, mix briefly and serve.

COLD FISH PIE

1³/₄ lb (800 g) monkfish

2 tbsp olive oil

4 tinned tomatoes

4 eggs

1 small bunch chives

butter

7 fl oz (200 ml) homemade or bought mayonnaise

salt and pepper

Wash the fish, drain and place in an ovenproof dish greased with a little butter; sprinkle with the oil and bake at 400°F (200°C) mark 6 for 20 minutes. Remove from the oven and leave to cool.

Chop the tomatoes, place them in a bowl and add the lightly beaten eggs, chopped chives, salt and pepper. Stir well. Flake the fish flesh off the bone and slice.

Grease a sheet of foil with butter and use it to line an ovenproof soufflé dish. Layer the ingredients as follows: one third of the fish slices, covered with one third of the egg and tomato mixture; place under a hot grill so that the egg mixture starts to set. Repeat these two layers twice more, grilling in the same way. Place the dish in a roasting tin and pour in enough hot water to come half way up the sides of the dish. Cook for 1 hour at 350°F (180°C) mark 4.

Take out of the oven, place a sheet of foil on top, weight this down with a plate and a weight on top and leave until cold. Slice the pie and serve with mayonnaise.

AVOCADO WITH HADDOCK PURÉE

1 lb (500 g) haddock fillets

3 juicy lemons

2 large ripe avocados

7 fl oz (200 ml) mayonnaise, preferably homemade

2 tsp mild French mustard (e.g. Dijon)

1 tbsp Worcester sauce

1–1¹/₂ tbsp chopped mild pickled gherkins

1 tbsp capers

salt and pepper

Use only extremely fresh fish for this dish. Cod, hake, salmon, sole or bream can also be used. Cut the fish into short, thin strips, slicing on the slant, and place in a bowl with the juice of 2 lemons. Sprinkle with a pinch of salt, stir gently and leave to marinate in the refrigerator for 2 hours.

Cut the avocados lengthwise in half, discard the stone, and sprinkle with juice of the remaining lemon all over the cut surfaces to help prevent discoloration, reserving 1 tbsp of the juice for later use. Scoop out most of the avocado flesh but leave a layer about $^1/_4$ in (10 mm) next to the skin.

Drain the marinated fish well and purée in the food processor with the avocado flesh until very smooth. Add the mayonnaise, mustard, Worcester sauce, 1 tbsp lemon juice, salt and freshly ground white or black pepper. Process for a few seconds to mix well, then transfer the purée to a bowl and stir in the chopped gherkins and half the capers, coarsely chopped. If preferred, dill-pickled gherkins can be used and the capers omitted. (Do not use gherkins pickled in very sharp vinegar or acetic acid.)

Spoon equal amounts of this mixture into the hollowed avocados. Serve lightly chilled.

SALT COD MOUSSE

$1^1/_4$ lb (600 g) presoaked and softened salt cod
3 tbsp olive oil
7 fl oz (200 ml) milk
1 small lemon
1 small bunch parsley

Before starting on this recipe, you must soak the salt cod in several changes of cold water for 24 hours. Poach the fish in 11 fl oz (300 ml) gently simmering water for 20–30 minutes, drain, remove all the bones and skin and reduce to a smooth pulp in the food processor.

Heat the oil in a large saucepan; add the fish, stir well then gradually beat in the milk. The mixture should be light and fluffy.

Transfer to a deep dish, heaping the mixture up in a mound. Refrigerate until just before serving. Sprinkle with 3 tbsp strained lemon juice and very finely chopped parsley. Serve chilled.

FISH SALAD WITH GRAPEFRUIT AND WALNUTS

7 oz (200 g) tuna tinned in oil
$3^1/_2$ oz (100 g) tinned salmon
$2^1/_4$ lb (1 kg) mussels (see method)
5 oz (150 g) cooked, peeled small prawns or shrimps
1 egg yolk
5 fl oz (150 ml) oil
1 tbsp Dijon mustard
1 tbsp brandy
paprika
1 pink grapefruit
few lettuce leaves
$3^1/_2$ oz (100 g) walnuts
salt and pepper

Scrub and trim the mussels, discarding any that are damaged or gape open. Heat briefly in a pan over a high heat to open, then remove the molluscs from their shells. Discard any that do not open. (If mussels in the shell are unavailable, use approx. 8 oz [225 g] frozen shucked mussels.)

Drain the tuna and salmon (pick out any bones or skin from the latter) and flake finely with a fork. Make the mayonnaise with 1 egg yolk, a pinch of salt and the oil (see page 37); add the mustard, brandy, a pinch of paprika and freshly ground pepper for extra flavour. Peel the grapefruit and remove the segments carefully from their thin inner membranous skins; cut these skinned segments lengthwise in half. Wash and dry the lettuce and use to line a salad bowl. Mix the mussels, tuna, salmon, prawns and grapefruit pieces briefly and gently. Pound all but 5 of the walnuts and sprinkle over the salad. Add a little freshly ground pepper. Sprinkle with the mayonnaise just before serving and decorate with the remaining 5 walnut halves.

SAVOURY TUNA ROLLS

| 1 lb (500 g) fresh tuna |
| $^1/_2$ lemon |
| 2 bay leaves |
| 1 carrot |
| 1 bouquet garni |
| 6 tbsp olive oil |
| 1 clove garlic |
| 1 tbsp capers |
| 1 small bunch parsley |
| 1 small loaf white bread, sliced |
| salt and pepper |

Bring $4^1/_2$ pints (2 litres) water to the boil in a large saucepan with 1 tsp coarse sea salt, a few peppercorns, a piece of lemon rind (with no pith), the bay leaves, the peeled and sliced carrot and the bouquet garni. Add the tuna then turn down the heat and poach for 15 minutes. Drain and dry well. Heat 4 tbsp of the oil in a saucepan and sauté the tuna until golden brown all over, turning several times. Take out of the pan, drain, and leave to cool. Slice very thinly. Chop the garlic capers and parsley very finely, add a little oil and some salt and freshly ground pepper. Spread a little of this mixture on to each tuna slice and roll up.

Arrange 2 or 3 of these tuna rolls on each slice of bread and serve as an appetizer or light snack.

FISH COCKTAIL

| 1 middle cut of smooth hound or shark weighing $1^1/_4$ lb (600 g) |

| 1 carrot |
| 1 onion |
| 1 bay leaf |
| 2 oz (60 g) butter |
| 2 hard-boiled eggs |
| $3^1/_2$ fl oz (100 ml) milk |
| 2 oz (50 g) mixed dill pickles |
| 4 large lettuce leaves |
| juice of 1 lemon |
| 1 small bunch parsley |
| salt and pepper |

Wash and dry the fish and place in a heavy-bottomed saucepan with the peeled carrot, onion and bay leaf. Add enough water to just cover the fish. Poach for 15 minutes or until done. Drain, pat dry with kitchen paper, remove any skin and bones and purée in the food processor. Transfer the fish purée to a bowl and work in the softened butter, the finely chopped eggs and pickles, the milk, salt, and pepper. Mix well.

Place a lettuce leaf in each of four small glass dishes or coupes and spoon the fish mixture into each lettuce leaf. Chill until just before serving; sprinkle with a little strained lemon juice and the finely chopped parsley.

PORTUGUESE SALT COD SOUP

| $1^1/_2$ lb (700 g) presoaked salt cod |
| 1 carrot |
| 1 celery stalk |
| 1 small onion |
| 1 small bunch parsley |
| $3^1/_2$ fl oz (100 ml) olive oil |
| plain flour |
| 3 cloves garlic |

1 small piece chilli pepper
8 fl oz (225 ml) rosé wine
8 tinned tomatoes
2¹/₂ pints (1.4 litres) fish stock (fumet) (see page 39)
2 potatoes
4 thick slices coarse white bread
salt

See recipe for Salt Cod Mousse on page 106 for instructions on how to prepare the salt cod. Peel and chop the carrot, celery and onion; chop the parsley. Cut the salt cod into bite-sized pieces and dust lightly with flour. Sweat the vegetable mixture in the oil, then add the salt cod pieces and sauté gently for 10 minutes. Chop 2 peeled garlic cloves and the chilli pepper and scatter over the fish. Sprinkle with the wine, add the coarsely chopped tomatoes and stir well.

 Cook for 5 minutes, then add the boiling fish stock (*fumet*), cover, and simmer for 1 hour. Add the peeled potatoes cut into fairly small pieces; cover and cook for a further 45 minutes. Both the potatoes and the fish should be very soft. Rub the surface of the bread with the cut surfaces of the remaining garlic clove and toast in the oven until crisp. Place a piece of bread in each of 4 soup bowls and ladle the soup on top.

FISH AND MUSHROOM SOUP

2³/₄ lb (1.2 kg) mixed fish (e.g. hake, cod, bream, mackerel)
1 carrot
1 clove garlic
1 small onion
parsley
5 tbsp olive oil
2 salted anchovies
1¹/₂ tbsp pine nuts

1 tbsp capers
4–5 dried mushrooms (e.g. ceps)
plain flour
salt and pepper

Prepare the fish (see page 9), trim, gut, fillet, remove the skin, wash, dry and cut into bite-sized pieces. Peel and finely chop the carrot, garlic and onion; chop the parsley; sauté this mixture in 4 tbsp oil in a saucepan, adding a little salt. Rinse the anchovies, remove their bones and crush with 1 tbsp oil; add this to the vegetable mixture, followed by the pounded pine nuts and the finely chopped capers. Drain the mushrooms, reserving the water, squeeze out any moisture and chop. Add to the mixture, and stir in 1 tbsp flour and a little freshly ground pepper. Cook, stirring, for 2–3 minutes; add the fish pieces, 18 fl oz (500 ml) water and the strained water from the mushrooms. Partially cover the pan, and simmer for 20–25 minutes. Draw aside from the heat, leave to stand for a minute or two and serve.

FISH RAVIOLI WITH TOMATO AND CHIVE SAUCE

10 oz (300 g) fillets of mixed fish (e.g. hake, cod, etc.)
3¹/₂ fl oz (100 ml) dry white wine
1 lettuce heart
3 tbsp double cream
2 oz (50 g) freshly grated Parmesan cheese
9 oz (250 g) plain flour
3 eggs
8 fl oz (225 ml) sieved tomatoes
3 tbsp butter
few chives
salt and pepper

Poach the washed fish for 10–15 minutes in the wine mixed with 18 fl oz (500 ml) water; drain well. Boil the lettuce in salted water for 4 minutes, drain, and chop finely together with the fish. Stir in 1 egg yolk, the cheese and a pinch of salt. Sift the flour into a mound on a pastry board, make a well in the centre, break 2 whole eggs into it and break these up by beating gently with a fork. Gradually work in the flour, stirring the eggs round and round, with your slightly cupped hand or a wooden spoon, until the dough is well blended, firm, smooth and elastic. Roll out to a thin sheet and cut into rectangles measuring about 3 × 5 in (8–12 cm). Place a little of the stuffing in the centre of each, fold lengthwise, enclosing the stuffing, and seal the longer edge by moistening slightly; twist the ends gently closed and pinch the twisted section to seal like sweet wrappers.

Cook in a large saucepan of boiling salted water for 10–12 minutes. Heat the sieved tomato in a small saucepan with the butter, cream, salt, freshly ground pepper and chopped chives. Drain the fish ravioli, mix gently with the sauce and serve.

TAGLIATELLE WITH TUNA

10 oz (300 g) fresh tuna

1/2 onion

1 small bunch parsley

6 tbsp oil

5 oz (150 g) frozen peas

1 stock cube (fish, vegetable or chicken)

10 fl oz (300 ml) sieved tomatoes

1 small piece chilli pepper

12 oz (350 g) tagliatelle

salt

Chop the peeled onion with the parsley and sauté in 3 tbsp oil in a saucepan. Add the still frozen peas, crumble in the stock cube, and pour in 4 fl oz (120 ml) water. Cover and simmer for 15–20 minutes.

Wash and dry the tuna; fry in the remaining

oil, add the tomato, crumbled chilli pepper, and a little salt; cover and simmer for 20 minutes. Flake the tuna with a fork.

Cook the pasta in plenty of boiling salted water until just tender (*al dente*), drain, and mix briefly in the hot pan with the tuna sauce and the flavoured peas. Serve in a very hot dish.

SPAGHETTI WITH TUNA AND PESTO

8 oz (200 g) fresh tuna

1 lb (500 g) ripe tomatoes

1 medium-sized onion

1 clove garlic

4 tbsp olive oil

1 tbsp pesto sauce

12 oz (350 g) spaghetti

salt and pepper

Blanch, peel and coarsely chop the tomatoes, discarding the seeds. Peel and chop the onion and garlic together and sauté in the oil. Cut the tuna into very small dice, add to the pan and fry gently until coloured. Add the tomatoes and a little salt. Cover and simmer gently for 20 minutes. Add the pesto sauce and stir well. Turn off the heat.

Cook the spaghetti in plenty of boiling salted water. Drain when tender but still retaining some bite and turn into the saucepan containing the sauce; heat through, stirring over a fairly high heat for 2 minutes. Serve at once.

SPAGHETTI WITH EEL

1 1/4 lb (500 g) eel

1 onion

2 cloves garlic

1 small bunch parsley

plain flour
1 oz (25 g) butter
4 tbsp oil
1¼ lb (600 g) tomatoes
1 small piece chilli pepper
3½ fl oz (100 ml) dry white wine
10 oz spaghetti
salt

Chop the garlic, onion and parsley very finely. Clean the eel and skin (see page 10), cut off the head, wash and dry, and slice into thin steaks. Roll the fish pieces in flour seasoned with salt and pepper and fry in the butter and 2 tbsp oil over a moderate heat. When lightly browned all over, transfer the pieces with a slotted spoon (to drain) on to a plate and leave to cool completely. Remove all the bones and chop the flesh into very small pieces. Sauté the garlic mixture in the remaining oil, add the blanched, peeled, seeded, and coarsely chopped tomatoes; sprinkle with a small pinch of salt, cover, and simmer gently for 20 minutes. Add the eel pieces, the finely crumbled chilli pepper, and the white wine and simmer for 15 minutes. Cook the spaghetti in plenty of boiling, salted water and drain when tender but still *al dente*. Transfer to the saucepan containing the fish sauce and stir over a high heat for 1 minute. Turn into a very hot serving dish and serve at once.

CHINESE GROUPER SOUP

head of 1 large grouper or sea bass (e.g. from a 4½-lb [2-kg] fish)
4 tbsp soy sauce
1 oz (25 g) dried Chinese mushrooms
5 tbsp sunflower oil
4 small onions or spring onions
3 tbsp dry sherry
1 tsp sugar
18 fl oz (500 ml) chicken stock

8 oz (200 g) bamboo shoots
1 tbsp sesame oil

Wash the fish head well, sprinkle all over with the soy sauce and leave to stand for 15 minutes then drain, reserving the soy marinade. Soak the dried mushrooms in warm water for 30 minutes.

Fry the fish head in the sunflower oil in a large, non-metallic, heavy-bottomed saucepan (fireproof earthenware is ideal) until browned all over. Add the peeled and sliced onions and the sherry; cover tightly and boil for 1 minute. Add the soy sauce drained from marinating the fish, the sugar and the stock. Increase the heat and bring to the boil. Add the thinly sliced bamboo shoots and the drained mushrooms. Cover and simmer for 30 minutes.

Just before serving, remove the fish head and flake off all the usable flesh; sieve this (or place in the food processor) together with the vegetables. Blend this mixture with the sesame oil and serve in little bowls, one for each person, at the same time as the hot broth.

FISH AND RICE MOULD

2 fillets of hake
2 fillets of lemon sole
2 small fillets of cod
9 oz (250 g) short grain rice (e.g. arborio)
plain flour
2 oz (60 g) butter
1½ tbsp oil
5 eggs
4 oz (100 g) frozen petit pois
5 oz (150 g) button mushrooms
2 oz (50 g) freshly grated Parmesan cheese
2 tbsp fine fresh breadcrumbs
salt and pepper

Boil the rice in plenty of salted water until tender but still with a little bite to it. Leave to cool.

Cut the fish into small pieces; season with salt and pepper and coat with flour, shaking off excess. Fry in half the butter and all the oil. Hard boil 3 of the eggs; cool under running cold water, shell and cut into wedges. Cook the peas as directed on the packet and drain. Rinse the mushrooms, slice finely and sauté with ¹/₂ oz (10 g) butter in a non-stick pan, seasoning with salt and pepper. Transfer the rice to a large bowl.

Lightly beat the 2 remaining eggs and add to the rice with the cheese. Mix thoroughly. Turn half this mixture into a charlotte mould or casserole dish, greased with butter. Cover the rice with the fish, peas, eggs and mushrooms and cover these in turn with the remaining rice. (If using a mould, pack the layers fairly firmly.) Sprinkle with the breadcrumbs. Cook at 425°F (220°C) mark 7 for 20 minutes (in a bain-marie if using a mould which is to be turned out on to a warmed plate).

HAKE AND POTATO PIE

1 lb (500 g) fillets of hake
1¹/₄ lb (600 g) waxy potatoes
1 oz (25 g) butter
2 cloves garlic
1 sprig rosemary
3 sage leaves
1 small bunch parsley
1 chilli pepper
juice of 1 lemon
oil
7 fl oz (200 ml) dry white wine
salt and pepper

Wash the potatoes and boil in their skins for 15 minutes; drain, peel and cut into slices of even thickness.

Grease a deep, oval ovenproof dish with butter and arrange the ingredients in layers, starting with the potatoes, then fish and so on, and sprinkling each layer with salt, freshly ground pepper and finely chopped garlic, rosemary, sage, parsley and chilli pepper, as well as a little lemon juice and oil. End with a potato layer on top. Pour in the wine and bake for 30 minutes at 350°F (180°C) mark 4. Serve hot.

BAKED HAKE WITH PEAS AND OLIVES

1 lb (500 g) fillets of hake
3 potatoes
plain flour
6 tbsp oil
14 fl oz (400 ml) sieved tomatoes
1 onion
1 clove garlic
1 bay leaf
4 oz (100 g) fresh or frozen peas
2 oz (50 g) green olives, stoned
3 tinned anchovy fillets
salt

Wash the potatoes, boil for 10 minutes, drain, peel and slice. Rinse and dry the hake, and cut into bite-sized pieces. Coat lightly with flour and sauté in 3 tbsp oil.

Pour the sieved tomatoes (if unavailable, sieve drained tinned tomatoes) into a saucepan, add the peeled garlic, bay leaf and salt. Simmer for 20 minutes; discard the garlic and bay leaf. Pour 3 tbsp oil into an ovenproof dish and fill in layers, starting with a layer of potatoes, then hake, tomato sauce, peas and olives. Scatter the anchovies, cut into small pieces, over the top and bake in a preheated oven at 400°F (200°C) mark 6 for 15–20 minutes. Serve immediately.

SAILOR'S PIE

1 lb (500 g) fillets of hake

juice of ¹/₂ lemon

10 oz (300 g) floury potatoes

3¹/₂ fl oz (100 ml) milk

1¹/₂ oz (40 g) butter

1¹/₂ tbsp béchamel sauce (see page 80)

breadcrumbs

salt

Wash the fish, drain and poach for 10 minutes in 18 fl oz (500 ml) water with a little salt and the lemon juice. Leave to cool in the liquid and then drain. Remove any remaining bones, reduce to a purée in the food processor and transfer to a bowl.

Boil the potatoes in salted water for 30–40 minutes; drain, peel and mash while hot. Work the potatoes into the fish, add the hot milk, the butter cut into small pieces, the béchamel sauce and a little salt. When well blended, grease a deep cake tin (8–9 in [20–23 cm] in diameter) with butter, sprinkle the inside with breadcrumbs and fill with the fish mixture. Top with a layer of breadcrumbs.

Place in a preheated oven at 400°F (200°C) mark 6 for 10–15 minutes. Brown the top under the grill for 2 minutes. Leave to stand for a minute before serving.

Note: This fish pie goes well with steamed broccoli.

SALT COD PIE

2¹/₄ lb (1 kg) presoaked salt cod

7 tbsp oil

1 lb (500 g) waxy potatoes

1 onion

1 clove garlic

1 small bunch parsley

1 oz (25 g) breadcrumbs

juice of 1 lemon

2–3 fennel seeds (optional)

salt and pepper

Soak the salt cod in cold water for 24 hours, changing the water several times, to soften and remove excess salt. Drain, pat dry and place in a large ovenproof dish or medium-sized roasting tin with 3 tbsp oil.

Peel and thinly slice the potatoes; arrange these so they cover the cod. Place the finely sliced onion on top, sprinkle with finely chopped garlic and the breadcrumbs, chopped parsley, salt and freshly ground pepper. Sprinkle with the strained lemon juice, 4 tbsp oil and 18 fl oz (500 ml) water.

Cover with foil and place in the oven, preheated to 350°F (180°C) mark 4; bake for 30 minutes, remove the foil, and cook for a further 5 minutes.

STOCKFISH LIGURIAN STYLE

1³/₄ lb (800 g) dried cod (stockfish)

1 small bunch parsley

1 clove garlic

2 tbsp pine nuts

3 walnuts

pinch cayenne pepper

4 large ripe tomatoes

4 tbsp oil

20 mixed green and black olives

2 large waxy potatoes

1 carrot

1 medium-sized aubergine

10 oz (300 g) spinach

salt

Soak the stockfish for at least 3 days before making this dish, changing the water at frequent intervals. When softened, drain and cut into bite-sized pieces. Chop the parsley and peeled garlic together finely; reduce the pine nuts to a paste with the walnuts using a pestle and mortar (or in the food processor). Mix all these chopped and pounded ingredients well, adding the cayenne pepper and a pinch of salt. Fry very gently in the oil for 1 minute, then add the fish, increase the heat and brown lightly all over. Add the peeled and roughly chopped tomatoes, and cook for 5–6 minutes; add 7 fl oz (200 ml) warm water, cook for a few minutes then add the olives. Cover and simmer slowly for 2 hours, adding a little water when necessary.

Peel and cut the potatoes, carrot and aubergine into very small pieces, and add to the pan half way through the cooking time (after 1 hour) together with the chopped spinach. Add a little salt if necessary, but take care not to over-season, and cook for a further hour. Serve with hot French bread or garlic bread.

COTRIADE

4 lb (1.8 kg) mixed fish (e.g. haddock, whiting, eel, bream, etc.)
2¹/₄ lb (1 kg) raw fish trimmings (e.g. heads and trimmings)
4 onions
3 cloves garlic
1 oz (25 g) butter
2 fl oz (50 ml) olive oil
7 fl oz (200 ml) dry white wine
1 bouquet garni
1³/₄ lb (800 g) small or new potatoes
8 thick slices French bread
salt and pepper

Peel the onions and slice very thinly; crush the garlic. Fry very gently in the oil and butter. Pour in the wine and add 4¹/₂ pint (2 litres) boiling water.

Add the well washed fish heads and trimmings, the bouquet garni, salt and pepper. Bring to the boil and then simmer for 20 minutes. Remove the fish heads, all the trimmings and the bouquet garni (use a slotted ladle); add the peeled and thickly sliced potatoes. Simmer for 30 minutes.

Add the washed, filleted selection of fish, cut into bite-sized pieces, and simmer for 12 minutes. Remove the fish pieces with a slotted ladle and keep hot. Crisp the slices of French bread slightly in the oven, place a piece in each individual soup plate and ladle in the broth. Serve the fish pieces afterwards, as a second course, with the potatoes.

MEDITERRANEAN FISH PASTA

14 oz (400 g) fresh tuna
1 green pepper
1 aubergine
1 lb (500 g) ripe tomatoes
4 tbsp olive oil
2 cloves garlic
12 black olives, stoned
1 tbsp capers
5 tinned anchovy fillets
1¹/₂ tbsp chopped fresh basil leaves
1 tsp finely chopped fresh rosemary leaves
12 oz (350 g) small pasta shapes
salt and pepper

Hold the green pepper over a gas burner on a long fork or place under the grill, turning frequently, to scorch and loosen the skin. Peel, discard the stalk, seeds and white membrane; cut into thin strips. Peel the aubergine and cut into small dice. Blanch and peel the tomatoes and chop coarsely.

Cut the tuna into small cubes and fry in the oil,

preferably in a fireproof earthenware casserole dish, for 3 minutes, turning frequently. Add the aubergine and continue frying while turning. Add the green pepper, tomatoes (drained if tinned), crushed garlic, olives, capers, coarsely chopped anchovies and the herbs. Add a little salt if necessary, stir well, cover and simmer very gently for 15 minutes.

Cook the pasta in plenty of boiling salted water until just tender; drain, turn into the cooking pot containing the tuna, and stir over a high heat for 1 minute. Transfer to a heated serving dish or individual plates.

BAKED GROUPER WITH MUSHROOM AND PRAWN STUFFING

1 packet (approx. 2 tbsp) dried mushrooms (e.g. ceps)
1 grouper weighing 2¹/₄–2¹/₂ lb (1 kg)
4 medium slices stale bread, crusts removed
4 oz (100 g) peeled prawns
2 oz (50 g) freshly grated Parmesan cheese
2 eggs
pinch grated nutmeg
1 oz (25 g) butter
7 fl oz (200 ml) dry white wine
salt and pepper

Soak the mushrooms in a cup of warm water for 20 minutes to soften while you prepare the fish. Gut the grouper; cut off the fins and remove the scales by scraping the blunt edge of a large kitchen knife along the fish from the tail towards the head, against the direction of the scales. Wash well and remove the backbone, slitting all the way down the centre of the fish (see page 9).

Soak the bread in warm water in a bowl for 5 minutes. Chop the prawns. Drain the mushrooms, rinse and chop coarsely. Squeeze as much moisture out of the bread as possible and crumble

into a large bowl. Mix with the prawns and mushrooms, gradually working in the eggs, grated cheese, a generous pinch of salt, some freshly ground pepper and the grated nutmeg. Mix thoroughly.

Stuff the fish with this mixture and secure with cocktail sticks or small skewers so that the stuffing will not ooze out during the cooking. Use the butter to grease a wide, shallow ovenproof dish; place the fish in this and season with a little more salt and pepper. Bake for 1 hour at 400°F (200°C) mark 6, pouring a little of the wine over the fish at frequent intervals.

GROUPER WITH PEPPERS

1 grouper weighing 2¹/₄–2¹/₂ lb (1 kg)
juice of 1 lemon
2 oz (50 g) streaky bacon
1 red pepper
2 oz (50 g) butter, melted
1 onion
1 green pepper
4 large ripe tomatoes
3¹/₂ fl oz (100 ml) single cream
1 tbsp Dijon (or ordinary) mustard
3 tbsp freshly grated Parmesan cheese
salt and pepper

Prepare the grouper (see page 9), gutting through the gill aperture. Wash well, dry and sprinkle inside with the lemon juice. Make small, deep incisions in the fleshiest parts of the fish and stuff these with a mixture of the bacon and the red pepper, cut into tiny strips. Sprinkle with a little salt and plenty of freshly ground pepper; place the fish in an ovenproof dish, liberally greased with butter, and sprinkle melted butter over the top.

Slice the peeled onion and the green pepper into very thin rings; blanch, skin and chop the tomatoes. Spoon round the fish. Bake at 400°F (200°C) mark 6 for 30 minutes, basting the fish with its own juices several times. Mix the cream with the mustard and cheese and pour over the fish 5 minutes before removing from the oven.

GROUPER EN PAPILLOTE

4 grouper steaks weighing 5 oz (150 g) each

20 clams (fresh or tinned)

12 mussels

12 Dublin Bay prawns

1 onion

1 small bunch parsley

juice of 2 lemons

olive oil

salt and pepper

An excellent choice for a dinner party, this dish will look much more decorative if you use clams and mussels still in their shells. Wash and scrub the molluscs; peel the Dublin Bay prawns if wished, removing the black intestinal tract which runs down the back (see page 16). Chop the onion and parsley very finely. Spread a little of the chopped mixture on to 4 large squares of foil, place a fish steak on top, season with salt and pepper and arrange some of the molluscs and crustaceans on each steak. Sprinkle with lemon juice and a little oil. Seal the packets securely, leaving an air space inside.

Place in the oven, preheated to 350°F (180°C) mark 4, and cook for 15–20 minutes. Serve the fish still wrapped in the packets.

GROUPER WITH CLAMS

4 slices grouper weighing 8 oz (200 g) each

2¼ lb (1 kg) mussels

1 onion

1 carrot

1 bouquet garni

3½ fl oz (100 ml) olive oil

2 egg yolks

juice of 1 lemon

1 tbsp finely chopped parsley

salt and pepper

Leave the mussels to stand in cold, salted water for an hour or two, then scrub well, removing their beards. Discard any that are open. Place in a large pan over a high heat for a few seconds to open; discard any that fail to open. Remove the molluscs from their shells and strain their liquid through a fine cloth. (If using frozen shucked mussels, substitute a little dry white wine for the mussel liquor.)

Wash the fish steaks and pat dry with kitchen paper. Thinly slice the peeled onion and carrot; pour 4 tbsp of the oil into a wide fireproof casserole dish, spread the sliced vegetables over the bottom, and place the steaks on top in a single layer. Add the bouquet garni and the mussel liquor (or white wine) and sprinkle with the remaining oil. Cover and cook briskly for 20 minutes, turning the fish half way through.

Remove the steaks from the pan and keep hot. Reduce the liquid a little over a high heat. Draw aside from the heat, pour about 3½ fl oz (100 ml) of the liquid into a bowl, beat in the egg yolks and stir into the liquid left in the casserole.

Stir continuously over a low heat but do not allow to boil; add the lemon juice a little at a time. Add the mussels and when heated through pour over the fish and serve at once.

FISH STEAKS IN SWEET-SOUR SAUCE

4 dogfish or huss steaks weighing 8 oz (225 g) each

3½ oz (100 g) sultanas

1 onion

115

1 clove garlic
1 carrot
1 celery stalk
1 small bunch parsley
2 bay leaves
1¹/₂ oz (30 g) butter
7 fl oz (200 ml) dry white wine
salt and peppercorns

Wash and dry the fish steaks, season with salt and freshly ground pepper and set aside on a plate. Soak the sultanas for 15 minutes in warm water, and squeeze out excess moisture before using. Finely chop the onion, garlic, carrot, celery and parsley. Transfer to a wide pan, add the bay leaves, the drained sultanas and the butter. Sauté gently for a few minutes.

Place the fish steaks in the pan and fry until lightly browned on both sides; pour in the wine and cook over a moderate heat for 20 minutes, turning the fish once very carefully after 15 minutes' cooking, with each piece between two fish slices or wide spatulas to prevent them breaking.

BAKED FISH STEAKS WITH SPINACH

1³/₄ lb (800 g) huss steaks
7 fl oz (200 ml) olive oil
2 large waxy potatoes
1 onion
1¹/₂ tbsp finely chopped parsley
2¹/₄ lb (1 kg) spinach
4 tinned tomatoes
3¹/₂ fl oz (100 ml) dry white wine
salt and pepper

Generously grease a deep, oval ovenproof dish with oil. Peel the potatoes and cut into very thin slices; use half of these to line the bottom of the dish and sprinkle with a little salt. Peel the onion, slice in thin rings and sprinkle half, together with half the parsley, over the potatoes. Spread half the spinach, torn into small pieces, on top and press down firmly. Place strips of two drained tomatoes over the spinach, then arrange the fish steaks on these. Season with salt and pepper and drizzle a little oil over the fish.

Repeat this layering in reverse order, using the remaining half of the ingredients: tomatoes, spinach, parsley and onions and finally, a topping of potatoes. Sprinkle with the remaining oil and wine. Cover with foil and bake in the oven, preheated to 400°F (200°C) mark 6 for 15 minutes. Turn down to 350°F (180°C) mark 4 and bake for a further 40 minutes. By now all the liquid should be absorbed; if necessary, remove the foil for the last 10 minutes' cooking, to brown the top.

CURRIED FISH STEAKS

8 thin huss steaks weighing 4 oz (100 g) each
3–4 tsp mild curry powder
2 oz (50 g) butter
2 oz (50 g) plain flour
1 pint (600 ml) milk
5 oz (150 g) breadcrumbs
oil
4 fl oz (100 ml) double cream
1 lemon
salt and pepper

Cut the steaks in half, removing the central bone. Rub these filleted half steaks with salt and ¹/₂–1 tsp curry powder all over and leave to stand in a cool place for 2 hours.

Melt the butter in a saucepan over a very gentle heat; mix in the flour, then beat in the hot milk, adding a little at a time; season with salt and a little pepper and stir in 2½ tsp curry powder. Cook very slowly for 10 minutes, stirring continuously.

Coat the fish steaks with breadcrumbs and fry in plenty of very hot oil. Drain, place on kitchen paper, and keep hot. Stir the cream into the sauce and reheat but do not allow to boil. Serve the fish, garnished with lemon wedges, handing round the sauce separately. Steamed or boiled potatoes provide a good foil to the spicy fish and sauce.

HUSS IN CREAMY MUSHROOM SAUCE

2³/₄ lb (1.25 kg) huss
20 baby onions
7 oz (200 g) button mushrooms
2½ oz (70 g) butter
4 tbsp oil
1³/₄ pints (1 litre) fish stock (fumet) (see page 39)
1 bouquet garni
1 oz (25 g) plain flour
7 fl oz (200 ml) single cream
1 egg yolk
1½ tbsp finely chopped parsley
salt and pepper

Prepare the fish (see page 9) and cut into small pieces, discarding the central bone. Peel the onions, wipe the mushrooms with a damp cloth or kitchen paper, leaving them whole.

Brown the fish pieces all over by frying in 1 oz (25 g) butter and 2 tbsp oil. Season with salt and freshly ground pepper and add the fish stock, the onions and bouquet garni. Reduce the heat, cover and simmer slowly for 20 minutes. Sauté the mushrooms separately with the same quantities of oil and butter; season. Remove the fish pieces and onions when cooked, using a slotted ladle, and keep hot. Measure out 18 fl oz (500 ml) of the liquid left over from cooking the fish and onions and strain.

Melt the remaining butter in a fairly large saucepan, stir in the flour, and beat in the hot stock a little at a time. Cook for 5–10 minutes. Lower the heat and stir in the cream. Add the fish and onions to this sauce, cover and simmer very slowly for 10 minutes.

Transfer the fish to a heated serving platter, using a slotted ladle, allowing most of the sauce to drain back into the pan; surround the fish with the mushrooms and onions. Add a few spoonfuls of the sauce to the lightly beaten egg yolk; stir well then add to the sauce in the saucepan, off the heat. Season with a little salt and pepper and return to a very gentle heat for 2 minutes, stirring continuously until the sauce thickens a little. Pour over the fish and sprinkle with the parsley. Serve at once.

FRIED HUSS STEAKS

2½ lb (1 kg) huss steaks
5 fl oz (150 ml) white wine vinegar
3½ fl oz (100 ml) olive oil
plain flour
1 lemon
1 lettuce
salt

Wash the steaks, cut in half, removing bones and any skin, and pat dry thoroughly. Trim off the fins, head and tail and gut the fish: be sure to discard the liver as it is toxic. Wash well, dry and skin (see pages 9–10). Pat dry and slice into 12 pieces of equal size.

Place the fish in a deep dish, sprinkle the vinegar all over, cover with cling film and leave to stand in a cool place for about 30 minutes, turning two or three times. Drain the fish pieces, dry with kitchen paper, and coat with flour, shaking off excess. Fry for 2–3 minutes on each side over a high heat in the oil (use an iron frying pan if possible). Reduce the heat and fry more gently for 5–6 minutes so that the fish cooks right through. Drain, place on a kitchen towel, and keep hot.

Spread out the lettuce leaves on a large serving platter and place the fish on top, garnished with lemon wedges. Serve at once.

LEMON-BAKED HAKE

1³/₄ lb (800 g) fillets of hake
2 oz (50g) butter
4 lemons
3 onions
1 tsp dried mixed herbs
3 tbsp finely chopped parsley
7 fl oz (200 ml) dry white wine
6 tbsp breadcrumbs
salt and pepper

Rinse the fillets thoroughly under running cold water, dry and cut into small, evenly-sized pieces. Grease a small, deep ovenproof dish with a little of the butter and pack half the fish pieces closely in a single layer covering the bottom of the dish. Slice the lemons thinly into rounds, discarding the seeds, and use half of them to cover the fish.

Peel and slice the onions into wafer-thin slices. Spread half of these on top of the lemon layer. Arrange three more layers, in the same order, using up the rest of the fish, lemons and onions. Sprinkle the top with mixed herbs and parsley, a little salt and plenty of freshly ground pepper. Sprinkle the breadcrumbs over the top; distribute small flakes of the remaining butter over the surface and bake for 30 minutes at 400°F (200°C) mark 6.

PORTUGUESE HAKE

2 hake weighing 1¹/₄ lb (600 g) each
1¹/₂ tbsp lemon juice
3 eggs
3 tbsp chopped chives or parsley
1 oz (25 g) butter
3 tbsp oil
salt and pepper

Trim off fins, heads and tails, and gut the fish (see page 9); dry well. Cut each fish into four thick steaks. Sprinkle with salt, freshly ground pepper and the lemon juice. Beat the eggs with a pinch of salt, pepper and three quarters of the chives or parsley. Coat the fish pieces in the beaten egg; melt the butter and oil ready in a pan and fry the fish for 3 minutes, turn and fry for 5 more minutes.

Pour the rest of the egg into the pan between and around the fish and beat with a fork as it cooks, to scramble. Do not over-cook, the egg should be quite creamy. Transfer the fish and scrambled egg to a warmed serving dish, sprinkle with the remaining chives or parsley and serve at once.

Note: 1 lb (500 g) cod fillets can replace the hake.

HAKE WITH CAPER MAYONNAISE

1 hake weighing 2¹/₄–2¹/₂ lb (1 kg)
1 onion
1 carrot
2 cloves
1 bay leaf
3¹/₂ fl oz (100 ml) white wine vinegar
7 fl oz (200 ml) mayonnaise (see page 37)
1 tbsp capers
salt and peppercorns

Make 5¹/₄ pints (3 litres) *court-bouillon* (see page 39) with water, the peeled and quartered onion, peeled and thickly sliced carrot, cloves, bay leaf, peppercorns, vinegar and salt. Boil for 30 minutes and strain into the fish kettle. Place the cleaned, prepared fish (see page 9) on the slotted rack and lower into the liquid. Poach at the gentlest possible simmer for 15–20 minutes. Leave to cool in the liquid.

Remove the fish very carefully from the liquid, transfer from the rack, and remove the skin. Arrange on a platter and serve with the mayonnaise mixed with chopped capers.

SPANISH SALT COD

approx. 1 lb 10 oz (750 g) presoaked salt cod

juice of 1 lemon

1 bay leaf

few peppercorns

$1^{1}/_{2}$ oz (40 g) butter

1 oz (25 g) plain flour

$3^{1}/_{2}$ fl oz (100 ml) fish stock (fumet) (see page 39)

7 fl oz (200 ml) dry white wine

5 oz (150 g) peeled shrimps or small prawns

3 oz (80 g) tinned anchovy fillets

2 egg yolks

salt and pepper

Soak the fish in several changes of cold water for 24 hours then wash under running cold water to remove lingering traces of salt. Remove any skin and bones; cut into small, bite-sized pieces. Place in a dish and sprinkle with the lemon juice. Leave to stand for 10 minutes. Bring a large saucepan of water with the bay leaf and a few peppercorns in it to the boil; drain off the lemon juice from the fish and poach for 10 minutes.

Remove the fish pieces from the pan with a slotted ladle. Melt the butter in a saucepan, stir in the flour, cook until slightly coloured then beat in the fish stock, wine and 2 tbsp lemon juice, adding a little at a time. Cook for a few minutes; the sauce should be fairly thin and very smooth. Add the fish pieces, the shrimps and the drained anchovy fillets.

Simmer for 5 minutes; mix 2 tbsp of the sauce with the lightly beaten egg yolks in a bowl, then stir into the saucepan, making sure the mixture does not boil from this point onwards. Add a little salt if necessary and some pepper before serving.

MARSEILLES SALT COD

$1^{1}/_{2}$ lb (700 g) presoaked salt cod

2 tbsp dried mushrooms (e.g. ceps)

1 onion

olive oil

$1^{3}/_{4}$ lb (800 g) waxy potatoes

8 ripe tomatoes

15 green olives, stoned

salt and pepper

Soak the salt cod for 24 hours in several changes of cold water then rinse thoroughly under running cold water. Soak the dried mushrooms in warm water for 1 hour to soften and plump up. Peel the potatoes. Chop the onion finely and fry gently in the oil in a large, deep saucepan. Add the blanched and peeled, seeded and coarsely chopped tomatoes (drain well if using tinned tomatoes). Cover and simmer for 10 minutes.

Cut the potatoes into small pieces and add to the saucepan, followed by $3^{1}/_{2}$ pints ($1^{1}/_{2}$ litres) water. Bring back to the boil and cook for 5 minutes; remove any skin and bones from the salt cod, cut into fairly small pieces, and add to the saucepan with the drained mushrooms and the olives. Cover and simmer gently for 20 minutes longer. Season and serve.

SALT COD FRITTERS

$1^{1}/_{4}$ lb (600 g) presoaked salt cod

1 bay leaf

1 small sprig thyme
6 oz (180 g) plain flour
2 small eggs
1 cup milk
oil for deep-frying
3 cloves garlic
1 tbsp tarragon vinegar
salt

Rinse the presoaked salt cod (see previous recipe) under running cold water thoroughly to remove any lingering traces of salt. Place in a large saucepan and pour in sufficient hot water to cover the fish; add the bay leaf and thyme. Bring to the boil, then simmer for 15 minutes. Leave to cool in the liquid, drain well, remove any bones or skin and reduce to a very thick purée in the food processor.

Make a batter, working the egg yolks gradually into the flour and then beating in the milk, adding a little at a time (the batter may be mixed in the blender). When the mixture is very smooth, add a pinch of salt and beat in 3 tbsp olive oil. Leave to stand. Peel the garlic cloves, crush or pound with a pestle and mortar, work in 1 tbsp olive oil and the tarragon vinegar. Stir this mixture into the fish purée and then amalgamate with the batter, mixing well. Beat the egg whites until stiff but not dry and fold gently but thoroughly into the batter.

Heat the oil to the correct temperature in the deep-fryer and when it is smoking hot, drop the mixture into the oil in tablespoonfuls, frying 3–4 fritters at a time: the batter mixture will puff up and bob up to the surface; fry each batch until crisp and golden brown. Remove with a slotted ladle, draining well, and keep hot, uncovered, on kitchen paper.

SALT COD WITH PEPPERS

1¹/₂ lb (700 g) presoaked salt cod
1 lb (500 g) ripe tomatoes
4 red peppers
2 large onions

2 bay leaves
3¹/₂ fl oz (100 ml) olive oil
salt and pepper

See previous recipes for preparation of salt cod. Remove any remaining bones and skin. Blanch, peel and seed the tomatoes and chop. Grill the peppers briefly, turning very frequently, to loosen the skin; peel, remove their stalks, seeds and pith and cut into thin strips. Peel and chop the onions finely; crumble the bay leaves.

Grease a deep casserole dish with oil and arrange a layer of cod, onion, bay leaf and tomatoes followed by a layer of peppers. Season with salt and pepper and sprinkle with a little oil. Repeat the layering, ending with a layer of cod, sprinkled with some onions and bay leaf.

Cover and cook over a very low heat (using a heat diffuser, if necessary) for 2¹/₂ hours, shaking the dish gently from time to time to prevent the ingredients sticking and burning.

DEEP-FRIED SALT COD

1¹/₂ lb (700 g) presoaked salt cod
6 oz (175 g) plain flour
1 egg, at room temperature
¹/₄ oz (10 g) fresh yeast
2 bay leaves
oil for deep-frying
6 fl oz (175 ml) dry white wine
salt

Soak the cod in cold water for 4–5 hours, changing the water frequently, even if presoaked, to make sure it is not too salty.

Sift the flour into a mound in a large mixing bowl, make a well in the centre and break the egg into the well. Add the yeast dissolved in 1–2 tbsp warm water, a pinch of salt, 2 tbsp oil and the white wine. Blend these ingredients gradually and thoroughly with the flour, using a wooden spoon or a balloon whisk. A coating batter (very thick but still of pouring consistency) is required. If too thick, add a little more wine. Cover the bowl with a clean cloth and leave to stand in a warm room for 2 hours.

Drain the cod well; pick out any remaining bones or pieces of skin; cut into bite-sized pieces. Heat the oil until very hot in the deep-fryer. Dip the salt cod pieces in the batter, making sure they are completely coated, and deep-fry a few at a time until crisp and golden brown on the outside.

Keep each batch hot, uncovered, on kitchen paper to finish draining while frying the succeeding batches.

STOCKFISH BERGEN STYLE

1³/₄ lb (800 g) presoaked stockfish (dried cod)

5 oz (150 g) butter

4 large onions

2 oz (50 g) plain flour

18 fl oz (500 ml) milk, or single cream

2 oz (50 g) grated Emmenthal cheese

salt

Stockfish must be soaked for 24 hours in at least 3 changes of water. Rinse the stockfish thoroughly, remove any skin and bones, and cut into small pieces. Melt 4 tbsp of the butter in a large, heavy-bottomed saucepan and sweat the peeled and very thinly sliced onions, with the lid on, for about 20 minutes or until transparent. Do not allow to colour; add a very little water from time to time to prevent this. Add a little salt and draw aside from the heat. Meanwhile, heat the milk to scalding point. Melt all but 1 tbsp of the remaining butter in a small saucepan, stir in the flour and gradually beat in the milk. Add salt and pepper and continue cooking, stirring continuously, for 10 minutes.

Use the remaining butter to grease a deep, wide casserole dish. Spread the onions over the bottom, place the fish on top, and cover with the sauce. Sprinkle with cheese and bake in a preheated oven at 375°F (180°C) mark 4 for 35–40 minutes.

WHITING PIE

1¹/₄ lb (600 g) fillets of whiting or cod

1¹/₂ oz (40 g) stale white bread (no crusts)

3¹/₂ fl oz (100 ml) milk

1 small bunch chervil

1 large floury boiled potato

2 oz (50 g) butter

4 eggs

12 oz (350g) frozen puff pastry

salt and pepper

Skin and finely chop the raw fish fillets and place in a large bowl. Soak the bread in the milk; squeeze out excess. Chop the chervil. Grease an 8–9-in (20–22-cm) spring-release cake tin or deep flan dish with butter.

Peel the boiled potato while still hot and push through a fine sieve. Mix with the fish. Add the finely crumbled bread, the remaining butter (softened at room temperature and cut into small pieces) and the chervil. Season with salt and freshly ground pepper and work in the egg yolks. Blend thoroughly.

Roll out the thawed pastry on a floured work surface and use to line the base and sides of the tin, allowing an extra ¹/₂-in (1¹/₂-cm) border all the way round if using a flan dish. Beat the egg whites with a pinch of salt until stiff but not dry and fold into the fish and potato mixture gently but thoroughly.

Fill the pie shell with the mixture; crimp the edge of the pastry between your thumb and index finger and fold over the filling. Bake at 350°F (180°C) mark 4 for about 40 minutes.

AMERICAN FISH MOULD

4 smooth hound steaks weighing 5 oz (150g) each

1¹/₂ tbsp finely chopped parsley

1 carrot

1 tbsp dried dill
2 lemons
7 fl oz (200 ml) dry white wine
7 fl oz (200 ml) double cream
4 eggs
salt and peppercorns

Wash and dry the fish steaks. Place in a frying pan in a single layer. Add the parsley, the peeled and coarsely chopped carrot and the dill. Sprinkle with 1 tbsp lemon juice, the wine and 9 fl oz (250 ml) hot water. Bring to a boil, reduce the heat, and simmer for 10 minutes.

Draw aside from the heat; transfer the fish steaks to a plate using a slotted fish slice, and remove the skin and backbone. Flake the flesh and place in a bowl.

Using a wooden spoon, stir in the cream and 2 egg yolks, blending until smooth. Season with salt and freshly ground pepper. Beat the 2 egg whites until stiff and fold gently but thoroughly into the fish mixture.

Lightly oil a charlotte or similar mould. Tap the base of the mould on the work surface as you fill it with the fish mixture to avoid air pockets. Smooth the surface and place in a preheated oven at 400°F (200°C) mark 6 for 30 minutes.

While the fish mould is cooking, hard-boil the eggs, cool quickly under running cold water and shell; cut lengthwise into quarters. Remove the mould from the oven, place a heated serving plate on top, turn upside down so that the moulded pie slides out on to the plate. Decorate with the egg wedges and lemon slices.

SPICED FISH STEAKS

4 huss steaks weighing 8 oz (225 g) each
1 tsp ground cumin
¹/₂ tsp ground chilli pepper
¹/₂ tsp real saffron powder or turmeric

2 fl oz (50 ml) oil
1 small bunch parsley or coriander
juice of 1 lemon
salt and pepper

Wash and dry the fish steaks and place each on a large square of foil.

Mix the cumin, chilli and saffron (or turmeric) with the lemon juice in a small bowl; gradually beat in the oil, adding a little at a time. Stir in the finely chopped parsley or coriander, a generous pinch of salt and a little freshly ground pepper. Blend well, then spoon an equal amount over each fish steak. Enclose the steaks in the foil, making sure that no juices can escape, and arrange these parcels in a single layer in a roasting pan or ovenproof dish. Place in the oven, preheated to 400°F (200°C) mark 6, to cook for 10 minutes.

Check to see whether the fish steaks are done before serving in their foil wrappings on warmed plates, accompanied by lemon slices if wished.

FISH STEAKS WITH BASIL AND OLIVES

4 smooth hound steaks weighing 8 oz (225 g) each
olive oil
1–2 tbsp basil leaves
3¹/₂ oz (100 g) black olives, stoned
14 oz (400 g) tomatoes
pinch dried oregano
2 tbsp capers
salt and pepper

Wash and dry the fish. Grease a wide, deep casserole dish with oil and sprinkle the chopped basil and the sliced olives over the bottom; add the fish steaks in a single layer and spoon over the roughly chopped, seeded tomatoes.

Sprinkle with the oregano and the rinsed, dried

capers. Season with salt and plenty of freshly ground pepper. Bake for 40 minutes at 350°F (180°C) mark 4. Serve straight from the casserole dish, piping hot.

SMOOTH HOUND WITH MUSHROOMS

8 slices smooth hound weighing 4 oz (120 g) each

14 oz (400 g) mushrooms

$^1/_2$ onion

1 small bunch parsley

1 clove garlic

olive oil

$3^1/_2$ fl oz (100 ml) dry white wine

1 large ripe tomato

salt and pepper

Trim the mushrooms, scraping off all the hard and gritty parts; wipe all over with a damp cloth. Slice thinly. Finely chop the onion, parsley and garlic; sweat gently in olive oil. Add the mushrooms, season with salt and pepper and sauté very gently for 5–6 minutes. Pour in the white wine, stir and continue cooking until the wine has evaporated. Add the blanched, peeled and chopped tomato. Check the seasoning, cover and simmer for about 10 minutes.

Trim the skin off the fish steaks; wash, dry and season with a little salt and pepper. Coat lightly with flour and fry until well browned. Drain well; transfer to a heated casserole dish; cover with the mushroom sauce and heat through for 5–6 minutes in the oven, preheated to 400°F (200°C) mark 6.

FISH STEAKS WITH ANCHOVIES

8 slices smooth hound weighing $3^1/_2$ oz (100 g) each

plain flour

7 fl oz (200 ml) olive oil

2 shallots

4 tinned anchovy fillets

1 tbsp finely chopped parsley

1 tsp capers

oregano

$3^1/_2$ fl oz (100 ml) dry white wine

salt and pepper

Wash and dry the fish steaks, remove the skin, season with salt and pepper and coat lightly with flour. Brown on both sides by frying in $3^1/_2$ fl oz (100 ml) hot oil. Remove from the pan, draining well, and keep hot.

Peel and finely chop the shallots, sweat gently in the remaining oil; add the finely chopped anchovies and parsley, the capers, a pinch of oregano and some freshly ground pepper. Pour in the wine and simmer until the wine has completely evaporated (15–20 minutes).

Place the fish steaks on a warmed serving platter, spoon the sauce over them and serve without delay.

SWORDFISH STEAKS IN TOMATO AND BLACK OLIVE SAUCE

4 swordfish steaks weighing 6 oz (175 g) each

2 salted anchovies

1 small bunch parsley

2 cloves garlic

olive oil

5 fl oz (150 ml) sieved tomatoes

1 tbsp capers

2 oz (50 g) black olives, stoned

salt and pepper

Rinse the anchovies to eliminate excess salt and remove their bones (1 tbsp chopped tinned anchovy fillets can be used instead). Chop the anchovies, parsley and peeled garlic and sauté gently in 4 tbsp olive oil, making sure the anchovies break up in the oil. Add the sieved tomatoes and 3^1/$_2$ fl oz (100 ml) water; cover and cook for 10 minutes. Add the capers and black olives. Simmer for 5 minutes.

Wash the fish steaks, pat dry, removing any skin; coat with flour, shake off excess and fry until golden brown in olive oil in a pan. Remove, draining off any oil, and place in the saucepan containing the tomato mixture. Cover, cook for 2 minutes over a gentle heat then serve.

GOURMET'S SWORDFISH STEAKS

4 swordfish steaks weighing approx. 8 oz (225 g) each
1 celery stalk
1 onion
2 cloves garlic
1 tbsp capers
2 oz (50 g) green olives, stoned
1^1/$_2$ tbsp sultanas
4 large ripe tomatoes
salt and pepper

Soak the sultanas in warm water for a few minutes to soften. Wash and dry the fish steaks; coat with flour, shaking off excess, and fry until lightly browned on both sides in 4 tbsp oil. Remove from the pan with a slotted fish slice, draining well, and keep hot.

Sauté the finely chopped celery, onion and garlic in the oil left in the pan; add the capers, olives and drained sultanas.

Cook for a further 4–5 minutes, add the blanched, peeled, seeded and roughly chopped tomatoes, season with salt and pepper and simmer for about 10 minutes. Oil an ovenproof dish and arrange the steaks in it in a single layer. Pour the

sauce over them and place in a preheated oven at 350°F (180°C) mark 4 for about 15 minutes.

LEMON AND GARLIC SWORDFISH STEAKS

4 swordfish steaks weighing approx. 8 oz (225 g) each
4 tbsp oil
juice of 1 lemon
1 clove garlic
oregano
salt and pepper

Prepare the marinade by mixing together the oil, strained lemon juice, very finely chopped garlic, 1 tbsp water, salt and freshly ground pepper.

Rinse the fish steaks and dry well with kitchen paper; leave to marinate in the prepared mixture, turning frequently, for about 1 hour. Drain well, reserving the marinade, and place under (or over, if barbecuing) a very hot grill and cook for 10 minutes, turning half way through this time. (Alternatively, place on a rack in a roasting tin in the oven, preheated to 425°F (220°C) mark 7, and cook for 10–15 minutes, turning once.) Heat the marinade over hot water for 5–10 minutes, adding a pinch of oregano. As soon as the fish is cooked, transfer to a warmed serving plate and sprinkle with the hot marinade. Serve.

SWORDFISH STEAKS AU GRATIN

8 swordfish steaks weighing approx. 4 oz (100 g) each
3 salted anchovies
1 small bunch parsley
2 sage leaves
1 sprig rosemary

2 cloves garlic

4 fl oz (120 ml) olive oil

juice of 1 lemon

4 tbsp breadcrumbs

salt

Rinse excess salt from the anchovies, remove their bones (6 tinned anchovy fillets can be used instead) and chop finely together with the parsley, sage, rosemary leaves and garlic. Place this mixture in a bowl and mix with the oil and the lemon juice.

Remove any skin from the fish steaks, rinse, dry well and sprinkle with a little salt. Grease a large, shallow ovenproof dish with oil and place the fish in it in a single layer. Spread some of the herb mixture on top of each slice and sprinkle with breadcrumbs. Place in a preheated oven at 425°F (220°C) mark 7 and cook, uncovered, for 15 minutes. Place under the grill for 5 minutes to brown well on top. Serve at once.

STUFFED SWORDFISH ROLLS

1³/₄ lb (800 g) swordfish, cut into 9 thin slices

2 cloves garlic

1 onion

5 tbsp oil

1 small bunch parsley

1 small bunch basil

2 tbsp breadcrumbs

1 tbsp capers

3¹/₂ oz (100 g) freshly grated hard cheese

2 eggs

1 chilli pepper

salt and pepper

mayonnaise or tartare sauce (see pages 37–38)

Wash the fish slices and dry thoroughly; remove the skin; cut the flesh of just one slice into small dice. Slice the peeled garlic and onion very finely and place in a saucepan with 2 tbsp of the oil, the finely chopped parsley and basil leaves, breadcrumbs, capers and the diced fish. Fry for 10 minutes, stirring frequently. Process the mixture in the food processor until smooth then spoon into a bowl.

Stir in the cheese, eggs, salt, freshly ground pepper and the finely crumbled chilli pepper. Spread some of this mixture over the top of each fish slice, roll the slices up, securing each with 3 cocktail sticks or small steel skewers. Brush with a little oil and grill for 10 minutes, turning fequently so that they cook evenly all the way round and right through, using 2 fish slices or special tongs. Serve as soon as they are cooked.

SWORDFISH SICILIAN STYLE

4 swordfish steaks weighing 5–7 oz (150–200 g) each

2 tbsp sultanas

plain flour

14 fl oz (400 ml) olive oil

1 onion

2 cloves garlic

1 celery stalk

2 tbsp pine nuts

1 tbsp salted capers

2 oz (50 g) green olives, stoned

1 lb (450 g) tinned tomatoes

2 bay leaves

salt and pepper

Wash and dry the fish slices. Soak the sultanas in warm water for 15 minutes; squeeze out excess moisture before using. Coat the fish steaks lightly with flour and fry until browned on both sides in the very hot oil. Use a slotted fish slice or ladle to transfer the fish slices from the frying pan to drain further on kitchen paper.

Strain the oil carefully when it has cooled a little and use half to fry the finely chopped onion, garlic, celery, pine nuts and raisins. Add the rinsed and dried capers and the olives. After a few minutes add the tomatoes, crushed with a fork. Cover and simmer for 10 minutes. Season with a very little salt and some freshly ground pepper. Place the fish slices in an ovenproof dish and pour the tomato sauce over them; add the bay leaves and a little more pepper. Cook at 400°F (200°C) mark 6 for 20 minutes. Serve hot, straight from the dish.

MONKFISH IN SAFFRON SAUCE

$1^3/_4$ lb (800 g) fillets of monkfish

1 onion

2 cloves garlic

7 fl oz (200 ml) good dry sparkling white wine

1 sachet real saffron

plain flour

3 oz (80 g) butter

1 lemon

2 oz (50 g) flaked almonds

salt and pepper

Wash and dry the filleted fish. Chop the peeled onion and garlic cloves roughly and liquidize with the wine and saffron in the food processor.

Lightly coat the fillets with flour and fry in $1^1/_2$ oz (40 g) butter until lightly browned on both sides, turning once only. Add the finely grated rind of the lemon, the remaining butter cut into small pieces, the liquidized mixture, and the lightly toasted flaked almonds. Season with salt and freshly ground pepper. Continue cooking over a moderate heat until the liquid and cooking juices have reduced and thickened a little, and serve.

MONKFISH AND VEGETABLE PIE

4 monkfish slices or steaks weighing approx. 7 oz (200 g) each

$1^1/_4$ lb (600 g) waxy potatoes

7 oz (200 g) celery

5 oz (150 g) carrots

1 shallot or 1 small mild onion

1 large ripe tomato

$3^1/_2$ fl oz (100 ml) olive oil

salt and pepper

Wash the fish slices; dry thoroughly. Wash the potatoes and boil for 5 minutes; drain, peel and cut into thin round slices. Wash and trim the celery and carrots; cut into small pieces; chop the peeled shallot very finely.

Line the bottom of a casserole dish with the potato slices; sprinkle them with the shallot, celery and carrot; place the fish on top in a single layer. Blanch and peel the tomato, cut into rough strips, and scatter over the fish. Sprinkle with the oil and season with salt and plenty of freshly ground pepper. Add enough hot water to just come up to the tomato layer. Bake in a preheated oven at 400°F (200°C) mark 6 for 40 minutes or until done.

SEAFOOD KEBABS

14 oz (400 g) monkfish

8 peeled Dublin Bay prawns

8 baby cuttlefish

1 small red pepper

8 button mushrooms, stalks trimmed

juice of 1 lemon

1 tbsp dry white wine

3 tbsp olive oil

parsley

salt and pepper

Prepare the Dublin Bay prawns and cuttlefish (see pages 16, 20) and pat the cuttlefish dry. Remove the skin from the monkfish tail (the only part of this fish that is ever used) and cut the flesh into 16 small, evenly sized cubes or pieces. Cut the red pepper into 16 pieces. Thread on to 8 wood or metal skewers in the following order: 1 Dublin Bay prawn, 1 cuttlefish, 2 pieces red pepper, 2 pieces monkfish, 1 mushroom. Place the skewers in a large ovenproof dish in a single layer.

Beat together the lemon juice, wine, oil, salt and freshly ground pepper until well blended, and sprinkle over the skewers; cover loosely with foil and place in a preheated oven at 400°F (200°C) mark 6 for 10 minutes, then remove the foil and place under a very hot grill for 6 minutes, turning once after 3 minutes. Leave to stand for a minute or two before serving.

MONKFISH WITH HERBS AND JUNIPER BERRIES

1³/₄ lb (800 g) filleted monkfish
1 sprig basil
1 small bunch chervil
1 sprig tarragon
2 cloves garlic
4 bay leaves
6 juniper berries
1 sprig rosemary
juice of 2 lemons
6 tbsp olive oil
2 oz (50 g) butter
salt and pepper

Spread out the rinsed and dried fish fillets on a large plate. Chop the basil with the chervil and tarragon; cut the peeled garlic cloves into wafer-thin slices; crumble the bay leaves finely; crush the juniper berries slightly and detach the rosemary leaves from their stems. Mix all these with the lemon juice and 4 tbsp of the oil and pour over the fish. Leave to marinate for 2 hours, turning from time to time.

Heat the butter in a large pan with the remaining oil until it begins to foam; add the drained fish fillets and fry until golden brown, turning once or twice and seasoning with salt and freshly ground pepper. Strain the marinade and use a few spoonfuls to moisten the fish. Cook briskly until the fish is done; serve without delay.

MONKFISH WITH MIXED VEGETABLES

1³/₄ lb (800 g) monkfish
3 potatoes
4 carrots
5 oz (150 g) French beans
5 tbsp olive oil
2 oz (50 g) butter
plain flour
3¹/₂ fl oz (100 ml) dry white wine
7 fl oz (200 ml) fish stock (fumet) (see page 39)
4 fl oz (120 ml) sieved tomatoes
5 fl oz (150 ml) single cream
1¹/₂ tbsp finely chopped parsley
salt and pepper

Peel and dice the potatoes and carrots and steam until tender but still firm. Trim the beans and boil in lightly salted water until tender but still crisp. Drain and sauté gently, together with the steamed vegetables, in half the butter and half the oil. Slice the fish into fairly thick round steaks. Season with salt and pepper and fry for 6–8 minutes in the remaining oil and butter, turning once. Remove from the pan with a slotted fish slice, draining well, and keep hot. Add the wine to the juices and oil remaining in the pan; cook, uncovered, until reduced by half, scraping the deposits from the bottom of the pan as you do so. Pour in the fish stock, the cream and the sieved tomatoes and simmer for 5 minutes.

Place the fish pieces on a heated serving dish; pour the sauce over them; arrange the vegetables decoratively between and around the fish, sprinkle with parsley and serve.

MONKFISH WITH HORSERADISH

1³/₄ lb (800 g) monkfish slices of even thickness
2 red peppers
5 shallots
2 cloves garlic
1 small bunch parsley
1 small piece fresh horseradish root, or 1 tbsp ready-grated fresh horseradish
2 tbsp tomato ketchup
large pinch paprika or small pinch cayenne pepper
3¹/₂ fl oz (100 ml) olive oil
salt and pepper

Wash the fish slices and dry well with kitchen paper. Grill the peppers, turning very frequently, to loosen their skins; peel, remove the seeds and inner membrane and cut into small dice. Peel the shallots and garlic; peel the horseradish root if using fresh (take care, as it will sting your eyes). Place half the diced peppers and all the other ingredients with the exception of the fish into the food processor and reduce to a purée.

Transfer the purée to a bowl, stir in the ketchup, the paprika (or cayenne pepper), salt and freshly ground pepper. Lay the fish slices out flat in an ovenproof dish, sprinkle with the oil and spoon an equal amount of the purée over each steak. Sprinkle the remaining diced peppers on top.

Cover with foil and bake at 350°F (180°C) mark 4 for 15–20 minutes or until the fish is cooked. Serve very hot, straight from the ovenproof dish.

MONKFISH IN RADICCHIO CREAM SAUCE

1¹/₄ lb (600 g) filleted monkfish
plain flour
4 oz (120 g) radicchio
1¹/₂ oz (40 g) butter
1¹/₂ tbsp oil
1 clove garlic
Worcestershire sauce
4 tbsp dry white wine
2 fl oz (50 ml) milk
3 tbsp single cream
salt and pepper

Wash and dry the fish very thoroughly. Cut into slices ¹/₂ in (1¹/₂ cm) thick and coat lightly with flour. Shred the radicchio into thin strips. Melt the butter with 1 tbsp oil in a large pan and sauté the whole, peeled garlic clove until lightly coloured, then remove and discard. Add the radicchio to the flavoured oil and butter, cover, and sweat gently for 5–10 minutes, stirring and turning now and then.

Add the fish pieces to the pan and sauté for a few minutes, turning once or twice; season with salt and pepper. Sprinkle a few drops of Worcestershire sauce into the pan, followed by the wine. Cook until the wine has almost completely evaporated, then pour in the milk and cream, heated together in a saucepan to scalding point. Simmer for 5–10 minutes. Check seasoning and serve.

Note: Garnish with uncooked radicchio leaves, if wished, and serve with boiled new potatoes.

SKATE WITH COURGETTES AND CREAM

---

4 wings of skate

---

2 courgettes

3¹/₂ fl oz (100 ml) double cream

---

salt and pepper

Poach the skate wings in salted water for 15 minutes. Drain. Remove the skin and cut into fairly small strips cutting along the long filaments of the wings, not across them. Arrange a circle of lightly steamed, thinly sliced courgettes on each of the warmed plates. Place the pieces of fish radiating out from the centre.

Simmer the cream gently for a few minutes, season with salt and freshly ground white pepper and pour all round the fish. Garnish decoratively with diced vegetables sautéed in butter and chopped chives, if wished (see illustration on page 104).

BRILL WITH SORREL

2¹/₄–2¹/₂ lb (1 kg) brill

---

7 fl oz (200 ml) milk

---

1 lemon

---

25 sorrel leaves

---

pinch nutmeg

---

2 eggs

---

1 tsp mild French mustard (e.g. Dijon)

---

salt and peppercorns

Prepare the fish as for flatfish (see page 9). Wash then poach in a very large saucepan or square fish kettle for 35–40 minutes in a mixture of 1³/₄ pints (1 litre) water, the milk and juice of half the lemon. Add more water if this is not sufficient to cover the fish. Boil 20 of the sorrel leaves in lightly salted water with a pinch of nutmeg and 2–3 peppercorns for 10 minutes; drain and sieve. Beat the eggs,

mustard and the juice of the remaining half lemon and blend well with the sorrel purée. Pour this sauce on to a warmed serving dish, place the well drained fish carefully on top and decorate with the remaining sorrel leaves.

BRILL WITH TRUFFLES AND MADEIRA

1³/₄ lb (800 g) fillets of brill

---

1 lb (500 g) raw fish trimmings (e.g. heads, bones, offcuts, etc.)

---

1 onion

---

1 carrot

---

1 bouquet garni

---

3 oz (80 g) butter

---

1 small truffle

---

4 oz (100 g) button mushrooms

---

1 tbsp plain flour

---

5 fl oz (150 ml) Madeira

---

1 tsp tomato purée

---

1 lemon

---

watercress

---

salt and cayenne pepper

Make a *court-bouillon* with the fish trimmings, the peeled and quartered onion, peeled and sliced carrot, the bouquet garni, a little salt and 1³/₄ pints (1 litre) water; boil gently for 1 hour.

Season the fish fillets lightly with salt and pepper; place in an ovenproof dish which has been greased with butter. Pour in the strained *court-bouillon*, dot 1 oz (25 g) butter, cut into tiny pieces, all over the fish, cover with foil, and bake in the preheated oven at 350°F (180°C) mark 4 for 10 minutes.

Wipe the truffle with a damp cloth and chop finely. Wipe the mushrooms and slice thinly.

Transfer the fish to a warmed serving dish, reserving the cooking liquid. Melt 2 oz (50 g) butter in a small saucepan, stir in the flour and cook for a minute or two, then gradually stir in the cooking liquid, adding a little at a time. Add the Madeira, followed by the tomato purée and the chopped truffle and mushrooms. Add a little salt to taste and simmer for 5 minutes, stirring continuously. Draw aside from the heat and stir in a pinch of cayenne pepper. Pour the sauce over the fillets and decorate with lemon slices and watercress. Serve at once.

TURBOT WITH PRAWNS AND SCALLOPS

2¼ lb (1 kg) turbot, net trimmed weight

4 oz (100 g) peeled small prawns

6 scallops

4½ pints (2 litres) court-bouillon (see page 25)

7 oz (200 g) button mushrooms

3 shallots

1 oz (25 g) butter

1 tbsp olive oil

1 oz (30 g) plain flour

3½ fl oz (100 ml) double cream

1 egg yolk

parsley

salt and pepper

Wash and shuck the scallops (see page 23), reserving only the circular white 'cushion' of meat and the orange roe. Rinse well and pat dry. (Thawed, frozen shucked scallops can be used, but they will have no roe.) Pour the cold *court-bouillon* into a very wide saucepan or a square fish kettle large enough to take the fish flat. Place the fish and the white scallop meat on the rack and lower into the liquid. Bring to the boil over a high heat; immediately reduce the heat to very low and barely simmer for 15 minutes. Turn off the heat and leave the fish in the *court-bouillon*.

Wipe and trim the mushrooms, slice thinly. Peel the shallots and chop very finely; sauté the mushrooms and shallots together in the butter and

oil for 15 minutes; sprinkle in the flour, mix well, then gradually add 9 fl oz (250 ml) of the strained cooking liquid, stirring continuously. Continue simmering until the sauce has thickened a little. Add the cream and the prawns, mix well, and simmer for a further 2–3 minutes.

Draw aside from the heat; crush 2 of the scallop roes (if available) with a fork and mix with the egg yolk. Add 2–3 spoonfuls of the sauce, blend well and stir into the sauce in the pan. Season with salt and pepper and stir briefly over a very low heat for a few seconds; do not allow to come near boiling point. Add the scallop meat, cut into thin slices. Remove the fish from the fish kettle, draining well; remove the skin and place on a warmed serving dish. Pour the sauce all round it, sprinkle the fish with chopped parsley, and serve.

BRILL WITH TOMATO AND SHERRY SAUCE

1½ lb (700 g) fillets of brill

juice of 1 lemon

1 clove garlic

2 onions

3 tbsp olive oil

10 oz (300 g) ripe tomatoes

plain flour

3½ fl oz (100 ml) medium or dry sherry

7 fl oz (200 ml) single cream

salt and pepper

Wash and dry the fish fillets, place on a plate, sprinkle with the lemon juice and leave to stand for 30 minutes. Peel and chop the garlic and onions very finely; fry in a heavy-bottomed saucepan or fireproof casserole dish in the oil for a few minutes. Add the blanched, peeled and seeded tomatoes cut into strips; season with salt and freshly ground pepper and cook, uncovered, over a high heat for 10 minutes. Leave to cool a little before processing in the blender until smooth. Return to the pan.

Drain the lemon juice from the fish fillets, coat lightly with flour and place in the pan containing the sauce. Simmer briefly, turning the fish carefully once or twice; add the sherry and cream and cook over a high heat for a few minutes to reduce and thicken the sauce a little. Sprinkle with plenty of freshly ground pepper.

BRILL IN MUSHROOM AND WHITE WINE SAUCE

2¼–2½ lb (1 kg) brill
14 oz (400 g) button mushrooms
2 oz (50 g) butter
1 clove garlic (optional)
1 shallot
1 sprig fresh basil
9 fl oz (250 ml) dry white wine
salt and pepper

Prepare the fish for cooking (see page 9, instructions for flat fish) leaving it whole. Wash under running cold water and dry well. Wipe the mushrooms with a damp cloth and slice thinly.

Sauté the finely chopped garlic and shallot in half the butter, using a heavy-bottomed casserole large enough to take the fish flat. Tear the basil leaves roughly into small pieces and add, together with the mushrooms. Season with salt and pepper, cook briskly for a few minutes, then place the fish in the casserole.

Pour in the wine, sprinkle a little more salt and pepper over the surface of the fish and bake in a preheated oven at 400°F (200°C) mark 6 for 40 minutes. Turn the fish very carefully only once, half way through cooking.

Use two large slotted fish slices or spatulas to remove the fish and place on a heated serving platter. Keep hot. Purée the juices and vegetables left in the pan in a blender, pour into a small saucepan, stir in the remaining butter (do not melt beforehand) and heat until nearly boiling. Pour immediately over the fish and serve.

BRILL BAKE WITH BRANDY

1¼ lb (600 g) fillets of brill
plain flour
5 tbsp olive oil
1 lb (500 g) waxy potatoes
1 lb (500 g) mild red onions
2 oz (50 g) butter
2 fl oz (50 ml) brandy
salt and pepper

Rinse and dry the fillets, coat lightly with flour and fry in the oil for 2–3 minutes on each side over a high heat to brown lightly. Boil the potatoes in their skins for 5–10 minutes, then peel and slice thickly. Peel the onions and cut into very thin rings. Use 1 oz (25 g) of the butter to grease a fairly deep ovenproof dish; layer the ingredients in the following order: half the potato slices, half the fish fillets, all the onions and the remaining fillets. Top with the remaining potato slices. Season with salt and freshly ground pepper, distribute the remaining butter in small flakes over the top, sprinkle with the brandy and 2 fl oz (50 ml) lightly salted water.

Cover with foil; bake at 350°F (180°C) mark 4 for 30 minutes, removing the foil for the last 10 minutes to brown.

TURBOT IN CORAL SAUCE

1 turbot weighing 3¼ lb (1½ kg)
1 hen lobster weighing approx. 1 lb (500 g)
3 oz (80 g) butter
7 fl oz (200 ml) champagne or dry sparkling wine
5 fl oz (150 ml) fish stock (fumet) (see page 39)
3 tbsp olive oil
1 shallot
½ clove garlic (optional)
1 small pinch dried tarragon

1 tbsp sieved tomatoes
1 tbsp brandy
1 tbsp plain flour
salt and pepper

Prepare, skin and fillet the fish (see pages 9–12) or ask your fishmonger to do this for you. Prepare the lobster (you must use a hen lobster for this recipe) as for grilling (see page 30); pound the greenish liver (tomalley) and the coral and the claw meat together with a pestle and mortar. Refrigerate while completing the preparations.

Remove the flesh from the lobster shell, cut into small cubes, and scatter these over the bottom of an ovenproof dish greased with butter. Place the fillets on top, dot 1 oz (25 g) butter cut into small flakes over the fish, and season with salt and pepper. Pour in the champagne and the *fumet*. Cover with foil and bake in a preheated oven at 350°F (180°C) mark 4 for 30 minutes, occasionally basting the fish with the cooking liquid. Keep the fish hot on a serving plate while you pour the liquid into a small saucepan and reduce by one third over a high heat.

Sauté the reserved pounded lobster mixture in the oil; add the cooking liquid, the very finely chopped shallot and, if used, the garlic, the tarragon, and tomato (do not use tomato purée, as it is too concentrated for this recipe). Stir and simmer for 10 minutes, then add the brandy, and boil gently for a few minutes; pour through a sieve into a small saucepan.

Mix the remaining butter with the flour into a *beurre manié* and add, in small lumps, to the sauce. Beat with a balloon whisk over a low heat to thicken the sauce.

Place the fish on a warmed serving platter, cover with the sauce, decorate with the lobster cubes and serve immediately.

TURBOT IN SHRIMP SAUCE

1 turbot weighing 3¼ lb (1½ kg)
1¼ pints (750 ml) milk

1 lemon
8 oz (250 g) shrimps
5 oz (150 g) butter
2 tbsp plain flour
nutmeg
salt and pepper

Prepare the fish, leaving it whole (see page 9, instructions for flat fish); wash and dry well. Place in an ovenproof dish large enough to take it flat; season with salt and pepper. Mix the milk well with an equal volume of water, and pour over the fish. Place 4 slices of lemon on top of the fish and bake in a preheated oven at 400°F (200°C) mark 6 for 30 minutes.

Meanwhile, prepare the sauce: peel the shrimps (see page 17) and fry in a pan in 1 oz (25 g) butter. Place the heads and shells in a large saucepan with 1 pint (600 ml) cold water, bring to the boil and boil hard for 10 minutes. Strain, discarding the heads and shells. Keep the stock hot.

Beat ³/₄ oz (20 g) butter in a bowl until pale and fluffy, then work in the flour thoroughly, followed by the hot fish stock, adding a little at a time and beating well with a balloon whisk. Transfer to a small saucepan, bring to the boil while stirring, then add the remaining butter and the shrimps. Add salt, pepper and freshly grated nutmeg to taste.

When the fish is cooked, take the 4 fillets carefully off the bone, place each on a hot plate and coat with the sauce.

TUNA WITH MINT AND GARLIC

1½–1¾ lb (700–800 g) fresh tuna
2 cloves garlic
10 mint leaves
2 oz (50 g) butter
7 fl oz (200 ml) dry white wine
2 tbsp olive oil
1 onion

14 fl oz (400 ml) sieved tomatoes

2 oz (50 g) green olives, stoned

salt and pepper

Wash and dry the tuna fish steaks, cut small slits in the flesh and insert pieces of thinly sliced peeled garlic and the mint leaves. Fry the fish in a single layer in the butter, season with salt and pepper, add the wine, and cook until it has evaporated. Keep hot.

Sauté the finely sliced onion in the oil until soft; add the sieved tomato and the olives and simmer for 15–20 minutes. Add the tuna steaks, moisten with 2 tbsp hot water, cover and simmer for 15 minutes. Serve.

TUNA WITH MARSALA

1 middle cut of tuna weighing 1 lb (500 g)

wine vinegar

3 oz (80 g) butter

1 onion

2 cloves garlic

1 small bunch parsley

1 bay leaf

7 fl oz (200 ml) dry Marsala

fish stock (fumet) (see page 39)

1 tbsp crushed anchovy fillets

1 tbsp capers

1 lemon

salt and pepper

Wash the tuna and blanch for 2 minutes in boiling water acidulated with 1 tbsp vinegar. Melt half the butter in a large, heavy-bottomed saucepan or casserole and sauté the finely chopped onion, the peeled and finely sliced garlic, the parsley leaves and the crumbled bay leaf. When the onions are tender, add the fish and brown all over. Pour the Marsala over the fish, turn up the heat and cook for 2 minutes, then pour in 8 fl oz (225 ml)

boiling hot *fumet*. Season with salt and pepper, reduce the heat and simmer for 40 minutes, moistening with more *fumet* whenever necessary.

Meanwhile cream 1½ oz (40 g) of the butter with the anchovies. When the fish is cooked, remove from the pan with two slotted fish slices, slice into steaks and keep hot. Sieve the juices remaining in the pan; pour into a small saucepan, stir in the anchovy butter, capers and lemon juice. Simmer, stirring, until the sauce is smooth. Season to taste; pour over the fish and serve.

BARBECUED MUSTARD TUNA

4 fresh tuna steaks weighing approx. 8 oz (225 g) each

5 oz (150 g) mild French (e.g. Dijon) mustard

1 tbsp plain flour

salt and pepper

Mix the mustard and flour thoroughly until completely smooth; add a pinch of salt and some freshly ground pepper. Spread over both sides of the tuna steaks and leave to stand for 20–30 minutes.

Barbecue or, alternatively, grill for 5–10 minutes or until cooked, turning once and spreading any spare mustard mixture over the second side. Serve at once.

STUFFED AMBERJACK

1 middle cut of amberjack weighing 2¾ lb (1 kg)

1 lb (500 g) mussels (in the shell) or 4 oz (120 g) shucked mussels

1 shallot

1 clove garlic

dry white wine

1½ tbsp finely chopped parsley

1 onion
3 tbsp olive oil
1 tbsp sieved tomatoes
1 tbsp breadcrumbs
1 hard-boiled egg
1¹/₂ oz (40 g) butter
1 oz (20 g) plain flour
1 egg yolk
salt and pepper

Scrub the mussel shells, removing beards and barnacles (see page 22) and place in a large fireproof casserole dish with the very finely chopped shallot, crushed garlic, 2 fl oz (50 ml) dry white wine and half the parsley. Cover and cook for a few minutes over a high heat to open the mussels; discard any which do not open. Remove the molluscs from their shells, reserve the liquor from the pan and strain.

Finely chop the onion and fry gently in the oil. Add the tomato, breadcrumbs, the remaining chopped parsley, sieved hard-boiled egg and salt and pepper. Stir for a few seconds and turn off the heat. Add the mussels.

Open up the gutted middle cut of fish, remove the backbone and the bones attached to it and stuff with the mussel mixture. Secure with cocktail sticks or small steel skewers.

Grease an ovenproof dish of a suitable size for the fish. Place the fish in it, sprinkle with a very little oil and bake in the oven, preheated to 350°F (180°C) mark 4, for about 45 minutes or until done. Sprinkle with a little white wine and a little oil at intervals to prevent the fish drying out.

Meanwhile, heat the strained mussel liquor in a small saucepan; work 2 tbsp butter with the flour and add this *beurre manié* to the liquid to thicken as it melts; stir continuously. Draw aside from the heat, beat in the egg yolk and stir for a minute over a very low heat. Pour the sauce over the fish and serve from the casserole dish.

Note: Garnish with lemon wedges and watercress and serve with steamed long-grain rice.

PIQUANT AMBERJACK

4 slices or fillets of amberjack weighing 7 oz (200 g) each
2 large peppers (1 yellow and 1 red)
1 clove garlic
pinch oregano
2 sprigs parsley
5 fl oz (150 ml) olive oil
2 tinned anchovy fillets
1 thick slice white bread
2 tbsp capers
3 small dill-pickled cucumbers or gherkins
butter
1 tbsp finely chopped shallot
4 tbsp white wine
1 small bay leaf
salt and pepper

Wash and dry the fish slices. Grill the peppers, turning frequently. Peel and cut into strips. Rub the inside of a bowl with half the clove of garlic. Place the pepper strips, a pinch of oregano, 1 tsp chopped parsley, 2 tbsp oil, salt and pepper in the bowl. Mix well and leave to stand for 30 minutes.

Place the remaining parsley, the anchovy fillets, crumbled slice of bread (without crusts), the garlic, strained and squeezed capers, dill pickles or gherkins, 3 tbsp oil, a generous pinch of salt and plenty of freshly ground pepper in a blender or food processor and reduce to a smooth purée.

Grease an ovenproof dish, large enough to take the fish in a single layer, and sprinkle the finely chopped shallot all over the bottom. Place the fish on top, sprinkle with 3 tbsp oil, season with salt and pepper, and pour the wine around the fish pieces. Add the bay leaf.

Cover with foil and bake for 10 minutes in a preheated oven at 400°F (200°C) mark 6. Transfer the fish pieces to a heated serving dish, coat them with the sauce and decorate with the strips of pepper.

SHARK ROLLS WITH SHRIMP AND OLIVE STUFFING

12 thin slices porbeagle shark

2 oz (50 g) peeled shrimps

2 oz (50 g) fine soft breadcrumbs

2 oz (50 g) freshly grated Parmesan cheese

2 oz (50 g) green olives, stoned

2 oz (50 g) black olives, stoned

1 tbsp capers

1 sprig parsley

1 chilli pepper

1 egg

4 tbsp olive oil

8 sage leaves

3¹/₂ fl oz (100 ml) dry white wine

salt and pepper

Chop the shrimps, mix with the breadcrumbs, cheese, chopped green and black olives, chopped capers, parsley and chopped chilli pepper. Blend well, adding the egg and 1 tbsp oil. Season with salt and pepper. Spread this mixture on top of the fish slices and roll them up, fastening securely by threading them, 3 at a time, on to pairs of thin wooden or steel skewers, placing a sage leaf between the rolls.

Heat the oil in a wide pan and sauté the skewered fish rolls, turning once and sprinkling with a little salt and with the white wine. Continue cooking for about 10 minutes, by which time the wine will have evaporated and the rolls will be well browned.

MARINATED SHARK STEAKS

4 shark steaks weighing 8 oz (225 g) each

2 cloves garlic

1 small bunch parsley

1 sprig thyme

1 sprig fresh oregano

1 small bunch chervil

2 bay leaves

3¹/₂ fl oz (100 ml) olive oil

juice of 1 lemon

salt and pepper

Wash and dry the fish steaks and place on a large plate. Chop one peeled clove of garlic with the parsley, thyme, oregano, chervil and bay leaves; transfer to a bowl, add all but 2 tbsp of the oil and the lemon juice. Mix thoroughly, add a little salt and pour all over the fish. Leave to marinate for 2 hours.

Slice the second garlic clove very thinly. Use the remaining oil to grease 4 large squares of greaseproof paper or foil; place a fish steak on each square, sprinkle each one with 2 tbsp of the marinade and place a few garlic slivers on top. Seal the paper or foil parcels securely and bake at 400°F (200°C) mark 6 for 10–15 minutes.

SHARK WITH PEAS

4 shark steaks weighing 8 oz (200 g) each

1 clove garlic

1 small bunch parsley

2 sprigs basil

4 tbsp olive oil

9 oz (250 g) tinned peas, drained

2 tbsp tomato purée

4 fl oz (120 ml) fish stock (fumet) (see page 39)

salt and pepper

Wash and dry the fish steaks. Chop the peeled garlic finely with the parsley and basil. Sauté this

135

mixture very gently in the oil in a heavy-bottomed saucepan or casserole for a minute or two. Add the peas, stir, then place the fish on top in a single layer.

Dissolve the tomato purée in the hot stock, pour over the fish and season with salt and freshly ground pepper. Simmer, uncovered, for 10 minutes. Transfer the fish steaks to a warmed serving dish, cover with the peas and tomato liquid and serve.

MIXED SEAFOOD AU GRATIN

14 oz (400 g) mixed filleted fish (e.g. haddock, whiting, John Dory or any fresh, white fish)

4 oz (100 g) peeled shrimps

3¼ lb (1½ kg) mussels (or 1 lb [500 g] shucked mussels)

3½ fl oz (100 ml) dry white wine

2 shallots

14 fl oz (400 ml) court-bouillon (see page 25)

2 oz (50 g) butter

2 oz (50 g) plain flour

4 oz (100 g) grated Emmenthal cheese

2 tbsp breadcrumbs

salt and pepper

Scrub and clean the mussels; pour the white wine into a large fireproof casserole dish or saucepan, add the thinly sliced peeled shallot and place the mussels on top; cover and place over a high heat for a few minutes, to make the mussels open. Drain the mussels, discarding any that remain closed. Remove the molluscs from their shells, saving all their juice and the liquid in the pan and strain through a cloth or very fine sieve.

Rinse the fish fillets, add to a pan or fish kettle containing the cold *court-bouillon* and bring slowly to the boil; immediately reduce the heat and simmer very slowly for 5 minutes. Melt all but ½ oz (10 g) of the butter in a small saucepan, stir in the flour and cook for a few seconds over a low heat. Beat in 14 fl oz (400 ml) strained *court-bouillon* and about 6 tbsp mussel liquor, adding a

little at a time. Simmer over a low heat for 7–8 minutes, stirring continuously. Turn off the heat, add a little salt and stir in the grated cheese.

Grease an ovenproof dish with the remaining butter; cover the bottom with the well drained fish fillets and cover these with the shrimps and the mussels. Coat with the sauce and sprinkle with the breadcrumbs. Place in a preheated oven at 425°F (220°C) mark 7 for 15 minutes.

HADDOCK WITH SMOKED BACON

1½ lb (700 g) fillets of haddock

4 oz (100 g) smoked streaky bacon cut in one thick slice

3½ fl oz (100 ml) dry white wine

salt and pepper

Cut the haddock into 1-in (3-cm) cubes. Cut the bacon into smaller cubes and sauté in a frying pan, preferably an iron one, over a high heat until they are golden brown and have released a lot of fat; use a slotted ladle or spoon to remove the bacon pieces, draining the fat back into the pan. Fry the fish cubes in the fat for about 10 minutes, turning carefully now and then. Sprinkle sparingly with salt and with plenty of freshly ground pepper.

Use a slotted ladle to remove the fish cubes from the pan, allowing as much fat as possible to drain off them; discard the fat, wipe the pan with kitchen paper and return the fish and bacon to it, sprinkling the wine all over them. Cook briskly for a minute or two until almost all the wine has evaporated. Serve hot.

·Crustaceans·

Prawns Belgian style

2
Palinurus vulgaris

6
Maia squinado

3
Nephrops norvegicus

5
Penaeus kerathurus

7
Palinurus Spp.

1

Dutch: Rivierkreeft
English: (Freshwater) crayfish
French: Écrevisse à pattes rouges
German: Europäischer flusskrebs
Italian: Gambero di acqua dolce
Spanish: Cangrejo de rio

2

Dutch: Pantserkreeft
English: Crawfish
French: Langouste
German: Languste
Italian: Aragosta mediterranea
Spanish: Langosta

3

Dutch: Noorse kreeft
English: Dublin Bay prawn
French: Langoustine
German: Kaisergranat
Italian: Scampo
Spanish: Cigala

4

French: Crevette rose du large
Italian: Gambero rosa
Spanish: Gamba

5

French: Caramote
Italian: Mazzancolla
Spanish: Lagostino

6

Dutch: Spinkrab
English: Spider crab
French: Araignée de mer
German: Seespinne
Italian: Grancevola
Spanish: Centolla

7

Italian: Aragosta atlantica

8

Dutch: Zeekreeft
English: Lobster
French: Homard
German: Hummer
Italian: Astice americano
Spanish: Bogavante

9

English: Shore crab
French: Crabe vert
Italian: Granchio comune
Spanish: Cangrejo de mar

10

Italian: Granchio di sabbia

11

English: Mantis shrimp
French: Squille
Italian: Canocchia
Spanish: Galera

12

English: Flat lobster
French: Grande cigale
Italian: Magnosa/Cicala
Spanish: Cigarra

13

French: Crevette rouge
Italian: Gambero rosso
Spanish: Carabinero

14

English: Florida lobster
Italian: Aragosta americana

15

English: Edible crab
French: Tourteau
Italian: Granciporro
Spanish: Buey

16

English: Brown shrimp
French: Crevette grise
Italian: Gamberetto grigio
Spanish: Quisquilla gris

17

French: Ériphie
Italian: Favollo
Spanish: Cangrejo moruno

1

Astacus fluviatilis

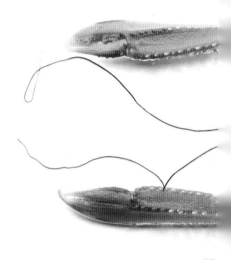

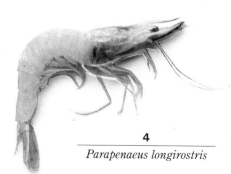

4

Parapenaeus longirostris

Crawfish and dill vol-au-vents

Lobster soup

13
Aristeus antennatus

14
Palinurus argus

15
Cancer pagurus

16
Crangon crangon

17
Eriphia verrucosa

8
Homarus americanus

9
Carcinus mediterraneus

10
Portunus holsatus

11
Squilla mantis

12
Scyllarides latus

Lobster in tomato sauce

CRAB-STUFFED PEACHES

5 large ripe peaches

juice of 1 lemon

7 oz (200 g) crabmeat

3¹/₂ fl oz (100 ml) double cream

1 tbsp brandy

generous pinch paprika

8 crisp lettuce leaves

salt and pepper

Blanch the peaches in boiling water very briefly to make them easier to peel. Cut them in half, remove the pit, and sprinkle with a little of the lemon juice. Chop one peach into very small pieces.

Pick out and discard any pieces of cartilage (hard, tough pieces) from the crabmeat. Mix with the chopped peach in a large bowl, sprinkle with the remaining lemon juice, stir in the cream and brandy, season with the paprika, a little salt and plenty of freshly ground white pepper. Mix well. Spread out the lettuce leaves on a serving platter; place a peach half, hollow side uppermost, on each lettuce leaf and pack the crab mixture into each hollow, heaping it up to form a small mound. Chill for 1 hour in the refrigerator before serving.

CRAB MOULD

5 oz (150 g) peeled, cooked shrimps or small prawns

4 fillets of lemon sole or plaice

6 oz (170 g) tinned crabmeat

1 oz (25 g) butter

3 tbsp mayonnaise (see page 37)

1 tbsp tomato ketchup

1 tsp mild mustard

1 sachet gelatine

9 fl oz (250 ml) whipping cream

1 escarole or curly endive

salt and pepper

Sauté the fish fillets in the butter, seasoning with salt and pepper. Remove any tough pieces of cartilage from the crabmeat before flaking it; chop the drained fillets and the shrimps. Place in a bowl. Stir in the mayonnaise, ketchup and mustard. Dissolve the gelatine completely in 3 tbsp extremely hot (but not boiling) water; warm gently over hot water while stirring if necessary. Allow to cool a little, then stir in 2 tbsp of the cream; mix thoroughly into the crabmeat mixture. Beat the remaining cream until very firm and fold gently but thoroughly into the crab mixture. Season with salt and pepper if wished. Rinse out a mould with cold water, spoon the creamy crab mixture into it, tapping the bottom of the mould on the work surface as you do so to avoid air pockets.

Smooth the surface level and chill for 6 hours. Turn out on to a serving plate and surround with escarole or curly endive leaves.

CRAB QUICHE

4 oz (120 g) cooked, peeled prawns

1 lb (500 g) mussels (in the shell) or 4 oz (120 g) thawed, frozen shucked mussels

6 oz (175 g) tinned crabmeat

3 eggs

2¹/₂ tsp lemon juice

1 tsp Worcestershire sauce

3¹/₂ fl oz (100 ml) single cream

12 oz (350 g) frozen puff pastry

salt and pepper

Prepare the mussels (see page 22). Heat for a minute or two in a large, covered pan, shaking the pan now and then to make them open. (Turn

145

the mussels if necessary.) Discard any which do not open. Take off the shell; leave to cool. If using unpeeled raw or cooked prawns you will need double the weight given above. Mix with the mussels and keep cool. Drain the crabmeat; pick out and discard any hard pieces; flake finely with a fork and mix with the mussels and prawns. Beat the eggs with the lemon juice, salt, pepper, Worcestershire sauce and cream. Stir into the crab mixture.

Roll out the thawed pastry and use to line a greased spring-release flan pan (or oven-to-table flan dish); spoon the crab and egg mixture into it. Place in a preheated oven at 375°F (180°C) mark 4 and bake for about 40 minutes.

CHILLED CRAB WITH PARSLEY AND LEMON

2¹/₄–2¹/₂ lb (1 kg) crab or crabs

juice of 2¹/₂ lemons

1 bay leaf

4 tbsp extra virgin olive oil

2 cloves garlic

finely chopped parsley

salt and pepper

If you have bought live crabs, soak these in cold salted water for 1 hour, then wipe well before cooking. Kill the crabs by pushing a skewer several times, at different angles, into the ventral nerve centre (lift up the little tail flap on the underside of the crab) and the brain (between the eyes, at the edge of the underside of the shell); ask your fishmonger to show you how or do it for you. (Never buy a dead raw crab which has not been killed while you wait.) Cook (for 10–15 minutes if small, 20–25 minutes if large) in a large saucepan of water with the juice of ¹/₂ lemon and the bay leaf. See page 19 for cooking hints. Drain well. If pre-cooked crabs are used, join the recipe at this point: remove the flesh from the body, the legs (if large enough) and from the claws (if present). Discard the leathery stomach sac and greyish,

feathery gills. Use the brownish very soft parts as well as the white flesh, as they are delicious. Place all the meat in a bowl and mix with a dressing made by beating together the oil, the juice of 2 lemons, very finely chopped garlic and parsley, salt and pepper. Chill in the refrigerator for 2–3 hours before serving.

MANTIS SHRIMP WITH PARSLEY

16 mantis shrimp

extra-virgin olive oil

juice of 1 lemon

3 tbsp chopped parsley

salt

Use a small piece of cocktail stick to plug the small hole in the rear of the mantis shrimp's shells. Rinse well and plunge into boiling, slightly salted water. Cook for a few minutes only: as soon as they change colour, they are done. Open with very sharp, pointed scissors (fish scissors are ideal) as shown on page 18 while still warm.

Place on a serving dish and sprinkle with a few tablespoons extra virgin olive oil, the strained lemon juice and the parsley. Serve.

LOBSTER WITH DILL

2 lobsters weighing approx. 1¹/₂ lb (700 g) each

few sprigs dill

1 lettuce

2 slices fresh or unsweetened tinned pineapple

3¹/₂ oz (100 g) button mushrooms

1 tbsp mayonnaise (see page 37)

9 fl oz (250 ml) whipping cream

pinch sugar

salt and pepper

Prepare the lobsters for cooking (see page 15) and add to a very large pan of boiling, slightly salted water; cook for 15–20 minutes. Drain, take all the meat out of the shells and claws and dice. Wash and dry the dill weed, snip off the small feathery leaves, reserving a sprig or two for decoration. Wash and dry the lettuce. Drain the pineapple well and cut into small pieces. Slice the mushrooms wafer-thin. Place all the ingredients except the lettuce and dill in a bowl and mix with the mayonnaise, then fold in the lightly beaten cream, flavoured with a pinch of sugar, salt and freshly ground white pepper.

Line a large salad bowl with the lettuce leaves; spoon in the lobster mixture and decorate with the reserved dill sprigs.

LOBSTER AND ARTICHOKE SALAD

2 lobsters weighing 1 lb (500 g) each
1 escarole or curly endive
4 artichokes
1/2 lemon
plain flour
butter
4 tbsp sunflower oil
2 tbsp tarragon vinegar
salt and pepper

Wash, trim and dry the escarole or endive. Wash the artichokes, trim down to their hearts and sprinkle these all over with lemon juice immediately to prevent them discolouring. Mix a little cold water with 1 oz (25 g) flour and then stir into 1³/₄ pints (1 litre) water; add 1 oz (25 g) butter, bring to the boil, and cook the artichokes for 10 minutes. Lower the lobsters into a very large pan of boiling salted water; cook fast for 2 minutes, remove from the pan and drain; detach the head and the claws. Return the claws to the boiling water to cook for 10 minutes more. Take the flesh out of the shell, cut into thick slices, and fry these gently in 1¹/₂ oz (40 g) butter for 1 minute on each side. Drain and leave to cool. Gradually beat the oil into the vinegar in a bowl, adding a little oil at a time; add salt and pepper.

Extract the claw meat and thinly slice the artichokes. Arrange all the lobster meat, salad leaves and artichokes attractively on a large plate and sprinkle with the dressing.

Note: Frozen or tinned artichoke hearts can be used for this recipe.

LOBSTER IN ASPIC

1 lobster weighing 1¹/₄ lb (600 g)
18 fl oz (500 ml) dry white wine
1 bouquet garni
1 lemon
1 sachet gelatine
¹/₄ red pepper
2 eggs
3 tbsp mayonnaise (see page 37)
1 sprig parsley
salt and pepper

Make a *court-bouillon* (see page 39) with the white wine, 5¹/₂ pints (2¹/₂ litres) water, 1 bouquet garni, the rind of ¹/₂ lemon (no pith), salt and a few peppercorns. Bring this *court-bouillon* to the boil again, plunge the lobster into it, and cook for 30 minutes. Leave to cool in the liquid; drain well, extract the meat from the body in a single piece, slice into fairly thick 'steaks' or medallions; reserve the largest 8 of these and chop the remaining meat (and the meat extracted from the claws) coarsely. Make the gelatine, using a total of 1 pint (600 ml) liquid (or use packet aspic powder). Leave to cool but do not chill.

Have 8 ramekins ready chilled in the freezer; pour a layer of aspic about 1 in (2.5 cm) thick into the bottom of each and return to the freezer for a few minutes to set; place a small piece of red pepper, decoratively cut, on the aspic with a parsley leaf pressed flat beside it; place a piece of lobster flat on top.

147

Hard-boil the eggs; cool and peel; process the yolks with the chopped lobster and mayonnaise; add 1 tbsp finely chopped parsley, salt and pepper to taste; continue processing until very smooth. Using a piping bag and fairly large-gauge fluted nozzle, pipe a large rosette in the centre of each slice of lobster in the moulds: leave a little space all round between the mayonnaise and lobster and the sides of the ramekins. Gently pour in enough aspic to fill the ramekin and chill for 3–4 hours. Unmould and serve.

WARM CRAB SALAD

12 oz (350 g) fresh, frozen or tinned white crabmeat

1 small Savoy cabbage

8 oz (225 g) French beans

1 tbsp sunflower or sesame oil

1 small clove garlic

1 tbsp light soy sauce

1 tbsp white wine or dry sherry

salt and pepper

Peel off the leaves of a very fresh, firm Savoy cabbage (discard the outer wilted and damaged leaves). Wash well, shake dry and cut out the larger central sections or 'ribs' before blanching them in boiling salted water. When the water comes back to the boil immediately remove the cabbage leaves; pat dry with kitchen paper and shred.

Trim the beans and boil in salted water for 10 minutes or until tender but still crisp. Drain well.

Heat the oil with the garlic over a low heat, discarding the garlic pieces when they have started to colour; add the shredded cabbage to this flavoured oil, season with a little salt and freshly ground pepper and stir-fry for two minutes. Add the soy sauce and white wine or sherry and stir-fry for 2 minutes. Turn into a salad bowl with the crabmeat and beans. Stir the salad briefly and serve while still warm.

PRAWN BEIGNETS

10 oz (300 g) peeled Dublin Bay prawns

3¹/₂ oz (100 g) chicken breast

¹/₂ onion

1 tsp finely chopped fresh ginger

¹/₂ tsp baking powder

1 tbsp sherry

1 tbsp cornflour

1 egg white

sunflower oil

salt

Chop the Dublin Bay prawns very finely with the raw chicken breast, add the finely chopped onion, ginger, baking powder, sherry and cornflour. Mix well. Gradually stir in the egg white (do not beat), adding a teaspoon at a time, and a pinch of salt. Blend well and leave to stand for 1 hour.

Heat the correct volume of sunflower oil in a deep-fryer until very hot. Shape the mixture into small balls and deep-fry a few at a time until light and golden brown. Place each batch on kitchen paper and keep hot (uncovered) while you fry the next batch. Serve immediately.

PRAWNS WITH AVOCADO

2¹/₄ lb–2¹/₂ lb (1 kg) Dublin Bay prawns, in the shell

2 large ripe tomatoes

1 avocado

juice of 1 lemon

9 oz (250 g) mayonnaise (see page 37)

1 tbsp brandy

1 tbsp tomato ketchup

3 mint leaves

salt and pepper

If using raw Dublin Bay prawns, pull off the heads and discard (unless needed for fish stock or soup); add the tails to boiling salted water and cook for 5 minutes. When cold, peel and chop. (If you buy frozen, cooked peeled prawns, thaw thoroughly before using.) Blanch the tomatoes, peel and remove the seeds. Dice.

Cut the avocado lengthwise in half, remove the pit, scoop out the flesh and cut into small cubes, sprinkling immediately with lemon juice to prevent discoloration. Mix with the brandy, ketchup and finely chopped mint leaves into the mayonnaise. Gently fold in the tomatoes, avocado and prawns. Serve chilled.

WARM PRAWN SALAD

20 Dublin Bay prawns
5 oz (150 g) butter
4 tbsp white wine vinegar
9 oz (250 g) button mushrooms
juice of 1 lemon
1 sprig tarragon
4 tbsp olive oil
1 lettuce
salt and pepper

Heat half the butter and cook the unpeeled Dublin Bay prawns for 2–3 minutes on each side. Add 2 tbsp vinegar, scrape the pan with a wooden spoon to release any cooking deposits and simmer over a very low heat for 10 minutes. Trim the mushrooms, slice thinly and fry in the remaining butter over a high heat for 1 minute; sprinkle with 2 tbsp lemon juice, season with salt and pepper and simmer for 5–6 minutes. Finely chop the tarragon. Mix the remaining vinegar in a bowl with the oil, salt, pepper and chopped tarragon.

Peel the prawns, reserving 4 for decoration, as soon as they are cool enough to handle. Place the lettuce leaves in 4 fairly deep individual dishes and sprinkle with a little of the tarragon dressing. Place

the prawns and mushrooms on the lettuce leaves and pour the remaining dressing over them. Garnish each serving with an unpeeled prawn and serve.

PRAWNS IN CHILLI MAYONNAISE

1 lb (500 g) Dublin Bay prawns
1³/₄ pints (1 litre) court-bouillon (see page 39)
1 egg yolk
1 tsp mustard
7 fl oz (200 ml) olive oil
1 chilli pepper
juice of 1 lemon
1 lettuce
salt

If using raw prawns, wash well, and cook in the *court-bouillon* for 5 minutes. Drain and leave to cool.

Liquidize the egg yolk with the mustard, the oil, chilli pepper, lemon juice and a pinch of salt to make a thick mayonnaise. Line a salad bowl with lettuce leaves. Stir the prawns into the mayonnaise (if using thawed frozen cooked prawns, drain and dry well and add them at this point). Spoon into the salad bowl and serve chilled.

PRAWNS IN ASPIC WITH RUSSIAN SALAD

10 oz (300 g) peeled cooked Dublin Bay prawns
gelatine (sufficient to set 1³/₄ pints [1 litre] liquid)
juice of 1 lemon

6 baby gherkins
1 hard-boiled egg
14 oz (400 g) tinned Russian salad
5 oz (150 g) stuffed green olives
1 black olive

Make enough gelatine or aspic, according to the manufacturer's instructions, to set 1³/₄ pints (1 litre) liquid. Stir in 1 tbsp lemon juice and leave to cool but do not chill. Rinse out the inside of a charlotte mould with cold water; pour in enough aspic to cover the bottom with a layer ¹/₄ in (1 cm) deep. Put in the freezer for a few minutes to set. Coat the inside of the mould with a thin film of aspic, returning to the freezer briefly to set.

Slice all but 2 of the gherkins and the hard-boiled egg. Arrange some of the gherkin slices on top of the aspic; gently press the egg slices flat against the sides of the mould; spoon in about 7 oz (200 g) of the Russian salad and smooth level. Arrange some of the prawns around the top edge of the Russian salad, pressed against the sides of the mould.

Pour in another layer of aspic and place in the freezer to set. Repeat this process twice more: the next layer will consist of the remaining Russian salad, with the olives around the top edge; cover with more aspic, then with a layer of gherkin slices with prawns round the edge. Cover with the remaining aspic and chill in the refrigerator for 3 hours. Dip the mould briefly in hot water to loosen, dry the outside and turn out on to a serving plate.

Place the black olive on top, slice the two gherkins into fans and use to decorate.

PRAWN AND MUSHROOM MOULDS WITH LETTUCE SAUCE

16 Dublin Bay prawns
10 oz (300 g) ceps (boletus edulis)
olive oil

2 eggs
12 fl oz (350 ml) single cream
nutmeg
1¹/₂ tbsp finely chopped basil, chervil and chives
2 tbsp butter
6 lettuce leaves
3¹/₂ fl oz (100 ml) milk
2 tbsp tomato ketchup
salt and pepper

If using raw Dublin Bay prawns, add to boiling salted water and poach for 3 minutes then drain and peel.

Cut off the mushroom stalks, slice the caps and sauté for 4 minutes in 3 tbsp very hot oil; drain and chop finely. Beat the eggs with a pinch of salt, 9 fl oz (250 ml) of the cream, freshly ground pepper and a pinch of nutmeg, the herbs and mushrooms.

Grease 4 earthenware ramekin or similar dishes with butter; place 2 prawns in the bottom of each. Spoon in the egg mixture (if you wish to unmould these, fill to the brim); place in a roasting tin, pour in sufficient hot water to come half way up the sides of the ramekins and cook in the oven, preheated to 400°F (200°C) mark 6, for about 25 minutes.

Shred the washed lettuce leaves, blanch for a few seconds in boiling salted water, drain well and place in a saucepan with the remaining cream, milk, ketchup, salt and pepper.

Cover and cook for 10 minutes over a low heat; sieve. Run the point of a sharp knife around the inside edge of the ramekins and unmould on to heated individual plates; spoon the lettuce sauce so that it surrounds each mould on the plate and garnish with the prawns. Serve very hot.

CHINESE PRAWNS

12 Dublin Bay prawns
18 fl oz (500 ml) dry white wine
1 bouquet garni

1 piece lemon rind
sesame oil
1 lettuce
1 cucumber
2 hard-boiled eggs
2 slices ham
8 spring onions
2 egg yolks
1 tsp mustard powder
3 tbsp sieved tomatoes or ketchup
pinch sugar
salt and pepper

If using raw Dublin Bay prawns, leave unpeeled and rinse under running cold water. Pour 1³/₄ pints (1 litre) water into a large saucepan. Add the white wine, bouquet garni, lemon rind and 2 tsp coarse sea salt and bring to the boil; simmer for 20 minutes. Add the prawns and cook for 12 minutes. Drain, peel and cut into pieces.

If using frozen peeled cooked prawns, thaw completely and follow the recipe from here on. Sprinkle with 1–2 tbsp sesame oil and stir. Line a salad bowl or cover a serving platter with large, crisp lettuce leaves; arrange the very finely sliced, peeled cucumber on top, then the prawns and, lastly, wedges of hard-boiled egg and chopped ham. Chop the spring onions and sprinkle over to decorate.

Mix the egg yolks with the mustard, tomato, pinch of sugar and salt, and a little freshly ground pepper. Whisk in 5 tbsp sesame oil and serve this dressing separately.

PRAWNS MANHATTAN

24 Dublin Bay prawns
1 shallot
1 clove

18 fl oz (500 ml) dry white wine
1 bay leaf
1 sprig thyme
1 lettuce
1 lemon
10 fl oz (300 ml) single cream
4 tbsp tomato ketchup
few drops Worcestershire sauce
1 small bunch parsley
1 small bunch chives
salt, peppercorns and cayenne pepper

Peel the shallot; push the sharp stalk of the clove firmly into it and place in a saucepan with 3¹/₂ pints (1¹/₂ litres) water, the wine, bay leaf, thyme, 1 tsp salt and a few peppercorns.

Bring to the boil, add the well rinsed prawns (if using raw), and poach for 5 minutes after the water returns to a gentle boil. Drain and leave to cool.

Cut the lettuce leaves into thin strips. Divide between 4 small, deep glass dishes or cocktail glasses and sprinkle with a little lemon juice.

Use a balloon whisk to beat the cream with the ketchup and Worcestershire sauce and season with cayenne pepper and salt.

Peel the prawns (if using thawed, frozen cooked prawns, add at this point) and place on top of the lettuce. Cover with the cream dressing. Decorate each serving with a slice of lemon, a sprig of parsley, and some chopped chives.

PRAWN CHOUX BUNS

5 oz (150 g) peeled cooked small prawns
3 oz (90 g) butter
1 oz (25 g) plain flour
10 fl oz (300 ml) milk
3 oz (80 g) grated Emmenthal cheese
20 home-made or commercially prepared choux buns

151

Make a white sauce: melt 1 oz (25 g) of the butter in a saucepan and add the flour. Gradually add the milk and bring to the boil, stirring continuously, until thick and smooth. Draw aside from the heat, season with salt and pepper and add 2 tbsp of the grated cheese, stirring well; add the remaining butter and the prawns. Cut off the tops of the choux buns; fill with the prawn mixture, using a teaspoon.

Grease a wide, shallow ovenproof dish with butter, place the choux buns in it, sprinkle the remaining cheese on top of each bun, and place in a preheated oven at 425°F (220°C) mark 7 for a few minutes until the cheese has melted.

Note: Tinned crabmeat can be used instead of prawns. For a special occasion, use finely chopped cooked lobster meat for the filling and stir 1 tbsp sherry into the prepared white sauce.

SEAFOOD MOULD

10 oz (300 g) shrimp
1¼ lb (600 g) fillets of hake
½ onion
2 cloves
1 sprig parsley
1 lemon
1 bay leaf
½ carrot
1 celery stalk
9 fl oz (250 ml) white sauce
2½ oz (70 g) grated Gruyère cheese
3 eggs, separated
2 oz (50 g) butter
breadcrumbs
3½ fl oz (100 ml) brandy
9 fl oz (250 ml) cream
salt and white peppercorns

Bring a fairly large saucepan of water to the boil with the half onion, 2 peppercorns, cloves, sprig of parsley, a wedge of lemon, bay leaf, carrot and celery. Simmer for a few minutes then add the hake fillets and poach gently for a few minutes until done.

Remove from the liquid, drain well and reduce to a purée in the food processor. Mix with the white sauce (for the recipe, see Prawn Choux Buns, page 151), add the Gruyère, egg yolks, salt and freshly ground white pepper.
Stir thoroughly; fold in the stiffly beaten egg whites.

Grease a ring mould with ½ oz (10 g) butter; sprinkle the breadcrumbs all over the inside; spoon the mixture in, tapping the bottom on the work surface to eliminate air pockets and smoothing the surface level. Cook in a roasting tin half filled with hot water in a preheated oven at 325°F (180°C) mark 4 for 45 minutes.

Heat the remaining butter in a small saucepan, add the prepared prawns and sprinkle with the juice of half a lemon, salt, pepper and the brandy. Cook, uncovered, until the brandy has evaporated; add the cream and simmer to reduce and thicken.

Turn the mould out on to a warmed serving plate and fill the central well with the prawns and sauce.

PRAWNS BELGIAN STYLE

10 oz (300 g) peeled prawns
2 large heads chicory
4 fl oz (100 ml) mayonnaise (see page 37)
1 tbsp lemon juice
3 tbsp single cream
pinch paprika
2 tbsp tomato ketchup
salt

If raw prawns are used, wash, boil gently in salted water for 4–5 minutes, sprinkle with a little salt and leave to cool. Reserve the largest chicory leaves, slicing half the rest into thin strips and mixing these with the prawns in a bowl (if thawed, frozen prawns are used, add them now). Mix the lemon juice, cream, paprika and ketchup into the mayonnaise, and stir into the contents of the bowl. Fill the large, reserved leaves with this mixture and arrange on a round serving plate, radiating like the spokes of a wheel.

SHRIMPS WITH MELON

8 oz (200 g) shrimps
2 small ripe Charentais or Cantaloupe melons
1 small green pepper
4 tinned palm hearts
4 tbsp olive or walnut oil
2 tbsp white wine vinegar or cider vinegar
few chives
salt and pepper

Slice the melons horizontally in half and scoop out the seeds. Use a melon baller to scoop out the flesh and place these melon balls in a bowl. Scoop out any remaining flesh, leaving the empty skins to serve as a container; chill. Dice the green pepper; drain the palm hearts and cut into small round slices. If raw shrimps are used, boil for 2 minutes in salted water, drain and peel. Place the vinegar, salt, pepper and chopped chives in a large bowl and beat in the oil; add the melon balls, green pepper, palm hearts and shrimps and mix gently but thoroughly. Fill the empty melon halves with this mixture and chill before serving.

PRAWNS WITH RASPBERRIES

1¼ lb (600 g) raw peeled prawns

18 fl oz (500 ml) dry white wine
1 slice lemon
1 bouquet garni
2 fl oz (50 ml) raspberry vinegar
5 tbsp best olive oil
1 bunch lamb's lettuce
12 raspberries
salt, peppercorns and pepper

Pour the wine and 1¾ pints (1 litre) water into a saucepan, add the lemon slice, bouquet garni, 1 tsp coarse salt and a few peppercorns. Bring to the boil and simmer for 15 minutes. Add the prawns and cook for 5–6 minutes. Drain and leave to cool. Mix well with the olive oil and the raspberry vinegar.

Mix the lamb's lettuce very gently with the prawns and the raspberries. Season with salt and pepper to taste. Serve.

PRAWN SALAD

40 prawns, in the shell
2 carrots
2 shallots
2 sprigs parsley
1 bay leaf
14 fl oz (400 ml) dry white wine
8 oz (225 g) mixed salad leaves (e.g. radicchio, escarole, watercress)
5 oz (150 g) French beans
½ cucumber
6 tbsp oil
3 tbsp wine vinegar
1 tbsp lemon juice
salt and white peppercorns

Cut one carrot and the shallots into small pieces, place in a large non-metallic saucepan with the parsley, bay leaf, 1 tbsp coarse sea salt, 6 peppercorns, the wine and 6½ pints (3 litres) water. Cover and boil for 10 minutes.

Add the raw prawns to the saucepan, bring back to the boil and cook for 3 minutes. Drain and peel all but 8. Boil the beans in salted water for 14 minutes. Cut the carrot into fine matchstick strips and blanch for 3 minutes in boiling salted water.

Mix the oil into the vinegar in a large bowl, add 1 tbsp lemon juice, salt and freshly ground pepper. Arrange the cooked vegetables attractively on a serving plate together with the peeled, diced cucumber and the prawns. Garnish with the 8 reserved, unshelled prawns and serve.

PRAWN TORTILLAS

12 oz (350 g) peeled prawns
7 oz (200 g) plain flour
3 oz (80 g) garbanzo flour
2 mild red onions
1 bunch parsley
oil
salt

Sift the two types of flour together into a large bowl. Gradually stir in enough cold water to make a fairly thick pouring batter. Chop the onions and parsley very finely and stir into the batter. Chop the prawns very coarsely and add to the batter. Add a generous pinch of salt, stir thoroughly, and leave to stand in a cool place or in the refrigerator for 3 hours. Stir well just before frying. Pour enough oil into a pan to completely cover the bottom and when very hot, add the batter in tablespoonfuls, making sure you have plenty of chopped prawns in each. Fry in small batches, turning when golden brown on the first side. Serve while still very hot and crisp.

CRAWFISH PARISIAN STYLE

1 crawfish weighing 2¼–2½ lb (1 kg)
4 carrots
2 onions
1 bouquet garni
10 oz (300 g) frozen diced mixed vegetables
4 oz (100 g) frozen small peas
6 eggs
2 sachets gelatine
9 fl oz (250 ml) olive oil
½ lemon
1 tbsp tomato ketchup
1½ tbsp finely chopped parsley
8 small tomatoes
1 lb (450 g) white bread (optional)
8 lettuce leaves
1 black truffle
butter
salt, peppercorns and pepper

Bring 6½ pints (3 litres) water to the boil in a deep, wide saucepan with the peeled and sliced carrots and onions, bouquet garni, 1 tbsp coarse sea salt and a few peppercorns. Boil this *court-bouillon* gently for 10 minutes.

Prepare the crawfish for cooking as shown on page 15, add to the *court-bouillon* and simmer for 30 minutes; leave to cool in the liquid.

Cook the diced vegetables and the peas in salted water according to the directions on the packets; drain and leave to cool.

Remove the crawfish from the *court-bouillon* and untie. Use a pair of sharp kitchen or fish scissors to cut along the edge of the underside, as directed for mantis shrimp (see page 18), free the thinner under shell and extract the flesh in one piece. Slice into 8 steaks and refrigerate. Hard-boil 4 eggs, cool under running cold water, and peel.

Make the gelatine or enough fish aspic to set 1¾ pints (1 litre) liquid, following the manufacturer's instructions; leave to cool until it has a slightly thickened, oily appearance; use a pastry brush to coat the crawfish slices with it and return them to the refrigerator. Make a mayonnaise by blending the remaining 2 egg yolks, 7 fl oz (200 ml) olive oil, salt and the lemon juice; stir in the mustard and mix three quarters with the mixed vegetables.

Slice the eggs in half, remove the yolks and crush with a fork, blending with the remaining mayonnaise. Flavour half this mixture with the tomato ketchup and half with the finely chopped parsley.

Slice off the tops of the tomatoes, scoop out the seeds and centres and fill with the vegetable mixture. Use a piping bag and a fairly large, fluted nozzle to pipe the two egg yolk mixtures into the hard-boiled whites.

Place a truffle slice on each crawfish piece, give them another coating of aspic (if this has set too thickly, warm briefly) and return to the refrigerator until set. Coat a third time and chill until set.

Arrange the empty crawfish shell on a large serving platter. (For a dramatic presentation, prop the shell against a crustless loaf of bread, cut diagonally and placed in such a way on the platter as to form a slightly sloping support. Arrange the shell so the tail is uppermost, with the claws gripping the sides of the bread.)

Surround the shell (and mask the bread support, if using) with lettuce leaves and place the stuffed eggs and tomatoes on top; press small pieces of butter on to the crawfish shell, down the centre, and press the aspic-covered steaks or medallions on these in a line down the back of the shell, slightly overlapping one another and with the slightly larger medallions starting nearest the head. Use the remaining aspic to coat the entire crawfish with a glaze.

Chill until just before serving. Serves 6–8.

CRAWFISH COCKTAIL

1 crawfish weighing approx. 1½ lb (700 g)
14 fl oz (900 ml) dry white wine
1 carrot
1 onion

1 celery stalk
1 bouquet garni
4 oz (100 g) button mushrooms
juice of 1 lemon
2 slices fresh pineapple
4 fl oz (100 ml) mayonnaise (see page 37)
4 fl oz (100 ml) double cream
1 small bunch dill
4 lettuce leaves
salt and white peppercorns

Prepare the crawfish as shown on page 15. Make the *court-bouillon*: pour the wine and 3½ pints (2 litres) water into a very large saucepan, add the cleaned and prepared carrot, onion, celery, bouquet garni, 2 tsp salt and a few peppercorns; boil for 15 minutes, add the crawfish and poach gently for 15 minutes. Draw aside from the heat, leave to cool completely. Take the flesh out of the shell in one piece, slice into steaks, and cut each of these into 4 quarters.

Slice the mushrooms thinly into a large bowl and sprinkle immediately with the lemon juice; add the crawfish pieces and the chopped pineapple slices. Combine the mayonnaise and cream, season with salt and freshly ground white pepper and fold into the crawfish mixture.

Place a large, crisp lettuce leaf in each of 4 glass dishes, fill each with a quarter of the crawfish cocktail and garnish with a sprig of dill. Serve slightly chilled.

CRAWFISH AND DILL VOL-AU-VENTS

1 crawfish weighing 1–1¼ lb (500–600 g)
12 medium-sized vol-au-vent cases
1 oz (25 g) plain flour

155

1¹/₂ oz (40 g) butter
3¹/₂ fl oz (100 ml) single cream
3¹/₂ fl oz (100 ml) dry white wine
4 oz (100 g) tiny button mushrooms
1 clove garlic (optional)
12 peeled prawns
1 sprig dill
salt and pepper

Prepare the crawfish (see page 15) and cook for approx. 25 minutes (see previous recipe for method). Leave to cool in the *court-bouillon*; drain, take the meat out of the shell and chop into small pieces.

Bake the vol-au-vent cases as directed and while they are cooking make the sauce: melt 1 oz (20 g) butter, stir in the flour then gradually add the cream, followed by 1¹/₂ tbsp of the wine. Cook, stirring, for 10 minutes. Cover and keep warm away from direct heat.

Chop the mushrooms coarsely; sauté in 1 oz (20 g) butter; sprinkle with the remaining white wine. Season with salt and pepper; cook gently for 15 minutes; stir these and the crawfish into the sauce. Mix carefully and add salt to taste.

Spoon the mixture into the vol-au-vent cases and heat briefly in a moderate oven. Take out of the oven and decorate each vol-au-vent with a couple of prawns and a small frond of dill.

Note: The filling can be made with prawns, if crawfish is unavailable. Serve the vol-au-vents with drinks.

PRAWN BISQUE

20 medium-sized raw prawns in the shell
1 carrot
1 onion
1 clove garlic

4 oz (110 g) butter
few sprigs thyme
1 bay leaf
few sprigs parsley
1 sprig tarragon
3¹/₂ fl oz (100 ml) brandy
14 fl oz (400 ml) dry white wine
3¹/₂ oz (400 g) rice
3¹/₂ fl oz (100 ml) single cream
salt and pepper

Raw unpeeled prawns are best for this recipe but unpeeled cooked ones can be used. Peel and trim the carrot, onion and garlic; chop all three very finely and fry gently in 2 oz (50 g) of the butter in a large, heavy-bottomed saucepan. Add the herbs, cover, and sweat very gently for 15 minutes. Add the peeled prawns, having removed the black vein or alimentary tract running down their backs.

Cook for a few minutes, stirring. Heat the brandy, pour into the saucepan, and set alight. Shake gently until the flames have died down, add the wine, 1¹/₄ pints (750 ml) boiling water, salt and freshly ground pepper and boil gently for 12 minutes. Cook the rice separately in 9 fl oz (250 ml) fast boiling salted water; cover tightly and continue boiling until the rice has absorbed all the water (about 20 minutes).

Peel the prawns when cooked and chop, reserving all the shells and heads; pound these and then liquidize with the rice and cooking liquid (in several batches). Pour through a fine sieve.

Heat the soup and boil for 1 minute, beating with a balloon whisk; draw aside from the heat and beat in the remaining butter, adding it in small pieces, followed by the cream and lastly the chopped prawns. Serve very hot, with an extra seasoning of freshly ground pepper.

Note: For a special occasion, ladle the soup into consommé bowls and garnish with thin half slices of lemon, a sprinkling of chopped fresh tarragon and a few extra whole cooked prawns.

PASTA WITH TOMATO AND PRAWN SAUCE

1 lb (500 g) cooked peeled prawns

¹/₂ celery stalk

1 small carrot

¹/₂ onion

3¹/₂ fl oz (100 ml) olive oil

6 ripe tomatoes or 6 oz (180 g) tinned tomatoes

¹/₂ chilli pepper

14 oz (400 g) pasta shapes

3 tbsp chopped parsley

2 cloves garlic, peeled and finely chopped

salt and pepper

Finely chop half the prawns. Prepare and peel or trim the carrot, celery and onion, chop very finely, and sauté in the oil in a large, heavy-bottomed saucepan. Add the blanched, peeled and chopped tomatoes, the chopped and whole prawns, a little crumbled dried chilli pepper and salt; cover and sweat over a very low heat for 15 minutes.

Cook the pasta in plenty of boiling salted water until just tender (*al dente*); drain well. While the pasta is cooking, stir the parsley and garlic into the prawn and tomato mixture and simmer for a minute. Serve the pasta as soon as it is cooked in deep, warm plates, with a generous topping of the sauce.

GREEN TAGLIATELLE WITH SHRIMP SAUCE

14 oz (400 g) shrimps

1 celery stalk

1 carrot

1 shallot

2¹/₂ oz (70 g) butter

7 fl oz (200 ml) single cream

14 oz (400 g) green tagliatelle

2–3 tbsp chopped parsley

salt and pepper

If the shrimps are raw, rinse well, and boil gently in 14 fl oz (400 ml) lightly salted water for 2–3 minutes. Drain, reserving the liquid.

Peel the shrimps and boil the shells in the cooking liquid until reduced by half. If you are using cooked unpeeled shrimps, just boil the heads and shells in the same volume of lightly salted water until reduced. Strain.

Prepare and chop the celery, carrot and shallot; sweat in the butter, adding the reduced liquid at intervals to moisten. Simmer to reduce further; add the shrimps and cream and season with salt and pepper. Cook gently for 5 minutes.

Cook the pasta in plenty of boiling, salted water till just tender but still with a little bite to it; drain and mix with the shrimp sauce and sprinkle with the parsley. Serve at once.

Note: For a delicious alternative shrimp sauce which is quick to prepare, heat 8 fl oz (225 ml) single cream, add 1 clove garlic, crushed, and 8 oz (225 g) cooked peeled shrimps. Add 1–2 tbsp dry white wine and season to taste. Stir into the cooked pasta and serve immediately.

PASTA WITH PRAWN AND VEGETABLE SAUCE

1 lb (500 g) prawns, heads removed

1 green pepper

4 tinned tomatoes

¹/₂ celery stalk

1 small carrot

¹/₂ onion

2 cloves garlic

3¹/₂ fl oz (100 ml) olive oil

3¹/₂ fl oz (100 ml) dry white wine

ground ginger

14 oz (400 g) pasta shapes (e.g. quills)

3¹/₂ fl oz (100 ml) single cream

6–8 basil leaves (or pinch dried basil)

salt and pepper

Grill the pepper, turning very frequently, to loosen the skin; peel and cut into thin strips. Seed the tomatoes and chop coarsely. Chop the carrot, celery, onion and garlic very finely and sweat in the oil for 10 minutes in a covered saucepan. Add the white wine and cook until it has evaporated. Add the green pepper, tomatoes, peeled prawns and a pinch of ginger. Season with salt and freshly ground pepper and simmer slowly for 5 minutes, stirring well.

Cook the pasta until just tender in a large saucepan of boiling salted water; drain well and mix with cream; turn into a deep, heated serving bowl and gently stir in the prawn sauce and the coarsely chopped fresh basil leaves. Serve at once.

FRENCH PRAWN SOUP

10 oz (300 g) prawns

3¹/₂ oz (100 g) rice (preferably short-grain risotto rice)

1³/₄ pints (1 litre) fish stock (fumet) (see page 39)

3¹/₂ oz (100 g) butter

¹/₂ onion

¹/₂ carrot

14 fl oz (400 ml) dry white wine

1 tbsp brandy

7 fl oz (200 ml) single cream

salt and white pepper

Bring the fish stock to the boil in a fireproof casserole dish, sprinkle in the rice, cover tightly, and place in a preheated oven at 350°F (180°C) mark 4 for 40 minutes or until the rice is very tender, having absorbed all the stock.

Sweat the onion, sliced wafer-thin, and the finely chopped carrot in 2 oz (50 g) of the butter. If raw prawns are used, boil gently for 4–5 minutes in lightly salted water, drain, reserving the liquid, and peel. If cooked unpeeled prawns are used, boil the shells and strain. Add the prawns to the onion and carrot mixture, pour in the brandy and cook until evaporated. Add some of the reserved cooking liquid and simmer for 20 minutes. Season with salt and pepper; liquidize with the rice until very smooth. Pour into another saucepan; reheat, stirring in the remaining cooking liquid to make up 1¹/₂ pints (800 ml) soup.

Beat in the remaining butter a small piece at a time and stir in the cream; do not allow the soup to boil after you have added it.

Note: Garnish with thin lemon slices.

PRAWN VERMICELLI

16 king prawns

3 tbsp olive oil

1 bay leaf

3 shallots

1 clove garlic

1 small bunch parsley

3 oz (80 g) tuna

2 tbsp brandy

¹/₂ chilli pepper

1 lb (500 g) tinned tomatoes

3¹/₂ fl oz (100 ml) dry white wine

3¹/₂ fl oz (100 ml) vegetable stock

14 oz (400 g) vermicelli

salt

If the prawns are raw, add to boiling salted water and cook for 2 minutes. Drain and peel. Add 10 of the prawns to the oil in a large saucepan and sauté with the bay leaf and a pinch of salt. Finely chop the shallots, garlic and parsley and add to the saucepan. Add the well drained, flaked tuna and stir gently. Pour in the brandy, add a little crumbled chilli pepper and the tomatoes. Cover and simmer for 35 minutes. Chop the remaining prawns finely and sauté in 2 tbsp oil. Add the wine and vegetable stock, cook for 10 minutes, then stir into the large saucepan.

Cook the vermicelli until just tender in plenty of boiling salted water; drain well, transfer quickly to a warmed tureen or serving bowl and mix with the sauce.

SHRIMP BROTH

1¹/₄ lb (600 g) raw shrimps or small prawns
1 shallot
1 carrot
1 celery stalk
1 bay leaf
1 small bunch chives
2 tbsp lemon juice
ground coriander
1 large spring onion
salt and white peppercorns

Rinse and peel the shrimps or prawns (see page 17). Boil the heads and shells hard in a saucepan containing 1³/₄ pints (1 litre) water for 15 minutes, together with the peeled and quartered shallot, carrot and celery. Add the bay leaf, a few peppercorns and some chives and continue boiling for another 10 minutes. Strain this broth, discarding the shrimp shells and vegetables, and return to the rinsed saucepan. Bring back to the boil and add the shrimps and the lemon juice. Simmer for 5 minutes; season to taste with salt,

freshly ground white pepper and a pinch of coriander, then ladle into warmed soup bowls; decorate with thinly sliced rounds of spring onion.

CREAM OF SHRIMP SOUP

1 lb (500 g) very small shrimps
2 carrots
2 onions
1 oz (25 g) butter
2 fl oz (50 ml) brandy
7 fl oz (200 ml) dry white wine
1³/₄ pints (1 litre) fish stock (fumet) *(see page 39)*
1 tbsp tomato purée
1 bouquet garni
3¹/₂ fl oz (100 ml) single cream
few chives
salt and pepper

Buy the freshest shrimps possible. Cook for 3 minutes, drain and peel.

Dice the carrots and onions; gently heat the butter in a large saucepan, add the shrimps, carrots and onions. Cook, stirring, over a low heat for 5 minutes; pour in the brandy and simmer for 9 minutes.

Add the fish stock and the white wine, the tomato purée and bouquet garni and season with salt and pepper. Cover and simmer very slowly for 30 minutes.

Remove and discard the bouquet garni, remove and reserve 12 shrimps and liquidize the contents of the saucepan. Reheat in a clean saucepan, add the cream and reserved shrimps and bring to the boil, stirring continuously. Season to taste with salt or pepper. Add the finely chopped chives (if unavailable, use parsley) and serve at once.

PRAWN CONSOMMÉ

24 king prawns

2 leeks

1 celery stalk

1 carrot

2 shallots

4 oz (100 g) mushrooms

butter

olive oil

1 clove garlic

1 onion

1 bouquet garni

1 tsp tomato purée

7 fl oz (200 ml) dry white wine

3½ fl oz (100 ml) port

1½ tbsp chopped parsley

salt and cayenne pepper

Trim and rinse the leeks thoroughly. Chop them, and the celery, carrot and mushrooms into very small pieces; sauté together in 1 oz (25 g) butter and 2 tbsp olive oil for 5 minutes in a large saucepan. Add 2¾ pints (1½ litres) hot water, the whole peeled garlic clove, onion and the bouquet garni; bring to the boil and cook for 25 minutes.

Remove and discard the onion, garlic and bouquet garni. Cook the prawns in boiling salted water for 5 minutes if raw, then drain. Peel.

Pound the heads and shells roughly and place in a deep pan with the tomato purée, the white wine, port, salt and pinch of cayenne pepper. Stir well and boil for 15 minutes. Strain and add to the vegetable broth in the saucepan. Add the prawns and bring to the boil.

Remove from the heat and add a little salt if needed. Pour into a warmed soup tureen, sprinkle with the parsley and serve very hot.

LOBSTER BISQUE

1 lobster weighing 3¼–3½ lb (1½ kg)

2 tbsp olive oil

1 oz (25 g) butter

7 fl oz (200 ml) brandy

1 carrot

2 shallots

1 celery stalk

1 onion

1 clove garlic

few sprigs parsley

1 bouquet garni

3 tbsp tomato purée

1¼ pints (750 ml) fish stock (fumet) (see page 39)

9 fl oz (250 ml) dry white wine

2 tbsp potato flour

2 egg yolks

3 fl oz (75 ml) double cream

salt and pepper

Use a cleaver or very sharp, heavy kitchen knife to cut the raw lobster in pieces, shell and all. Discard the stomach sac (found in the 'head') and transfer the lobster, making sure you collect any juices released, to a large saucepan containing the very hot oil and butter, together with the creamy liver and coral, if any. Sauté until the flesh has turned opaque and the shell is red.

Drain off the cooking juices, oil and butter and reserve; heat 2 fl oz (50 ml) of the brandy, pour over the lobster and flame. When the flames have subsided, return the reserved cooking juices, etc., to the saucepan, add all the vegetables and the parsley, finely chopped, the bouquet garni, the tomato purée mixed with the hot fish stock and the wine. Add a little salt and freshly ground white pepper, cover and simmer for 20 minutes. Allow to cool a little. Remove the lobster pieces from the saucepan, extract all the flesh and set aside. Place the pieces of lobster shell and the slightly cooled contents of the saucepan in a large blender (or blend in several batches) and process at length until the shells have totally disintegrated and blended with the liquid. Strain through a very fine sieve. Mix the potato flour with the lightly beaten eggs and the cream (potato flour is available at good delicatessens; if unavailable, use 1 large sieved boiled floury potato). Bring the soup back to the boil; draw aside from the heat and stir in the egg and cream mixture. Heat very gently while stirring continuously; do not allow to boil. Cut the lobster flesh into small pieces; place in a bowl, pour the remaining brandy over them; place an equal number of these in heated soup plates and ladle the hot soup over them.

LOBSTER SOUP

1 lobster weighing approx. 1¹/₂ lb (700 g)
1 onion
1 carrot
1 celery stalk
7 fl oz (200 ml) dry white wine
1 bouquet garni
2 oz (50 g) butter
3 shallots
3¹/₂ fl oz (100 ml) brandy
1¹/₂ oz (40 g) plain flour
3 ripe tomatoes
1 small bunch chives
salt and peppercorns

Tie the lobster before cooking, if wished, as shown on page 15. Bring 3¹/₂ pints (2 litres) water to the boil in a very large saucepan with the peeled and quartered onion, carrot, celery, the white wine, bouquet garni, 2 tsp coarse sea salt and a few peppercorns; boil for 15 minutes. Add the lobster and cook for 30 minutes. Leave to cool in the liquid, drain, take all the flesh out of the shell, slicing this into fairly thick steaks (medallions),

and chopping the flesh from the claws. Strain the cooking liquid.

Sweat the finely chopped shallots in the butter in a large saucepan or deep pan. Add the chopped claw meat and fry briskly, stirring and turning. Sprinkle with the brandy and flame. Blend the flour into 7 fl oz (200 ml) of the strained stock and add to the pan; stir well as it heats through and thickens. Add the tomatoes, followed by 15 fl oz (450 ml) more of the stock. Simmer gently, uncovered, for 15 minutes.

Allow to cool a little; process in the liquidizer or food processor until very smooth. Reheat, add salt and freshly ground white pepper if needed, and the medallions of lobster meat. When nearly boiling, serve in individual bowls sprinkled with chopped chives.

Note: Serve with crisply toasted French bread, if wished.

PASTA WITH MANTIS SHRIMP

20 mantis shrimp
6 tbsp olive oil
juice of 1 lemon
3 tbsp finely chopped parsley
1 clove garlic (optional)
14 oz (400 g) spaghetti
salt and pepper

If you cannot buy fresh or frozen mantis shrimp use Dublin Bay prawns instead. Wash the mantis shrimp well, boil for 3 minutes in a little lightly salted water; leave to cool in the water. Drain (strain and reserve the cooking liquid), remove from their shells as shown on page 18, and arrange on a large, fairly deep plate. (If precooked crustaceans are purchased, simply peel and arrange on the plate.)

Prepare the dressing: beat the oil, strained lemon juice, parsley, peeled crushed garlic clove, salt and freshly ground pepper. Sprinkle over the crustaceans and leave to marinate.

161

Cook the spaghetti until just tender in a large saucepan containing the reserved cooking liquid, topped up with water and adding a little more salt. Drain well; drain off the marinade from the mantis shrimp into the saucepan containing the spaghetti, stir well for a few seconds over a moderate heat, turn into a large, heated serving dish and surround with the mantis shrimp. Serve at once.

SHELLFISH RISOTTO

1½ lb (700 g) mixed shellfish (e.g. small crabs [softshell if available], prawns or Dublin Bay prawns)
1 carrot
1 celery stalk
½ onion
1 bay leaf
few sprigs parsley
2 fl oz (50 ml) olive oil
1 oz (25 g) butter
1 onion
8 fl oz (225 ml) dry white wine
10 oz (300 g) short-grain risotto rice (e.g. arborio)
salt and peppercorns

Vary your choice of shellfish according to personal preference or availability. Peel or shuck (with the exception of softshell crabs which are trimmed in a special way) and chop the flesh. Place all the shells and heads in a large saucepan with 2¾ pints (1½ litres) water, the peeled and coarsely chopped vegetables (use ½ onion, reserving the whole one), bay leaf, parsley, salt and a few peppercorns. Boil for 30 minutes; strain and keep very hot.

Heat the oil and butter in a heavy-bottomed saucepan; when the butter starts to foam, add the finely sliced whole onion, followed by the meat from the crustaceans. Sauté for a few minutes, then add the wine. Simmer for 5 minutes, sprinkle in the rice; add 4 fl oz (125 ml) of the hot strained stock; cook until this has been absorbed by the rice, then add another 4 fl oz (125 ml) stock. Keep

cooking until the rice is tender, adding more stock; if you use Italian arborio rice (the best for risottos) it will absorb a lot of liquid. Serve with a little bit of extra butter stirred into the risotto when cooked.

SEAFOOD PANCAKES WITH SMOKED SALMON SAUCE

1 small crawfish
1 lb (500 g) mixed Dublin Bay prawns and small prawns
5 oz (150 g) butter
5 tbsp plain flour
brandy
2 eggs
4 oz (100 g) smoked salmon
14 fl oz (400 ml) single cream
salt and pepper

Prepare and cook the crawfish (see page 15) and remove the flesh from the shell. Rinse the prawns if uncooked and sauté for 5–6 minutes in 3 oz (80 g) of the butter in a large pan. Peel. (If precooked prawns are used, do not cook in the butter, simply peel them.) Chop all the meat from all the crustaceans fairly coarsely and return to the pan (if cooked prawns are used, add 2 oz [50 g] butter now and 2 tbsp water). Heat through, then stir in 1½ tbsp of the flour; add the brandy, salt and pepper and cook for 10 minutes, stirring.

Make a thin batter with the beaten eggs, combined with the remaining flour, 7 fl oz (200 ml) cold water, salt and pepper. Leave to stand for ½ hour. Heat a little butter in a small, non-stick pan or special omelette pan. Pour in a little batter, and tilt the pan gently. Cook over a moderate heat until golden underneath, then turn and cook the other side. Repeat until all the batter has been used up.

Spoon a little of the seafood mixture on to each pancake and fold to enclose this filling. Place the filled pancakes in a large, shallow ovenproof dish, greased with butter, and heat through for 8–10 minutes at 400°F (200°C) mark 6 in a preheated oven.

Process the cream and chopped smoked salmon together briefly in the liquidizer; heat the resulting sauce to just below boiling point; pour over the hot pancakes, and serve at once.

DUMPLINGS WITH PRAWN FILLING

20 peeled Dublin Bay prawns
5 tbsp sherry
pinch Chinese (or mild Indian) curry powder
2 cloves garlic
10 oz (300 g) plain flour
2 eggs
soy sauce
salt and pepper

Place the Dublin Bay prawns in a bowl; sprinkle with the sherry and add the curry powder, peeled and chopped garlic cloves, a pinch of salt and a little freshly ground white pepper. Marinate for 1 hour.

Sift the flour into a mound in a large mixing bowl or on to a pastry board. Make a well in the middle; break the eggs into it and add a pinch of salt. Beat the eggs very briefly with a fork, then use your slightly cupped hand or a wooden spoon to stir them gently round and round, gradually incorporating the flour. Add a little cold water if necessary to make a smooth, elastic dough, easy to roll out on a floured working surface. Roll out into a thin sheet with a floured rolling pin. Use a fluted or plain round pastry cutter (about 3 in [8 cm] in diameter) to cut into circles; cover these discs with a clean cloth to prevent them from drying out. Drain the prawns thoroughly, chop finely, and place about 1 tsp on each disc; fold the discs in half, enclosing the filling; press closed along the edges of the semicircles, moistening a very little to make them adhere better.

Boil the dumplings in a large saucepan of boiling salted water, or steam for about 20 minutes. Drain well and sprinkle with a little light soy sauce. Serve at once.

PRAWN SOUP WITH LEMON AND VODKA

1 lb (500 g) Dublin Bay prawns, in the shell
2 shallots
1 clove garlic
2 fl oz (50 ml) olive oil
2 lemons
9 fl oz (250 ml) dry white wine
7 fl oz (200 ml) sieved tomatoes
1 tbsp tomato purée
10 fl oz (300 ml) fish stock (fumet) (see page 39)
7 fl oz (200 ml) single cream
1 oz (25 g) butter
1 oz (25 g) plain flour
pinch sugar
2 tbsp vodka
salt and cayenne pepper

Chop the peeled shallots and garlic very finely. Peel the prawns (see page 16) and split in half lengthways down the middle. Pound all the heads and shells thoroughly and add to the oil, ready heated in a saucepan with the shallot and garlic mixture. Fry gently, stirring, for 5 minutes. Add the juice of the lemons and the white wine and boil hard, uncovered, for 6 minutes. Strain into another saucepan; add the sieved tomatoes and the tomato purée, the hot fish stock and the cream. Cover and simmer for 10 minutes. Knead or mix the butter with the flour and half the grated lemon rind; add this *beurre manié* in small pieces to the soup and stir over a gentle heat until the soup thickens a little. Add the prawns, a pinch of cayenne pepper, salt, a pinch of sugar and the vodka and simmer for a further 5 minutes. Ladle into a warmed tureen or individual soup plates and sprinkle with the remaining finely grated lemon rind.

Note: Garnish with lemon slices or chopped chives, if wished.

PRAWN AND OYSTER SOUP

16 Dublin Bay prawns (scampi)

3¹/₂ oz (100 g) butter

olive oil

3 carrots

1 onion

18 fl oz (500 ml) dry white wine

5 fl oz (150 ml) single cream

24 oysters

1 leek

12 baby onions

1 sprig chervil

salt and pepper

Peel the prawns (see page 16) and pound the heads (if sold with the heads on) and shells; fry gently in 1 oz (25 g) of the butter and 2 tbsp oil in a saucepan with a peeled diced carrot and sliced onion. Season with salt and pepper, stir well, cover and cook gently for 10 minutes. Add 12 fl oz (350 ml) water and continue cooking for 30 minutes. Strain into another saucepan; add the white wine and boil hard until reduced by a quarter in volume. Add the cream and simmer for 5 minutes, stirring continuously. Turn the heat down as low as possible and use a balloon whisk to beat in the remaining butter, adding a small piece at a time. Draw aside from the heat.

Open the oysters (see page 22), reserving and straining all their juice into a small saucepan. Boil this liquid until reduced by half.

Wash and prepare the remaining carrots and the leek; slice into very thin matchstick strips. Blanch for 3 minutes in boiling salted water; drain. Peel the baby onions and boil in salted water for 15 minutes. Drain.

Steam the prawns for 6 minutes if raw. Heat the oysters in their reduced juice for a few seconds only. Add all the vegetables, the juice in which the oysters have been heated and salt and pepper to the soup; reheat, without boiling; add the prawns and oysters and serve without delay, sprinkled with chopped chervil.

CRAWFISH SOUP

1 crawfish weighing approx. 1³/₄ lb (800 g)

1 shallot

2 oz (50 g) butter

16 black olives

1–2 tbsp pine nuts

10 fl oz (300 ml) sieved tomatoes

1 bay leaf

1 onion

2 celery stalks

1 small bunch parsley

1 lemon

8 thick slices coarse white or French bread

salt and pepper

Extract the meat from the crawfish tail in one piece and slice across into 8 steaks. Chop the peeled shallot finely and fry in the butter; add the pitted olives, pine nuts, sieved tomato and bay leaf, and season with salt and freshly ground pepper. Cook, stirring occasionally, for 20 minutes. Meanwhile, chop the shell into fairly large pieces and boil for 20 minutes in 1¹/₂ pints (900 ml) water with the chopped onion and celery, a slice of lemon and a few sprigs of parsley. Strain the resulting stock and stir into the tomato mixture; add the crawfish pieces and the remaining, finely chopped parsley. Simmer for 10–20 minutes, uncovered. When the sauce has thickened considerably turn off the heat and leave to stand for 1 minute before serving with the crisp, oven-toasted slices of bread.

RICE TIMBALÉS WITH CRAWFISH SAUCE

1 crawfish weighing approx. 1¹/₂ lb (700 g)

5 oz (150 g) short-grain risotto rice (e.g. arborio)

3 onions
1 bouquet garni
1 celery stalk
14 fl oz (400 ml) dry white wine
butter
1 sachet real saffron powder
1 tbsp plain flour
18 fl oz (500 ml) single cream
tomato ketchup
salt and white peppercorns

Remove the crawfish's head; remove the undershell, following the same method as given for mantis shrimp on page 16 and extract the flesh; chop into fairly small pieces (remove the black alimentary canal thread first, which runs down the centre of the back). Place the shell and head, etc., in a large saucepan with 1 onion, bouquet garni, celery, salt and a few peppercorns, 7 fl oz (200 ml) of the wine and 18 fl oz (500 ml) water. Boil for about 1 hour; strain through a fine sieve.

Peel and finely chop one of the remaining onions, sweat with 1 oz (25 g) of the butter until transparent, add the rice and continue cooking for a minute, stirring. Sprinkle in 3½ fl oz (100 ml) of the wine and cook until it has evaporated.

Stir the saffron into 10 fl oz (300 ml) of the hot, strained stock and add to the rice. Bring to the boil, cover tightly, and place in a preheated oven at 350°F (180°C) mark 4 to cook for 16–17 minutes (or until the rice has absorbed all the moisture without becoming dry).

Sauté the third, peeled and finely chopped onion in 1½ oz (40 g) butter; add the crawfish pieces and continue cooking over a higher heat. Sprinkle evenly with 1 tbsp flour, season with salt and freshly ground pepper and add the remaining wine and cook until it has almost completely evaporated. Lower the heat, stir in the cream and 1 tbsp tomato ketchup; cover and keep hot.

Fill four 8-fl oz (225-ml) capacity timbale moulds or ramekins with rice, pressing down firmly without crushing the grains. Place in a very hot oven for 2 minutes, then turn out on to individual heated plates. Surround with the crawfish mixture and serve at once.

CATALAN ZARZUELA

1 lb (500 g) mussels in the shell
14 oz (400 g) cuttlefish or squid
12 Dublin Bay prawns
1 crawfish
14 oz (400 g) hake
10 oz (300 g) eel
2 onions
2 cloves garlic
3½ fl oz (100 ml) olive oil
10 oz (300 g) tinned tomatoes
2 red peppers
1 small bunch parsley
7 fl oz (200 ml) dry white wine
4 oz (100 g) small black olives, stoned
1 sachet real saffron powder
salt and pepper

Leave the mussels to stand in cold salted water for 2–3 hours. Prepare and clean the cuttlefish or squid (see page 20) and cut them into strips. Peel the prawns and remove the black thread or intestinal tract which runs down their backs. Cut the raw crawfish tail into steaks, slicing through the shell at the joints. Scrub and prepare the mussels, removing all beards and barnacles. Discard any that do not close when tapped sharply. Prepare and clean the hake (see page 10, top left) and the eel (see page 11). Peel and finely chop the onions and garlic and fry gently in the oil in a very large, deep casserole dish. Add the chopped tomatoes, the peppers, cut into thin strips, and the chopped parsley. Cook for a few minutes before adding all the seafood. Add the wine, season with plenty of freshly ground pepper and a little salt; mix the saffron with 2 fl oz (50 ml) hot water and add.

Cover and cook for 20 minutes once the liquid has reached a gentle simmer. Add the stoned olives and cook for a few minutes more. Serve straight from the casserole. Serves 6–8.

PAELLA

8 Dublin Bay prawns
1¹/₄ lb (600 g) baby cuttlefish
8 small clams, in the shell
8 dog cockles, in the shell
16 mussels, in the shell
1 small chicken
3 onions
2 celery stalks
3–4 cloves garlic
1 leek
1 bouquet garni
1 tbsp paprika
3 peppers (2 red, 1 yellow)
8 oz (225 g) chorizos (Spanish sausages)
8 ripe tomatoes
8 oz (225 g) frozen peas
9 oz (250 g) rice
4 tbsp olive oil
1 sachet real saffron powder
salt and peppercorns

Joint the chicken into 8 pieces, taking the breast meat off the bone. Reserve. Break the backbone and place the carcass in a large saucepan with the peeled, quartered onion, the celery, the unpeeled garlic cloves, leek, bouquet garni, paprika, salt and a few peppercorns. Add enough water to cover and bring slowly to the boil, removing all the scum that rises to the surface with a slotted ladle or spoon. Simmer for 1 hour.

Peel and chop the remaining onions; slice the peppers into strips. Slice the chorizos into thick rounds. Prepare the baby cuttlefish or squid (see page 20). Place in a saucepan with just enough water to cover, bring to the boil, drain immediately, and rinse in a sieve under running cold water. Cut into thin strips. Blanch, peel and roughly chop the tomatoes.

Heat the oil, preferably in a special iron or stainless steel paella pan (or very wide pan which can go in the oven). Add the well drained chicken pieces and fry for 15 minutes or until done, turning so that they brown all over; set aside on a plate. Add the chorizo slices to the oil in the pan and fry lightly; add the onion, peppers and cuttlefish or squid. Cook over a moderate heat for a few minutes. Add the tomatoes and cook until most of their juices have evaporated.

Add the rice, stir well and return the chicken pieces to the pan. Add the cleaned and prepared seafood, followed by the peas. Mix the saffron into 1 pint 2 fl oz (625 ml) of the hot strained chicken stock and pour over the rice. Season with salt and pepper. Bring to the boil, cover tightly (use foil if necessary) and place in the oven, preheated to 425°F (220°C) mark 7, to cook for 25 minutes. Turn off the oven and leave the paella in it for a further 5 minutes.

Paella is traditionally served from its pan, the word originally meaning a pot. Serves 6–8.

PRAWNS À L'AMÉRICAINE

1³/₄ lb (800 g) Dublin Bay prawns, in the shell
1 carrot
1 celery stalk
1 large onion
3 tbsp olive oil
3 oz (75 g) butter
1 clove garlic
1 bay leaf
1 sprig thyme
8 fl oz (220 ml) brandy
10 oz (300 g) sieved tomatoes
1 small piece chicken stock cube
plain flour
1 tsp lemon juice
¹/₂ tbsp finely chopped fresh tarragon or parsley
7 fl oz (200 ml) single cream

14 oz (400 g) rice
salt and pepper

This recipe is best made with raw Dublin Bay prawns, but can also be made with cooked, frozen or fresh crustaceans. Rinse the prawns and dry on kitchen paper. Chop the trimmed and washed carrot, celery and the peeled onion very finely and sauté in 1 oz (25 g) butter for 5 minutes in a large saucepan; add the whole peeled clove of garlic, the bay leaf and thyme.

When the contents of the pan start to colour, add the whole prawns, in their shells, and cook briskly for 5 minutes, stirring. Sprinkle with half the brandy, heat through and set alight. Shake the pan gently until the flames die down; stir in the tomatoes and the small piece of stock cube. Bring back to the boil and remove the prawns with a slotted spoon, allowing as much liquid to drain back into the pan as possible.

Boil the rice in salted water until tender; drain and mix with 1 oz (25 g) butter in a heated serving dish. Cover and keep hot. Peel the prawns, while the rice cooks, saving as much of their juices as possible, add this liquid to the contents of the pan and put through the food mill or blend briefly in the food processor. Reheat together with 1 oz (25 g) butter mixed with 1 tsp flour, stirring well. Add the prawns, 1 tsp lemon juice, the tarragon or parsley, the rest of the brandy and the cream.

Bring almost back to the boil, then serve with the rice.

CREOLE CRAB

4 crabs
4 tbsp olive oil
1 onion
1 clove garlic
1 lemon
1 sprig thyme
1 bay leaf
1 chilli pepper

rice
salt

Rinse the crabs under running cold water, stop up any gaps in their shells with compressed bread, and boil in lightly salted water for about 10 minutes depending on size. Drain, detach their claws and remove all the meat from these and their shells (see page 19).

Fry the crabmeat gently in the oil for about 15 minutes; add enough water to just cover. Add the very finely chopped, peeled onion and garlic, lemon juice, thyme, bay leaf and chilli pepper, bring back to the boil, then simmer very slowly for 30 minutes; add salt to taste.

Boil the rice for about 18 minutes. Remove and discard the chilli pepper, thyme and bay leaf from the crab mixture. Stir in the rice and serve very hot.

CRAB SALAD WITH BEAN SPROUTS

1 king crab or large Dungeness or common crab weighing 2¼–2½ lb (1 kg)
2 carrots
2 celery stalks
3 shallots
1 onion
1 leek
5 sprigs parsley
20 white peppercorns
18 fl oz (500 ml) dry white wine
1 clove
5 oz (150 g) rice
5 oz (150 g) button mushrooms
½ lemon
4 oz (100 g) bean sprouts
2 ripe tomatoes
soy sauce

167

mint leaves

salt and peppercorns

Wash, trim and prepare all the vegetables. Chop all except the mushrooms, bean sprouts and tomatoes into small pieces. Place in a saucepan with the white wine, 1³/₄ pints (1 litre) water, 6 peppercorns, the clove and 1 tbsp salt. Cover and boil for 30 minutes. Meanwhile, cook the rice in boiling salted water for 18 minutes; drain, rinse under running cold water and drain thoroughly. Wipe the mushrooms with a damp cloth, slice thinly, and sprinkle with the lemon juice; mix well.

Cook the crab in the vegetable broth for 15 minutes; drain, then open and extract all the flesh (and from the claws if using a Dungeness or common crab) discarding the gills and intestines. Rinse the bean sprouts, discard any empty green seed cases; cut the tomatoes into quarters.

Mix the rice in a bowl with the crabmeat, mushrooms, bean sprouts and tomatoes. Dress with 3 tbsp soy sauce and a little freshly ground pepper. Decorate with mint leaves and serve.

TEMPURA

2 fillets of summer flounder
12 king prawns or very large prawns, peeled but tail fan left on
1 egg yolk
4 oz (120 g) plain flour
12 fresh or frozen asparagus tips or spears about 1¹/₂ in (4 cm) long
8 large spring onions
1 large aubergine
1 large carrot
7 fl oz (200 ml) oil
cornflour or plain flour
salt
assorted Japanese hot (peppery) sauces

The ideal way to enjoy this dish is to have an efficient fondue set, so that each person can fry their own selection of foods at the table, but you can also cook Tempura conventionally in the kitchen. Provided the items are freshly fried and not kept waiting, they will still be delicious.

The lightness of the batter is most important: beat the egg yolk in a bowl, beat in 8 fl oz (225 ml) iced water, adding a little at a time to blend thoroughly. Pour all the flour into the bowl at once and beat just enough to make sure that all the flour is moistened. Do not overbeat: it does not matter if there are a few lumps and prolonged beating would make the batter much less light and delicate. Chill in the refrigerator for 1 hour.

Prepare, rinse, and dry the asparagus and prawns; cut the flounder into short, thin strips. Trim the onions and cut lengthwise in half. Cut the trimmed and peeled carrot and the aubergine into small slices just under ¹/₄ in (¹/₂ cm) thick. Thread an assortment of all these ingredients on to bamboo skewers or satay sticks, dust lightly with cornflour or ordinary flour and place on a plate, ready for cooking. Heat the deep-fryer to 325°F (180°C) mark 4 (if frying at the table, test for temperature, by dropping a small cube of bread into the oil: if bubbles immediately form all round the cube and it starts to cook at once, the oil is ready). Have steamed rice and a selection of sauces in small bowls by each person's table setting.

Take the batter out of the refrigerator at the last minute; the colder it is, the lighter the batter. Each person dips a skewer into the batter and fries his selection of food. (The onions and asparagus will take about 5–6 minutes to cook; the fish fillets, prawns and aubergine about 2 minutes.)

CRAWFISH BORDELAISE

1 crawfish weighing 2¹/₄–2¹/₂ lb (1 kg)
2 tbsp olive oil
2 oz (50 g) butter
2 fl oz (50 ml) good brandy

1 onion
1 carrot
1 small white celery heart
2 cloves garlic
2 shallots
11 fl oz (325 ml) good red Bordeaux wine
2 tbsp tomato purée
1 bouquet garni
few sprigs parsley
8 triangles white bread
salt and pepper

A live crawfish is traditional for this dish. Use a cleaver or sharp, heavy kitchen knife to cut off the head and slice the body into 'steaks', cutting through the shell where the rings are jointed together. Remove and discard the black intestinal tract and the sand sac or stomach (found in the head). Crush the thin legs, collecting the juice which runs out and place in a bowl, together with the liver; reserve the coral if you have a hen (female) crawfish.

Heat 2 tbsp oil in a large, deep pan with 1 oz (25 g) butter; add the slices of crawfish (still in the shell) and fry briskly until the shell is red. Transfer to a very hot flameproof dish, pour the heated brandy over them, and flame.

Add the cleaned, prepared and finely chopped vegetables to the oil, butter and juices left in the pan and fry gently till tender, then pour in the wine, the juice from the lobster, tomato purée, bouquet garni, salt and freshly ground pepper. Simmer for 15 minutes, discard the bouquet garni, and liquidize the sauce. Return to the pan and add the crawfish pieces; cook gently for 10 minutes. Weigh the coral if present, then weigh out an equal amount of butter softened at room temperature and work the coral into it; add 2 tbsp of the sauce from the pan and mix well, then stir into the saucepan. Cook over the lowest possible heat for 10 minutes more.

Serve the crawfish pieces coated with sauce and surrounded by small triangles or shapes of bread, toasted or lightly fried in butter.

SWEET AND SOUR CRAWFISH

1 crawfish weighing 2¼–2½ lb (1 kg)
18 fl oz (500 ml) dry white wine
2 carrots
2 celery stalks
1 onion
1 bouquet garni
2 shallots
1½ oz (40 g) butter
3 tbsp oil
7 fl oz (200 ml) sparkling white wine
14 oz (400 g) ripe tomatoes
1 tsp sugar
salt and peppercorns

Make the *court-bouillon* in which to cook the lobster with the white wine, all the vegetables except the shallots (prepared and cut in pieces), the bouquet garni, 1½ tsp coarse sea salt, a few peppercorns and water. Prepare the crawfish as shown on page 15, add to the boiling *court-bouillon*, and cook gently for about 30 minutes. Drain well and when slightly cooler, cut lengthwise down the middle. Remove the flesh carefully, reserving the shells.

Peel and finely chop the shallots, fry in 1½ oz (40 g) butter and 3 tbsp oil; add the sparkling wine and reduce by half; blanch, peel and seed the tomatoes, chop and add to the pan. Boil for 10 minutes, uncovered, to reduce and thicken, and season with salt and pepper. Add the sugar, simmer for 10 minutes more, then add the crawfish flesh (still in two halves). Stir gently while cooking in the sauce for 5 minutes.

Use 2 slotted fish slices or similar to remove the lobster halves from the sauce and replace them in the half shells, on a heated serving plate. Coat them with a little sauce and serve the rest in a sauceboat.

Note: Serve with a mixed salad.

CRAWFISH À L'AMÉRICAINE

1 crawfish weighing 2¹/₄–2¹/₂ lb (1 kg)

2 tbsp olive oil

4¹/₂ oz (120 g) butter

3¹/₂ fl oz (100 ml) brandy

6 shallots

7 fl oz (200 ml) dry white wine

7 fl oz (200 ml) fish stock (fumet) (see page 39)

4 fresh or tinned tomatoes

1 sprig tarragon

1 tbsp finely chopped parsley

salt and pepper

Buy a live crawfish if possible and kill it. Chop into fairly large pieces, shell and all, collecting and reserving the juices. Discard the sand sac and remove the alimentary tract; reserve the greenish tomalley (the liver) and the coral, if any.

Fry the crawfish pieces briskly, stirring in 1 oz (30 g) butter until their shell has turned bright orange-red. Drain off excess butter and pour in the brandy; heat and flame.

Peel and finely chop the shallots, sweat in 1¹/₂ oz (40 g) butter in a wide, fairly deep pan or sauteuse; add the white wine and continue cooking until this has evaporated. Add the crawfish pieces, their reserved juice and the hot fish stock. Add the blanched, peeled, seeded and chopped tomatoes and the sprig of tarragon. Simmer for 15 minutes. Work the coral into 2 oz (50 g) butter softened at room temperature. Remove the crawfish pieces with a slotted spoon or ladle and place in a heated serving dish. Discard the tarragon.

Add the coral butter to the sauce in the pan, stir gently as the butter melts, and add the chopped parsley. Season to taste with salt and freshly ground pepper, pour over the crawfish and serve at once.

LOBSTER THERMIDOR

1 lobster weighing 2¹/₄–2¹/₂ lb (1 kg)

3¹/₂ fl oz (100 ml) white wine vinegar

1 carrot

1 onion

1 celery stalk

1 bouquet garni

3¹/₂ fl oz (100 ml) sherry

7 fl oz (200 ml) fish stock (fumet) (see page 39)

7 fl oz (200 ml) dry white wine

4 tbsp white sauce

1 tsp English mustard powder or French mustard

2 oz (50 g) freshly grated Parmesan cheese

butter

salt and peppercorns

Prepare the lobster for cooking as shown on page 15. Make a *court-bouillon* with 3¹/₂ pints (2 litres) water, the vinegar, prepared vegetables, bouquet garni, 1¹/₂ tsp coarse sea salt and a few peppercorns. Bring to the boil, add the lobster and cook over a moderate heat for 20 minutes; drain, cut lengthwise in half, take the flesh from each half, and reserve the shells; extract the meat from the claws. Cut the meat into small pieces, place in a saucepan and add the sherry; cook over a very low heat, stirring, until the sherry has evaporated. Reduce the fish *fumet* and wine together in another saucepan to one third of the original volume. Stir in the white sauce and mustard; cook over a low heat, beating with a balloon whisk.

Pour half the sauce carefully into the empty lobster shells on a hot fireproof serving plate, fill the shells with the lobster pieces and coat with the remaining sauce. Sprinkle with the grated cheese, dot a few flakes of butter on top and place under the grill at medium heat for a minute or two.

170

CRAWFISH FLAMBÉ

2 crawfish or lobsters weighing approx. 1¹/₄ lb (600 g) each

butter

brandy

salt and pepper

Rinse the crawfish or lobsters under running cold water; dry with kitchen paper and cut lengthwise in half, using a very strong, heavy kitchen knife. Remove the sand sac in the head and the black thread running down the back (the intestinal tract). Season with salt and freshly ground pepper and generously brush all over the cut surface with melted butter. Place the lobsters, cut side uppermost, in the grill pan and grill for 20 minutes, turning twice and brushing frequently with more melted butter.

Place on a very hot serving plate, heat 3 tbsp brandy, pour over the crawfish or lobsters and set alight. Place on the table while still flaming.

LORD NELSON'S LOBSTER

1 lobster or crawfish weighing 2¹/₄–2¹/₂ lb (1 kg)

3¹/₂ oz (100 g) butter

8 oysters

6 tinned anchovy fillets

1¹/₂ oz (40 g) fine breadcrumbs

olive oil

salt and pepper

Buy a live lobster, preferably, for this recipe but a fresh or frozen cooked lobster will be almost as good. Split the lobster lengthwise in half with a very sharp, heavy kitchen knife; remove the sandy sac in the head and the black intestinal tract which runs down the back. Preheat the oven to 350°F

(180°C) mark 4 and place the lobster halves, cut side uppermost, in a heatproof dish; season with salt and plenty of freshly ground pepper, dot the surface with half the butter, in small pieces, and cook for 20 minutes. The lobster can also be grilled (have the grill at medium heat).

While the lobster is cooking, prepare the oysters: scrub under running cold water, open (see page 22), and take out the molluscs, reserving all their juice and straining it into a bowl; stir in the breadcrumbs, finely chopped anchovies and a very little olive oil; mix thoroughly into a spreadable mixture.

When the lobsters are cooked, take out of the oven, place 4 raw oysters on each cut surface, spread the anchovy mixture all over the top and dot with tiny pieces of the remaining butter. Return to the oven and cook at the same temperature for 10 minutes. Serve very hot.

BARBECUED CRAWFISH

2 crawfish or lobsters weighing 1¹/₄ lb (600 g) each

oil

4 oz (125 g) stale white bread, without the crust

5 tbsp red or white wine vinegar

6 tinned anchovy fillets

3 gherkins or small dill pickles

2 oz (50 g) capers

1 clove garlic

butter

fine dry breadcrumbs

salt and pepper

Use a heavy, sharp kitchen knife or cleaver to cut the crawfish or lobsters lengthwise in half. Remove the sand sac from the head and discard; take out the black alimentary tract which runs down the back.

Have the barbecue ready and glowing hot. (If cooking indoors, use a barbecue-type electric grill or a griddle, at a moderate setting.) Place the crawfish halves, shell side down, on the grid and grill for 15–20 minutes. Brush the surface frequently with oil and turn 2–4 times. When they are nearly done, season with salt and freshly ground pepper.

Crumble the stale bread into a small bowl, add the vinegar, stir and leave to soak; squeeze out excess moisture, then process in the food processor with the well drained anchovies, gherkins or dill pickles, capers and garlic until smooth.

As soon as the crawfish are cooked, spread the mixture over the exposed meat, sprinkle with melted butter, top with the fine dry (or toasted) breadcrumbs and brown under a hot grill for a few minutes.

ORIENTAL CRAB WITH MUSHROOMS

4 oz (100 g) dried Chinese mushrooms
8 small snow crabs or 4 medium-sized crabs
3 tbsp melted pork fat or bacon fat
4 baby onions or spring onions
3 tbsp dry sherry
3¹/₂ fl oz (100 ml) chicken stock
4 egg whites
3 tbsp cornflour
2 tbsp sunflower oil
salt

Soak the Chinese mushrooms in hot water for 1 hour, to soften. Wash the raw, freshly killed (or cooked) crabs under running cold water; remove their claws and legs, crack the claws if present and crush the legs lightly with a hammer or rolling pin; remove all the flesh from the shell and claws, discarding the grey feathery gills and intestines. Heat the fat in a frying pan or wok over a high heat, add the peeled, whole onions or spring onions and stir-fry for a minute or two; add the crabmeat and

the crushed legs (which will release juice as they cook); sprinkle with a little salt and the sherry and keep stir-frying as you add half the chicken stock. Cook for 8–10 minutes. Remove and discard the thin legs, squeezing out their juices into the pan. Beat the egg whites lightly in a bowl; mix the cornflour with 1–2 tbsp cold water, then mix into the remaining chicken broth. Beat into the egg whites. Drain the Chinese mushrooms well, squeeze out excess moisture, and chop roughly. Heat the sunflower oil in a small saucepan and cook the mushrooms for 10 minutes, adding a little salt. Add to the crab mixture and cook, stirring, for 3 minutes. Mix in the beaten egg white mixture, stirring as you add it. Cook for a further 2 minutes; serve at once.

LOBSTER WITH MARSALA

2 lobsters weighing approx. 1¹/₂ lb (700 g) each
3 oz (75 g) butter
brandy
7 fl oz (200 ml) Marsala
7 fl oz (200 ml) single cream
salt and pepper

Cut the heads off the lobsters using a sharp, heavy kitchen knife. Cut the head lengthwise and reserve the coral and tomalley (discard the sand sac, or stomach). Twist off the two large claws where they join the body and crack open but do not extract the meat; sauté the claws briskly in 1 oz (25 g) of the butter and all of the oil. Slice the lobster thickly into medallions, shell and all, cutting where the shell is jointed, and remove the black thread-like alimentary canal running down the lobster's back. Add these to the pan and fry, stirring, until the shell is bright red.

Drain off the fat from the pan; pour in the brandy, heat and flame. Add the Marsala and the cream; lower the heat, season with salt and pepper, cover and simmer slowly for 15 minutes. Arrange the lobster pieces on a heated serving plate, together with the meat extracted from the cooked claws. Cover and keep warm, preferably over hot water, while you melt the remaining butter in a small saucepan with the coral and tomalley (greenish liver); add to the Marsala cream sauce and cook for 1 minute, beating with a fork or small balloon whisk. Pour over the lobsters and serve at once.

LOBSTER WITH MIXED HERBS AND VERMOUTH

2 lobsters weighing 1¼ lb (600 g) each
2 onions
2 shallots
1 leek
1 carrot
1 celery stalk
1 large ripe tomato
2 oz (50 g) butter
3½ fl oz (100 ml) dry white vermouth
9 fl oz (250 ml) single cream
3 tbsp mixed, finely chopped fresh herbs (e.g. parsley, tarragon, chives, chervil, basil)
salt
black and white peppercorns

Bring 7 pints (4 litres) water to a boil in a very large cooking pot or saucepan with the peeled, halved onion, 1½ tsp coarse sea salt and a few black or white peppercorns.

If using a live lobster, prepare for cooking (see page 15) and add to the boiling water. Cook for 25 minutes, then leave to cool in the liquid. Drain and extract the meat from the shells, keeping the meat from one in a single piece (snip away at each side of the undershell as shown for mantis shrimp on page 18).

Wash, prepare and finely chop the remaining vegetables and sweat in half the butter until tender; add the vermouth and cook until it has evaporated. Add the blanched, skinned and seeded tomato cut into strips. Pour in the cream, season with salt and

freshly ground white pepper and simmer gently for 15 minutes.

Cut the lobster flesh into fairly thick slices or medallions. Place the whole lobster shell (minus its underside, which will not show) on an ovenproof serving platter. Make sure the top surface of the shell is dry and arrange the slices of lobster flesh all along the top, overlapping each other slightly (have the larger slices nearer the head and graduate to smaller slices near the tail). Process the sauce in a blender until smooth; return to the pan over a low heat. Knead the butter, softened at room temperature, with the herb mixture (and with the coral if there is any) and stir into the sauce. When almost at boiling point, pour carefully over the line of medallions on the lobster's back and heat in a preheated very hot oven for 4–5 minutes.

LOBSTER WITH APPLES AND CALVADOS

1 lobster or crawfish weighing approx. 2½ lb (1 kg)
1 small carrot
1 leek
1 small onion
3 apples
2½ pints (1.4 litres) dry cider
2 tbsp sultanas, soaked in water
3 tbsp double cream
1½ tbsp Calvados or applejack
2 oz (50 g) unsalted butter
salt and pepper

Use a firm variety of apple that will not disintegrate when cooked. Cut the carrot into small pieces, the leek into rings and chop the onion coarsely; place in a deep, non-metallic saucepan. Remove the core from one apple but do not peel; cut into small pieces and add to the saucepan. Add all but 3½ fl oz (100 ml) of the cider and season with salt and a little freshly ground white or black pepper.

173

Bring to the boil and boil for 2 minutes. If you are using a live crawfish or lobster, add it to the fast boiling liquid now; cover and cook for 10 minutes.

Peel, core and thinly slice the remaining apples and use to cover the bottom of a wide, shallow ovenproof dish. Sprinkle with the well drained sultanas. Spoon half the cream and the remaining cider over the apples. Place in the oven, preheated to 400°F (200°C) mark 6, uncovered, for 10 minutes.

Drain the lobster. Boil the cider stock fast until reduced to about 1 pint (600 ml); draw aside from the heat and when it has cooled a little, liquidize until smooth. Return to the saucepan with the rest of the cream and the Calvados and boil over a moderate heat until it has reduced further and thickened slightly. Remove from heat; beat in the butter a small piece at a time. Add salt and freshly ground pepper to taste.

If you have cooked the lobster in the cider, cut lengthwise in half at this point. If you have bought your lobster ready cooked, place cut sides down on top of the apple slices for their last 5 minutes' baking in the oven to warm through and take up a little of the apple and cider flavour. Remove and discard the small legs and antennae, the stomach sac, spongy gills and intestinal tract. Place each half on a heated plate; arrange the baked apple slices and raisins on top and coat with the sauce. Serves 2 generously.

LOBSTER IN TOMATO SAUCE

2 lobsters weighing approx. 1¹/₂ lb (700 g) each
2 carrots
12 baby onions or spring onions
2 oz (50 g) butter
3 tbsp olive oil
¹/₂ celery stalk
1 shallot
1 leek
7 fl oz (200 ml) dry white wine
4 tbsp sieved tomatoes
1¹/₂ tbsp finely chopped parsley
salt and pepper

Finely chop all the vegetables (use only the white part of the leek for this recipe) except the onions or spring onions. Take the cooked lobster meat out of the shell in one piece (cut open along the underside) and slice into thick slices or medallions; fry in 3 tbsp oil and 1 oz (25 g) butter, turning once or twice, for 5 minutes; remove from the pan and set aside to keep warm. Add the chopped vegetables to the oil, butter and juices in the pan and sweat gently for 4–5 minutes. Pour in the white wine and cook over a slightly higher heat for 5 minutes. Stir in the sieved tomatoes and 10 fl oz (300 ml) water, season with salt and pepper and boil gently, uncovered, for 20 minutes.

Process in a blender until smooth (or sieve), return to the saucepan with the lobster slices, and simmer for 10 minutes. Use a slotted spoon to transfer the medallions to a heated serving dish; boil the sauce hard for a few minutes to thicken slightly and pour over the lobster. Sprinkle with parsley and serve.

PRAWNS IN PINK SAUCE

24 Dublin Bay prawns, in the shell
9 fl oz (250 ml) dry white wine
4 tbsp olive oil
2 cloves garlic
7 fl oz (200 ml) brandy
4 oz tinned tomatoes, drained
7 fl oz (200 ml) single cream
salt and pepper

Raw Dublin Bay prawns are best for this recipe, but you can use cooked ones successfully too, in which case omit the initial cooking stage of this recipe. Remove the heads from the raw prawns and cook for 5 minutes in a saucepan containing 3¹/₂ pints (2 litres) boiling water, the wine, 1¹/₂ tsp coarse sea salt and a few peppercorns. Drain the prawns and peel when cool enough to handle.

Heat the oil in a pan and fry the peeled garlic cloves until pale golden brown, then crush

the cloves with a fork to release the juice and
discard them. Add the prawns (whether freshly
cooked or precooked) to the flavoured oil and heat
through, stirring. Pour in the brandy and allow to
evaporate.

Remove the prawns from the oil with a slotted
spoon and keep warm; add the tomatoes to the
pan and cook over a high heat for a further 10
minutes. Pour in the cream and simmer very gently
for 10 minutes longer, stirring from time to time.
Return the prawns to the pan, stir and serve hot.

SEAFOOD MEDLEY

7 oz (200 g) Dublin Bay prawns
1 crawfish weighing approx. 1¹/₂ lb (700 g)
7 oz (200 g) small octopus
wine vinegar
1 carrot
1 onion
1 celery stalk
1 sprig thyme
1 bay leaf
few sprigs parsley
2 aubergines
olive oil
1 celeriac
7 oz (200 g) baby onions or spring onions
1 clove garlic
1 tsp sugar
12 oz (350 g) ripe tomatoes
1 tbsp capers
plain flour
3 eggs
salt and pepper

Pour 2³/₄ pints (1¹/₂ litres) water into a large
saucepan, add 3¹/₂ fl oz (100 ml) vinegar, the
prepared and quartered carrot, onion, celery stalk,

thyme, bay leaf and a few parsley leaves and bring
to the boil.

Prepare the crawfish for cooking as shown on
page 15 and add to the boiling water; cook for 35
minutes. Turn off the heat, and cool in the liquid.

Slice the aubergines and fry in plenty of very hot
oil in a non-stick frying pan; remove, draining well
and keep hot. Peel and wash the celeriac, cut into
matchstick pieces, and fry in the same oil. Drain
and keep hot. Boil the peeled baby onions in
salted water for 15 minutes then simmer for 30
minutes with ¹/₂ clove garlic (finely chopped), the
sugar, 1 tbsp vinegar, the blanched, peeled and
quartered tomatoes and the capers. Prepare the
octopus (see page 21 for method) and cut into
fairly small pieces, rinse under running cold water,
and dry. Coat lightly with flour and fry briefly in the
hot oil, adding more oil if necessary. Chop the
remaining garlic and parsley.

Drain the crawfish, take the meat out of the shell
and cut into fairly small pieces. Add these and all
the other ingredients to the tomato and onion
sauce; simmer for a few minutes, then leave to
cool. If raw Dublin Bay prawns are used, simmer
for 3–4 minutes in the cooking liquid used for the
crawfish, drain and add to the crawfish mixture.

Transfer the contents of the saucepan to a large,
fairly deep serving plate and serve cold, garnished
with quarters of hard-boiled egg.

PRAWNS NEW ORLEANS STYLE

20 Dublin Bay prawns
4 shallots
2 cloves garlic
1 red pepper
few sprigs parsley
1 small piece fresh horseradish root
2 tbsp tomato ketchup
1 tbsp mild mustard
1 tbsp paprika
3¹/₂ fl oz (200 ml) olive oil
salt

If raw Dublin Bay prawns are used, remove their heads, blanch in boiling salted water for 1 minute, drain and peel. Place the peeled garlic and shallots, the red pepper (stalk, seeds and pale inner membrane removed), the parsley and the peeled and chopped horseradish in the food processor with the ketchup and mustard and process until very smooth.

Arrange the prawns in a single layer in a shallow ovenproof dish; sprinkle them with the oil and then with the processed mixture. Sprinkle over the paprika. Cover the dish with foil and place in a preheated oven at 425°F (220°C) mark 7 for 15 minutes. Serve from the ovenproof dish.

SPICED PRAWNS WITH PEPPERS

24 Dublin Bay prawns
1 carrot
1 onion
2 sprigs parsley
1 sprig thyme
1 bay leaf
1/2 green pepper
1/2 red pepper
1 oz (25 g) butter
1 tbsp oil
2 shallots
1 tsp curry powder
3¹/2 fl oz (100 ml) medium dry white wine (e.g. Riesling)
9 fl oz (250 ml) single cream
juice of 1 lemon
salt and cayenne pepper

Bring 5¹/4 pints (3 litres) water to the boil in a large saucepan with 1 tbsp coarse sea salt, the peeled and coarsely chopped carrot and onion, parsley, bay leaf and thyme. Boil for 15 minutes, then add the prawns and cook for 5 minutes.

Cut the peppers into thin strips; blanch these in boiling salted water for 3 minutes, drain and set aside.

Heat the butter and oil together in a deep pan and sweat the finely chopped shallots until tender. Sprinkle in the curry powder, add the wine and simmer until it has almost completely evaporated. Stir in the cream; simmer for about 10 minutes to reduce. Season with salt and a pinch of cayenne pepper and stir in the lemon juice. Strain and spoon an equal amount into each of 4 small heated ramekin dishes or bowls; add 6 prawns to each, decorate with the green and red peppers and serve immediately.

PRAWNS THERMIDOR

24 large Dublin Bay prawns
3¹/2 oz (100 g) butter
1 tbsp plain flour
9 fl oz (250 ml) milk
nutmeg
2 oz (50 g) freshly grated Parmesan cheese
7 fl oz (200 ml) single cream
2 tbsp olive oil
3¹/2 fl oz (100 ml) brandy
1 small black truffle (optional)
salt and pepper

If you have bought raw prawns, still with their heads on, take these off, peel (see page 16), remove the black thread-like intestinal tract which runs down their backs, rinse and dry.

Make a thin white sauce: heat 2 oz (50 g) of the butter, stir in the flour when the butter starts to foam, remove from the heat and stir in the very hot milk; cook over a gentle heat, stirring continuously for 10 minutes; season with a little salt, freshly grated nutmeg and pepper; stir in the grated cheese and cream. Do not allow to boil again; set aside and keep warm. Heat the remaining butter with the oil in a very wide pan, add the prawns and fry over a high heat, stirring, for a few minutes. Pour in the brandy and set alight when hot. Season with salt and freshly ground white pepper; add the sauce.

Heat briefly over a very low heat and as soon as the sauce shows signs of coming to the boil, remove from the heat and serve. Garnish with slivers of truffle if wished.

PRAWNS WITH GIN

1¼ lb (600 g) Dublin Bay prawns

3½ fl oz (100 ml) dry white wine

3 tbsp gin

few drops Worcestershire sauce

4 oz (100 g) bacon

few sage leaves (or pinch dried sage)

1 green pepper

8 baby onions or spring onions

8 mushroom caps

olive oil

1 lemon

salt and pepper

The prawns' heads should be removed. Peel and prepare the raw prawns (see page 16 and previous recipe). Place in a deep dish. Mix together the wine, gin, Worcestershire sauce, season with salt and freshly ground pepper and sprinkle over the prawns, making sure they are well coated. Cover and marinate in the refrigerator for 1 hour.

Cut the bacon slices into pieces just long enough to wrap around one of the prawns. Drain the marinade from the prawns, soak up excess moisture with kitchen paper, wrap each in a piece of bacon and thread on to wooden skewers or satay sticks, alternating them with sage leaves, small pieces of pepper, onions or spring onions, and the mushroom caps. Place on a grid in the grill pan, brush generously with oil and grill under a high heat, turning several times and brushing with more oil if necessary. Serve piping hot.

PRAWNS FLAMED IN PERNOD

24 Dublin Bay prawns

1 carrot

1 onion

1 shallot

1 small bulb fennel

4 tinned tomatoes

3 oz (80 g) butter

2 tbsp oil

7 fl oz (200 ml) Pernod

14 fl oz (400 ml) dry white wine

salt and pepper

Raw prawns are best for this recipe. Rinse under running cold water. Clean and prepare the vegetables and dice. Blanch, peel and seed the tomatoes; chop coarsely. Melt half the butter with all the oil in a large, heavy-bottomed saucepan and sweat the vegetables over a low heat, stirring occasionally until they are all tender. Add the prawns, still with their heads on and unpeeled, and sauté over a higher heat, stirring, until they are cooked.

Pour in the Pernod, heat through then set alight to flame. Shake the pan gently until the flames have gone out, and add the white wine, a little salt and plenty of freshly ground pepper; cover and simmer for 5 minutes.

Take the prawns out of the pan with a slotted spoon, draining any sauce back into the pan; peel them and keep hot in a fairly deep serving dish. Use a small teaspoon to scoop out the soft, flavoursome contents of their heads and add to the still simmering sauce in the pan; this should have reduced by about half and thickened somewhat. Allow to cool a little before liquidizing until very smooth; reheat in a smaller saucepan; reduce the heat and beat in the remaining butter with a balloon whisk, adding a small piece at a time. Add a little more salt if necessary. Pour this sauce over the prawns and serve.

Note: Brown rice and a crisp green salad would go well with this dish.

177

PRAWNS AU GRATIN

2³/₄ lb (1.2 kg) Dublin Bay prawns

4 oz (120 g) butter

12 oz (350 g) fresh ceps (boletus edulis) or 3 packets dried ceps

1 onion

2 cloves garlic

3¹/₂ fl oz (100 ml) brandy

1³/₄ pints (1 litre) court-bouillon (see page 39)

7 fl oz (200 ml) single cream

2 tbsp plain flour

2 fl oz (50 ml) milk

2¹/₂ oz (75 g) grated Gruyère cheese

salt and pepper

Sauté the raw prawns for 10 minutes, unpeeled and still with their heads on, in 1¹/₂ oz (40 g) of the butter, stirring continuously. Clean and prepare the mushrooms and slice finely. (If using dried ceps, soak in hot water and drain before use.) Finely chop the peeled onion and garlic.

Transfer the prawns, using a slotted spoon, to another saucepan; pour in the brandy, heat and flame. Add the boiling hot *court-bouillon* and boil for 5 minutes. Draw aside from the heat. Peel when cool enough to handle.

Sauté the chopped onion and garlic in 1 oz (25 g) butter in a pan, add the mushrooms and sauté over a high heat until all excess moisture has evaporated. Turn down the heat, pour in the cream and add the prawns. Stir well, seasoning with salt and freshly ground white pepper, and simmer for 5 minutes.

Make a white sauce: heat the remaining butter, stir in the flour and draw aside from the heat; add the very hot milk, stirring vigorously. Continue stirring over a medium heat for 10 minutes. Season and add to the prawn mixture.

Butter a shallow, wide ovenproof dish, transfer the prawns mixture to it, and distribute evenly; sprinkle with the Gruyère cheese and place in the oven, preheated to 425°F (220°C) mark 7, for 7–8 minutes to brown lightly.

CURRIED PRAWNS

24 large Dublin Bay prawns

2 oz (50 g) butter

2 cloves garlic

3¹/₂ fl oz (200 ml) saké or sherry

7 fl oz (200 ml) single cream

1 tbsp Chinese or mild Indian curry powder

salt

Choose a pan wide enough to take all the prawns in a single, close-packed layer, melt the butter, add the raw prawns and fry over a fairly high heat for a few minutes, or until they are just cooked. Sprinkle with the saké and cook until it evaporates. Pour in the cream, simmer for 10 minutes, uncovered, then stir in the curry powder, season with salt and simmer briefly before serving.

MEDITERRANEAN KEBABS

16 large Dublin Bay prawns

4 thick slices white bread

1 large Italian mozzarella cheese

4 oz (100 g) stuffed green olives

1 small onion or shallot

few sprigs basil

1 clove garlic

1 oz (25 g) butter

1 lb (500 g) ripe tomatoes

olive oil

salt and pepper

Rinse and peel the prawns. Cut the crusts off the bread slices and cut each into 4 squares. Slice the mozzarella cheese into ¹/₂-in (1-cm) cubes and allow the whey to drain off. Thread the ingredients on to wooden skewers in the following order: bread, prawn, mozzarella, olive.

Chop the onion or shallot with the basil leaves and peeled garlic; sweat gently in the butter and 2 tbsp olive oil; add the blanched, peeled, seeded and chopped tomatoes, season and simmer, uncovered, for 30 minutes.

Pour enough olive oil into a very wide pan to cover the bottom. Heat and add the kebabs; brown lightly, turning several times. Pour the tomato sauce all over the kebabs and cook in the oven, at 350°F (180°C) mark 4, for 20 minutes.

EBI SHIOYAKI (GARLIC PRAWNS)

8 large Dublin Bay prawns
4 lemons
5 fl oz (150 ml) oil
9 cloves garlic
5 oz (150 g) butter
1 tbsp finely chopped parsley
salt and pepper

Mix the juice of 3 lemons with the oil and add the juice from 6 crushed garlic cloves. Season with salt and freshly ground pepper. Spread the prawns out in a non-metallic dish or bowl and pour the marinade all over them. Cover the dish tightly and leave in the refrigerator for 3 hours. Turn the prawns several times so that they marinate evenly. Get the barbecue ready, or preheat the grill and grill the prawns for about 10 minutes, turning once. Heat the butter until it shows signs of colouring slightly, add the juice of the remaining lemon, the juice of the remaining, crushed cloves of garlic, salt, pepper and the parsley.

Serve at once, handing the garlic and lemon butter sauce round separately.

FLAT LOBSTERS WITH CAPERS

16 flat or slipper lobsters

3 oz (80 g) fine fresh breadcrumbs
2 oz (50 g) capers
6 tbsp olive oil
salt and pepper

Rinse the lobsters thoroughly under running cold water, trim off their legs and soak in a large bowl of cold salted water for 1 hour. Drain and cut lengthwise along their undersides through the shell (do not cut the flesh more than you can help) with a pair of strong kitchen scissors. Remove the underside of the shell and place, upside down, flesh exposed, on foil in a roasting tin.

Mix together the breadcrumbs, chopped capers, 3 tbsp oil, salt and freshly ground pepper; fill the opening you have cut along what was the lobsters' underside with this mixture, packing it in firmly; sprinkle or brush with a little more oil and bake in the oven, preheated to 325°F (180°C) mark 4, for 10–15 minutes. If the lobsters become too dry while cooking, cover with a sheet of foil.

MANTIS SHRIMP WITH TOMATO SAUCE

3¹/₄–3¹/₂ lb (1¹/₂ kg) mantis shrimp
1 lb (500 g) ripe tomatoes
2 onions
2 cloves garlic
5 tbsp olive oil
sugar
1 small bunch parsley
salt and pepper

Wash the mantis shrimp thoroughly under running cold water, snip off their legs and cartilaginous protuberances and trim off the 'scalloped' bits of their shells on each side to neaten. Blanch, peel and sieve the tomatoes (or use 16 fl oz [450 ml] Italian tomato *passato*, available in cartons). Chop the peeled onions and garlic very finely and fry in the oil; add the drained mantis shrimp and cook for 5 minutes, stirring, before adding the sieved tomatoes. Season, add a pinch of sugar and simmer for 5 minutes more. Turn into a serving dish and sprinkle with chopped parsley.

TUNA-STUFFED MANTIS SHRIMP

$1^3/_4$ lb (800 g) mantis shrimp

$3^1/_2$ fl oz (100 ml) dry white wine

4 oz (100 g) tuna

2 cloves garlic

1 small bunch parsley

1 tbsp capers

1 oz (25 g) fine soft breadcrumbs

fish stock (fumet) *(see page 39)*

1 small piece chilli pepper

2 oz (50 g) dry breadcrumbs

4 tbsp olive oil

1 bay leaf

salt and pepper

Soak the mantis shrimp in the wine mixed with an equal volume of water for 1 hour. Drain, trim off their legs, the cartilaginous pieces on the underside and side protuberances using strong kitchen scissors and cut open as shown on page 18. Flake the tuna very finely and mix with the finely chopped garlic, parsley and capers; soak the breadcrumbs in the stock, squeeze out excess moisture and combine with the tuna mixture, adding the finely crumbled chilli pepper, dried breadcrumbs, salt and freshly ground pepper. Add 4 tbsp olive oil and blend well.

Use this mixture to stuff the mantis shrimp. Place them on lightly oiled foil in an ovenproof dish, with their remaining (back) shells downwards and stuffing uppermost. Sprinkle with the crumbled bay leaf then with the remaining oil and bake at 350°F (180°C) mark 4 for 8–10 minutes, or until browned and crisp.

CRAB AU GRATIN

4 medium-sized crabs

1 small onion

2 oz (50 g) butter

Worcestershire sauce

1 tsp strong English mustard powder

1 oz (25 g) plain flour

7 fl oz (200 ml) milk

breadcrumbs

salt and pepper

Soak the crabs in a large bowl of cold water for at least 2 hours, then add to a saucepan full of boiling salted water and cook for 20 minutes. Leave them to cool in the water, drain and remove all the meat from their bodies, claws, legs, discarding the feathery gills ('dead men's fingers') and the intestines.

Peel the onion and slice wafer-thin; fry very gently in 1 oz (25 g) butter, add the crabmeat and cook gently for 5 minutes. Sprinkle with a few drops of Worcestershire sauce and the mustard powder. Stir well and continue cooking gently for a few minutes; return equal quantities of this mixture to the trimmed and washed half shells.

Make a white sauce with the remaining butter, flour and milk and season with salt and freshly ground pepper. Cover the crabmeat in the shells neatly with this; sprinkle the breadcrumbs on top, and place in a preheated oven at 400°F (200°C) mark 6 for 15 minutes to heat through and brown.

CRAB BELLEVUE

4 crabs

1 celery heart

2 waxy potatoes

2 tbsp mayonnaise *(see page 37)*

2 tbsp double cream

2 tbsp brandy

1 tsp tomato ketchup

1 tbsp Worcestershire sauce

4 large, crisp lettuce leaves

1 hard-boiled egg

4 black olives

salt and pepper

Rinse the crabs, cleaning where necessary, and cook for 10–15 minutes, depending on their size, in *court-bouillon* (see page 25). Leave to cool in the liquid, drain, and open carefully, extracting all the meat (discarding the greyish feathery gills and intestines). Wash the top half of the shell thoroughly, and trim back along the curved line along the underside where the centre section has been detached. Chop the meat from the body and claws very coarsely (do not neglect the soft, brownish meat, which is also delicious) and place in a saucepan with the washed, trimmed celery heart and the peeled potatoes, both cut into very small dice. Add just enough lightly salted water to enable you to cook these ingredients for 10 minutes, adding more water when necessary. Mix the mayonnaise, cream and brandy in a bowl, add the ketchup and Worcestershire sauce, salt and freshly ground pepper. Dry the clean, empty crab shells, line each with a lettuce leaf and fill with the crab mixture. Spoon about 1 tbsp of the mayonnaise mixture on top. Sprinkle with a little finely chopped hard-boiled egg and finish each with the black olives, cut in half and stoned.

PRAWNS MARINARA

32 large or king prawns

4 oz (120 g) butter

4 shallots (or 2 small onions)

1 bouquet garni

1¼ pints (750 ml) dry white wine

1 oz (25 g) plain flour

3 tbsp chopped parsley

salt and pepper

Rinse and peel the prawns, removing their black intestinal tracts. Heat 2½ oz (70 g) of the butter in a frying pan until foaming, add the prawns, and fry briskly for about 5 minutes, turning frequently. Add the finely chopped shallots and the bouquet garni and season with salt and plenty of freshly ground pepper. Cook, stirring continuously, for a further 2 minutes over a gentle heat. Add the wine, cover and boil for 10 minutes. Remove the prawns with a slotted spoon and keep hot in a serving dish. Increase the heat and reduce the liquid in the pan by half. Work the flour into 1 oz (25 g) butter, add to the liquid, and stir to thicken the sauce as the butter melts and releases the flour gradually. Cook for 2 minutes. Add a further 1 oz (25 g) (solid) butter and beat into the sauce with a whisk over the lowest possible heat. Remove and discard the bouquet garni, add a little more salt to taste, stir and pour over the prawns. Decorate with parsley.

PRAWNS AU GRATIN

3¼–3½ lb (1½ kg) medium-sized prawns

1 shallot

1 small onion

1 carrot

4 oz (100 g) butter

olive oil

3½ fl oz (100 ml) brandy

18 fl oz (500 ml) dry white wine

1 tbsp sieved fresh or tinned tomatoes

2 sprigs tarragon

1 tbsp plain flour

9 fl oz (250 ml) single cream

1 truffle (optional)

salt and cayenne pepper

Rinse the prawns and boil for 5 minutes in salted water. Drain, peel and remove the intestinal tract; pound the heads and shells.

Heat 1 oz (25 g) of the butter with 3 tbsp of the oil; add the cleaned, prepared and finely diced

181

vegetables, cover and sweat over a very low heat for 30 minutes. Add the heads and shells, 2 fl oz (50 ml) brandy, heat through and flame; pour in the wine and 3½ fl oz (100 ml) water. Stir in the sieved tomato and add the tarragon, cayenne pepper and a pinch of salt.

Cover and simmer for 20 minutes; strain into a clean saucepan. Melt 2 oz (50 g) butter over a low heat, stir in the flour, cook for a minute and then stir in the strained liquid. Stir for a little while, then add the cream and salt and pepper to taste. Simmer for a further 3–4 minutes.

Sauté the prawns in 1 oz (25 g) butter for 5 minutes, add the remaining brandy, and stir in the creamy sauce (a few truffle peelings are an optional addition at this stage). Transfer to a fairly shallow heatproof dish and place under a hot grill for a minute or two to brown slightly.

PRAWN FRICASSÉE

32 large prawns
1 carrot
2 shallots
1 onion
1 bouquet garni
4 oz (120 g) butter
3½ fl oz (100 ml) champagne brandy
9 fl oz (250 ml) good dry white wine (e.g. Chablis)
14 fl oz (400 ml) single cream
salt and pepper

Rinse and peel the prawns, removing the intestinal tract. Peel the carrot, shallots and onion and chop finely. Sauté in 2 oz (50 g) butter till tender. Melt 2½ oz (70 g) butter in another, much larger pan; add the prawns and fry for a few minutes, turning frequently. Pour in the brandy, increase the heat and allow to evaporate. Add the vegetables, salt and pepper followed by the white wine and the bouquet garni. Cover and cook fast for 10 minutes. Remove the prawns with a slotted spoon and keep hot in a serving dish. Add the cream and reduce

over a high heat until the sauce has thickened a little. Discard the bouquet garni. Pour the sauce over the prawns and serve.

PRAWN MOULDS

1¼ lb (600 g) medium-sized prawns
1 large egg
9 fl oz (250 ml) double cream
Tabasco sauce
1 tbsp truffle paste
2 oz (50 g) butter
1 shallot
3½ fl oz (100 ml) dry white wine
salt and pepper

Rinse and peel the prawns, removing their intestinal tract (a black thread running down the back). Reserve the heads and shells. Place the prawn meat in the food processor or liquidizer with the egg, just over 5 fl oz (150 ml) of the cream, a few drops of Tabasco sauce, the truffle paste, a pinch of salt and pepper. Process until very smooth and perfectly blended.

Grease 4 moulds or ramekin dishes with butter and fill with the mixture; place in a roasting tin and pour enough hot water into the pan to come half way up the sides of the moulds. Cook in the oven, preheated to 350°F (180°C) mark 4, for about 20 minutes or until firmly set.

Meanwhile, melt 1 oz (25 g) butter in a fairly large saucepan, sweat the finely chopped shallot until transparent, add the prawn heads and shells and stir; add the wine, salt and pepper and cook fast for 10 minutes. Discard the heads, draining any liquid from them back into the pan; allow to cool a little before processing in the blender or food processor at maximum speed until the shells have totally disintegrated and the mixture is very smooth. Strain into a clean saucepan, add the remaining cream and a little salt if needed and heat very gently for a few minutes. Turn the moulds out on to individual heated plates, spoon the sauce around them and serve.

PRAWN AND SWEETCORN OMELETTE

16 jumbo prawns

7 oz (200 g) frozen artichoke hearts

1¹/₂ oz (40 g) butter

4 tbsp oil

1 clove garlic

2 leeks

³/₄ cup tinned sweetcorn, drained

6 eggs

3 tbsp single cream

1 tbsp chopped fresh tarragon

salt and pepper

Slice the thawed artichoke hearts thinly and fry in half the butter and 1 tbsp oil for 6–7 minutes with the finely chopped garlic clove and a little salt and pepper, stirring gently.

Trim the leeks and wash very thoroughly. Using only the white part, slice into thin rings and sweat with the remaining butter and 1 tbsp oil. Add the sweetcorn, a little salt and pepper and cook for 3–4 minutes. Cook the prawns in boiling salted water for 2 minutes, if raw; peel and chop into pieces. Beat the eggs with the cream, season to taste and add the tarragon, followed by the artichoke hearts, leek and sweet cornmixture, and the prawns. Stir well.

Heat 3 tbsp oil in a large frying pan; pour the mixture into the pan and cook until set. This omelette should be firm: turn once and cook until set on the other side.

PRAWNS IN MUSHROOM AND CREAM SAUCE

32 medium-sized prawns

1 carrot

1 onion

1 shallot

5¹/₂ oz (160 g) butter

9 oz (250 g) tiny button mushrooms

juice of 1 lemon

2 tbsp olive oil

5 fl oz (150 ml) dry white wine

4 tbsp plain flour

18 fl oz (500 ml) milk

3¹/₂ fl oz (100 ml) single cream

1 truffle (optional)

salt and pepper

Rinse the prawns and remove the black intestinal tract. Peel the carrot, onion and shallot and chop very finely; sweat in 1 oz (25 g) butter for 5 minutes. Rinse and dry the mushrooms; sprinkle with a little lemon juice.

Bring 9 fl oz (250 ml) water to the boil with the remaining lemon juice, 1 oz (25 g) butter, salt and pepper; add the mushrooms and boil for 5 minutes. Drain well.

Sauté the prawns in 2 oz (50 g) butter and the oil for a few minutes; add the sautéed chopped vegetables, the wine, salt and pepper and cook for 10 minutes. Make a white sauce with 1¹/₂ oz (40 g) butter, the flour and the hot milk; cook, stirring continuously, for 10 minutes, season with salt and pepper. Transfer the prawns to a heated serving dish, leaving their cooking juices, etc., behind; sprinkle the prawns with the truffle, sliced wafer-thin (or use drained, tinned truffle peelings) and add the mushrooms. Keep hot.

Process all the heads and shells of the prawns and the contents of the pan in which they were cooked in a blender at maximum speed until very smooth; strain and stir into the white sauce; add the cream and 1 oz (20 g) butter (solid) and beat with a balloon whisk over a very low heat until the butter has completely melted; pour over the prawns and serve.

Note: Garnish with chopped parsley or chives, if wished.

PRAWN AND SHERRY OMELETTE

10 oz (300 g) peeled prawns

6 eggs

2 tbsp dry sherry

2 spring onions

pinch garlic powder

3 tbsp oil

salt and pepper

Beat the eggs with salt, freshly ground pepper and the sherry. Rinse the spring onions and snip the green part only into rings. Sprinkle the prawns with the garlic powder, stir and leave to stand for 20 minutes. Mix the prawns and the spring onions into the egg mixture. Heat the oil in a large, non-stick frying pan and cook the omelette, starting off at a high heat for 30 seconds, then reducing the heat and cooking more gently until set; turn if you want a firm omelette and finish cooking on the other side.

SHRIMPS IN SPARKLING WINE

1¹/₂ lb (700 g) cooked, peeled shrimps or small prawns

2 oz (50 g) butter

2 oz (50 g) plain flour

9 fl oz (250 ml) milk

4 oz (120 g) smoked cheese

10 fl oz (300 ml) dry sparkling white wine

salt and pepper

Choose a variety of smoked cheese that will melt well. Make a white sauce with 1¹/₂ oz (40 g) of the butter, the flour and hot milk; season and cook the sauce while stirring for 10 minutes, add the grated cheese and when it has melted add the wine, stirring well over a low heat. Place the shrimps in

an ovenproof dish, greased with butter, pour the sauce all over them and place, uncovered, in a preheated oven at 400°F (200°C) mark 6 for 25–30 minutes.

SAVOURY PRAWNS

14 oz (400 g) medium-sized prawns

2 cloves garlic

2 onions

few sprigs parsley

1 bay leaf

7 fl oz (200 ml) dry white wine

olive oil

plain flour

1 tsp tomato ketchup

1 tsp mild French mustard

2 tbsp single cream

salt and pepper

Peel the prawns and place the heads and shells in a large saucepan with the peeled and sliced garlic and one onion, a sprig of parsley and the bay leaf. Add the wine diluted with an equal quantity of water and season with salt and pepper. Bring to the boil and continue boiling until the liquid has reduced by half. Rind and chop the remaining onion and sauté until golden brown in 4 tbsp oil. Dry the prawns, coat lightly with flour, and add to the sautéed onion; cook, stirring for a few minutes, then add the ketchup, mustard and cream. Mix well and add the strained stock from the shells. Stir well and serve, decorated with a little chopped parsley.

·MOLLUSCS·

BAKED OYSTERS

p. 193

Time: 50 minutes
Difficulty: Very easy
Hot appetizer

OYSTERS WITH SPINACH

p. 193

Time: 30 minutes
Difficulty: Easy
Hot appetizer

OYSTERS WITH CHAMPAGNE

p. 193

Time: 1 hour
Difficulty: Very easy
Hot appetizer

OYSTERS IN CREAM AND VEGETABLE SAUCE

p. 194

Time: 1 hour 15 minutes
Difficulty: Easy
Hot appetizer

SCALLOPS WITH TUNA

p. 194

Time: 1 hour
Difficulty: Very easy
Cold appetizer

SCALLOPS WITH CORAL SAUCE

p. 195

Time: 2 hours 20 minutes
Difficulty: Fairly easy
Hot appetizer

EXOTIC SCALLOPS

p. 195

Time: 30 minutes
+ 2 hours marinating time
Difficulty: Very easy
Cold appetizer

SCALLOPS WITH MUSHROOMS AND BRANDY

p. 195

Time: 1 hour
Difficulty: Easy
Hot appetizer

SCALLOPS WITH THYME

p. 196

Time: 25 minutes
Difficulty: Very easy
Hot appetizer

SCALLOP GALETTES

p. 196

Time: 1 hour 15 minutes
Difficulty: Easy
Hot appetizer

CLAM SALAD

p. 197

Time: 1 hour
Difficulty: Very easy
Cold appetizer

CLAMS IN WINE SAUCE

p. 197

Time: 1 hour
Difficulty: Very easy
Hot appetizer

Spaghetti with mussels and mushrooms

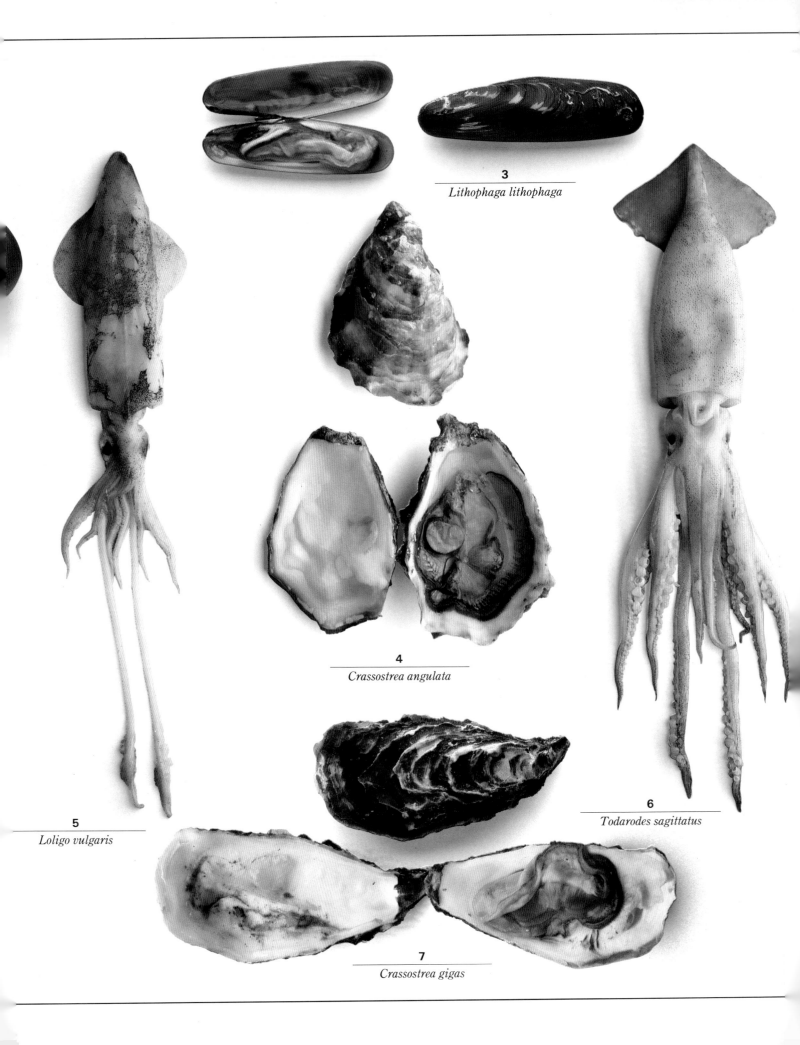

3
Lithophaga lithophaga

4
Crassostrea angulata

5
Loligo vulgaris

6
Todarodes sagittatus

7
Crassostrea gigas

1

English: Smooth Venus
Italian: Fasolaro/Cappa liscia
Spanish: Almeión brillante

2

English: Cuttlefish
French: Seiche
German: Tintenfisch
Italian: Seppia
Spanish: Sepia

3

English: Date-shell
French: Datte de mer
German: Seedattel
Italian: Dattero di mare
Spanish: Dátil de mar

4

English: Portuguese oyster
French: Huître portugaise
German: Portugiesische Auster
Italian: Ostrica portoghese
Spanish: Ostra de Portugal

5

Dutch: Pijlinktvis
English: Squid
French: Calmar
German: Kalmar
Italian: Calamaro
Spanish: Calamar

6

English: Flying flusk
French: Calmar
Italian: Totano

7

English: Pacific oyster
German: Lange japanische Auster
Italian: Ostrica giapponese

8

English: Clam, Warty Venus
French: Praire
German: Wartzige Venusmuschel
Italian: Tartufo di mare
Spanish: Escupina gravada

9

English: Cockle
French: Coque
German: Gewöhnliche Herzmuschel
Italian: Cuore edule
Spanish: Berberecho

10

Dutch: Oester
English: Oyster
French: Huître
German: Auster
Italian: Ostrica piatta
Spanish: Ostra

11

English: Curled octopus
French: Eledone
Italian: Moscardino bianco

12

Dutch: Mossel
English: Mussel (Blue mussel)
French: Moule
German: Miesmuschel, Pfahlmuschel
Italian: Mitilo, Cozza
Spanish: Concha, Muscle

13

English: Razor shell
French: Couteau
Italian: Cannolicchio
Spanish: Navaja

14

English: Top shell
French: Bigorneau
Italian: Chiocciola di mare
Spanish: Caracol gris, Caramujo

15

Dutch: Sint Jakobsschelp
English: Scallop
French: Coquille Saint-Jacques
German: Pilgermuschel, Jacobsmuschel
Italian: Conchiglia di San Giacomo
Spanish: Concas peregrina

16

English: Sea-urchin
French: Oursin
Italian: Riccio di mare
Spanish: Erizo de mar

17

Dutch: Middellandse-Zee-tapijtschelp
English: Carpet shell
French: Clovisse, Palourde
German: Teppichmuschel
Italian: Vongola verace
Spanish: Almeja

18

Dutch: Achtarmige poliep, Kraak
English: Octopus
French: Poulpe, Pieuvre
German: Gemeine Krake, Meerpolyp
Italian: Polpo
Spanish: Polipo

19

English: Golden carpet shell
French: Clovisse
Italian: Vongola grigia
Spanish: Amayeula

1

Callista chione

2

Sepia officinalis

Cuttlefish with peas

Stuffed squid with olives

Scallops with mushrooms and brandy

14
Nassa mutabilis

16
Paracentrotus lividus

15
Pecten jacobaeus

19
Venus gallina

17
Tapes decussatus

18
Octopus membranaceus

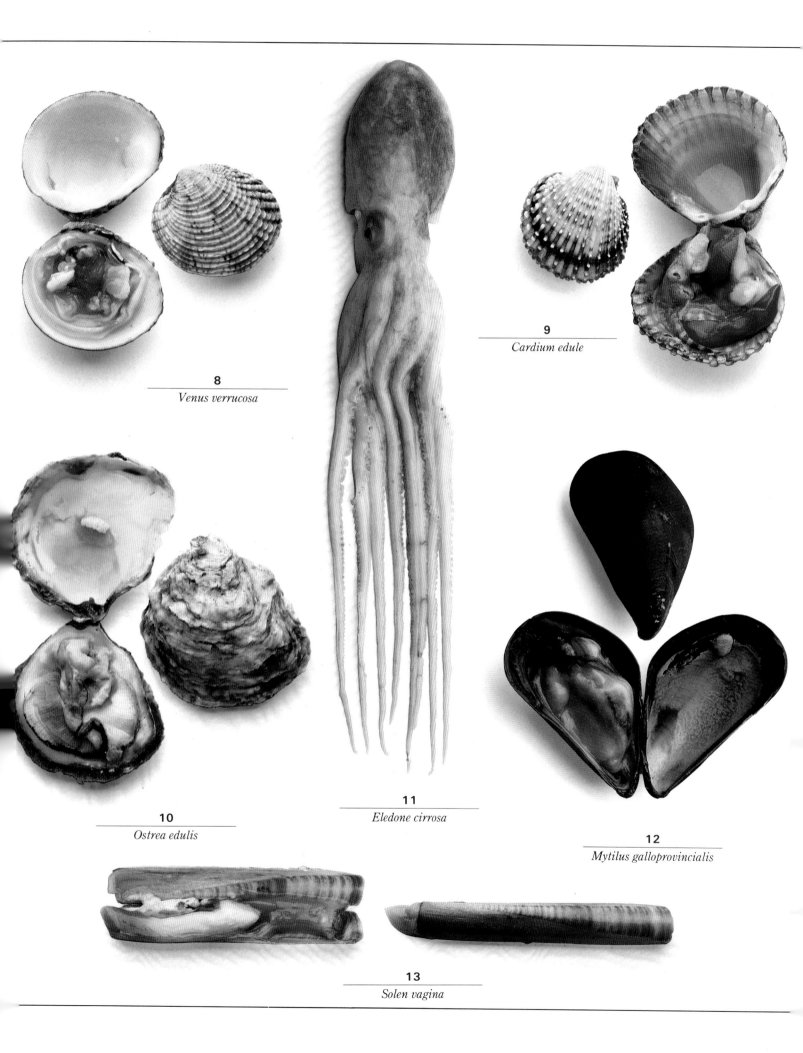

8
Venus verrucosa

9
Cardium edule

10
Ostrea edulis

11
Eledone cirrosa

12
Mytilus galloprovincialis

13
Solen vagina

*Green tagliatelle
with scallops*

BAKED OYSTERS

24 large oysters

2¹/₂ oz (70 g) butter

3 tbsp chopped parsley

2 tbsp chopped fresh tarragon

1 shallot

1 clove garlic

12 peeled and crushed peanuts

1 tsp anise liqueur

1 tbsp fine breadcrumbs

salt

Wash and scrub the oysters and shuck (see page 22), drain off their juices and lightly squash the oysters flat with your thumb on the half shell.

Work the butter (softened at room temperature), herbs, the finely chopped shallot and garlic with the pounded peanuts and liqueur. Spread a little of this mixture over the oysters on their half shells. Sprinkle with the breadcrumbs and place the oysters on a bed of coarse salt in a roasting tin (or use heatproof oyster plates).

Place in the oven, preheated to 400°F (200°C) mark 6, and remove as soon as the butter has melted.

OYSTERS WITH SPINACH

12 large oysters

5 oz (150 g) frozen chopped spinach

2 tbsp olive oil

2 cloves garlic

¹/₂ oz (10 g) butter

1 egg

7 fl oz (200 ml) plain yoghurt

1 tsp mild curry powder

salt and pepper

Clean the oysters and steam them open in a perforated steamer over boiling water. Detach the molluscs from their shells, draining well, and reserve the half shell from which you detach each mollusc.

Sauté the frozen spinach gently over a low heat with the oil and peeled garlic cloves, stirring so that the moisture evaporates as it thaws. Season with salt and freshly ground pepper; turn off the heat when all the moisture has evaporated. Stir in the butter and fill the empty, deeper half shells with a little of this mixture, to make a bed on which each mollusc is then replaced; top each with its original flat, half shell and replace in the steamer. While the oysters are heating through, beat the egg with the yoghurt, curry powder and a little freshly ground pepper; stir over a low heat to reduce and thicken a little.

Serve the oysters with the hot yoghurt sauce handed round separately.

OYSTERS WITH CHAMPAGNE

24 oysters

12 fl oz (350 ml) champagne

4 egg yolks

2 tbsp double cream

pepper

Clean the oysters, shuck them (see page 22), and reserve their juices. Detach each mollusc from its half shell, wash both halves of each shell thoroughly, and place in the oven at a fairly low heat to dry out.

Pour the champagne into a saucepan and boil until reduced by three quarters in volume (you should be left with about 7 fl oz [200 ml]); allow to cool slightly away from the heat and then beat in the egg yolks, cream and 2 tsp of their reserved juice (strained through a fine sieve). Beat this mixture in a bowl or double boiler over hot (not boiling) water until light and frothy; draw aside from the heat and keep warm over the hot water. Bring the oyster juice to a very gentle boil and blanch the oysters in it for 30 seconds. Drain well,

193

reserving the juice, and return the molluscs to the deeper half shells. Beat the hot juices in which the oysters were blanched into the sauce, adding a little at a time; season with freshly ground pepper. Arrange the oysters in a single layer in a very wide, ovenproof dish and heat under a very hot grill for 30 seconds. Serve at once.

OYSTERS IN CREAM AND VEGETABLE SAUCE

24 oysters
2¹/₄–2¹/₂ lb (1 kg) large mussels
1 medium-sized onion
2 leeks
3 oz (80 g) butter
7 fl oz (200 ml) dry white wine
2 small tender carrots
2 small celery stalks
3¹/₂ fl oz (100 ml) single cream
salt and pepper

Soak the mussels in cold, salted water for 1–2 hours, then scrub under running cold water and trim off their beards. Peel and finely chop the onion; wash the leeks thoroughly and chop the white part only of one of them; fry very gently with the onion in 1 oz (25 g) butter. Add the mussels and wine, cover and bring to the boil to make the mussels open. Discard any which do not open after a few minutes' fast cooking. Strain the cooking liquid and juices from the mussels through a very fine sieve: it is this liquid which is important for this recipe; the mussels themselves can be reserved for a seafood salad. If you cannot buy fresh unshucked mussels, use clam juice from tinned clams or a little more dry white wine instead. Prepare all the remaining vegetables, cut into fine matchstick strips, and blanch for 2 minutes in boiling salted water. Drain well.

Shuck the oysters (see page 22), saving and straining all their juices; pour half into a saucepan and add the mussel liquid. Boil until reduced by half. Stir in the cream.

Simmer for 3 minutes, draw aside from the heat and beat in the remaining butter with a balloon whisk, adding a small, solid piece at a time. Add the blanched vegetables to this sauce and heat very gently over a low heat; do not allow to boil. Add the remaining oyster juices and season with salt and a little freshly ground white pepper. Stir and serve.

SCALLOPS WITH TUNA

12 scallops
¹/₂ oz (10 g) butter
1 tbsp fish stock (fumet) (see page 39)
1 tbsp dry white wine
6 oz (170 g) tinned tuna
3 tbsp thick mayonnaise
few sprigs parsley
salt and pepper

Wash the scallops in their shells under running cold water, scrubbing the outside of the shells clean. Open (see page 23) and detach the mollusc from its shell (use the pale round 'cushion' of flesh and the orange coral or roe, discarding everything else). Clean and dry the deep half shells in a hot oven for 10 minutes.

Melt the butter in a non-stick pan and fry the scallops in it for 2 minutes, turning them carefully once. Add the fish stock and white wine, cover and simmer over a gentle heat for 3–4 minutes. Season with salt and freshly ground white pepper. Drain the tuna well and reduce to a smooth paste in the food processor or put through a food mill; transfer to a bowl and mix in the mayonnaise and a little pepper. Fill a piping bag with this mixture and using a fluted, large-gauge nozzle pipe an equal amount into the cooled and cleaned half shells. Place the mollusc on top of the tuna, pressing down very lightly into the tuna mixture. Decorate with a few parsley leaves and serve.

SCALLOPS WITH CORAL SAUCE

8 scallops

3 small carrots

5 leeks (white part only)

1 onion

1 shallot

2 oz (50 g) butter

1 tbsp olive oil

juice of 1 lemon

1/2 cucumber

5 fl oz (150 ml) double cream

salt and pepper

Slice 1 carrot, 1 leek, the onion and the shallot very thinly and sauté in a saucepan for 4 minutes with 1 oz (25 g) of the butter and the oil. Add a little salt, the lemon juice and 2³/4 pints (1¹/2 litres) hot water; cook, uncovered, for 30 minutes. Strain the liquid.

Slice the remaining leeks very finely and cook in 1 oz (25 g) butter, covered, over a fairly high heat for 5 minutes. Add a pinch of salt, 3¹/2 fl oz (100 ml) of the strained liquid; simmer, uncovered, for 20 minutes.

Wash and shuck the scallops (see page 23), detach the molluscs from the shell; snip the coral away from the white part very carefully, set aside; cut the white part into 2 or 3 slices, depending on how large they are, using a very sharp knife. Reserve 3¹/2 fl oz (100 ml) of the remaining stock and pour the rest into a deep pan. Heat to boiling point, add the remaining carrots, finely sliced, and simmer for 15 minutes. Add the sliced cucumber, simmer for 3 minutes, then add the sliced white scallop meat and half the roes (orange parts). Simmer for a further 3 minutes.

Process the leeks and reserved liquid with the cream and remaining raw, orange roes in a blender. Heat this sauce in a saucepan, seasoning with salt and pepper. Arrange the scallop slices and corals in a heated serving dish with the drained carrots and cucumber. Coat with some of the sauce, serving the rest in a sauceboat.

EXOTIC SCALLOPS

8 scallops

2 shallots

5 tbsp olive oil

5 tbsp peanut oil

3 tbsp chopped chives

3 lemons

2 tbsp tinned green peppercorns

coarse sea salt

Wash the outside of the scallops' shells thoroughly and place flat in a very wide pan over a high heat for a few seconds to open. Detach the round piece of white meat and the orange coral, separate the two carefully and cut the white meat in thin slices.

Chop the peeled shallots finely and place in a non-metallic bowl with the olive oil, the peanut oil, chives, juice of 2 lemons and the drained green peppercorns. Add the scallops to this marinade, stir carefully, and leave to stand for 2 hours in a cool place.

Sprinkle plenty of coarse sea salt over the bottom of a roasting tin, press the cleaned deeper shell halves into this stabilizing layer of salt and lay the sliced marinated scallops in them with a little strained marinade. Decorate with lemon slices and serve.

Note: the coral can be used to flavour sauces or other seafood dishes.

SCALLOPS WITH MUSHROOMS AND BRANDY

12 scallops

4 oz (100 g) carrots

2 shallots or 1 small onion

4 oz (120 g) butter

1 tbsp olive oil

4 oz (100 g) button mushrooms

195

2 fl oz (50 ml) brandy
2 fl oz (50 ml) dry white wine
2 fl oz (50 ml) single cream
salt and pepper

Cut the peeled carrots and onions into matchstick pieces. Sweat for 5 minutes in a covered pan with 1 oz (25 g) of the butter and the oil. Add the finely sliced mushrooms, salt and pepper and cook for a further 5–6 minutes, stirring occasionally.

Wash the scallops and open as directed on page 23, and separate the white cushions of flesh from the coral. Wash, dry and cook the white part for 2 minutes, turning once, in 1 oz (25 g) of the butter. Sprinkle with the brandy, then with the white wine, and add a pinch of salt. Remove from the pan with a slotted spoon and keep warm in a covered dish.

Add all the vegetables to the juices and liquid left behind after cooking the scallops; add the cream and the remaining butter. Reduce the liquid, cooking over a high heat, uncovered and stirring with a wooden spoon as the mixture thickens. Add a little salt and freshly ground pepper if necessary.

Place equal quantities of the cooked white scallop meat, the uncooked coral roe (3 roes to each portion) in 4 little ramekin dishes, covering each portion with some of the vegetable sauce. Place these on a heat diffuser or in the oven to heat through for a few minutes only; they should not reach boiling point. Serve at once.

SCALLOPS WITH THYME

12 scallops
1 oz (25 g) butter
powdered dried thyme
juice of 1 lemon
1¹/₂ tbsp finely chopped parsley
coarse sea salt and pepper

Preheat the oven to 475°F (240°C) mark 9. Open the scallops (see page 23), detach the white meat, rinse well and cut into thin slices. Wash 4 of the deeper half shells, dry and grease them liberally with some of the butter. Sprinkle with sea salt which will adhere to the butter. Place a very thin slice of butter on each scallop slice and arrange an equal number of these slices slightly overlapping one another in each shell. Dot with small flakes of the remaining butter and sprinkle each portion with a small pinch of powdered thyme, freshly ground pepper and a little more sea salt. Place on a baking sheet or directly on to the middle grid or shelf in the oven and bake for 2 minutes. Take out of the oven and sprinkle each portion with lemon juice and chopped parsley. Serve.

SCALLOP GALETTES

16 scallops
12 oz (350 g) frozen puff pastry
1 red pepper
1 shallot
3¹/₂ fl oz (100 ml) dry white wine
1 tbsp white wine vinegar
2 tbsp double cream
4 oz (120 g) butter
1¹/₂ tbsp finely chopped parsley
salt and pepper

Thaw the puff pastry at room temperature; roll out in a thin sheet on a floured work surface; cut into 4 pieces, about 4¹/₂ in (12 cm) square. Place these on one or two non-stick baking sheets rinsed in cold water. Place a sheet of foil loosely on top of the pastry and cook in a preheated oven at 400°F (200°C) mark 6 for 10 minutes. Remove the foil and cook for a further 3 minutes. Grill the red pepper to loosen the skin, peel and cut half into thin strips. Chop the other half very finely.

Place the peeled and very finely chopped shallot in a saucepan with the wine and vinegar and boil until only 1 tbsp liquid remains. Lower the heat and when very low, beat in the cream, followed by the butter, adding a small piece at a time. Add a little salt and the sliced half pepper and process until very smooth in the blender. Correct the seasoning, adding pepper if wished. Open the scallops (see page 23), detach and rinse the white meat (reserve the coral or orange roes for use in sauces, etc.) and cut into thin slices; place these on the pastry bases. Brush the scallop slices lightly with melted butter, season with salt and freshly ground pepper and place under a medium hot grill for 3 minutes.

Transfer the galettes to individual heated plates and decorate with chopped red pepper and parsley. Serve the creamy sauce separately.

CLAM SALAD

$5^1/_2$ lb ($2^1/_2$ kg) small clams, in the shell
3 leeks
1 large ripe tomato
1 small mild onion
1 tbsp finely chopped parsley
1 tbsp wine vinegar or cider vinegar
4 tbsp olive oil
salt and pepper

Prepare the clams for cooking (see page 23). Place in a very large pan over a high heat, cover and heat for a minute or two, shaking the pan now and then; discard any clams which have not opened. Remove the molluscs from their shells, strain all their juice and reserve. (If using tinned clams, two 10-oz [275-g] tins should be sufficient; reserve the juice.)

Wash the leeks very thoroughly; cut the white part only into thick rings and blanch for 5 minutes in boiling salted water. Drain and leave to cool. Blanch, peel and quarter the tomato; discard the seeds and dice the flesh. Peel the onion, slice wafer-thin, and soak these slices in cold water for 30 minutes. Pour 3 tbsp of the clam juice into a bowl, add the parsley, vinegar, salt and freshly ground pepper, then beat in the oil with a balloon

whisk, adding a little at a time.

Arrange the leeks in a layer on a serving plate, place the clams on top and decorate with the diced tomato and the well drained onion rings. Sprinkle with the dressing and serve.

CLAMS IN WINE SAUCE

$1^3/_4$ lb (800 g) clams, in the shell
2 bay leaves
generous pinch powdered thyme
1 onion
1 small bunch parsley
3 tbsp olive oil
7 fl oz (200 ml) dry white wine
1 oz (25 g) butter
1 tbsp plain flour
pepper

Rinse the clams thoroughly under running cold water, place in a large, heavy-bottomed saucepan or fireproof casserole dish with 2 bay leaves, a pinch of thyme, the peeled chopped onion, a few sprigs of parsley and the oil.

Pour in the wine, cover and cook over a high heat for a few minutes, stirring and turning once if necessary; discard any clams which have not opened.

Draw aside from the heat and when cool enough to handle, detach the top, empty valve of the shell, leaving each mollusc on the half shell. Transfer these to individual heated plates and keep warm.

Heat the butter in a small saucepan, stir in the flour, then gradually beat in the strained juices and wine. Continue stirring for 5 minutes as the sauce thickens and cooks. Season with salt and freshly ground pepper.

Pour the sauce over the clams, sprinkle with finely chopped parsley, and serve.

Note: Lemon wedges and a few sprigs of watercress are an optional, decorative garnish.

197

PORTUGUESE SEAFOOD SALAD

9 oz (250 g) cleaned and prepared squid

1 onion

3 large ripe tomatoes

2 gherkins

1 yellow pepper

1 tin sardines, drained

2 oz (50 g) stuffed green olives

4 tbsp olive oil

2 tbsp red or white wine vinegar

2 hard-boiled egg yolks

1 sprig parsley

salt and pepper

Clean and prepare the squid (see page 20). Cut the squid into thin strips and boil gently in water for 20 minutes; reserve 2 tbsp of the cooking liquid. Leave to cool completely.

Peel the onion, slice into very thin rings, and soak these in cold water for 30 minutes. Blanch, peel and halve the tomatoes, extract the seeds and cut the flesh into strips. Slice the gherkins into thin rounds. Grill the yellow pepper to loosen the skin, peel and cut into strips. Drain the sardines thoroughly, reserving the oil, remove their bones, and flake with a fork. Slice the olives into rounds.

Mix all the above-mentioned prepared ingredients in a salad bowl. Put the vinegar, reserved cooking liquid, salt and freshly ground pepper in a small bowl and beat in the sardine oil.

Work the egg yolks with a fork to a dry paste and gradually beat in the olive oil, adding a very little at a time as you would for mayonnaise; combine with the sardine oil mixture and sprinkle over the contents of the salad bowl.

Chill the Portuguese seafood salad in the refrigerator for 30 minutes and then serve, in the large bowl or in individual glass dishes, sprinkled with finely chopped parsley.

SQUID SALAD

8 squid

1 carrot

1 celery stalk

¹/₂ onion

1 bay leaf

5 tbsp olive oil

juice of 1 lemon

2 small bunches lamb's lettuce

salt

Prepare the squid (see page 20) and boil gently for 15–20 minutes in 2³/₄ pints (1¹/₂ litres) water with the peeled and sliced carrot, sliced celery, peeled and quartered onion, and the bay leaf. Do not boil for longer, as lengthy boiling toughens squid. Leave to cool in the liquid.

Add a pinch of salt to the lemon juice and beat in a little oil at a time so that the mixture emulsifies. Drain and dry the squid and cut into small strips or pieces. Place in a bowl and mix with the dressing. Stir in the washed and dried lamb's lettuce leaves just before serving.

SQUID WITH CHILLI

1 lb (500 g) small squid

2 cloves garlic

5 tbsp olive oil

1 small bunch parsley

2 tinned anchovy fillets

pinch chilli powder

7 fl oz (200 ml) dry white wine

7 fl oz (200 ml) fish stock (fumet) (see page 39)

salt

Prepare and wash the squid (see page 20). Slice into rings. Fry the peeled garlic cloves in the oil; as soon as they turn pale golden brown, remove and discard them. Add 1½ tbsp chopped parsley to the flavoured oil together with the squid.

Add the well drained, chopped anchovies, the chilli powder and a pinch of salt and cook over a fairly high heat for 20 minutes, stirring as necessary. Add the wine and cook until it has evaporated; pour in the fish *fumet*, cover tightly and cook for a further 20 minutes.

BABY CUTTLEFISH WITH PARSLEY AND BASIL

1¼ lb (600 g) small cuttlefish
1 celery stalk
1 carrot
2 sprigs parsley
3½ fl oz (100 ml) wine vinegar
6 tbsp olive oil
1 clove garlic
1 sprig fresh basil (or pinch dried basil)
juice of 1 lemon
salt and peppercorns

Prepare and wash the cuttlefish (see page 20 for method).

Bring a large saucepan of water to the boil with the prepared celery, carrot, 1 sprig parsley, vinegar, salt and a few peppercorns, and add the cuttlefish. Boil gently for 10 minutes, then leave to cool in the cooking liquid. Heat the oil in a saucepan and add the peeled and chopped garlic, the remaining chopped sprig of parsley, basil and strained lemon juice. Season with salt and freshly ground pepper. Stir while sautéeing gently for 4–5 minutes. Draw aside from the heat. Drain the cuttlefish thoroughly, transfer to a heated serving dish, pour the warm dressing all over them and serve, garnished with extra basil leaves, finely chopped, if wished.

MUSSEL SOUFFLÉ

3¼–3½ lb (1½ kg) mussels
7 fl oz (200 ml) dry white wine
1 onion
juice of 1 lemon
2 oz (50 g) butter
1 oz (25 g) plain flour
4 eggs
nutmeg
salt and pepper

Scrub the mussels well, removing their beards and barnacles and soak them in cold, salted water for 1–2 hours.

Place the drained mussels in a deep, wide pan with the wine, sliced onion, lemon juice and freshly ground pepper. Cover and place over a high heat to make the mussels open (stir once or twice). Discard any that fail to open. Take the molluscs off the shell when they are no longer too hot to handle; strain the juices and cooking liquid.

Melt 2 oz (50 g) butter, stir in the flour and cook gently until lightly coloured; stir in 9 fl oz (250 ml) of the cooking liquid and continue cooking, stirring continuously, for 5–6 minutes over a low heat. Remove from the heat.

Process half the mussels in the food processor until very finely chopped and mix into the sauce, followed by the 4 egg yolks, salt and pepper to taste and a pinch of nutmeg. Add the remaining, whole molluscs.

Beat the eggs with a pinch of salt until stiff but not dry; fold in the mussel mixture.

Transfer to a buttered soufflé dish (choose a size which this mixture will two-thirds or three-quarters fill) and place in a preheated oven at 400°F (200°C) mark 6 for about 20 minutes, or until well risen and golden brown on top. Serve at once.

Note: As with all soufflés, this must be served as soon as it is taken out of the oven, or it will begin to sink.

AVOCADO AND MUSSEL COCKTAIL

$1^3/_4$ lb (800 g) mussels
2 avocados
1 onion
3 shallots
2 cloves garlic
1 small bunch parsley
2 tbsp white wine vinegar
4 tbsp olive oil
salt and cayenne pepper

Soak, wash and scrub the mussels (see page 22 and preceding recipes) and place in a large saucepan. Cover and cook briefly for a few minutes over a high heat to make them open, stirring and turning once or twice (discard any mussels which fail to open). Detach the molluscs from their shells and place in a salad bowl.

Peel the onion, shallot and garlic, chop finely with the parsley and mix in a bowl with a pinch each of salt and cayenne pepper; stir in the vinegar and the oil. Blend well. Add the hot, strained juice from the mussels. Cut the avocados lengthwise in half and remove the pit. Scoop out the flesh with a spoon, keeping the half skins intact. Sprinkle the flesh with a little lemon juice and cut into small cubes; fold these gently into the mussel mixture. Sprinkle with the dressing, stir once more and fill the empty skins with this mixture. Serve at once, while still slightly warm.

FRIED BREADED MUSSELS

$2^1/_4$–$2^1/_2$ lb (1 kg) large mussels
1 clove garlic
2 eggs
$3^1/_2$ oz (100 g) plain flour
4 oz (100 g) breadcrumbs
7 fl oz (200 ml) oil
1 lemon
salt

Thoroughly clean and prepare the mussels (see preceding recipes and page 22), place in a wide saucepan with 3 tbsp water and the whole peeled garlic clove. Cover and cook for a few minutes over a high heat to make the mussels open; detach the molluscs from their shells. Discard any that fail to open.

Beat the eggs with a little salt in a bowl; coat the mussels lightly with flour, shaking off excess, then dip in the beaten egg and finally roll in the breadcrumbs to coat well. Heat the oil in a non-stick pan and fry the mussels a few at a time until golden brown. Remove with a slotted spoon and keep warm on kitchen paper to finish draining.

Transfer to a heated serving dish, garnish with lemon wedges and serve at once.

CLAM AND MUSSEL APPETIZER

1 lb (500 g) small clams
1 lb (500 g) mussels
5 tbsp olive oil
1 clove garlic
few sprigs parsley
2 tbsp sieved tomatoes
juice of $1/_2$ lemon
pepper

Clean the clams and mussels (see pages 22, 23 and preceding recipes). Place in a wide saucepan or deep frying pan with the oil, peeled garlic clove and a sprig of parsley. Cover and place over a high heat for a minute or two to make the bivalves open, stirring and turning once or twice. Take the molluscs off their shells, cover and keep warm. Discard the garlic and parsley and strain the liquid into a small saucepan. Heat the liquid, stir in the sieved tomatoes, the strained lemon juice and a little freshly ground pepper. Add the clams and mussels, heat through for 1–2 minutes over a low heat (do not allow to boil) and serve at once.

SEAFOOD FLAN

1 lb (500 g) mussels
1 lb (500 g) date-shells or medium-sized clams
1 lb (500 g) small curled octopus
4 oz (100 g) peeled prawns or shrimps
2 cloves garlic
1 small bunch parsley
3 tbsp olive oil
5 oz (150 g) frozen peas
7 fl oz (200 ml) dry white wine
14 oz (400 g) frozen puff pastry (thawed)
3 eggs
5 fl oz (150 ml) single cream
salt and pepper

Soak and then scrub the molluscs (see pages 22, 23 and previous recipes); place in a wide saucepan, cover and heat quickly to make them open, stirring once if necessary; discard any that fail to open. Detach the molluscs from their shells.

Clean the baby curled octopus (see page 20; the method is the same), wash thoroughly, and dry with kitchen paper. Cut into small pieces. Chop the peeled garlic with the parsley and sauté gently in the oil in a deep pan. Add the octopus and the peas and cook until the peas are done; add a pinch

of salt and the wine, cover and simmer gently for 15 minutes.

Remove the lid and boil fast over a high heat to reduce the liquid almost to nothing. Reduce the heat, add the molluscs and prawns, stir and cook gently for 15 minutes. Have the pastry ready thawed at room temperature and roll out into a thin sheet; use to line the base and sides of a 9½–10-in (24-cm) spring-release cake tin, deep flan tin or ceramic flan dish, prick the surface with a fork and fill with the seafood mixture.

Beat the eggs with the cream, salt and freshly ground pepper and pour all over the surface of the seafood filling. Place in a preheated oven at 400°F (200°C) mark 6 and bake for about 35 minutes.

MUSSELS AFRICAINE

2¾ lb (1.2 kg) mussels
7 fl oz (200 ml) dry white wine
2 onions
½ oz (10 g) butter
2 tbsp olive oil
1 tbsp plain flour
1 egg yolk
4 tbsp double cream
1 tbsp lemon juice
1 sachet real saffron powder
1½ tbsp finely chopped parsley
salt and peppercorns

Prepare the mussels (see page 22 and previous recipes in this section). Place in a wide saucepan with the wine and 4 coarsely crushed peppercorns, cover and cook for 1–2 minutes over a high heat to open. Detach and discard the empty half shell of each mussel. Strain the juices from the mussels and liquid from the pan.

Peel and finely chop the onions; sweat in the butter and oil. Sprinkle with the flour and cook for

1 minute over a low heat while stirring. Add the strained liquid and simmer very gently for about 7 minutes.

Beat the egg yolk into the cream, add the lemon juice and then stir this into the onion mixture. Cook over the lowest possible heat (the mixture must not reach boiling point), stirring continuously. Mix in the saffron, remove from the heat and add a little salt. Place the mussels on their half shells in a single layer in a wide, heatproof serving platter, cover with the sauce, and place in the oven for 3 minutes at 425°F (220°C) mark 8. Sprinkle with the parsley and serve.

FRENCH OCTOPUS SALAD

3 lb (1.3 kg) octopus

2 cloves garlic

8 oz (250 g) frozen French beans

20 black olives, stoned

1¹/₂ tbsp chopped parsley

6–7 tbsp olive oil

juice of 1 lemon

1 small jar cocktail sauce or 4 fl oz (125 ml) mayonnaise (see page 37) mixed with 1 tbsp tomato ketchup

salt and pepper

Clean and prepare the octopus (see page 21). Wash well and place in a fireproof earthenware cooking pot with the peeled cloves of garlic; cover tightly and cook over a very low heat for 2 hours (the moisture contained in the octopus will prevent it from drying out, provided no steam can escape from the pot). When the octopus is cooked, remove the lid, leave to cool then cut into small pieces. Boil the French beans in salted water until just tender; drain, leave to cool then cut into short lengths. Place the octopus pieces, beans and olives in a bowl and sprinkle with a dressing made from the oil, lemon juice, parsley and freshly ground pepper. Chill briefly before serving. Serve the cocktail sauce separately.

SPECIAL SEAFOOD SALAD

10 oz (300 g) octopus

7 oz (200 g) salmon

7 oz (200 g) tinned tuna

7 oz (200 g) prawns or shrimps

2 oz (50 g) salted anchovies or 8 tinned anchovy fillets

1 tbsp caviar or black lumpfish roe

7 oz (200 g) mixed salad leaves (e.g. escarole, lamb's lettuce and radicchio)

2 large ripe tomatoes

1 clove

¹/₂ bay leaf

9 fl oz (250 ml) mayonnaise

3¹/₂ fl oz (100 ml) olive oil

juice of 1 lemon

12 deep scallop shells

salt

Rinse excess salt from the anchovies and remove bones (or drain if using tinned fillets). Place in a deep dish with the oil and leave to stand for 20 minutes. Trim, wash and shred the salads; blanch, peel and seed the tomatoes then chop. Boil the octopus gently in 1³/₄ pints (1 litre) water with a slice of lemon and the clove for 35–40 minutes. Leave to cool in the cooking liquid. Poach the salmon in just enough water to cover with the half bay leaf.

Drain the octopus, peel off its skin and cut the flesh into small pieces. Place 3 scallop shells on each plate; fill one shell with a quarter of the octopus meat, and the second with a quarter of the drained salmon, cut into fairly small pieces. Dress the prawns with oil and lemon juice and place in the third shell. Repeat for each plate.

Top the octopus-filled shell with a little mixed salad, tomato pieces, some flaked tuna, oil and lemon juice and 2 tbsp mayonnaise. Top the salmon-filled shells with 1 tsp caviar. Chop the anchovy fillets and place on top of the prawns. Chill for 30 minutes before serving.

SQUID WITH RICE

$2^1/_4$–$2^1/_2$ lb (1 kg) whole small squid

4 cloves garlic

1 small bunch parsley

6 tbsp olive oil

pinch mild curry powder

10 fl oz (300 ml) dry white wine

10 oz (300 g) long-grain non-stick rice

1 oz (25 g) butter

$3^1/_2$ fl oz (100 ml) single cream

salt and pepper

Clean and prepare the squid (see page 20). Cut their sacs into rings about $^3/_8$ in (1 cm) wide; cut the tentacles into small pieces. Chop the peeled garlic and the parsley.

Heat the oil in a pan, add the squid, and cook over a moderate heat, stirring for 6–7 minutes; add the garlic and parsley and season with salt, freshly ground pepper and the curry powder. Stir well and pour in the wine, diluted with $3^1/_2$ fl oz (100 ml) water. Cover and simmer gently for 30 minutes, stirring occasionally.

Cook the rice in plenty of boiling salted water for 15 minutes; drain well, transfer to an ovenproof dish and dot small pieces of butter over the top. Sprinkle with a little salt and pepper; place in the oven, at 250°F (130°C) mark $^1/_2$, for 5 minutes to dry. Stir the cream into the squid mixture when its simmering time is up; cook gently for 5 minutes. Add a little salt and pepper if needed. Spoon all over the rice; sprinkle with the chopped parsley and serve immediately.

LINGUINE WITH BABY SQUID

1 lb (500 g) baby squid

1 large onion

2 cloves garlic

1 small bunch parsley

1 small piece chilli pepper

$3^1/_2$ fl oz (100 ml) olive oil

7 fl oz (200 ml) dry white wine

12 oz (350 g) linguine

salt and pepper

Clean and prepare the baby squid (see page 20). Peel and finely chop the onion and garlic, chop the parsley and chilli pepper and sweat in the oil for a few minutes in a large heavy-bottomed saucepan.

Add the squid and fry for 4–5 minutes; season with salt and pepper, cover and simmer very gently for 20 minutes. Add the wine and an equal quantity of water, replace the lid and simmer slowly for a further 20 minutes.

Cook the pasta in plenty of boiling salted water until tender but still with a little bite to it, drain, add to the saucepan containing the squid and stir well very briefly over a high heat. Serve without delay, in heated plates.

MUSSELS WITH CHERVIL

$2^1/_4$–$2^1/_2$ lb (1 kg) mussels, in the shell

1 leek

2 waxy potatoes

1 oz (25 g) butter

18 fl oz (500 ml) milk

4 slices white bread

$1^1/_2$ tsp finely chopped fresh chervil

1 tbsp tomato purée

salt and pepper

Clean and prepare the mussels (see page 22 and previous recipes for mussels in this section). Transfer to a wide saucepan with $3^1/_2$ fl oz (100 ml) water, cover and place over a high heat to open (stir if necessary). Remove from the heat

203

immediately the mussels have opened, discarding any which remain closed. Take the molluscs off their shells and strain the liquid from the pan.

Rinse the leek thoroughly to eliminate any grit; slice the white part only into thin rings; peel and dice the potatoes, add salt and pepper and sweat both in the butter in a covered saucepan for 10 minutes over a low heat. Heat the milk to boiling point and pour into the saucepan containing the vegetables. Add the finely crumbled bread (no crusts), cover and cook over a very gentle heat for a further 30 minutes. Liquidize the contents of the saucepan together with the tomato purée and the strained liquid from the mussels. Pour into a saucepan, add the mussels, a little more salt and freshly ground pepper if necessary and reheat gently. Sprinkle with the finely chopped chervil and serve.

SPAGHETTI WITH MUSSELS AND MUSHROOMS

$2^1/_4$–$2^1/_2$ lb (1 kg) mussels, in the shell
6 tbsp olive oil
2 tsp anchovy paste or anchovy sauce
9 oz (250 g) button mushrooms
$3^1/_2$ fl oz (100 ml) dry white wine
12 oz spaghetti
finely chopped parsley
1 clove garlic
salt and pepper

Clean and prepare the mussels (see page 22 and earlier recipes in this section). Place in a wide saucepan containing 2 tbsp oil; cover tightly and place over a high heat for a minute or two to open the mussels. Discard any that do not open. Take the molluscs off the shell. Save all the juices and oil, strain and pour into a deep dish and add the mussels.

Pour the remaining oil into a saucepan and add

the anchovy paste, blending it into the oil over a low heat; add the finely sliced mushrooms and stir well. Pour in the wine, add a little salt if necessary and a generous amount of freshly ground pepper and cook gently for 10 minutes, stirring occasionally.

Cook the spaghetti in plenty of boiling salted water until tender but still firm. A few minutes before it is done, add the mussels to the mushroom mixture together with the finely chopped garlic and parsley. Heat through. Drain the spaghetti, pour a very little olive oil over it and then mix in the mussel and mushroom mixture. Serve at once.

MUSSEL SOUP

$3^1/_4$–$3^1/_2$ lb ($1^1/_2$ kg) mussels, in the shell
1 clove garlic
$^1/_2$ small onion
$^1/_2$ celery stick
$^1/_2$ carrot
1 small bunch parsley
4 tbsp olive oil
$^1/_2$–1 chilli pepper
$3^1/_2$ fl oz (100 ml) dry white wine
7 fl oz (200 ml) sieved tomatoes
thick slices French bread
salt and pepper

Scrub and clean the mussels as directed on page 22; place in a wide saucepan with 1 peeled clove garlic, cover tightly and place over a high heat for a few minutes to open. Discard any mussels that fail to open. Take the molluscs out of the pan and keep warm. (If you prefer, take the mussels off their shells.) Strain the liquid from the pan and reserve.

Chop the onion, celery, carrot, remaining garlic and the parsley very finely; fry gently in 4 tbsp oil. Add the crumbled chilli pepper and pour in the white wine. Cook fast until the wine has evaporated; pour in the strained reserved liquid.

As soon as this comes to the boil, stir in the sieved tomatoes and $3^{1}/_{2}$ fl oz (100 ml) water. Add the mussels and cook for a further 3 minutes. Season with plenty of freshly ground pepper and serve with the bread, baked until crisp and golden brown in the oven.

rice has absorbed all the liquid but is still moist (it will not be tender yet). Draw aside from the heat and stir in the lightly beaten eggs and a generous pinch of salt. Add the remaining hot fish stock and place in a preheated oven, at 350°F (180°C) mark 4, to bake for 15–20 minutes by which time the rice should have absorbed the liquid and be very tender.

RICE, POTATO AND MUSSEL PIE

10 oz (300 g) mussels
7 oz (200 g) clams
3 tbsp olive oil
1 onion
2–3 fresh or tinned sardines
3 waxy potatoes
2 ripe tomatoes
$^{1}/_{2}$ sachet real saffron powder
14 oz (400 g) risotto rice (e.g. arborio)
$1^{3}/_{4}$ pints (1 litre) fish stock (fumet) (see page 39)
2 eggs
salt

Clean and prepare the mussels and clams (see pages 22–23); transfer to a very wide saucepan, add 2 tbsp water, cover tightly, and cook over a high heat for 1–2 minutes to open the molluscs. Remove the clams and mussels from their shells, straining and reserving their juices.

Sauté the very finely chopped onion in the oil in a fireproof casserole dish until pale golden brown; add the chopped sardines (bones removed) and the peeled potatoes cut into fairly small pieces, the peeled and chopped tomatoes and the saffron mixed with the strained liquid. Cook over a moderate heat for about 15 minutes; add the molluscs and the rice. Stir for 1–2 minutes, add just over half the hot fish stock and cook until the

TAGLIATELLE WITH MUSSELS

$4^{1}/_{2}$ lb (2 kg) mussels, in the shell
4 cloves garlic
4 shallots
$3^{1}/_{2}$ oz (100 g) butter
7 fl oz (200 ml) dry white wine
1 tbsp mild curry powder
1 tsp cumin seeds
1 oz (25 g) plain flour
7 fl oz (200 ml) single cream
9 oz (250 g) tagliatelle
salt and pepper

Soak, scrub and clean the mussels (see page 22). Place in a very wide saucepan containing the peeled, crushed garlic cloves, the peeled and thinly sliced shallots, $2^{1}/_{2}$ oz (70 g) butter, the wine and freshly ground pepper. Cover the pan tightly and cook for a few minutes, to open the mussels; discard any that fail to open. Take all the mussels off the shell except for 15 which will be used for decoration, draining their juices back into the pan. Strain these juices and the liquid in the pan.

Pour the liquid into a small saucepan and stir in the curry powder and the cumin seeds (or use a generous pinch of ground cumin). Heat gently.

Work the flour into 1 oz (25 g) softened butter, add this to the liquid away from the heat and beat with a balloon whisk as it melts. Return to a very low heat (do not allow to boil) and stir in the cream. Heat gently, then add the mussels and a little salt if wished.

Cook the tagliatelle in a large pan of boiling salted water until tender but still firm, and drain. Mix the curry and mussel sauce into the pasta; cover and place in a preheated oven at 425°F (220°C) mark 8 for 4 minutes. Decorate with the reserved mussels in the shell and serve.

CLAM CHOWDER

4 dozen clams
4 oz (125 g) salt pork, in one piece
2 onions
14 oz (400 g) tinned tomatoes
1 celery stalk
1 carrot
few sprigs parsley
1 sprig fresh thyme
1 bay leaf
2 large potatoes
4 crackers
salt and pepper

Wash the clams thoroughly, place in a deep pan or cooking pot with 1¼ pints (750 ml) water or sufficient to cover them and set over a high heat. Bring to the boil, then reduce the heat and simmer until the shells open. (If one or two clams fail to open, discard them.) Place a clean piece of muslin in a sieve and strain the liquid drained from the clams.

Remove the clams from their shells and chop finely. Finely dice the salt pork and fry in a deep, heavy-bottomed saucepan until most of its fat has been rendered; remove the salt pork with a slotted spoon and discard. Peel and finely chop the onions and fry in the pork fat until transparent. Add the chopped tomatoes and simmer, uncovered, while stirring until some of their liquid has evaporated. Chop the celery and carrot and add to the pan, together with the herbs and the strained clam broth. Cover and simmer gently for about 1 hour; add the peeled and diced potatoes and boil for a further 15 minutes or until tender.

Add the chopped clams and simmer to heat through. Add salt to taste and plenty of freshly ground pepper. Crumble the crackers coarsely into the bottom of heated soup bowls and ladle in the soup.

Note: This is an alternative, less rich version of the more traditional New England chowder which has no tomato in it and 16 fl oz (450 ml) milk and 12 fl oz (350 ml) double cream (heated) added after the clams.

SEAFOOD RICE PILAF

1³/₄ lb (800 g) mussels
1³/₄ lb (800 g) small clams
1 lb (500 g) prawns, heads removed
1 shallot
3¹/₂ fl oz (100 ml) dry white wine
1 small onion
7 tbsp olive oil
10 oz (300 g) risotto rice (e.g. arborio)
1 sachet real saffron powder
18 fl oz (500 ml) chicken stock
2 leeks
1 oz (25 g) butter
3¹/₂ fl oz (100 ml) single cream
1 tsp finely chopped fresh chervil
salt

Wash and prepare the mussels and clams (see page 22–23). If you have bought raw prawns, add them to boiling salted water and cook for 2 minutes once the water has returned to the boil. Drain and peel.

Put the mussels and clams in a large saucepan with the peeled and finely sliced shallot, the wine and 2 tbsp of the oil. Cover and bring to the boil, removing the clams with a slotted spoon as soon as they open. Strain the liquid. Take the molluscs out of their shells and keep warm.

Peel and finely chop the onion and fry until pale golden brown in 4 tbsp oil. Add the rice and stir to coat with the oil over a moderate heat. Stir the saffron into 3½ fl oz (100 ml) of the hot strained broth and add to the rice together with the boiling hot chicken stock. Stir and as soon as the liquid has returned to the boil, cover tightly and place carefully in the oven, preheated to 400°F (200°C) mark 6, for 15–17 minutes, by which time the rice should have absorbed all the liquid.

While the rice is cooking, wash the leeks thoroughly and chop the white part only; sweat in the butter and the remaining oil until tender. Add a pinch of salt and the cream and cook, uncovered, for 1–2 minutes over a low heat. Add the prawns, mussels and clams to this sauce and heat through.

Take the rice from the oven when done, spoon the seafood and sauce mixture over the top and sprinkle with the chervil. Serve at once.

cooking gently, stirring and turning, for a few minutes; add the sieved tomatoes, cover and simmer for 10 minutes.

Wash and scrub the shells of the molluscs thoroughly, removing beards and barnacles. Discard any that do not close when tapped. Place in a pan with the bay leaf and the finely sliced shallot. Cover and place over a high heat; remove from the heat as soon as the molluscs have opened, discarding any which fail to open. Take the molluscs off their shells, strain all their juice and reserve.

Add the mussels and clams to the tomato mixture, together with the olives; simmer gently for 3–4 minutes. Cook the spaghetti until tender but still *al dente*, drain and add to the tomato mixture. Stir over a high heat for 1–2 minutes; serve immediately.

SPAGHETTI WITH MUSSELS AND CLAMS

2¼–2½ lb (1 kg) mussels
2¼–2½ lb (1 kg) small clams
1 yellow pepper
2 cloves garlic
4 tbsp olive oil
10 fl oz (300 ml) sieved tomatoes
1 bay leaf
1 shallot
12 black olives, stoned
14 oz (400 g) spaghetti
salt and pepper

Place the pepper under the grill and turn frequently to scorch and loosen the skin; peel and cut into thin strips; fry the peeled and finely chopped garlic in the oil, add the pepper strips and continue

MIXED TAGLIATELLE WITH SEAFOOD

2¼–2½ lb (1 kg) mussels
2¼–2½ lb (1 kg) small clams
4 scallops
7 oz (200 g) prawns, heads removed
2 shallots
1 oz (25 g) butter
1 tbsp olive oil
7 fl oz (200 ml) single cream
5 oz (150 g) egg tagliatelle
5 oz (150 g) green tagliatelle
salt and pepper

Scrub and wash the mussels and clams (see pages 22–23). Place the mussels in one saucepan, the clams in another, add 6 fl oz (180 ml) water to each, cover both and cook very briefly over a high heat to open. Take all but a few (reserve these for decoration) off the shell. Strain the cooking liquid and the juices they produce.

Wash the scallops well, open in a covered pan over a high heat. Take the white cushion of meat and the orange roe off the shell; cut the white part into thin slices. Cook the prawns for 2 minutes in boiling water if raw. Peel.

Sauté the peeled and finely chopped shallots in the butter and oil; add the scallop slices and fry for 1 minute, turning once.

Pour in 9 fl oz (250 ml) of the strained cooking liquid from the mussels and clams. Simmer until the liquid has reduced by half. Add the cream, prawns, mussels and clams. Simmer for 3–4 minutes.

Cook both kinds of tagliatelle together in plenty of boiling salted water, drain and mix with the seafood sauce. Season to taste. Transfer to heated individual plates and decorate with the reserved molluscs in the shell.

RICE SALAD WITH SHELLFISH

1 lb (500 g) mussels
1 lb (500 g) smooth Venus clams
1 lb (500 g) warty Venus clams
14 oz (400 g) fresh or frozen peas
9 fl oz (250 ml) dry white wine
1 onion
9 oz (250 g) long-grain non-stick rice
2 fl oz (50 ml) mayonnaise
2 fl oz (50 ml) single cream
1 tbsp tomato ketchup
1¹/₂ tsp finely chopped fresh celery leaves
1¹/₂ tsp chopped chives
1¹/₂ tsp chopped chervil
1 tsp finely chopped parsley
salt and cayenne pepper

Boil the peas for 5–10 minutes or until tender. Drain and rinse under running cold water.

Prepare the mussels and clams as directed on page 22 and place in a very large, deep pan with the wine and finely chopped onion. Cover and place over a high heat. Remove from the heat as soon as they open. Drain well, straining all the liquid and topping up to 1 pint (¹/₂ litre) with water. Take the molluscs off their shells.

Bring the liquid to the boil in a large saucepan. Sprinkle in the rice, cover tightly and cook for 18 minutes over a very low heat. The rice should absorb all the liquid and be moist and fluffy without sticking and burning on the bottom of the pan. Turn into a bowl and mix with the peas. Add the mayonnaise, mixed with the cream and tomato ketchup, the chopped celery leaves and herbs (except the parsley), and season with a pinch of cayenne pepper and a little salt and freshly ground pepper to taste. Stir briefly and gently; add the seafood and sprinkle with the parsley.

PASTA WITH MIXED SEAFOOD

1 lb (500 g) mussels
1 lb (500 g) tiny curled octopus
14 oz (400 g) baby cuttlefish
2 cloves garlic
3¹/₂ fl oz (100 ml) dry white wine
1 large yellow pepper
1 small bunch parsley
3 tbsp olive oil
9 oz (250 g) ripe tomatoes
1 tsp chopped fresh oregano (or pinch dried)
10 oz (300 g) pasta shapes (e.g. shells)
salt and pepper

Soak, scrub and prepare the mussels (see page 22), place in a saucepan with the garlic and wine, cover and cook for a few minutes over a high heat to make the mussels open.

Drain the mussels well, straining and reserving

the liquid. Take half the molluscs off their shells and leave the others on the half shell, discarding the empty half. Keep warm. Clean and prepare the curled octopus and the cuttlefish (see page 20) and boil them gently in salted water for 20 minutes. Leave to cool in the liquid, then drain and cut into small pieces. Grill the yellow pepper to loosen the skin, peel and cut into strips. Chop a peeled garlic clove with the parsley and fry these together in the oil. Add the pepper, the blanched, skinned and coarsely chopped tomatoes, the octopus and cuttlefish, oregano, salt and freshly ground pepper. Cover and simmer for 10 minutes, adding the mussels after 8 minutes. Boil the pasta in plenty of boiling salted water until just tender, drain, and mix with the sauce. Garnish each serving with some of the mussels on the half shell.

VENETIAN SEAFOOD RISOTTO

10 mussels
2 oz (50 g) peeled prawns
6 Dublin Bay prawns
2 oz (50 g) butter
¹/₂ onion
3¹/₂ fl oz (100 ml) brandy
1 sachet real saffron powder
4–5 fresh or tinned tomatoes
1 chicken leg
10 oz (300 g) risotto rice (e.g. arborio)
salt and pepper

Place the cleaned and prepared mussels in a wide pan, cover, and place over a high heat for 1–2 minutes to make them open. Detach the molluscs from the shells. Sauté the finely chopped onion in 1 oz (25 g) of the butter. Add the mussels and both types of prawn (rinse these first if raw); simmer

gently for 2–3 minutes, then add the brandy. Stir in the saffron powder mixed with a little water and the sieved tomatoes. Simmer for 5 minutes; add 1 pint (600 ml) boiling water and simmer for 10 minutes more. Take the chicken flesh off the bone, discarding the skin; shred the meat and fry in the remaining butter then add to the tomato sauce. Season with salt and freshly ground pepper to taste.

Sprinkle in the rice, stir and cover tightly; place in a preheated oven at 340°F (170°C) mark 3 to bake for 15–20 minutes.

SCALLOP RISOTTO WITH YELLOW PEPPER SAUCE

8 scallops
5 fl oz (150 ml) fish stock (fumet)) (see page 39)
2 yellow peppers
4 shallots
3 fl oz (90 ml) olive oil
3 fl oz (90 ml) single cream
¹/₂ onion
2 oz (50 g) butter
14 oz (400 g) risotto rice (e.g. arborio)
salt and pepper

Make the *fumet* as directed. Grill the pepper, turning frequently, to loosen the skin; peel and cut into thin strips. Finely chop 2 shallots and sweat in 3 tbsp of the oil; add the yellow pepper and sauté for 5–6 minutes. Process half the peppers with the cream in a blender and pour this mixture over the remaining pepper strips; season with salt and pepper and simmer for 5 minutes.

Wash the scallops well, open in a pan over a high heat, detach the molluscs from their shells and poach the white meat for 3 minutes in the *fumet*. Turn off the heat and leave to cool slightly in the liquid. Remove and set aside. Peel and chop the remaining shallots and the $\frac{1}{2}$ onion; sweat in 1 oz (25 g) butter and 2 tbsp oil until transparent.

Sprinkle in the rice and stir over a moderate heat for 1–2 minutes; pour in the strained, reheated fish stock, stirring continuously. When the rice is tender, draw aside from the heat and gently mix in 1 oz (25 g) butter. When this has melted, making the rice glossy, add the yellow pepper sauce and the thinly sliced scallops. Season with freshly ground pepper and serve.

BUTTERFLY PASTA WITH SCALLOPS

$2^1/_4$–$2^1/_2$ lb (1 kg) mussels
12 scallops
2 shallots
$\frac{1}{2}$ oz (10 g) butter
2 tbsp olive oil
1 clove garlic
1 bay leaf
1 sprig thyme
7 fl oz (200 ml) dry white wine
1 tbsp tomato purée
14 oz (400 g) butterfly pasta shapes
3 tbsp single cream
salt and pepper

Wash the mussels and scallops (see pages 22–23). Place the mussels in a large pan and the scallops in a wide pan, cover and cook for 1–2 minutes over a high heat to open. Detach the molluscs from their shells and strain the liquid produced by the mussels. Discard all but the white cushion of meat and orange roe from the scallops.

Peel and finely chop the shallots and sweat until transparent in the butter and oil. Cut the white part of the scallops in half and add to the shallots together with the mussels, the peeled and crushed garlic, bay leaf and thyme. Season with salt and

pepper, add the wine, the strained juices and the tomato purée. Stir well, cover and simmer for 10 minutes. Remove and discard the thyme and bay leaf. Cook the pasta in plenty of boiling salted water until just tender; drain and turn into the seafood mixture. Stir in the cream, simmer for a minute or two and serve at once.

GREEN TAGLIATELLE WITH SCALLOPS

12 scallops
2 large red peppers
1 medium-sized onion
2 cloves garlic
2 oz (50 g) butter
1 tbsp olive oil
1 pint 7 fl oz (800 ml) fish stock (fumet)) (see page 39)
$3^1/_2$ fl oz (100 ml) single cream
10 oz (300 g) green tagliatelle
1 tbsp chopped parsley
salt and pepper

Grill the peppers to loosen the skin, peel and dice. Peel and finely chop the onion and garlic and sweat in $\frac{1}{2}$ oz (10 g) butter and the oil. Add the peppers, salt and pepper, then cover and simmer for 5 minutes. Process in a blender with $3^1/_2$ fl oz (100 ml) *fumet* until very smooth. Pour into a small saucepan, add the cream and simmer slowly for 7–8 minutes while stirring. Scrub the scallop shells under running cold water and open them with an oyster knife or strong, sharp knife. Detach the white meat and coral from the shell, rinse and add the white part only to the *fumet*; bring slowly to the boil, reduce the heat, and poach gently for 3 minutes. Leave to cool in the liquid.

Cook the tagliatelle in plenty of boiling, salted water until just tender but still firm. Drain, mix with the sauce, $1^1/_2$ oz (40 g) melted butter, the sliced white scallop meat, the coral or roe, and season generously with freshly ground pepper. Sprinkle with chopped parsley and serve at once.

SEAFOOD AND WHISKY SOUP

1¹/₂ lb (700 g) assorted clams

4 oz (100 g) baby curled octopus

5 oz (150 g) mantis shrimp

10 oz oz (300 g) king prawns

5 fl oz (150 ml) olive oil

3 cloves garlic

1 small onion

1 small bunch parsley

3 large ripe tomatoes

7 fl oz (200 ml) whisky

thick slices of French bread

salt and pepper

Sauté 1 peeled clove garlic gently in 4 tbsp oil until soft; crush it with a fork to release the juices then discard. Add the peeled and finely chopped onion and chopped parsley to the flavoured oil. Fry gently for 5 minutes. Blanch, peel and seed the tomatoes, chop and add to the onion and parsley.

Rinse the mantis shrimp (small pieces of lobster or other crustaceans may be substituted) under running cold water and add to the tomato mixture; simmer for 25–30 minutes. Put through a food mill (shells and all) or process in the blender and then strain and reserve.

Sauté another garlic clove in 4 tbsp olive oil in another saucepan until pale golden brown, crush gently, then remove and discard; add all the cleaned and prepared molluscs and crustaceans (see pages 17, 20 and 23) to this flavoured oil and heat through. Pour in the whisky, cook, uncovered, until it has evaporated. Add the reserved sauce and simmer for about 20–25 minutes.

Toast the bread slices in the oven until crisp. Cut the remaining garlic clove in half and rub over the bread to flavour. Place a slice of bread in the bottom of each heated soup bowl; ladle in the piping hot soup and serve.

MEDITERRANEAN MUSSEL SOUP

3¹/₄–3¹/₂ lb (1¹/₂ kg) mussels

3¹/₂ fl oz (100 ml) olive oil

2 cloves garlic

1 sprig parsley

1 small piece chilli pepper

coarse white or French bread (optional)

Soak the mussels in cold salted water for 1–2 hours then scrub well. (See page 22 and earlier recipes in this section.) Peel and finely chop the garlic and parsley and sauté gently in a deep pan in the oil; add the mussels and the crumbled chilli pepper.

Cover and cook over a moderate heat for 20 minutes, stirring the mussels once or twice. Serve straight from the pan into heated bowls (discarding any mussels that have failed to open) with, if wished, thick bread slices, baked in the oven till golden brown and crisp.

SAILOR'S SOUP

7 oz (200 g) mussels

5 oz (150 g) baby curled octopus

4 Dublin Bay prawns

5 oz (150 g) small clams

1 gilt-head bream weighing approx. 1¹/₄ lb (600 g)

1 clove garlic

6 tbsp olive oil

1 tbsp plain flour

parsley

9 oz (250 g) fresh or tinned tomatoes

thick slices of French bread

1 lemon

salt and pepper

Trim and gut the fish and wash well; prepare the mussels and clams (see pages 22–23 and earlier recipes in this section). Peel and finely chop the garlic, fry gently in the oil in a large, fireproof casserole dish. Add all the rinsed and dried ingredients (shucked frozen or tinned mussels and clams may be used if fresh are unavailable) to the pan and fry for 2–3 minutes, stirring over a high heat. Sprinkle with the flour, lower the heat and stir for 3–4 minutes.

Add 1¹/₂ tbsp finely chopped parsley, salt and freshly ground pepper. Blanch and peel the tomatoes, chop and lay over the fish. Pour enough hot water into the pan to come half way up the fish. Bake in a preheated oven at 475°F (240°C) mark 9 for 20 minutes or until done. Transfer an equal amount of the various ingredients and liquid to heated individual bowls and serve with lemon wedges and the bread slices, toasted in the oven until crisp.

TAGLIATELLE WITH OYSTERS

20 oysters
2 tbsp olive oil
1¹/₂ tbsp brandy
1 large clove garlic
1 tbsp finely chopped parsley
10 oz (300 g) tagliatelle
2 tbsp double cream
salt and pepper

Scrub the oysters well under running cold water before shucking them (see page 22 for method). Discard the shells and juices.

Pour the oil and brandy into a large saucepan (large enough to accommodate the tagliatelle when they are cooked). Crush the garlic clove and add its juice to the pan, followed by the chopped parsley and the oysters. Season with salt and freshly ground white or black pepper.

Add the tagliatelle to a large pan of boiling salted water; fresh tagliatelle will only take a very few minutes to cook. While the pasta is cooking, warm the oyster mixture over a very low heat for 2–3 minutes, stirring very gently. When the tagliatelle are done, drain and quickly add to the saucepan containing the oysters. Stir briefly, draw aside from the heat and stir in the cream. Serve at once.

BLACK RISOTTO

14 oz (400 g) cuttlefish (with ink sacs)
1 onion
1 clove garlic
5 tbsp olive oil
1 small bunch parsley
7 fl oz (200 ml) dry white wine
10 oz (300 g) risotto rice (e.g. arborio)
2 tbsp sieved tomatoes
1³/₄ pints (1 litre) fish stock (fumet) (see page 39)
salt

Prepare the cuttlefish (see page 20) and snip the ink sacs free taking care not to puncture them. Wash the cuttlefish thoroughly under running cold water and dry with kitchen paper. Cut into fairly thin rings.

Peel the onion and slice wafer-thin; sauté until pale golden brown with the peeled garlic clove and chopped parsley in the oil in a large saucepan. Stir well, remove and discard the garlic, add the cuttlefish, and cook for 6–7 minutes. Pour in the wine and cook, uncovered, until it has evaporated, then sprinkle in the rice. Continue cooking, stirring to coat the rice with oil, then add the tomatoes and a little of the hot fish stock. Keep adding the fish stock as and when the rice has absorbed the previous addition of liquid, simmering over a moderate heat.

About 7 minutes after the first addition of fish stock, add the ink from the ink sacs and stir well. Continue cooking and adding the fish stock until the rice is tender. Serve without delay.

BLACK SPAGHETTI

14 oz (400 g) cuttlefish (with ink sacs)

3 large ripe tomatoes

½ onion

3 tbsp olive oil

2 cloves garlic

4–5 baby onions

12 oz (350 g) spaghetti

salt and pepper

Prepare and clean the cuttlefish as shown on page 20. Remove the ink sacs carefully so that they do not break at this point as the ink is used to colour and flavour this dish. Blanch, peel and seed the tomatoes, then cut into small pieces.

Pour the oil into a deep pan, ideally a fireproof earthenware cooking pot, and sauté the finely chopped onion and garlic together. Add the baby onions, cut lengthwise in half, and continue cooking for 2–3 minutes. Add the tomatoes and season with pepper and salt. Cook for 2 minutes while stirring, then add the well washed and dried cuttlefish bodies, cut into rings; simmer for 25 minutes. Snip the ink sacs so that they release their ink (strain through a very small, fine mesh sieve if wished) and stir this liquid into the pan. Simmer for a further 15 minutes. Cook the spaghetti until tender in plenty of boiling salted water, drain and mix with the contents of the pan.

NEAPOLITAN SPAGHETTI

4 oz (100 g) baby cuttlefish

10 oz (300 g) mussels

10 oz (300 g) small clams

4 oz (100 g) prawns (weight with heads removed)

5 tbsp olive oil

4 cloves garlic

7 fl oz (200 ml) dry white wine

1 small bunch parsley

1 small piece chilli pepper

10 oz (300 g) spaghetti

salt and pepper

If the prawns are raw, boil gently in salted water for 5 minutes. Drain and peel.

Peel the garlic cloves and fry them gently until pale golden brown in the oil in a fairly deep, wide saucepan; crush with a fork to release their juices and then discard the cloves. Prepare the cuttlefish (see page 20; if they are very small you will not need to slice their bodies) and add to the flavoured oil with the soaked and scrubbed mussels and clams (or use frozen or tinned shucked mussels and clams), the wine, 1½ tbsp finely chopped parsley, the crumbled piece of chilli pepper, salt and freshly ground pepper. Cover and cook for 5–6 minutes or until the molluscs' shells have opened; drain well, straining this liquid into another saucepan; add the molluscs to the strained liquid, taking the mussels and clams off the shell if you like. Add the prawns when the spaghetti is nearly done, and heat for 1–2 minutes, stirring.

Cook the spaghetti in plenty of boiling salted water until tender but still firm, drain, add the seafood mixture and serve at once.

PASTA WITH BABY CUTTLEFISH

1 lb (500 g) baby cuttlefish

7 oz (200 g) celery hearts

2 shallots

1 clove garlic

1 oz (25 g) butter

2 tbsp olive oil

3½ fl oz (100 ml) dry white wine

½ stock cube (vegetable or chicken)

12 oz (350 g) fusilli *(spiral pasta shapes)*
3¹/₂ fl oz (100 ml) single cream
1¹/₂ tbsp finely chopped parsley
1 lemon
nutmeg
salt and pepper

Prepare the cuttlefish (see page 20 and previous recipe). Wash them well and dry with kitchen paper. If large enough, cut the bodies into strips and the tentacles into pieces.

Peel and chop the shallots and garlic and sweat in the butter and oil; add the finely chopped celery hearts, stir and cook for 3 minutes over a low heat before adding the cuttlefish. Simmer, stirring for 3 more minutes, pour in the wine and boil over a higher heat until the wine has evaporated. Add 7 fl oz (200 ml) boiling water and the crumbled half stock cube. Stir well, cover, and simmer gently for 20 minutes.

Cook the pasta in a large pan of boiling salted water until *al dente* (tender but still firm), drain, and add to the cuttlefish mixture. Mix well over a high heat for 1–2 minutes. Sprinkle with the parsley, grated lemon rind, plenty of freshly ground pepper and a grating of nutmeg. Serve.

CLAM RISOTTO

2–2¹/₂ lb (1 kg) clams in the shell or 1 1-lb (450-g) tin shucked clams in brine
16 fl oz (450 ml) dry white wine
2 tbsp dried caps (boletus edulis)
1 small carrot
1 small onion or shallot
¹/₂ celery stalk
5 tbsp olive oil
10 oz (300 g) risotto rice (e.g. arborio)
2 tbsp brandy
1 tbsp tomato purée

1¹/₂ pints (900 ml) chicken stock
1 oz (25 g) butter
salt and pepper

Wash the clams thoroughly if they are still in the shell; put them in a large saucepan with half the white wine, cover and place over a high heat until all the shells have opened. Take the clams off their shells and pour the cooking liquid through a very fine sieve. If using tinned clams, drain off the liquid, mix with the white wine and boil over a high heat until reduced to approx. 14 fl oz (400 ml).

Soak the mushrooms in warm water until soft. Peel the carrots and chop finely; sweat in the oil, together with the finely chopped onion and celery, until tender. Cut the drained mushrooms into strips and add to the pan, together with the clams. Pour in 3¹/₂ fl oz (100 ml) of the wine and clam juice mixture. Season with salt and pepper.

Boil gently for 4 minutes before sprinkling in the rice; add the brandy, the remaining wine and clam juice and the tomato purée and continue cooking until the rice has absorbed all the liquid, stirring frequently. Keep the chicken stock hot and add a little at a time to the rice as it cooks until tender (this will take about 20 minutes). The risotto should be moist but not soggy. Draw aside from the heat, stir in the butter gently to allow it to melt and give the risotto a glossy appearance. Serve very hot.

FISHERMAN'S MUSSEL STEW

4¹/₂ lb (2 kg) mussels, in the shell
2 fl oz (50 ml) olive oil
1 clove garlic
1 small piece chilli pepper
4 oz (120 g) fresh or tinned tomatoes
1 small bunch parsley
salt

Prepare the mussels for cooking (see page 22 and earlier recipes in this section). You can use shucked thawed frozen mussels if preferred. Pour the oil into a deep saucepan or cooking pot and add the whole, peeled garlic clove, the finely chopped chilli pepper and parsley and the tomatoes (blanched, peeled and chopped). Cook for 15 minutes, then add a pinch of salt. Remove and discard the garlic clove, add the mussels, cover and cook fast for 10–12 minutes. Discard any mussels that have failed to open. Serve hot.

STUFFED SQUID WITH OLIVES

2¼–2½ lb (1 kg) squid
1 tbsp capers
1 small bunch parsley
1 clove garlic
7 tbsp olive oil
1 lb (450 g) tinned tomatoes (do not drain)
12 black olives, stoned
2 tbsp breadcrumbs
1 hard-boiled egg
1 onion
salt and pepper

Prepare the squid as shown on page 20, detaching the tentacles from the body sacs. Chop the tentacles very finely and place in a saucepan with 4 tbsp of the oil and the finely chopped capers, parsley and garlic. Fry for 3 minutes, then add 2 tinned tomatoes, the coarsely chopped olives and the breadcrumbs. Cook, uncovered, until any excess moisture has evaporated, then stir in the finely chopped hard-boiled egg. Stir well. Use this mixture to stuff the body sacs of the squid, sew up the openings or secure tightly with cocktail sticks or small skewers.

Chop the onion finely and sweat in 3 tbsp oil in a fireproof casserole dish; add the remaining tomatoes and juice together with 4 fl oz (120 ml) water. Arrange the stuffed squid in a single layer in this dish; season with salt and pepper, cover tightly and simmer over a very low heat for 1 hour.

SQUID WITH ANCHOVIES

2¼–2½ lb (1 kg) small squid
4 tbsp olive oil
1 small bunch parsley
4 tinned anchovy fillets
3½ fl oz (100 ml) dry white wine
1¼ lb (600 g) fresh or tinned tomatoes
½ chilli pepper
salt and pepper

Prepare, wash and dry the squid (see page 20), cut their bodies into rings and chop the tentacles coarsely.

Sweat the finely chopped parsley in the oil in a large casserole dish or fireproof cooking pot (ideally earthenware). Add the drained, chopped anchovy fillets and crush into the oil until completely broken up. Add the squid and the wine. Cook over a moderate heat, uncovered, until the wine has reduced by half then add the chopped tomatoes.

Crumble the chilli pepper into the casserole dish; season with salt and freshly ground pepper. Cover tightly and simmer slowly for 20 minutes. Serve straight from the casserole dish or cooking pot.

Note: Serve with moulded steamed rice and French bread.

SQUID EN PAPILLOTE

8 squid
3½ oz (100 g) peeled prawns
3½ oz (100 g) tinned crabmeat
1 small bunch parsley
2 cloves garlic

4 tbsp freshly grated Parmesan cheese
3 tinned tomatoes
5 tbsp breadcrumbs
5 tbsp olive oil
1 egg
salt and pepper

Prepare and clean the squid for cooking (see page 20) detaching the tentacles from the body sacs (these will be stuffed). Chop the prawns and place in a bowl. Add the drained, flaked crabmeat (pick out any pieces of cartilage and discard), the finely chopped parsley and garlic, grated cheese and the drained, seeded and chopped tomatoes. Fry the breadcrumbs in 3 tbsp of the oil and add to the bowl. Stir in the lightly beaten egg, season with salt and freshly ground pepper, mix thoroughly and use this mixture to stuff the body sacs of the squid, securing with cocktail sticks or small skewers. Take 4 large squares of heavy duty greaseproof paper or foil and place 2 stuffed sacs and some of the tentacles in the centre of each. Drizzle a little oil over and seal the parcels securely. Bake at 400°F (200°C) mark 6 for 30 minutes.

SCALLOP KEBABS

16 scallops
3 oz (80 g) butter
1 tbsp olive oil
8 mushrooms
juice of ¹/₂ lemon
1 shallot
7 oz (200 g) breadcrumbs
salt and pepper

Place the well washed and scrubbed scallops flat in a very wide pan over a high heat to open. Rinse the white 'cushion' of meat and the coral carefully, dry and fry for 3 minutes in 1 oz (25 g) butter with 1 tbsp oil, turning once; do not allow to brown at all. Drain, reserving the liquid, and set aside on a plate.

Wipe the mushrooms with a damp cloth, remove the stalks and sprinkle the caps with lemon juice. Slice the caps horizontally in half to form two discs. Peel and finely chop the shallot and sauté in the scallop cooking juices. Add the mushrooms after 2 minutes, season with salt and pepper and sauté for another 2 minutes.

Thread the prepared ingredients on to 4 wooden skewers or satay sticks, alternating the scallops (white meat and coral) and mushrooms. Melt the rest of the butter, season it with salt and freshly ground pepper and roll the kebabs in this, then roll in the breadcrumbs. Grill for 6 minutes, turning once half way through this time.

CHINESE SCALLOPS

12 scallops
2 carrots
2 courgettes
10 oz (300 g) French beans
plain flour
4 tbsp sunflower oil
¹/₂ oz (10 g) butter
1 oz (25 g) dried Chinese (wood ear) mushrooms
7 oz (200 g) bean sprouts
1 tbsp paprika
1 tbsp soy sauce
salt and cayenne pepper

Wash and trim the vegetables; soak the mushrooms in hot water to soften and plump up. Shred the carrots and courgettes in the food processor or cut into thin, matchstick strips; cut the beans into lengths to match the carrots and courgettes .

Open the scallops as shown on page 23; take the white meat and coral off the shells and rinse under running cold water. Thawed frozen scallops can also be used. (The coral is not used for this recipe; reserve for use in a sauce or another dish if wished.) Stir-fry the scallop meat for 2 minutes in 2 tbsp very hot oil; transfer it to a dish and keep warm. Stir-fry the carrots, courgettes and beans in 2 tbsp very hot oil with the butter in another pan. Rinse and drain the soaked mushrooms, squeeze out excess moisture and mix with the other vegetables; cover and cook gently for 8 minutes. Turn up the heat, add the bean sprouts, paprika and cayenne pepper and stir-fry for a minute or two. Add the soy sauce and salt and pepper if needed. Stir quickly, add the scallops, cover and simmer for 2 minutes. Serve at once.

MUSSEL TARTLETS

20 large mussels
3¹/₂ oz (90 g) butter
9 oz (250 g) frozen whole leaf spinach
nutmeg
12 oz (350 g) frozen puff pastry
1 small onion
1 shallot
2 tbsp finely chopped parsley
3¹/₂ fl oz (100 ml) double cream
2 egg yolks
3¹/₂ fl oz (100 ml) dry white wine
salt and pepper

Thaw the spinach completely; chop coarsely and add to 1¹/₂ oz (40 g) melted butter; cover and cook over a very low heat for 10 minutes. Season with a little salt, nutmeg and freshly ground pepper when cooked.

Roll the thawed pastry out into a thin sheet and use to line four lightly buttered 4¹/₂- or 5-in (12-cm) tart pans. Prick the bottom of each tart shell with a fork to prevent puffing during baking. Bake in a preheated oven at 425°F (220°C) mark 7 for 12 minutes or until done.

Prepare the mussels (see page 22) and place in a large saucepan with the onion, the peeled and chopped shallot, the parsley and 1 oz (25 g) of the butter. Take the molluscs off their shells; strain all the liquid produced during cooking (through a piece of muslin placed in a fine sieve) and reduce considerably over a high heat. Turn down the heat and stir in the cream; beat in 1 oz (25 g) solid butter with a balloon whisk, adding a small piece at a time. Continue simmering over a very low heat while stirring with a wooden spoon until the mixture coats the back of the spoon.

Place the egg yolks in a heatproof bowl or top of a double boiler, add the wine and continue stirring over barely simmering water with a palette knife as it thickens. When the mixture is thick enough to coat the back of a metal spoon, combine it with the cream sauce, season with salt and pepper to taste, stir in the mussels and heat very gently for 1–2 minutes, stirring continuously.

Spread out one quarter of the spinach in each pastry shell, cover with 2 tbsp of the mussel mixture and place under a preheated grill to brown lightly. Serve without delay.

MUSSELS À LA GRECQUE

4¹/₂ lb (2 kg) mussels
7 oz (200 g) long-grain non-stick rice
2 tbsp currants
2 onions
8 tbsp olive oil
3 tbsp pine nuts
1¹/₂ tbsp chopped parsley
pinch ground cinnamon
salt and pepper

Cook the rice in plenty of boiling salted water until tender but still firm. Drain well and spread out on a clean dry cloth, using your fingers to ensure that the grains are well separated. Soak and scrub the mussels (see page 22), place in a large pan, cover and put over a high heat to make them open,

217

turning them over once or twice. Drain, reserving and straining all the juices released during cooking. Remove and discard the empty half of the bivalves.

Soak the currants in hot water for 15 minutes to soften, then squeeze out excess moisture. Peel and finely chop the onion. Sweat in 3 tbsp of the oil until transparent and add the drained currants and the pine nuts. Cook for 1 minute, stirring, then add the parsley, salt, freshly ground pepper and the cinnamon. Add the rice and stir gently but thoroughly.

Pack a little of this mixture around each mussel on the half shell. Place in a single layer in a very wide, shallow pan and cover each mollusc with a few drops of oil. Pour the strained and reserved cooking juices into the pan (make up to about 8 fl oz (225 ml) with water if necessary), cover and simmer gently for about 20 minutes.

MUSSELS WITH CORIANDER

$2^1/_4$–$2^1/_2$ lb (1 kg) mussels
2 shallots
1 small bunch fresh coriander leaves
1 oz (25 g) butter
7 fl oz (200 ml) dry white wine
7 fl oz (200 ml) mayonnaise
1 egg white
salt and pepper

Prepare the mussels for cooking (see page 22). Finely chop the shallots and coriander leaves.

Melt the butter in a large cooking pot and sweat the shallots for 3 minutes; pour in the wine, bring to the boil, then add the mussels, some freshly ground pepper, and $1^1/_2$ tbsp of the chopped coriander. Cover and cook over a high heat briefly until the mussels open. Discard any that fail to do so.

Drain, strain the liquid and mix 5 tbsp of it into the mayonnaise, followed by 1 tsp of the chopped coriander; mix well and chill in the refrigerator. Leave the mussels on the half shell, arranging

them on a large serving plate and discarding the empty half shells.

Beat the egg white until stiff and fold half of it into the mayonnaise; place a very small amount of this mixture on each mussel and hand round any remaining mayonnaise separately.

STUFFED MUSSELS

$2^1/_4$–$2^1/_2$ lb (1 kg) large mussels
2 cloves garlic, finely chopped
$1^1/_2$ tbsp parsley, finely chopped
2 oz (60 g) freshly grated hard cheese
2 tbsp fine breadcrumbs
2 eggs
1 tbsp olive oil
salt and pepper

Soak, scrub and prepare the mussels (see page 22). Place them in a large pan with 3 tbsp water, cover and place over a high heat to make them open. Keep the molluscs on their half shells, discarding the empty halves. Transfer to a large, shallow fireproof dish containing $3^1/_2$ fl oz (100 ml) water. Cook gently for 4 minutes.

Make the stuffing: mix the last six ingredients listed above very thoroughly and leave to stand for 5 minutes. Heap a small amount of this stuffing on top of each mussel. Place under a preheated grill and cook for about 5 minutes or until brown and crisp on top.

MUSSELS WITH GINGER

$2^1/_4$–$2^1/_2$ lb (1 kg) large mussels
2 onions
2 oz (50 g) fresh ginger
2 cloves garlic
2 green chilli peppers

1 tbsp ground cumin

1 tsp freshly ground pepper

2 cloves

4 tbsp oil

salt

Scrub the mussels with a stiff brush under running cold water to remove beards and barnacles. Place in a large bowl of salted cold water and leave to stand for 2 hours, changing the water twice and adding salt each time. Peel the onions and slice into very thin rings. Peel the fresh ginger root and the garlic and slice wafer-thin. Remove the core, seeds and white membrane and slice the chilli pepper. Mix the sliced onion, ginger, garlic and chilli with the well drained mussels (still in their shells) in a large bowl, add the cumin and cloves; leave to stand for 10 minutes.

Heat the oil in a large pan and add the entire contents of the bowl. Cover tightly and cook fast for 5 minutes, removing the lid only to stir the mussels once or twice. Pour in 4 fl oz (100 ml) water, add a little salt, and turn down the heat. Replace the lid and simmer for 20 minutes. Serve very hot.

BAKED MUSSELS

1 lb (500 g) mussels

8 oz (250 g) baby squid

14 oz (400 g) small shrimps

1 small bunch parsley

3 cloves garlic

3 tbsp freshly grated hard cheese

2 tbsp breadcrumbs

3 eggs

6–8 thick slices white bread

dry white wine

butter

salt and pepper

Clean and prepare the mussels (see page 22 and earlier recipes in this section) and place in a large saucepan over a high heat with the lid on and cook briefly to open. Prepare (see page 20) and wash the squid and boil gently in salted water for 10 minutes. Drain and cut into small pieces. If the prawns are raw, boil for 1 minute in salted water. Drain and peel.

Chop the parsley and garlic together and mix in a bowl with the cheese and the breadcrumbs. Beat the eggs lightly in a bowl with salt and pepper, add the mussels, squid pieces and prawns and stir. Remove the crusts from the bread slices, line the bottom of a lightly buttered ovenproof dish neatly with them, and sprinkle with just enough white wine to moisten. Pour in the egg mixture, distributing the molluscs and crustaceans evenly, sprinkle the garlic mixture all over the surface and bake at 400°F (200°C) mark 6 for 25 minutes.

AMALFI SALAD

2¼–2½ lb (1 kg) mussels

2¼–2½ lb (1 kg) small clams

4 scallops

3 large waxy potatoes

7 fl oz (200 ml) dry white wine

2 shallots

1 oz (25 g) butter

7 fl oz (200 ml) single cream

few sprigs parsley

salt and pepper

Choose a variety of potato which will remain firm when cooked, and boil until tender, then slice into thin rounds. Clean and prepare the mussels and clams (see pages 22, 23), rinse well and place in a large cooking pot with the wine and the finely chopped shallots. Cover and cook briefly over a high heat to make them open, turning once or twice. Unless you have bought frozen ones, open the scallops (see page 23), detach the white cushion of meat, rinse well and slice thinly. Take the mussels and clams off their shells; strain and reserve the liquid.

Sauté the scallop slices in the butter for only a few seconds. Reduce the strained mussel and clam liquid by half over a high heat, lower the heat, stir in the cream and season with salt and freshly ground pepper. Arrange the potato slices in a serving bowl and add the molluscs. Give the cream sauce a final stir and pour it all over; sprinkle with 1½ tbsp finely chopped parsley.

TOP SHELLS WITH WHITE WINE

2¼–2½ lb (1 kg) top shells

1 onion

olive oil

1 bay leaf

1 green chilli pepper

3½ fl oz (100 ml) dry white wine

2 large ripe tomatoes

salt

Wash the top shells thoroughly, add to boiling salted water and cook for 15 minutes. Drain and extract the mollusc from inside each shell with a pin or small skewer. Peel the onion and slice very thinly; sweat in 3 tbsp olive oil, add the molluscs, the bay leaf, chilli pepper and a pinch of salt. Fry briskly for about 5 minutes.

Remove and discard the bay leaf and chilli pepper; sprinkle the wine all over the molluscs and cook over a high heat until evaporated. Add the blanched, peeled, seeded and chopped tomatoes (tinned tomatoes can also be used) and simmer uncovered for 15–20 minutes.

TOP SHELLS WITH DUCK

1¾ lb (800 g) top shells

1 bay leaf

1 sprig thyme

1 small oven-ready duck

3½ fl oz (100 ml) dry sherry

2 slices ham

salt and pepper

Cook the top shells for 15 minutes in plenty of boiling salted water together with the herbs and a few peppercorns. Drain and extract the molluscs with a small skewer or pin. Lower the duck into a large pan full of boiling water, leave for 1 minute, then remove, drain and dry with kitchen paper. Pour 5 tbsp water into a wide, deep pan or casserole dish and place the duck in it. Heat until the water comes to the boil, cover tightly and cook over the lowest possible heat for 1 hour, turning the duck now and then. After 1 hour, pour the sherry over the duck, and add the diced ham and the molluscs. Stir, bring the liquid to the boil, cover tightly again and cook very slowly for a further 30 minutes. Stir and turn to prevent the ingredients sticking and burning, then cook for a final 30 minutes, by which time all the liquid should have evaporated. Cut the duck meat into small pieces, draining off as much fat as possible and transfer to a heated serving dish with the molluscs and ham. Serve very hot.

BRAISED OCTOPUS

3¼–3½ lb (1.5 kg) small octopus

2–3 cloves garlic

3½ fl oz (100 ml) oil

1 small bunch parsley

1 chilli pepper

4–5 large fresh or tinned tomatoes

thick slices of French bread

salt

Clean and prepare the octopus (see page 21). Peel and crush the garlic and sauté in a cooking pot or deep fireproof casserole dish (earthenware is best) in the oil. Add the octopus, fry for 2–3 minutes, stirring, then add the finely chopped parsley and chilli pepper, the blanched, peeled and seeded, chopped tomatoes and a pinch of salt. Place a piece of greaseproof paper over the top of the cooking pot, tie tightly in place with string and then place the lid on top (the octopus must cook slowly with only the moisture of the tomatoes and its own moisture so as little steam as possible must escape). Simmer over the lowest possible heat using a heat diffuser if necessary for $2\frac{1}{2}$ hours. (Do not remove the lid or paper to check on the octopus.) Serve with oven-browned slices of bread.

OCTOPUS SALAD

2 octopus weighing approx. $1\frac{1}{2}$–$1\frac{3}{4}$ lb (750 g) each

1 bay leaf

1 onion

1 carrot

2 waxy potatoes

$3\frac{1}{2}$ oz (100 g) green olives, stoned

5 tbsp olive oil

juice of 1 lemon

few sprigs parsley

salt

Clean and prepare the octopus (see page 21). Add them to a large pan full of cold water with the bay leaf, chopped onion and carrot and 1 tsp coarse sea salt. Bring to the boil and simmer for 35–40 minutes. Leave the octopus to cool in the cooking liquid.

Boil the washed potatoes until tender; peel and dice. Cut the olives in half and mix with the potatoes in a salad bowl. Drain the octopus, cut off the suckers, slice the flesh into small pieces and mix with the potatoes and olives.

Beat together the olive oil, strained lemon juice, very finely chopped parsley and a pinch of salt. Pour over the salad, stir briefly, and serve.

SEAFOOD BAKE

4 baby octopus

4 small cuttlefish

4 small squid

1 scorpionfish or rockfish weighing approx. $1\frac{3}{4}$ lb (800 g)

8 Dublin Bay prawns

8 tbsp olive oil

4 medium-sized potatoes, parboiled

2 oz (50 g) freshly grated Parmesan cheese

2 tbsp breadcrumbs

1 small bunch parsley

2 cloves garlic

salt

Prepare the octopus, cuttlefish and squid (see pages 20, 21) and cut into small pieces. Trim, gut and clean the fish and slice into fairly small pieces. Blanch the prawns in boiling salted water for 4 minutes if raw, drain and peel.

Grease a large ovenproof dish or casserole with 4 tbsp oil and place the seafood mixture in it; lay the peeled and sliced potatoes on top, seasoning with salt and freshly ground pepper if wished. Sprinkle with the Parmesan cheese (or any hard grating cheese), breadcrumbs, finely chopped parsley and garlic. Sprinkle with the remaining oil, cover tightly with a sheet of foil and bake in a preheated oven at 425°F (220°C) mark 7 for 30 minutes. Remove the foil and cook for a further 15 minutes to brown. Serve at once, straight from the cooking dish.

Note: Serve with a crisp green salad and lightly boiled courgettes.

CUTTLEFISH PRIMAVERA

$2^1/_4$–$2^1/_2$ lb (1 kg) small cuttlefish

$3^1/_2$ fl oz (100 ml) olive oil

few sprigs parsley

2 cloves garlic

8 fl oz (225 ml) dry white wine

juice of $^1/_2$ lemon

1 bay leaf

15 black olives, stoned

1 small onion

$^1/_2$ oz (10 g) butter

5 oz (150 g) frozen peas

3 small carrots

$^1/_2$ stock cube (vegetable or chicken)

few leaves lamb's lettuce

salt and pepper

Prepare and clean the cuttlefish (see page 20), but do not slice. Grease a casserole dish with oil, spread the whole cuttlefish over the bottom and sprinkle with the finely chopped parsley and garlic. Pour in the white wine, sprinkle with the lemon juice, salt and the crumbled bay leaf; add the olives and sprinkle with 4 tbsp oil. Cover with a sheet of foil and bake at 400°F (200°C) mark 6 for 40 minutes.

Finely chop the onion and fry until pale golden brown in 2 tbsp oil and the butter. Add the still frozen peas and the diced carrots, and cook gently, stirring, for 3–4 minutes. Add the stock cube dissolved in $3^1/_2$ fl oz (100 ml) hot water, cover and cook slowly for 20 minutes.

Take the casserole dish out of the oven and place over a high heat to reduce the liquid to almost nothing. Add the peas and carrots, season with a little freshly ground pepper, and mix carefully over a moderate heat for 2–3 minutes. Sprinkle with the torn salad leaves and serve at once while still very hot.

Boiled new potatoes and a green vegetable, e.g. French beans, broccoli or broad beans, would make a suitable accompaniment.

CUTTLEFISH KEBABS

$1^3/_4$ lb (800 g) cuttlefish

4 cloves garlic

1 tbsp chopped fresh rosemary

5 oz (150 g) fine dry breadcrumbs

7 fl oz (200 ml) olive oil

1 lemon

salt and pepper

Prepare the cuttlefish (see page 20), wash and dry well; cut each one in half or into three.

Finely chop the peeled garlic cloves and mix with the rosemary in a large bowl; add the breadcrumbs, oil, salt and freshly ground pepper, and stir well. Roll the cuttlefish pieces in this mixture, coating them well all over. Thread on to skewers and grill under a moderately hot grill turning several times. (Alternatively, cook in the oven at 325°F (180°C) mark 4 for about 40 minutes or until done.) Serve very hot, with lemon wedges.

CUTTLEFISH WITH VEGETABLE STUFFING

$2^1/_4$–$2^1/_2$ lb (1 kg) cuttlefish

1 shallot

4 tbsp olive oil

$3^1/_2$ oz (100 g) red pepper

$3^1/_2$ oz (100 g) aubergine

4 oz (120 g) courgettes

5 oz (150 g) button mushrooms

1 onion

2 oz (50 g) butter

1 egg

3 tbsp freshly grated Parmesan cheese

2 tbsp breadcrumbs

1¹/₂ tbsp finely chopped parsley

salt and pepper

Prepare the cuttlefish (see page 20). Boil the body sacs in salted water gently for 20 minutes. Chop the tentacles and fry in 2 tbsp of the oil with the thinly sliced shallot; add a pinch of salt, cover and simmer very slowly for about 20 minutes until the cooking juices have reduced almost to nothing.

Shred the pepper into strips; coarsely chop the aubergine or cut into small dice; grate the courgettes. Slice the mushrooms thinly. Sweat the finely chopped onion in ¹/₂ oz (10 g) butter and 2 tbsp oil. Add all the vegetables and the mushrooms, season with salt and pepper and cook, stirring, for 5–6 minutes.

Add the tentacles to the vegetables, continue cooking for 3–4 minutes then turn off the heat. Beat the eggs and cheese together and add to the pan, mixing well. Stuff the body sacs with this mixture and secure with small skewers or cocktail sticks.

Transfer to a casserole dish greased with butter, sprinkle with the breadcrumbs mixed with the parsley, drizzle 1 oz (25 g) melted butter over the surface and place in a preheated oven at 400°F (200°C) mark 6 to bake for 15 minutes.

CUTTLEFISH WITH PEAS

2¹/₄–2¹/₂ lb (1 kg) cuttlefish

few sprigs parsley

2 cloves garlic

6 tbsp olive oil

3¹/₂ fl oz (100 ml) dry white wine

1 tsp tomato purée

¹/₂ onion

10 oz (300 g) peas

1 stock cube (vegetable or chicken)

salt and pepper

Prepare the cuttlefish (see page 20). Reserve one of the ink sacs and one of the sacs containing the yellowish liquid. Slice the bodies into rings and the tentacles into small pieces. Wash thoroughly and dry. Fry the finely chopped parsley and garlic in 6 tbsp of the oil; add the cuttlefish and fry gently, stirring and turning, for a few minutes. Pour in the white wine and cook over a slightly higher heat until it has evaporated. Season with a little salt and plenty of freshly ground pepper and add 3 tbsp hot water with the tomato paste dissolved in it. Cover and simmer over a very low heat for 45 minutes.

Sauté the finely chopped onion in 3 tbsp oil in a saucepan. Add the peas and crumbled stock cube; cover and cook very gently for 15 minutes. Add the contents of this pan to the cuttlefish after it has cooked for the 45 minutes, stir in the ink and the yellow liquid; continue cooking for 5 minutes longer, then serve.

BAKED CUTTLEFISH

2¹/₄–2¹/₂ lb (1 kg) small cuttlefish

3¹/₂ fl oz (100 ml) olive oil

3 cloves garlic

3¹/₂ fl oz (100 ml) dry white wine

3 tbsp finely chopped parsley

2 tbsp fine breadcrumbs

3 tbsp freshly grated hard cheese

salt and pepper

Prepare the cuttlefish (as shown on page 20), separating the tentacles from the body sacs. Wash them thoroughly, and dry with kitchen paper; fry in the very hot oil and season with salt and pepper.

Reduce the heat, add the finely chopped garlic and the wine, cover and simmer gently for 15 minutes. Remove the lid, sprinkle with a mixture of the parsley, breadcrumbs and cheese, then scoop up some of the cooking juices and sprinkle over the surface; place, uncovered, in a preheated oven to bake for 10 minutes at 425°F (220°C) mark 7 or until golden brown.

SEAFOOD STEW

7 oz (200 g) baby cuttlefish
10 oz (300 g) mussels
10 oz (300 g) small clams
7 oz (200 g) shrimps or small prawns
7 oz (200 g) tinned crabmeat
7 oz (200 g) fillets Dover sole
7 oz (200 g) fillets of cod, hake or haddock
7 oz (200 g) mantis shrimp (optional)
7 fl oz (200 ml) olive oil
1 green pepper
1 lb (450 g) tinned tomatoes
1 small bunch parsley
2 cloves garlic
7 oz (200 g) spinach
3–4 basil leaves
salt and pepper

Trim, clean, and prepare all the seafood and fish (see pages 9–23). Boil the spinach for up to 5 minutes or until tender using only the water that clings to the leaves. Squeeze out excess moisture. Heat the oil in a very large deep casserole dish. Add the diced pepper and drained and seeded tomatoes, the chopped parsley and garlic, the spinach, basil, salt and freshly ground pepper. Sauté, stirring continuously, for 5–6 minutes, then add the peeled shrimps or prawns (see page 17), the cuttlefish, drained crabmeat (remove any pieces of cartilage) and the mantis shrimp if used; cover and simmer for 15 minutes.

If unshucked mussels and clams in their shells are used, open by heating over a high heat and detach the molluscs from their shells. (If frozen or tinned shucked mussels and clams are used, thaw or drain.) Add the fish fillets, cut into bite-sized pieces, to the pan, followed by the molluscs. Add 14 fl oz (400 ml) water and salt and pepper to taste, then bring to the boil and simmer for 15 minutes. Serve with rice.

·FRESHWATER FISH·

RAINBOW TROUT MOUSSE

p. 233

Time: 1 hour 30 minutes
Difficulty: Easy
Hot appetizer

SALMON SOUFFLÉ

p. 233

Time: 1 hour 15 minutes
Difficulty: Easy
Hot appetizer

SMOKED SALMON HORS D'OEUVRES

p. 233

Time: 20 minutes
+ chilling time
Difficulty: Very easy
Cold appetizer

SMOKED SALMON IN ASPIC

p. 234

Time: 40 minutes
+ 3 hours chilling time
Difficulty: Easy
Cold appetizer

Harlequin pike

CHILLED SALMON AND PRAWN FLAN

p. 234

Time: 40 minutes
+ cooling and defrosting time
Difficulty: Very easy
Cold appetizer

SMOKED SALMON NORWEGIAN STYLE

p. 235

Time: 20 minutes
Difficulty: Very easy
Cold appetizer

FRESHWATER SHAD WITH ANCHOVY DRESSING

p. 235

Time: 1 hour
+ marinating time
Difficulty: Very easy
Hot appetizer

CHAR MOUSSE

p. 235

Time: 1 hour 15 minutes
Difficulty: Very easy
Hot appetizer

EEL WITH TARTARE SAUCE

p. 236

Time: 45 minutes
Difficulty: Easy
Hot appetizer

HARLEQUIN PIKE

p. 236

Time: 1 hour
Difficulty: Fairly easy
Hot appetizer

CARP PÂTÉ

p. 237

Time: 2 hours
Difficulty: Fairly easy
Cold appetizer

PASTA WITH SALMON

p. 237

Time: 30 minutes
Difficulty: Very easy
First course

CHEF'S TROUT

p. 238

Time: 1 hour 30 minutes
Difficulty: Fairly easy
First course

EEL RISOTTO

p. 238

Time: 1 hour 10 minutes
Difficulty: Easy
First course

BARBEL WITH PINE NUT SAUCE

p. 238

Time: 1 hour 30 minutes
Difficulty: Very easy
Main course

2
Coregonus oxyrhynchus

4
Lucioperca lucioperca

6
Alosa fallax lacustris

7
Barbus barbus

8
Anguilla anguilla

1

Dutch: Snoek
English: Pike
French: Brochet
German: Hecht
Italian: Luccio
Spanish: Lucio

2

English: Houting
French: Bondelle
German: Schnäpel
Italian: Coregone bondella

3

Dutch: Zalm
English: Salmon
French: Saumon
German: Lachs
Italian: Salmone
Spanish: Salmón

4

Dutch: Snoekbaars
English: Pike-perch
French: Sandre
German: Zander
Italian: Lucioperca
Spanish: Luciperca

5

Dutch: Karper
English: Carp
French: Carpe
German: Karpfen
Italian: Carpa
Spanish: Carpa

6

German: Alse
Italian: Agone

7

Dutch: Barbeel
English: Barbel
French: Barbeau
German: Barbe
Italian: Barbo
Spanish: Barbo

8

Dutch: Aal
English: Eel
French: Anguille
German: Aal
Italian: Anguilla gialla
Spanish: Anguila

9

Dutch: Steur
English: Sturgeon
French: Esturgeon
German: Störe
Italian: Storione
Spanish: Esturion

10

English: Largemouth black
bass
French: Perche-truite
German: Forellenbarsch
Italian: Persico trota

11

Italian: Anguilla argentata

12

English: Butterfish
French: Perche-soleil
German: Sonnenbarsch
Italian: Persico sole

13

English: Channel catfish
French: Poisson-chat
German: Gatüpgelter
Gabelwels
Italian: Pesce gatto

14

English: Whitefish (Pollan)
French: Lavaret du bourget
German: Blaufelchen
Italian: Coregone lavarello

15

Dutch: Zeelt
English: Tench
French: Tanche
German: Schleie
Italian: Tinca
Spanish: Tenca

16

Dutch: Regenboog forel
English: Rainbow trout
French: Truite arc-en-ciel
German: Regenbogenforelle
Italian: Trota iridea

17

Dutch: Kopvoorn
English: Chub
French: Chevaine
German: Döbel
Italian: Cavedano

18

Dutch: Kwabaal
English: Burbot
French: Lotte de rivière
German: Aalquappe
Italian: Bottatrice
Spanish: Lota

19

Dutch: Baars
English: Perch
French: Perche
German: Barsch
Italian: Persico comune
Spanish: Perca

1

Esox lucius

3

Salmo salar

5

Cyprinus carpio

Salmon tartare

SALMON COULIBIAC

p. 250

Time: 1 hour 30 minutes
+ 20 minutes standing time
Difficulty: Fairly easy
Main course

GRILLED SALMON STEAKS WITH ANCHOVY BUTTER

p. 251

Time: 15 minutes
+ time for desalting anchovies
Difficulty: Very easy
Main course

BARBECUED SALMON

p. 251

Time: 1 hour
Difficulty: Very easy
Main course

STURGEON STEAKS WITH TARRAGON AND SHERRY VINEGAR

p. 252

Time: 20 minutes
Difficulty: Very easy
Main course

SWEET-SOUR STURGEON STEAKS

p. 252

Time: 45 minutes
Difficulty: Very easy
Main course

EEL WITH ARTICHOKES AND OLIVES

p. 252

Time: 1 hour 30 minutes
Difficulty: Very easy
Main course

Pike savarin mould

BRAISED EEL

p. 253

Time: 1 hour
Difficulty: Easy
Second course

EEL IN RED WINE

p. 253

Time: 45 minutes
Difficulty: Very easy
Main course

EEL WITH MIXED VEGETABLES

p. 254

Time: 1 hour 15 minutes
Difficulty: Easy
Main course

EEL STEW WITH BEER

p. 254

Time: 1 hour 10 minutes
+ soaking time
Difficulty: Fairly easy
Main course

EEL IN WHITE WINE

p. 255

Time: 2 hours
Difficulty: Very easy
Main course

EEL MASCAGNI

p. 255

Time: 1 hour
Difficulty: Easy
Main course

Sturgeon steaks with tarragon and sherry vinegar

EEL IN BRANDY SAUCE

p. 256

Time: 2 hours
Difficulty: Easy
Main course

FRIED BREADED EEL

p. 256

Time: 2 hours
Difficulty: Easy
Main course

EEL WITH PEAS

p. 256

Time: 1 hour 10 minutes
Difficulty: Easy
Main course

EEL WITH SPINACH, NETTLES AND SORREL

p. 257

Time: 1 hour
Difficulty: Fairly easy
Main course

PIKE WITH HERBS AND MUSHROOMS

p. 257

Time: 1 hour 10 minutes
Difficulty: Easy
Main course

STUFFED ROAST PIKE

p. 258

Time: 1 hour 40 minutes
Difficulty: Fairly easy
Main course

PIKE LOMBARDY STYLE

p. 258

Time: 50 minutes
Difficulty: Easy
Main course

231

16
Salmo gairdnerii

13
Ictalurus natalis

17
Leuciscus cephalus

18
Lota lota

15
Tinca tinca

19
Perca fluviatilis

9
Acipenser trasmontanus

10
Micropterus salmoides

11
Anguilla anguilla

14
Corégonus lavaretus

12
Eupomotis Gibbosus

Rainbow Trout Mousse

1¼ lb (600 g) rainbow trout

3¼ pints (1.8 litres) court bouillon *(see page 39)*

4 egg whites

7 fl oz (200 ml) whipping cream

nutmeg

1 oz (25 g) butter

salt

Prepare the *court bouillon*, warm over a gentle heat, and add the prepared trout to it. The liquid should cover the fish. Heat to a very gentle boil and then simmer slowly for about 25 minutes; leave the trout to cool in the liquid before lifting out and removing the skin and bones. Place in the food processor and blend with 2 egg whites.

Transfer the fish mixture to a bowl and lower this bowl into a larger bowl half filled with ice cubes; beat the mixture for 5 minutes; the ice cubes in the bowl below will cool the mixture rapidly. Beat the remaining 2 egg whites with a generous pinch of salt until stiff but not dry and fold gently but thoroughly into the fish mixture. Whip the cream with a pinch of grated nutmeg and fold into the fish mousse.

Grease a non-stick pudding mould lightly with the butter; turn the mousse mixture into this mould and place in a roasting tin in a preheated oven at 400°F (200°C) mark 6; pour boiling water to halfway or three quarters of the way up the sides of the mould. Bake for 40 minutes or until firm to the touch when pressed lightly in the centre and pale golden brown on top. Remove from the oven and from the pan; leave to stand and 'set' in the bowl for 5 minutes. Unmould to serve.

Salmon Soufflé

14 oz (400 g) fresh salmon

3½ fl oz (100 ml) olive oil

4 eggs

7 fl oz (200 ml) whipping cream

½ lemon

1 oz (25g) butter

salt and pepper

Brush the salmon lightly all over with a little oil and grill for about 20 minutes or until just done, turning several times and brushing with more oil at intervals (alternatively, bake in foil in the oven). Remove the skin and bones and process the salmon in the food processor to a smooth paste. Transfer to a mixing bowl.

Beat the egg yolks into the salmon paste one at a time with a wooden spoon, blending thoroughly; season with salt and freshly ground pepper. Beat the cream until fairly stiff and fold into the salmon mixture. Add a pinch of salt to the egg whites and beat; add a few drops of lemon juice and continue beating until very stiff but not dry. Fold the egg whites gently but thoroughly into the salmon cream mixture. Transfer the mixture to a well-buttered soufflé dish (choose a size that this quantity will three quarters fill) and place in a preheated oven (at 400°F 200°C mark 6). Bake for about 30 minutes or until well risen and golden brown on top. Serve at once.

Smoked Salmon Hors D'Oeuvres

7 oz (200 g) smoked salmon

1 tbsp lemon juice

1 tbsp double cream

5 oz (150 g) cream cheese

1 small bunch dill

salt and pepper

Cut the smoked salmon into fairly small pieces and place in the food processor with the lemon juice and cream; reduce to a smooth, very thick

233

purée. Transfer to a bowl and mix thoroughly with the cream cheese. Season with salt and plenty of freshly ground white pepper and chill in the refrigerator for 1 hour.

Scoop tablespoons of the cold mixture with your hands and roll these into small balls. Roll in the finely chopped dill. Place on a serving plate and chill until time to serve.

Note: Smoked salmon trimmings can also be used for this recipe.

SMOKED SALMON IN ASPIC

5 oz (150 g) thinly sliced smoked salmon
2 sachets gelatine (or sufficient to set 1³/₄ pints [1 litre] liquid)
2 tbsp port
1 medium-sized packet frozen mixed diced vegetables (Russian salad mixture)
7 fl oz (200 ml) mayonnaise
4 oz (100 g) cooked, peeled prawns
salt

Chill a fluted pudding or bavarois mould to ice-cold in the freezer. Make up 1³/₄ pints (1 litre) aspic following the manufacturer's instructions. Stir in the port and leave to cool until the mixture begins to thicken slightly, acquiring the consistency of oil. Pour just enough aspic to coat the bottom and sides of the chilled mould with a thin layer (slightly deeper at the bottom). Chill in the refrigerator until set. Cook the frozen vegetables until tender in boiling salted water; drain, allow to cool completely and mix with the mayonnaise.

Take the mould out of the refrigerator; arrange the prawns over the aspic lining on the bottom and sides, using a little of the remaining aspic to affix the prawns to the side. Arrange one or two slices of smoked salmon on top and cover with half the Russian salad mixture; arrange another layer of salmon, the remaining Russian salad, and finish with a salmon layer. Try not to dislodge the prawns as you fill the mould and leave a small space between the sides of the mould and the layers as you fill it. Pour in the remaining aspic, filling the gap down the sides of the mould, and fill the

mould to the brim. Chill for at least 3 hours. Run the point of a knife around the top inside edge of the mould, invert the mould on to a serving plate, and wrap a warm cloth round it to loosen. Unmould carefully to serve.

CHILLED SALMON AND PRAWN FLAN

7 oz (200 g) smoked salmon
1 lb (500 g) frozen puff pastry
1¹/₂ oz (40 g) butter
1 tbsp plain flour
1 cup milk
2 leaves isinglass weighing ¹/₄ oz (5 g) each or 1 sachet gelatine
5 fl oz (150 ml) whipping cream
3¹/₂ oz (100 g) cooked prawns
salt and pepper

Thaw the pastry at room temperature; roll out into a sheet ¹/₈ in (3 mm) thick; cut out a circle just over 10 in (26 cm) in diameter. Grease an 8¹/₂-in (22-cm) cake tin or deep flan dish with butter and line with the disc of pastry; fold the extra pastry which overlaps the edge of the tin or dish back over itself round the edge of the tin and pinch all the way round to form a scalloped border.

Cover the pastry shell with foil or waxed paper, fill with dried beans, and bake blind in a preheated oven at 375°F (180°C) mark 4 for about 25 minutes or until done. Take out of the oven, remove the beans and foil or paper and leave to cool.

Melt the butter in a small saucepan; stir in the flour and cook for a few minutes until slightly coloured; beat in the hot milk off the heat, making sure there are no lumps. Return to the heat and cook for 10 minutes, stirring continuously. Season with salt and pepper. Draw aside from the heat. Soak the isinglass leaves in cold water to soften, then squeeze out excess moisture. If using gelatine, dissolve completely in a very little hot water. Stir the isinglass or gelatine into the white sauce. Mix very thoroughly. Cool but do not refrigerate.

Process the smoked salmon with 1–2 tbsp of the cream until smooth. Whip the rest of the cream. Stir the salmon into the sauce and then fold in the cream. Fill the cold pastry shell with this mixture, smooth the surface level, and decorate with the prawns. Chill until shortly before serving.

SMOKED SALMON NORWEGIAN STYLE

12 slices smoked salmon

3¹/₂ oz (100 g) cream cheese

3¹/₂ fl oz (100 ml) soured cream

12 slices rye bread

¹/₂ oz (10 g) butter

2 hard-boiled eggs

1 large mild onion

1 small bunch dill

1 lettuce

salt

Mix the cream cheese in a bowl with the soured cream and a pinch of salt. Spread an equal amount of this mixture over each smoked salmon slice and roll up. Trim the bread slices into broad fingers so they are just large enough to accommodate the smoked salmon rolls and spread a little butter on each slice. Place the salmon rolls on the bread fingers.

Peel the eggs and slice into rounds; peel the onion and cut into wafer-thin rings. Spread the crispest lettuce leaves over a serving plate; arrange the salmon rolls on them, with the egg slices and onion rings in between.

FRESHWATER SHAD WITH ANCHOVY DRESSING

2¹/₄–2¹/₂ lb (1 kg) freshwater shad

juice of 1 lemon

8 fl oz (225 ml) olive oil

plain flour

3 salted anchovies (or 6 tinned anchovy fillets)

1 tbsp vinegar

pinch mustard powder or 1 tsp mild French mustard

1¹/₂ tbsp finely chopped parsley

salt

Trim, descale if necessary, gut, wash and dry the fish. Sprinkle with the lemon juice and 1 tbsp vinegar. Leave to marinate for 3–4 hours. Drain, coat lightly with flour, and fry in half the remaining oil; drain on kitchen paper and keep hot.

Chop the anchovies very finely (if salted anchovies are used rinse off excess salt and remove the bones) and blend thoroughly with the remaining oil, vinegar, mustard and chopped parsley; leave this dressing to stand for 5 minutes.

Arrange the fish on a warmed serving dish, give the cold dressing a final stir and pour all over the fish. Serve at once.

CHAR MOUSSE

1 char weighing approx. 1¹/₂ lb (700 g)

7 fl oz (200 ml) double or whipping cream

3 eggs

1 black truffle (optional) or 2 oz (50 g) button mushrooms

3¹/₂ fl oz (100 ml) fish stock (fumet) (see page 39)

1 oz (25 g) butter

salt and pepper

Trim off the char's head and fins, gut it and fillet; remove the skin (see pages 9–12).

Process the fillets to a smooth paste in the food processor; beat the cream if whipping cream is used, and blend into the fish purée; lightly beat 2 whole eggs and 1 yolk and stir thoroughly into the fish mixture. Season with a pinch of salt and plenty of freshly ground white pepper. Grease a non-stick mould with butter and fill to the brim with the mixture. Cook in the oven at 350°F (180°C) mark 4 in a bain-marie (standing in a pan of hot water which should come halfway to two thirds of the way up the sides of the mould) for about 30 minutes or until done.

Brush and wipe the truffle or button mushrooms, slice wafer-thin and fry in the butter; pour in the *fumet* and simmer until the liquid has reduced by one third of its original volume. Turn the hot mousse out on to a warmed serving dish and pour the sauce over it.

EEL WITH TARTARE SAUCE

2 eels weighing 1¹/₄ lb (600 g) each
2 hard-boiled eggs
1 tbsp wine vinegar
10 fl oz (300 ml) olive oil
1 egg yolk
1 tbsp mild mustard
juice of 1 lemon
1 tbsp capers
3 gherkins or small dill pickles
salt and pepper

Clean and prepare the eels (see pages 9 and 11) and cut them into 2-in (5-cm) lengths without skinning them. Place in a roasting tin with a little water (just enough to prevent the oil they produce as they cook overheating and spattering) and cook in the oven, preheated to 425°F (220°C) mark 7, for 5 minutes, then lower the heat to 325°F (170°C) mark 3 and cook for 20–25 minutes.

Meanwhile, prepare the sauce: chop the hard-boiled egg yolks very finely and work in the vinegar and 3¹/₂ fl oz (100 ml) of the oil. Set aside. Make a mayonnaise with the raw egg yolk, salt, pepper, mustard and lemon juice, gradually beating in the remaining olive oil. Mix this with the reserved hard-boiled egg yolk paste, followed by the finely chopped capers and gherkins.

HARLEQUIN PIKE

10 oz (300 g) fillets of pike or trout
5 fl oz (150 ml) low-fat natural yoghurt
2 eggs
1 tbsp tomato purée
7 oz (200 g) cooked spinach
butter
7 oz (200 g) French beans
1 lb (450 g) tinned tomatoes, drained
10 basil leaves
salt and pepper

Chop the fish fillets and process in the food processor until they form a smooth paste. Transfer to a bowl, mix in the yoghurt and season with salt and pepper; beat the egg whites with a pinch of salt until very stiff and fold into the fish mixture; divide this equally into three bowls.

Stir the tomato purée very thoroughly into one batch of fish mixture. Squeeze all the moisture out of the spinach, and reduce to a purée in the food processor. Mix this spinach purée with one of the remaining two lots, leaving the final one uncoloured. Lightly brush a turban, ring mould or rectangular mould with melted butter or oil; spoon the green mixture carefully into the mould in a neat layer and smooth level. Cover this layer with the white mixture, then finish with a third (red) layer. Tap the bottom of the mould gently against the work surface after each layer to release trapped air bubbles. Place the mould in a roasting tin in a preheated oven at 350°F (180°C) mark 4; pour in sufficient hot water to come two thirds of the way up the outside of the mould and cook for 30 minutes. Boil the French beans until tender in salted water. Remove the seeds from the drained tomatoes and liquidize until very smooth; pour into a saucepan and add salt, freshly ground pepper and the chopped basil leaves. Cook, uncovered, over a moderate heat until slightly thickened. Pour a little tomato sauce on to individual heated plates; arrange three small bundles of beans on each plate; unmould the mousse and slice carefully, placing three slices on each plate, on top of the sauce.

CARP PÂTÉ

1 carp weighing approx. 2³/₄ lb (1 kg)

3¹/₂ fl oz (100 ml) double or whipping cream

8 oz (225 g) cooked, peeled prawns

1¹/₂ sachets gelatine

1 tbsp tomato purée

1 tbsp anchovy paste

1¹/₂ tbsp finely chopped fresh herbs (e.g. chervil, chives, fennel, dill)

stuffed green olives

1 large ripe tomato

1 green pepper

salt and pepper

For the *court-bouillon*:

13 fl oz (350 ml) dry white wine

2 onions

2 carrots

1 sprig thyme

1 bouquet garni

generous pinch real saffron powder

1 celery stalk

1 chilli pepper

fish bones and trimmings

Chill a ring tube mould or rectangular mould in the freezer. Place all the *court-bouillon* ingredients in a saucepan, adding a pinch of coarse sea salt and 10 peppercorns; bring to the boil, then simmer gently for 25 minutes. Strain into a fish kettle or large oval fireproof casserole dish. Clean and prepare the carp, descaling, gutting it, and removing the head; lower into the lukewarm *court-bouillon*, bring just back to the boil, then reduce the heat so that the liquid barely simmers and cook for about 20 minutes. Remove carefully from the *court-bouillon*, drain and leave to cool.

Remove the skin and bones and purée the carp flesh in the food processor. Transfer this purée to a bowl and set aside. Process half the prawns in the food processor to a smooth paste, adding a very little of the *court-bouillon* to make this easier. Stir into the carp purée. Make up the gelatine following the manufacturer's instructions and leave to cool. When cold and beginning to thicken slightly, stir 8 fl oz (225 ml) of the gelatine mixture into the fish purée. Add the cream (beaten, if whipping cream is used), the tomato purée, anchovy paste (or anchovy sauce), the herbs and a small pinch of salt. Blend thoroughly.

Cover the bottom of the chilled mould with a ³/₄-in (2-cm) thick layer of gelatine, returning the mould to the freezer briefly to help it set quickly. Fill the mould with the fish mixture, smoothing the surface level. Chill in the refrigerator until set, then turn out and decorate with the remaining prawns, sliced stuffed olives, peeled sliced tomatoes and strips of green pepper.

PASTA WITH SALMON

6 oz (170 g) tinned salmon, drained

1 onion

1 small bunch parsley

2 cloves garlic

3¹/₂ fl oz (100 ml) olive oil

1 small piece chilli pepper

3¹/₂ fl oz (100 ml) dry white wine

14 oz (400 g) spaghetti or tagliatelle

salt

Peel and chop the onion, parsley and garlic very finely and sweat gently in the oil until the onion is transparent and soft. Crumble the chilli pepper and add to the pan. Stir well. Remove any pieces of bone or skin from the salmon and flake it. Stir into the pan, add the wine and simmer gently for 5 minutes.

Cook the pasta in plenty of boiling salted water until just tender but still firm. Drain and transfer to a heated serving dish; add the salmon mixture, stir and serve.

Note: Tinned tuna can replace the salmon.

237

CHEF'S TROUT

1 rainbow trout weighing approx. 1³/₄ lb (800 g)

3¹/₂ fl oz (100 ml) olive oil

6 cloves garlic

1¹/₂ oz (40 g) butter

7 oz (200 g) Dublin Bay prawns

1 lb (450 g) mixed shellfish (e.g. small clams and mussels)

3¹/₂ oz (100 g) peeled shrimps or small prawns

14 oz (400 g) tinned tomatoes

salt and pepper

Prepare the trout (see page 9), rinse and dry. Fry the whole, peeled garlic cloves in the oil in a wide frying pan until pale golden brown; remove and discard. Add the trout to the flavoured oil; cook for 10–15 minutes, turning once. Season with salt and pepper. Remove from the pan, draining as much oil as possible back into the pan, and set aside in a large ovenproof dish to keep warm.

Clean all the shellfish and place in a large pan over a high heat to open; take them off their shells and add to the oil. (Use one third net weight if using frozen or tinned shucked shellfish.) Add the prawns. Cook, stirring, for 10–15 minutes then add the sieved tomatoes. Season with salt and pepper and simmer for 10 minutes.

Cover the trout with the tomato and shellfish sauce and place in the oven at 400°F (200°C) mark 6 for 10–15 minutes. Serve straight from the dish.

EEL RISOTTO

1 eel weighing approx. 1¹/₄ lb (600 g)

1 clove garlic

2 fl oz (50 ml) olive oil

1 bay leaf

juice of 1 lemon

12 oz (350 g) Italian risotto rice (e.g. arborio)

3¹/₂ fl oz (100 ml) dry white wine

1¹/₂ pints (900 ml) fish stock (fumet) (see page 39) or chicken stock

1¹/₂ tbsp finely chopped parsley

salt and pepper

Prepare and skin the eel (see pages 9–11), rinse and cut into pieces.

Fry the whole, peeled garlic clove in the oil in a large saucepan or cooking pot; add the bay leaf and the eel pieces. Season with salt and pepper, cover and cook for 30–35 minutes. Remove the eel pieces, draining as much oil, etc., as possible back into the pan, place them in an ovenproof dish, sprinkle with the lemon juice and keep hot.

Remove and discard the garlic clove and bay leaf and add the rice to the oil and juices in the pan. Stir well while cooking for 1–2 minutes, then pour in the wine and cook until it has evaporated. Add 8 fl oz (225 ml) boiling hot *fumet* or chicken stock, then add about 4 fl oz (125 ml) at a time when each previous addition of liquid has been absorbed by the rice and continue cooking, stirring occasionally, until the rice is tender (approx. 18 minutes but it may take longer).

When the rice is nearly done, add the eel pieces and the parsley, stir and serve.

BARBEL WITH PINE NUT SAUCE

1 barbel weighing approx. 2³/₄ lb (1.2 kg)

fish trimmings (e.g. bones, heads, etc., from flatfish such as sole or flounder)

2 carrots

3 onions

1 bouquet garni

few sprigs parsley

2 oz (50 g) butter

18 fl oz (500 ml) dry white wine

7 oz (200 g) long-grain rice
7 fl oz (200 ml) single cream
1¹/₂ tbsp pine nuts
salt and pepper

Place the fish trimmings in a bowl and run cold water on to them for 10 minutes. Slice all the carrots and 1 onion into rounds; place in a large pan with all the fish trimmings, bouquet garni and half the parsley. Add plenty of water, bring to the boil, and simmer for 30 minutes.

Grease a fireproof casserole dish with butter, peel the remaining onions, slice wafer-thin, and spread over the bottom of the dish; finely chop the remaining parsley and sprinkle over; place the cleaned, prepared (see page 9) fish on top. Strain the fish stock. Pour the wine over the fish, then add just enough fish stock to cover. Season with salt and pepper; cover with a lightly buttered sheet of foil. Heat to boiling point on the hob, then place in a preheated oven at 400°F (200°C) mark 6 and cook for about 30 minutes.

Cook the rice in plenty of boiling salted water until just tender, and drain. Rinse small moulds or ramekins with cold water and press the rice into them. When the fish is done, remove carefully from the casserole and place on a large warmed serving platter.

Strain the cooking juices into a small saucepan; beat in the cream over a gentle heat, followed by the butter, adding this in small pieces. If the rice is not ready, keep the sauce warm over hot water. Coat the fish with some of the sauce, and serve the rest separately. Place the rice moulds in the oven for a few minutes then turn out around the fish and sprinkle with the pine nuts.

TROUT PARCELS WITH MUSHROOM AND BRANDY SAUCE

4 trout weighing 8 oz (250 g) each

3¹/₂ fl oz (100 ml) dry white wine
2 shallots
2 sprigs thyme
5 bay leaves
2 carrots
5 oz (150 g) button mushrooms
juice of 1 lemon
1 oz (25 g) butter
4 thin rashers smoked bacon
olive oil
3¹/₂ fl oz (100 ml) brandy
1 tbsp cornflour
2 tbsp double cream
salt and pepper

To make the sauce: pour the wine into a small saucepan, add the peeled and finely chopped shallots, one sprig of thyme, one bay leaf, the carrots (sliced into small cubes), a pinch of salt and a little freshly ground pepper. Bring to a gentle boil, reduce the heat to a minimum and leave the sauce to simmer very slowly.

Wipe the mushrooms with a damp cloth, slice thinly into a bowl and mix with nearly all the lemon juice. Drain; fry in the butter over a low heat for 15–20 minutes. Clean and prepare the trout (see page 9). Season each fish with salt and pepper, then wrap a bacon rasher round each. Place each fish on a large piece of lightly oiled foil, sprinkle with a few of the remaining thyme leaves, and place a bay leaf on each one. Fold into secure parcels, leaving an air space inside and place in the oven, preheated to 425°F (220°C) mark 7. After 5 minutes, lower the heat to 350°F (180°C) mark 4 and bake for a further 12 minutes.

While the fish are cooking, combine the wine mixture with the mushrooms, stir in the brandy and heat; remove and discard the bay leaf and the thyme.

Mix the cornflour with 1 tbsp cold water and stir into the sauce. Bring to the boil, stirring continuously; turn off the heat. Add the cream and a few drops of lemon juice, mix thoroughly and pour into a sauceboat or jug. Serve the trout in the sealed parcels, to be opened at table.

TROUT WITH MUSHROOMS AND ALMONDS

4 trout weighing 8 oz (250 g) each

3¹/₂ oz (100 g) butter

5 oz (150 g) button mushrooms

1 oz (30 g) slivered or flaked almonds

1 shallot

3¹/₂ fl oz (100 ml) brandy

14 fl oz (400 ml) single cream

salt and pepper

Clean and prepare the trout (see page 9), rinse well and dry. Brown lightly on both sides in a large pan in half the butter. Transfer to an oven-to-table casserole and season with salt and pepper.

Wipe the mushrooms with a damp cloth, chop coarsely, and sauté with the almonds in all but 1 oz (25 g) of the remaining butter over a low heat; when pale golden brown, add the very finely chopped shallot, pour in the brandy and continue cooking while mixing in the deposits from the bottom of the pan. Add the cream, season with salt and freshly ground pepper and simmer, uncovered, until reduced by one third. Pour this sauce all over the trout, cover with a sheet of foil, greased with butter, and place in a preheated oven at 400°F (200°C) mark 6 to bake for 15–20 minutes. Serve straight from the casserole dish.

SALMON TROUT IN CHAMPAGNE

1 salmon trout weighing 2¹/₄–2¹/₂ lb (1 kg)

2 carrots

2 potatoes

2 celery stalks

1 onion

1 clove garlic

10 fl oz (300 ml) champagne or dry sparkling white wine

7 fl oz (200 ml) mayonnaise

1 sachet gelatine (sufficient to set just over 18 fl oz [500 ml] liquid)

2 oz (50 g) mixed dill pickles

salt and pepper

Cut all the vegetables into small pieces and boil gently for 1 hour in just over 1³/₄ pints (1 litre) lightly salted water. Strain and pour into a fish kettle or deep oval pan; add the champagne. Clean and prepare the fish (see page 9), rinse very thoroughly and lower into the cooking liquid. Poach very gently for 40 minutes or until done; leave to cool in the liquid. Remove the fish, draining well, pat dry with kitchen paper and remove the skin carefully (leave the head in place). Transfer to a serving dish. Pipe the mayonnaise decoratively around and on the fish, using a fairly wide nozzle. Decorate with the drained pickles.

Make up the gelatine following the instructions, leave until cold and just starting to set, then brush or spoon all over the salmon trout to glaze with a fairly thick layer. Chill for a few hours before serving.

Note: Serve with potato salad and Russian salad on a bed of crisp lettuce.

TROUT WITH LEMON BUTTER STUFFING

4 trout weighing 8 oz (250 g) each

4 oz (125 g) butter

few sprigs parsley

2 lemons

7 fl oz (200 ml) dry white wine

5 fl oz (150 ml) single cream

salt and pepper

Prepare the trout (see page 9), gutting through the gill aperture if possible; rinse well and dry. Mix all but 1 oz (25 g) of the butter (softened at room temperature) with the finely chopped parsley, the juice of 1 lemon, salt and freshly ground pepper. When well blended, place an equal quantity inside each fish's ventral cavity.

Use the remaining butter to grease a casserole dish large enough to accommodate the fish in a single layer and place the trout in it, alternating heads to tails. Pour the wine all over the fish. Cover with the lid or a sheet of foil and bake in a preheated oven at 400°F (200°C) mark 6 for 10 minutes. Uncover and continue cooking at 325°F (180°C) mark 4, for a further 10 minutes. Serve straight from the casserole dish, garnished with the remaining lemon, cut into wedges.

TROUT À LA MEUNIÈRE

4 trout weighing 8 oz (250 g) each
7 fl oz (200 ml) milk
3 tbsp plain flour
3¹/₂ oz (100 g) butter
7 fl oz (200 ml) olive oil
juice of 2 lemons
1¹/₂ tbsp finely chopped parsley
salt and pepper

Trim and gut the trout (see page 9), rinse well under running cold water and dry thoroughly. Mix the cold milk with a little salt, dip the fish in it and then coat with flour. Heat 1¹/₂ oz (40 g) of the butter and all the oil in a very wide pan and fry the fish for about 15 minutes, turning just once half way through this cooking time.

Transfer the well-browned fish to a warmed serving plate, draining off as much fat as possible. Heat the remaining butter in a small saucepan until it turns golden brown (*noisette*), then pour over the fish; sprinkle with the lemon juice and parsley. Serve at once.

Note: This is a classic, delicious preparation suitable for small whole fish or large fish cut into steaks or fillets.

TROUT WITH PARMA HAM

4 trout weighing 8 oz (250 g) each
few sprigs parsley
1 clove garlic
few leaves marjoram
4 large thin slices Parma ham
plain flour
2 eggs
breadcrumbs
7 fl oz (200 ml) olive oil
1 bay leaf
1 lemon
salt and pepper

Trim the fish; slit open right down their bellies to gut, wash well, dry and open out flat; carefully remove the backbone, together with all the bones attached to it, snipping free at both ends with scissors. Remove the heads if wished. Season with salt and freshly ground pepper.

Chop together the parsley, the peeled garlic clove and marjoram very finely and sprinkle this herb mixture inside the fish. Cover with a slice of Parma ham, pressing the slice firmly against the fish to ensure it adheres well.

Dust the trout lightly all over with flour; beat the eggs lightly in a dish and dip the floured fish carefully, taking care not to dislodge the Parma ham slice. Coat with breadcrumbs, pressing so that they adhere well.

Heat the oil with the bay leaf in a very wide pan and fry the fish one at a time, turning once. Drain briefly on kitchen paper and keep hot on a large serving platter or individual warmed plates while you fry the remaining fish. Garnish each fish with a slice of lemon.

Note: Serve the trout with braised fennel, spinach in butter and mashed potatoes.

241

BAKED TENCH WITH MIXED SPICE STUFFING

4 tench weighing 8 oz (250 g) each

4 tbsp breadcrumbs

4 tbsp freshly grated Parmesan cheese

few sprigs parsley

1 clove garlic

1¹/₂ tsp mixed spices (cinnamon, cloves, nutmeg and pepper)

1¹/₂ oz (40 g) butter

5 tbsp oil

5–6 bay leaves

salt and pepper

Soak the tench in cold, salted water for 1–2 hours; rinse thoroughly under running cold water (see page 9), rinse again and dry. Make the stuffing: mix the breadcrumbs, cheese, the finely chopped parsley and garlic, a generous pinch of salt and the spices. Place some of this mixture in the ventral cavity of each fish, using about two thirds and reserving the rest. Press the cut edges closed and place the fish, head to tail, in a single layer in a casserole dish containing the melted butter, 3 tbsp of the oil and the bay leaves. Sprinkle the reserved stuffing mixture over the fish, drizzle the remaining oil and a pinch of salt over them, and bake in the oven, preheated to 350°F (180°C) mark 4, for about 40 minutes, basting the fish at frequent intervals with the cooking juices.

TENCH WITH BEANS, BASIL AND TOMATOES

1 2¹/₄–2¹/₂-lb (1-kg) tench

1 medium-sized tin (14 oz/450 g) white haricot beans

2 fl oz (50 ml) olive oil

7 fl oz (200 ml) good-quality dry red wine

6 large ripe tomatoes

1 bunch basil or ¹/₂–1 tsp dried basil

1 bay leaf

1 sprig thyme or ¹/₂ tsp dried thyme

salt and pepper

Drain the beans well in a sieve, rinse thoroughly in cold water and drain well. Wash the tench thoroughly in running cold water before and after gutting it. Scrape off the scales with the back of a kitchen knife working from tail to head and trim off the fins (see page 9).

Heat the oil in a large, wide pan and fry the fish in it, turning once and seasoning with salt and freshly ground pepper. Pour the red wine over the fish and continue cooking briskly until the wine has almost completely evaporated. Peel the tomatoes and chop roughly; add to the fish with the basil, bay leaf and thyme. Cook for 15 minutes, turning the fish carefully half way through this cooking time. Add the beans, cook for a final 4–5 minutes, adding a little hot water to moisten if necessary. Discard any stalks which remain from the herbs. Serve the tench in portions with the tomato and juices spooned over them.

WHITEFISH WITH SALMON ROE AND HERB STUFFING

1 whitefish weighing 2³/₄ lb (1.2 kg)

3¹/₂ oz (100 g) salmon roe or red lumpfish roe (Danish caviar)

2¹/₂ oz (70 g) butter

9 oz (250 g) mushrooms

1 clove garlic

2 small onions

3 tbsp finely chopped mixed herbs (e.g. parsley, basil, chervil, thyme, tarragon)

1¹/₂ pints (900 ml) dry white wine

2 tbsp breadcrumbs

salt and pepper

Prepare the whitefish (see page 9), trimming, descaling and gutting it; rinse and dry well. Grease a fairly shallow ovenproof dish with butter and place the fish in it.

Chop the mushrooms; peel and finely chop the onions and garlic. Mix these and the mushrooms with the chopped herbs. Stir in the salmon roe (or lumpfish roe) and season with salt and pepper. Spread some of this mixture underneath the fish, some inside the ventral cavity, and some on top.

Dot the fish with pieces of butter, pour 8 fl oz (225 ml) of the wine into the dish, and place in a preheated oven at 425°F (220°C) mark 7 to cook for 35 minutes; take the dish out of the oven, sprinkle the fish with the breadcrumbs, increase the temperature to 425°F (230°C) mark 8, and return to the oven for a further 10 minutes.

WHITEFISH SAUTÉED IN BUTTER

4 whitefish weighing 8 oz (250 g) each
plain flour
3¹/₂ oz (100 g) butter
1 small bunch parsley
juice of 1 lemon
salt

Trim, descale and gut the fish (see page 9). Rinse thoroughly, dry well and sprinkle with flour inside and out.

Melt the butter in a very wide, preferably non-stick pan and when it starts to foam, place the fish in the pan, head to tail and fry gently until golden brown. Cook in two batches if necessary. Do not allow the butter to get too hot. Turn the fish carefully and cook for a further 15 minutes or until done.

Transfer the fish to a warmed serving dish. Finely chop the parsley and sprinkle over the fish, followed by the lemon juice and a little salt. Serve very hot.

GRAYLING À LA MEUNIÈRE

2¹/₄–2¹/₂ lb (1 kg) grayling
plain flour
4 tbsp olive oil
3¹/₂ oz (100 g) butter
1 lemon
few sprigs parsley
salt and pepper

Prepare the fish, trimming and gutting them (see page 9). Rinse briefly under running cold water and dry well. Sprinkle a little salt into their ventral cavities and coat lightly with flour, shaking off excess.

Heat the oil and half the butter in a very large pan, add the fish, and fry gently for 5–6 minutes on each side, turning carefully with a fish slice. Drain off as much fat as possible from the fish as you transfer them to a heated serving dish; keep hot. Pour away the oil and butter left in the pan, wipe the pan, and heat the remaining butter. As soon as it starts to foam, add the juice of half the lemon and some freshly ground pepper. Sprinkle the fish with a little salt; pour the butter and lemon juice over them, sprinkle with the chopped parsley and garnish with the remaining half lemon, cut into thin round slices.

GRAYLING BAKED IN WINE

2¹/₄–2¹/₂ lb (1 kg) grayling
3 oz (80 g) butter
3¹/₂ fl oz (100 ml) dry white wine
salt and pepper

Trim, gut (see page 9) and rinse the fish and dry well. Melt the butter in a fireproof casserole dish, arrange the fish heads to tails in a single layer in it and fry gently, turning once, until golden brown on both sides. Sprinkle with a little salt, freshly ground pepper and the white wine. Bake, uncovered, in a preheated oven at 400°F (200°C) mark 6 for about 15 minutes, by which time the wine will have almost completely evaporated and the fish will be crisp on the surface. Serve straight from the casserole dish.

DEEP-FRIED GRAYLING

2¹/₄–2¹/₂ lb (1 kg) grayling
plain flour
oil for deep-frying
salt

Clean, gut (see page 9) and wash the fish and dry well. Coat with flour all over, shaking off excess. Heat the correct amount of oil to 350°F (180°C) in a deep-fryer or suitable large saucepan and deep fry the fish in small batches until golden brown. As each batch is done, remove with a slotted ladle and finish draining, uncovered, on kitchen paper. Sprinkle the fish with a little salt and serve as quickly as possible.

WHITEFISH WITH ONION AND TOMATO SAUCE

4 whitefish weighing approx. 8 oz (250 g) each
10 oz (300 g) mild onions
6¹/₂ fl oz (190 ml) olive oil
3 cloves garlic
14 oz (400 g) tinned tomatoes
1 bay leaf
1 tbsp wine vinegar
pinch sugar
few sprigs parsley
1 sprig rosemary

2 sage leaves
8 tbsp fine breadcrumbs
salt and pepper

Clean, trim, descale and gut the fish (see page 9), rinse well under running cold water and dry thoroughly. Sprinkle inside and out with a little salt.

Peel the onions and slice into wafer-thin rings; sweat these in 4 tbsp of the oil for 15 minutes; add two of the garlic cloves, peeled and lightly crushed with the flat of a knife blade, the sieved tomatoes, the bay leaf, vinegar, a generous pinch of sugar and a little salt and freshly ground pepper. Stir well and simmer, uncovered, over a low heat for 25 minutes. Chop the parsley finely with about 1¹/₂ tsp rosemary leaves, the sage leaves and the remaining peeled garlic clove; mix with the breadcrumbs. Roll the fish in this mixture and fry in a large pan in 6 tbsp hot oil.

When done and golden brown, transfer to a heated serving dish with a slotted fish slice, draining off as much oil as possible and serve, handing round the onion and tomato sauce separately.

WHITEFISH WITH HERBS AND NUTMEG

1¹/₄ lb (600 g) fillets of whitefish
1 sprig parsley
4–5 basil leaves
rosemary
1 clove garlic
1 lemon
3¹/₂ oz (100 g) fine breadcrumbs
nutmeg
3¹/₂ oz (100 g) plain flour
1 egg
3¹/₂ fl oz (100 ml) olive oil

2 oz (50 g) butter

white wine vinegar

salt and pepper

Rinse and dry the fish fillets. Chop the parsley and basil finely, mix with a few rosemary leaves, the crushed garlic, 1 tsp finely grated lemon rind, a pinch of grated nutmeg, the breadcrumbs, salt and freshly ground pepper.

Coat the fillets with flour, shaking off excess, and dip in the lightly beaten egg. Spread out two thirds of the breadcrumb mixture in a plate and coat the dipped, drained fillets with it, pressing to make the breadcrumbs stick. Fry in very hot oil in a non-stick pan. Drain well when done and keep hot in a single layer in a serving dish.

Melt the butter in a small saucepan, add the remaining third of the breadcrumb mixture, mix well, and cook for 4–5 minutes, stirring continuously with a wooden spoon. Add the lemon juice, an equal quantity of vinegar and a pinch of salt. Cook gently for a minute, then pour over the fish and serve.

CARP WITH SULTANAS AND ALMONDS

4 mid-section carp steaks weighing approx. 8 oz (250 g) each

1 carrot

1 small onion or shallot

1 tbsp honey

1 bay leaf

1 clove

2 coriander seeds

1 lemon

3¹/₂ oz (100 g) sultanas

5 oz (150 g) slivered, flaked or chopped almonds

salt and pepper

Bring 1¹/₂ pints (1 litre) water to the boil in a wide saucepan with the sliced carrot, the coarsely chopped onion, honey, bay leaf, clove, coriander seeds and the sliced lemon. Boil for 40 minutes. Add the fish steaks; top up the water if necessary to cover the fish. Bring back to a gentle boil; add the sultanas and the almonds. Simmer slowly for 45–50 minutes. Season with salt and freshly ground pepper and serve.

STUFFED CARP IN RED WINE

1 carp weighing 2³/₄ lb (1.2 kg), preferably with its liver

1¹/₂ oz (40 g) butter

3 tbsp olive oil

1 onion

1 clove garlic

few sprigs parsley

1 2-oz (50-g) thick slice bread (no crusts)

3¹/₂ fl oz (100 ml) milk

1 egg

2 oz (50 g) plain flour

7 oz (200 g) mushrooms

3¹/₂ fl oz (100 ml) dry red wine

salt and pepper

Clean, trim and gut the carp (see page 9); cut down to the backbone along its back, carefully remove the backbone and all the smaller bones attached to it (see page 12). Sauté the peeled and finely chopped onion in ¹/₂ oz (10 g) of the butter and 1 tbsp oil; add the finely chopped parsley and garlic and the chopped carp liver. Season with salt and freshly ground pepper and sauté for 10–15 minutes; process in the food processor to a smooth paste. Heat the milk to lukewarm, soak the bread in it and squeeze out excess milk; stir into the paste. Beat the egg lightly and blend with the bread and paste mixture.

Stuff the carp with this mixture, tie up or secure (not too tightly) and coat with flour; heat the remaining butter and 2 tbsp oil and fry the fish until golden brown, then turn and colour evenly on the other side. Pour in the wine and cook for 10 minutes longer.

Place the carp in a casserole dish, add the sliced mushrooms, the strained cooking juices and liquid and bake for 30 minutes at 400°F (200°C) mark 6, basting with the cooking juices at frequent intervals.

Note: Serve the stuffed carp with baked potatoes, glazed carrots and cauliflower in white sauce.

SALMON WITH GREEN OLIVES

14 oz (400 g) tinned salmon
1 onion
2 oz (50 g) butter
1 tbsp plain flour
5 fl oz (150 ml) single cream
2¹/₂ oz (70 g) green olives, stoned
breadcrumbs
salt and pepper

Drain the salmon, straining and reserving the liquid. Remove and discard any bones and skin. Peel and finely chop the onion and sweat in the butter over a low heat in a saucepan. Sprinkle in the flour and stir, seasoning with plenty of freshly ground pepper and a pinch of salt, then add the liquid and the cream. Continue stirring over a very low heat until the sauce has thickened.

Chop the olives into thin strips and add to the sauce with a little more salt if necessary. Do not flake the salmon but divide into bite-sized pieces. Place these in the saucepan and heat through, turning carefully once or twice. Transfer to a casserole dish, sprinkle with a thin topping of breadcrumbs, and brown in a preheated oven at 400°F (200°C) mark 6 for 15 minutes.

Note: Serve with rice, and a selection of salads, e.g. celery and tomato, cucumber and dill, and potato and spring onion.

SALMON EN PAPILLOTE

4 salmon steaks weighing approx. 5 oz (150 g) each
10 fl oz (300 ml) dry white wine
4 tbsp lemon juice
3–4 fish heads or 5 oz (150 g) fish trimmings
5 egg yolks
9 oz (250 g) butter
salt and black and green peppercorns

Make the fish stock: pour 7 fl oz (200 ml) of the wine and an equal quantity of water into a saucepan, add a generous pinch of coarse sea salt and a few black peppercorns and boil hard until the liquid has reduced to only 3¹/₂ fl oz (100 ml) in volume. Wash and dry the salmon steaks, place each on a large square of foil, and moisten with a little white wine, 1 tbsp lemon juice, 1 tbsp of the reduced fish stock, 2 green peppercorns and a pinch of salt. Fold up the parcels, sealing securely but leaving an air space inside. Bake for 10 minutes in the oven, preheated to 425°F (230°C) mark 8. Beat the egg yolks with 5 tbsp cold water in a heatproof bowl over hot water, season with salt and pepper and gradually beat in the melted butter, adding a little at a time. Add a few drops of lemon juice. Continue beating until the sauce has increased in volume and is light and velvety. Serve the salmon in their foil parcels and hand round the sauce in a warmed sauceboat.

SALMON FILLETS WITH GREEN AND PINK PEPPERCORNS

8 thin fillets of salmon
2¹/₂ oz (70 g) butter
3¹/₂ fl oz (100 ml) dry white wine
3¹/₂ (100 ml) fish stock (fumet) *(see page 39)*
1 tbsp clear honey

3¹/₂ fl oz (100 ml) double cream

¹/₂ lemon

16 green peppercorns

16 pink peppercorns

salt and cayenne pepper

Sprinkle a little salt on to the salmon fillets, then roll them up and fasten securely with cocktail sticks. Grease a casserole dish with butter and arrange the salmon rolls in it in a single layer. Sprinkle with melted butter and place in the oven, preheated to 350°F (180°C) mark 4, to cook for 8 minutes, turning the rolls carefully half way through this time. Pour the wine, *fumet*, honey and cream into a small saucepan and bring to a gentle boil; reduce the heat to very low and beat in 1 oz (25 g) butter, adding it gradually in small, solid pieces and beating each piece into the sauce until it has melted completely. Add a little salt and cayenne pepper. Cook for a minute or two longer without allowing the sauce to boil. Stir in a little lemon juice.

Transfer two salmon rolls to each individual heated plate, removing the cocktail sticks or skewers very carefully; pour a small quantity of sauce over each helping and decorate each portion with 4 pink peppercorns and 4 green peppercorns.

SWEET-SOUR SALMON STEAKS IN ASPIC

4 salmon steaks weighing approx. 7 oz (200 g) each

7 fl oz (200 ml) white wine vinegar

3 medium-sized onions

1 tbsp sugar

1 bay leaf

4 cloves

1 sachet gelatine (sufficient to set 18 fl oz (500 ml) liquid)

12 thin round slices cucumber

12 thin round slices raw carrot

salt

Sprinkle a little of the vinegar into a fairly deep dish, place the salmon steaks in it and sprinkle with a little salt and the remaining vinegar. Cover and leave to stand in a cool place for 2 hours. Drain off the vinegar, transfer the steaks to a fish kettle or saucepan in a single layer, and pour in 14 fl oz (400 ml) water; add the thinly sliced onions, the sugar, bay leaf, cloves and a pinch of salt.

Bring the liquid just to boiling point, reduce the heat as low as possible, cover and slowly simmer for 20 minutes. Drain the salmon steaks well and transfer to a serving dish; remove and discard the bay leaf and cloves. Strain the cooking liquid and use it to make the gelatine according to the manufacturer's instructions (top up with a little water if necessary).

Place 3 slices of cucumber, slightly overlapping, on each salmon steak; do likewise with the carrot slices. Arrange the onion rings around the fish. Use 8 fl oz (225 ml) of the gelatine mixture to coat the fish and the onions with a fairly thin layer of aspic. Chill (place in the freezer for a short time if your dish is freezer-proof) until this layer has set, then repeat with the remaining aspic. Chill for at least 2 hours or until shortly before serving.

SALMON ROULADES WITH OYSTER SAUCE

8 fillets of salmon weighing approx. 3 oz (80 g) each

4 fillets of Dover sole

12 oysters

7 fl oz (200 ml) double or whipping cream

8 large crisp spinach leaves

dry white wine

3¹/₂ oz (100 g) butter
9 fl oz (250 ml) fish stock (fumet) (see page 39)
salt and pepper

Process the sole fillets in the food processor to a smooth paste, transfer to a bowl, season with salt and pepper, and place in the refrigerator for 30 minutes to chill thoroughly. Beat 3 fl oz (80 ml) of the chilled cream and fold into the cold fish purée. Open the oysters, saving their juice (strain and reserve in a bowl).

Rinse the spinach leaves well and wrap one oyster in each leaf in a neat parcel. Spread the salmon fillets with the creamy fish paste, and roll up fairly tightly, enclosing a spinach and oyster parcel in each roll. Secure with cocktail sticks or small steel skewers. Grease a heavy-bottomed frying pan liberally with butter; place the rolls in it in a single layer and sprinkle with the strained oyster juice and with sufficient wine to come about one third of the way up the sides of the rolls. Poach over the lowest possible heat for 10 minutes. Season lightly with salt and freshly ground white pepper.

Meanwhile, make the sauce: pour the fish stock and the remaining cream into a small saucepan and boil, uncovered, until reduced by half. Lower the heat and beat the butter into the sauce a small, solid piece at a time, allowing each piece to melt before adding the next. Continue beating until the sauce is light and velvety. Season. Chop the remaining oysters and stir into the sauce, allowing them to heat through for a minute. As soon as the salmon rolls are cooked, transfer to warmed plates and coat with the oyster sauce.

SALMON WITH BROCCOLI PURÉE

8 slices or thin steaks salmon weighing 2 oz (50 g) each
10 oz (300 g) broccoli
4 carrots
3 tbsp olive oil
salt and pepper

Divide the broccoli into florets. Steam or boil in lightly salted water until tender. Drain and process to a smooth purée in a blender, with a very little water. Transfer the purée to a heatproof bowl or top of a double boiler and keep hot over simmering water. Boil the carrots until tender, cut crosswise in half, and keep warm. Heat the oil in a non-stick pan and fry the salmon slices for 3 minutes on each side; season with salt and pepper. Cover the centre section of 4 warmed plates with the broccoli purée. Carefully remove the skin and central bone from each salmon slice and place two slices on each bed of broccoli purée, opening the slices out slightly into a V shape and overlapping them into a fan-like decorative effect. Trim the carrot halves into neat oval shapes and garnish each serving with 2 of these.

STUFFED SALMON EN CROÛTE

1 salmon weighing 2¹/₄–2¹/₂ lb (1 kg)
10 oz (300 g) fillets of hake, cod or haddock
2 eggs
10 fl oz (300 ml) single cream
8 oz (225 g) carrots
4 oz (100 g) onions
few sprigs parsley
1 sprig thyme
1 bay leaf
9 fl oz (250 ml) champagne or sparkling dry white wine
1 lb (500 g) frozen puff pastry, thawed
salt and pepper

Gut the salmon (see page 9), scraping away and rinsing any blood from the ventral cavity. Use a sharp knife to cut down the back to the backbone and work the fillets away from the bones which radiate from the backbone just enough to be able to free the backbone and its attached bones (you will need to snip through the backbone just behind the head and at the tail end to free it). The object is to have a salmon which looks intact but which has been boned. If you are nervous of doing this yourself, ask your fishmonger to prepare the fish for you.

Process the white fish fillets to a very smooth paste with 1 egg white and 3½ fl oz (100 ml) of the cream. Season. Peel the carrots and cut half of them into very small dice, cook these in boiling water for 10 minutes, drain and refresh under running cold water. Fold them into the white fish mixture. Season the salmon inside and out; stuff with the white fish mixture and press the cut edges back into place. Secure the salmon loosely with kitchen string to keep it in shape. Grease a large roasting tin liberally with butter, place the fish carefully in it and place in the oven, preheated to 400°F (200°C) mark 6, cook for 15 minutes; reduce the heat to 350°F (180°C) mark 4. Slice the remaining carrots into rounds, peel and finely chop the onions and lay both around the salmon after the first 15 minutes' cooking time, together with the chopped parsley, thyme leaves and crumbled bay leaf. Cook the salmon for a further 20 minutes, basting it at frequent intervals with champagne, then transfer very carefully to a large platter.

Pour the remaining champagne into the roasting tin and cook over a high heat, stirring and scraping the bottom of the pan to loosen any deposits; when the liquid has reduced considerably, lower the heat and add the cream. Keep stirring as the sauce reduces and thickens. Allow to cool a little, then process in a blender until very smooth. Keep hot in a double boiler. Carefully remove the string from the salmon; peel off the skin. Roll out the thawed pastry into one sheet, large enough to envelop the salmon, and cut the sheet in half. Lay the salmon gently on one half; cover with the other half of the pastry sheet. (If liked, trim this pastry case into a fish shape.) Brush the edge of the lower pastry surface with cold water and press the pastry edges firmly closed. Lightly beat 2 egg yolks and brush all over the surface of the pastry as a glaze. Rinse a very large non-stick baking sheet with cold water, place the pastry case on it, and bake in the oven, preheated to 400–425°F (200–220°C) mark 6–7 for 30 minutes or until the pastry is well-risen, crisp, and pale golden brown.

Serve cut in slices with the champagne sauce.

SALMON TERIYAKI

4 salmon steaks weighing approx. 8 oz (250 g) each
2 onions
7 fl oz light soy sauce
7 fl oz (200 ml) saké or dry sherry
1 tsp sugar
salt

Remove the skin and centre bone from the salmon steaks and cut into small, even-sized cubes. Peel the onions, cut into quarters, and separate the layers. Thread the onion pieces and salmon cubes alternately on to skewers (wooden satay sticks or steel skewers) and place these in a wide, fairly deep dish.

Make the marinade: mix the soy sauce with the saké (or sherry) and the sugar until the sugar has dissolved. Pour over the salmon skewers and leave to stand for 15–20 minutes, turning once or twice. Drain well, reserving the marinade, and grill or barbecue for about 15 minutes or until done, basting at frequent intervals with the marinade. Season with salt if wished.

SALMON TARTARE

12 oz (350 g) very fresh salmon
4 very large peeled prawns
4 tinned anchovy fillets
1½ tbsp mixed chopped fresh herbs (e.g. parsley, chervil, chives)
2 eggs
1 tbsp wine vinegar
1 tbsp fish stock (fumet) (see page 39), or water or white wine
1 tbsp brandy
Tabasco sauce
Worcestershire sauce

3¹/₂ fl oz (100 ml) oil	*2 tbsp olive oil*
1 tbsp capers	*3 basil leaves*
salt and pepper	*juice of ¹/₂ lemon*

Remove the skin and bones from the raw salmon and chop it very finely or put through the food processor with the prawns and the well-drained and dried anchovies; if you use a food processor, be careful not to over-process these ingredients as the mixture should not be like a paste or purée (see illustration on page 226).

Stir in the chopped herbs, the egg yolks, vinegar, *fumet* (or substitute), brandy, 4 drops Tabasco sauce, 8 drops Worcestershire sauce, the oil, chopped capers, salt and freshly ground pepper. Mix well.

Rinse your hands in cold water and shape the mixture into round portions to look like very thick hamburgers; place these on individual plates and decorate with parsley sprigs, lemon slices, radishes cut into flower shapes, etc. Serve at once or refrigerate for a very short time.

Note: It cannot be stressed enough that only the freshest salmon should be used for this recipe.

SALMON SAVARINS

5 oz (150 g) salmon
4 oz (100 g) peeled prawns
1 oz (30 g) butter
few sprigs parsley
1 shallot
3¹/₂ oz (100 g) fillets of sole
1 egg
5 fl oz (150 ml) double cream
juice of ¹/₂ lemon
2¹/₂ oz (70 g) black olives, stoned
salt and pepper
For the sauce (optional):
2–3 ripe tomatoes

Sauté the prawns for 4 minutes in the butter with the very finely chopped shallot and parsley; season with salt and pepper and leave to cool. Remove any bones or skin from the salmon and place in the food processor with the white fish fillets; reduce to a smooth paste; add the egg, half the cream, and salt and pepper, and process at maximum speed for 15 seconds to blend well. Mix the prawns with the remaining cream, the lemon juice and the coarsely chopped olives.

Grease 4 small ring tube moulds, ramekins or timbale moulds with butter; place a layer of the prawn and cream mixture in the bottom of each mould and top with the salmon mixture. Cover each with a lightly buttered piece of foil and bake in the oven in a bain-marie (in a pan with sufficient hot water to come half way up the sides of the moulds) at 350°F (180°C) mark 4 for 30 minutes.

Serve the savarins hot or cold with the following sauce if wished: combine the blanched, peeled and seeded tomatoes in a blender with the other sauce ingredients until smooth. Pour a little on to each plate, and unmould the savarins on to this pool of sauce.

SALMON COULIBIAC

8 salmon slices cut ¹/₄ in (¹/₂ cm) thick
12 oz (350 g) frozen puff pastry
3 oz (80 g) butter
1 onion
3¹/₂ oz (100 g) small button mushrooms
3¹/₂ oz (100 g) rice
18 fl oz (500 ml) fish stock (fumet) (see page 39)
few sprigs parsley
1 small bunch chives

1 hard-boiled egg

salt and pepper

Thaw the pastry at room temperature. Remove the skin and central bone neatly from each salmon slice. Heat half the butter in a pan and fry the salmon slices until only just done, turning once and seasoning with salt and pepper.

Peel the onion and slice wafer-thin; slice the mushrooms very thinly. Sweat the onion until very soft in the butter used to cook the salmon; add the mushrooms and cook gently, stirring, for 15 minutes. Leave to cool.

Add the rice to the boiling fish stock, cover tightly, turn the heat down very low and continue cooking until the rice has absorbed all the liquid and is tender. Stir in the finely chopped parsley and chives. Roll the pastry into a single, thin rectangular sheet. Place 4 salmon slices in a line down the middle of the rectangle, working along the length of the rectangle and leaving a little space at either end. Cover each slice with some of the mushroom and onion mixture, reserving half of it; cover with a layer of rice, using a quarter of the rice for each slice. Cover with the remaining onions and mushrooms and chopped hard-boiled egg and top with the remaining 4 salmon slices. Sprinkle any remaining cooking juices and a very little melted butter over the salmon; fold the pastry over the salmon and fold over the ends, pinching tightly closed, to form a rectangular parcel. Make a very small hole through the top of the pastry and place a small tube of cardboard or foil in it to allow the steam to escape during cooking.

Transfer very carefully to a large non-stick baking tray, greased with butter, and leave to stand for 20 minutes. Bake in a preheated oven, at 400–425°F (200–220°C) mark 6–7, for about 30 minutes. Remove the foil or cardboard and pour a little melted butter into the hole. Slice and serve.

GRILLED SALMON STEAKS WITH ANCHOVY BUTTER

4 salmon steaks weighing approx. 6 oz (180 g) each

3¹/₂ oz (100 g) butter

3¹/₂ oz (100 g) salted anchovies or tinned anchovy fillets

1 lemon

2 tbsp oil

salt

Make the anchovy butter: cut the butter into small pieces and leave to soften at room temperature for 1 hour in a bowl. Rinse the salted anchovies under running cold water to eliminate excess salt and remove their bones. Soak these fillets in cold water for 1 hour. Drain and dry. If tinned anchovies are used, drain off all the oil and pat dry with kitchen paper. Using a pestle and mortar, pound the anchovies to a smooth paste and gradually work in the butter, adding a small piece at a time. (Or process the anchovies in a food processor, transfer to a bowl and work in the butter gradually with a large wooden spoon.) Keep at room temperature until needed.

Brush the salmon steaks with oil and grill at a very high temperature for 2–3 minutes on each side. Sprinkle with a little salt when cooked. They are done when the salmon has turned a much paler colour.

Serve immediately, topped with a piece of anchovy butter and garnished with lemon wedges.

BARBECUED SALMON

1 salmon weighing 2¹/₄–2¹/₂ lb (1 kg)

1 lemon

1 onion

1 small bunch parsley

4 tbsp olive oil

9 fl oz (250 ml) mayonnaise

2 gherkins or dill pickles

1 small bunch chives

1 tsp Worcestershire sauce

2 tbsp lemon juice

salt and pepper

Prepare the salmon for cooking, slitting open its belly and gutting it; cut off the head, trim off the fins and tail. Extend the ventral incision right down to the tail, open the fish out so that you can gradually work the backbone away from the flesh, together with all the connected bones, using a very sharp pointed knife and scissors. Rinse the salmon thoroughly, rubbing away any lingering traces of blood. Season inside with salt and pepper, fill the inside with thin slices of lemon and onion and chopped parsley then close up the fish again.

Brush a very large piece of foil with the oil and wrap the fish in this. Place on the grid above the glowing hot charcoal embers of the barbecue (about 7–8 in [18–20 cm] away from the embers) and cook for 30 minutes, turning twice very carefully. (Alternatively, bake in the oven, preheated to 300°F [150°C] mark 2, for about 45 minutes–1 hour or until done.)

Transfer the salmon to a very large plate and remove the foil, saving all the cooking juices. Remove and discard the lemon and onion slices; cut the fish into thick steaks and place on heated plates, sprinkling with the juices. Hand round a sauce made by mixing the mayonnaise with the chopped gherkins and chives, the Worcestershire sauce, lemon juice and a little freshly ground pepper.

STURGEON STEAKS WITH TARRAGON AND SHERRY VINEGAR

4 sturgeon steaks weighing 6 oz (180 g) each
1 shallot
3¹/₂ fl oz (100 ml) dry white wine
1 tbsp sherry vinegar
3¹/₂ fl oz (100 ml) single cream
2 oz (50 g) butter
2 fresh or tinned tomatoes
1 small sprig tarragon
salt and pepper

Peel and slice the shallot and place in a fish kettle or oval fireproof casserole dish. Pour in the wine, sherry vinegar and cream. Place the fish in the kettle or pan, season and poach gently for 10–12 minutes. Transfer the fish to a heated serving plate and keep warm. Boil the liquid gently until it has reduced by one third, then beat in the butter a small piece at a time; add the blanched, peeled and seeded tomatoes, finely diced, stir and draw aside from the heat. Mix in a few chopped tarragon leaves and ladle the sauce over the fish.

SWEET-SOUR STURGEON STEAKS

4 sturgeon steaks weighing approx. 8 oz (250 g) each
plain flour
4 tbsp oil
7 fl oz (200 ml) dry white wine
1 tbsp capers
4 pickled onions
¹/₂ stock cube (vegetable or chicken)
pepper

Remove the skin from the fish steaks, wash and dry them, coat generously with flour and fry in the oil in a large pan. Sprinkle the wine over the steaks and cook, uncovered, for 5–10 minutes over a moderate heat to reduce the wine. Add the chopped capers and onions, the crumbled half stock cube and freshly ground pepper. Cover and simmer for 10–15 minutes.

EEL WITH ARTICHOKES AND OLIVES

1 eel weighing 2¹/₄–2¹/₂ lb (1 kg)
2 oz (50 g) butter

1 sprig basil

1 oz (25 g) mushrooms preserved in oil

2–3 artichoke hearts preserved in oil

1 oz (25 g) green olives, stoned

7 fl oz (200 ml) dry white wine

juice of 1 lemon

4 thick slices coarse white bread or French bread

salt and pepper

Prepare the eel (see page 11). Cut the fish into short portions or steaks. Grease a casserole dish with butter and place the fish pieces in it in a single layer. Dot with small flakes of butter, season with salt and pepper, and sprinkle with chopped basil leaves (or a pinch of dried basil). Bake at 400°F (200°C) mark 6 for about 40 minutes or until done, turning the pieces frequently and moistening with a little of the wine.

Chop the mushrooms, artichoke hearts and olives. Transfer the cooked eel pieces to a warmed plate, reserving the cooking juices, and keep warm in the oven. Stir the chopped mixture, the remaining wine and the lemon juice into the cooking juices and cook over a low heat, stirring continuously, to reduce and thicken a little. Add the eel pieces to this sauce, and turn them in it to flavour. Place a crisply toasted piece of bread in each of 4 warmed deep dishes, place a few pieces of eel and some of the juices on top, and serve at once.

BRAISED EEL

1 eel weighing 2¹/₄–2¹/₂ lb (1 kg)

1 onion

3 tbsp olive oil

1¹/₂ oz (40 g) butter

1 lb (450 g) fresh or tinned tomatoes

3¹/₂ fl oz (100 ml) dry red or white wine

plain flour

1 celery stalk

2 cloves garlic

1 small bunch parsley

4 sage leaves

salt and pepper

Prepare the eel for cooking (see page 11). Slice. Chop the onion and sweat in the oil and butter in a pan.

Blanch, peel and seed the tomatoes; chop coarsely and add to the pan. Season with salt and pepper and simmer for 10 minutes. Pour in the wine, roll the fish pieces in flour to coat, and add to the pan. Simmer, uncovered, for a few minutes. Finely chop the celery, garlic, parsley and sage and sprinkle into the pan. Add salt and freshly ground pepper to taste. Cover and simmer slowly for about 35 minutes or until the eel is cooked, adding a little water if necessary.

EEL IN RED WINE

1 eel weighing 2¹/₄–2¹/₂ lb (1 kg)

2 onions

2 cloves garlic

1 small bunch parsley

1 sprig thyme

1 bay leaf

dry red wine

2 fl oz (50 ml) brandy

1 oz (25 g) butter

1 tbsp plain flour

salt and pepper

Clean and gut the eel (see pages 9 and 11), but do not skin. Cut into pieces and place in a saucepan with the peeled and coarsely chopped onions, the peeled and sliced garlic, parsley and thyme leaves and the bay leaf. Pour in just enough red wine to cover the eel pieces and then add the brandy. Season, bring to the boil, cover and reduce the heat. Simmer for 30 minutes.

253

Take the fish pieces out of the pan with a slotted spoon and set aside. Strain the liquid into a smaller saucepan. Work the butter with the flour (do not melt the butter beforehand) and add to the sauce in a solid piece; stir continuously over a low heat; as the butter melts and releases the flour, the sauce will thicken. Correct seasoning. Return the fish pieces to this sauce and heat through.

EEL WITH MIXED VEGETABLES

2 eels weighing approx. 1¹/₄ lb (600 g) each
1 celery stalk
1 large carrot
2 onions
few sprigs parsley
1 clove garlic
1 lemon
1 tbsp tomato purée
3 tbsp wine vinegar
few basil leaves
4 slices white bread
salt and pepper

Chop the celery and the peeled carrot; peel the onions and chop coarsely; peel the garlic and chop finely; place all these ingredients, together with the chopped parsley, in a large saucepan or fireproof casserole dish. Add just enough water to cover. Cut off a strip of lemon rind and add to the pan, followed by ¹/₂ tbsp salt. Cover and boil gently for 20–25 minutes, adding a little water if the liquid reduces.

Prepare the eels (see page 11): skin them and remove their heads. Coil each one round to form a circle, fastening the tail end to what was the 'neck' with a skewer. Use a slotted ladle or spoon to transfer half the cooked vegetables to another pan, draining them well. (Reserve the vegetable cooking liquid.) Place the eel circlets on top and cover with the remaining vegetables, also well drained. Cook over a low heat for 1 minute, stirring

with a wooden spoon; stir the tomato paste into the vegetable liquid and add to the pan. If this liquid does not cover the eels, add a little water.

Cover tightly (use a sheet of foil under the lid if necessary to ensure no steam escapes) and simmer over a very low heat for about 30 minutes. Add the vinegar and a little salt if necessary. Season with freshly ground pepper and continue cooking for a further 10 minutes. Decorate the eels with a few fresh basil leaves and serve with the bread slices, toasted and cut into small triangles.

EEL STEW WITH BEER

1 eel weighing 2¹/₄–2¹/₂ lb (1 kg)
vinegar
2 onions
2 oz (50 g) butter
2 cloves
parsley
marjoram
lemon rind
basil
generous pinch real saffron powder
7 fl oz (200 ml) beer
¹/₂ stock cube (vegetable or chicken)
1 tbsp plain flour
4 potatoes
salt and pepper

Soak the eel for 1–2 hours in a bowl containing equal parts vinegar and water; change the liquid for fresh halfway through the soaking time. Clean, prepare and skin the eel (see pages 9 and 11).

Liberally grease a deep cooking pot or heavy-bottomed saucepan with butter, place the peeled and sliced onion in it with the cloves, parsley, a pinch of marjoram, a small strip of lemon rind, 2–3 basil leaves or a pinch of dried basil, the saffron, freshly ground pepper and salt. Dot small pieces of butter all over these ingredients and add the eel, fastened securely in a circlet (tail to neck, head removed) with a skewer, preferably of wood. Pour in the beer (this should be at least $^3/_4$ in [2 cm] deep if it is to cook the eel satisfactorily; add more if necessary).

Bring to the boil, cover, and cook over a moderate heat for 30–35 minutes or until the eel is done. Wash and boil the potatoes. Transfer the eel to a warmed dish, reserving the cooking liquid; remove and discard the bay leaf, lemon rind, and cloves and liquidize the juices and contents of the pan with the $^1/_2$ stock cube and the flour until very smooth. Pour into a saucepan and heat, stirring continuously, for 5–10 minutes or until the sauce has thickened. Return the eel to this sauce and heat through; serve with the boiled potatoes.

EEL IN WHITE WINE

1 eel weighing 2$^1/_4$–2$^1/_2$ lb (1 kg)
1 oz (25 g) butter
1 oz (25 g) plain flour
14 fl oz (400 ml) dry white wine
4 small onions
1 bouquet garni
1 stock cube (vegetable or chicken)
5 oz (150 g) button mushrooms
salt and pepper

Prepare the eel as directed on pages 9 and 11 and slice into steaks of even thickness. Melt the butter in a large, heavy-bottomed saucepan or fireproof casserole dish, stir in the flour, and cook the resulting roux for a few minutes; heat the wine with an equal quantity of water to lukewarm and gradually mix into the roux, taking care that the mixture does not form lumps. Cook gently while stirring for a few minutes, then add the peeled onions, bouquet garni and the crumbled stock cube. Add a little salt and freshly ground pepper. Simmer over an extremely low heat for 1 hour, stirring occasionally. Add the eel pieces to this liquid and cook gently for 10 minutes. Thinly slice the mushrooms and add to the eel; simmer for 15 minutes. Serve very hot.

EEL MASCAGNI

1 eel weighing 2$^1/_4$–2$^1/_2$ lb (1 kg)
18 fl oz (500 ml) dry white wine
2 bay leaves
1 sprig thyme
generous pinch allspice
2 oz (50 g) butter
breadcrumbs
1 onion
2 shallots
1 tbsp plain flour
$^1/_2$ lemon
1 small bunch parsley
1 sprig chervil
salt

Clean, gut and skin the eel as directed on pages 9 and 11. Cut through the eel below the head and discard the head; trim off the fins. Form a circlet with the eel, fastening securely with a wooden skewer. Pour the wine into a large fireproof casserole dish, add the bay leaves, thyme and allspice, and bring to a gentle boil. Add the eel and simmer for about 20 minutes or until done. Leave to cool in the liquid.

Drain off the liquid and reserve; remove the skewer and straighten out the eel just sufficiently to make it easy to handle; brush with melted butter all over and roll in the breadcrumbs.

Heat 1 oz (25 g) butter in a pan and fry the eel until golden brown, turning once or twice. Sprinkle with the finely chopped onion and shallots; fry for 2 minutes. Sprinkle with the flour, pour in the strained reserved cooking liquid and boil gently to reduce and thicken the liquid.

Transfer the eel to a heated serving plate, draining well. Rearrange it into a circlet. Beat the remaining butter into the sauce in the pan, adding small pieces at a time; stir in a little lemon juice to taste and the finely chopped parsley and chervil. Beat until light and frothy. Heat just to boiling point, season then pour over the eel.

EEL IN BRANDY SAUCE

1 eel weighing 2¹/₄–2¹/₂ lb (1 kg)

3¹/₂ (90 g) butter

2 onions

1 clove garlic

dry white wine

12 mushroom caps

1 bouquet garni

16 large peeled prawns

brandy

7 fl oz (200 ml) double cream

1 tbsp plain flour

salt and pepper

Prepare the eel as directed on pages 9 and 11. Cut it into very short lengths or thick steaks. Heat 1¹/₂ oz (40 g) of the butter, add the finely chopped onions and garlic and sweat gently until the onions are transparent. Add the eel pieces, fry until lightly coloured all over, then pour in sufficient wine to just cover; season with salt and pepper, add the bouquet garni and simmer, uncovered, for about 20 minutes, by which time the wine should have reduced to one third of its original volume.

Fry the mushroom caps in 1 oz (25 g) butter; reduce the heat, cover, and cook gently for 20 minutes.

In a separate pan or small saucepan, sauté the prawns in ¹/₂ oz (10 g) butter, add the mushrooms, the brandy and 3¹/₂ fl oz (100 ml) wine. Season lightly with salt and pepper and simmer for 5 minutes. Draw aside from the heat.

Use a slotted spoon to transfer the eel, mushrooms and prawns to a warmed dish. Combine all the cooking juices, strain them into one of the pans, bring to the boil then stir in the cream. Work the remaining butter and flour together well and add in one piece to the liquid; cook over a low heat for 5 minutes, stirring, to thicken the sauce. Add a little more salt and pepper if needed. Add the eel, mushrooms and prawns to this sauce, stir over a very gentle heat for a minute or two, then serve while very hot.

FRIED BREADED EEL

1 eel weighing 2¹/₄–2¹/₂ lb (1 kg)

1 oz (25 g) butter

2 carrots

1 onion

1 small bunch parsley

1 clove garlic

14 fl oz (400 ml) dry white wine

1 bay leaf

1 sprig thyme

breadcrumbs

2 eggs

7 fl oz (200 ml) oil

salt and peppercorns

Gut the eel, skin and cut off its fins (see pages 9 and 11); cut into pieces of even thickness.

Peel the carrots and onions, slice very thinly, and fry in the butter with the chopped parsley and crushed garlic; pour in the wine and boil.

Add the eel pieces, bay leaf, thyme, pinch of salt and a few peppercorns. Boil gently for 15 minutes, turn off the heat and leave to cool. The liquid will become gelatinous as it cools.

Take the eel pieces out of the pan, draining well, and roll in the breadcrumbs; dip in lightly beaten egg and then roll in the breadcrumbs again to coat thickly.

Heat the oil in a pan and fry the eel until golden brown all over. Drain on kitchen paper and serve while still very hot.

Note: Accompany with a home-made tomato sauce, if liked.

EEL WITH PEAS

1 eel weighing 2¹/₄–2¹/₂ lb (1 kg)

1 onion

4 tbsp oil
1 lb (500 g) frozen peas
1 small bunch parsley
1 oz (25 g) butter
1 tbsp plain flour
salt and pepper

Get the eel ready for cooking as directed on pages 9 and 11; wash very thoroughly and cut into 2-in (5-cm) lengths. Fry the thinly sliced onion in the oil until pale golden brown, add the eel pieces and fry, turning carefully so that they do not break up.

Add the peas and the finely chopped parsley; season with salt and pepper. Cover the pan tightly and simmer very gently for 40–45 minutes, adding a very little hot water now and then to prevent the eel sticking or becoming too dry. About 5 minutes before the cooking time is up, work the butter with the flour and add to the pan, stirring so that the juices thicken. Cook for a few minutes more, then serve very hot.

Note: Serve with mashed potatoes.

EEL WITH SPINACH, NETTLES AND SORREL

1 eel weighing 2¼–2½ lb (1 kg)
2½ oz (70 g) butter
2 tbsp oil
3 shallots
2 onions
18 fl oz (500 ml) dry white wine
7 fl oz (200 ml) fish stock (fumet) (see page 39)
1 sprig sage
1 sprig parsley
2 oz (50 g) young nettle tops or shoots

2 oz (50 g) young spinach leaves (no stalks)
2 oz (50 g) sorrel leaves
juice of ½ lemon
1 tbsp plain flour
salt and pepper

Prepare the eel, skin (see pages 9 and 11) and cut into slices of even thickness. Fry these in 1½ oz (40 g) of the butter and all the oil for 2–3 minutes, turning several times. Peel and thinly slice the shallots and onions and scatter them over the eel pieces; cover and cook over a lower heat for 5 minutes. Add the wine and *fumet*; tie together the sprigs of sage and parsley and add to the pan as a bouquet garni. Simmer very gently over an extremely low heat for 20 minutes.

Wash the nettles (wear rubber gloves to prevent them stinging), the spinach and sorrel; cut into fairly broad strips and add to the eel; cook for 10 minutes. Work the remaining butter with the flour to form a solid ball of *beurre manié*; transfer the eel pieces to a heated plate; remove and discard the sage and parsley; add the butter and flour mixture to the liquid in the pan and stir over a gentle heat until the sauce has thickened. Add the lemon juice and salt and pepper and cook for a further 3–4 minutes stirring continuously. Pour this sauce over the eel and serve.

PIKE WITH HERBS AND MUSHROOMS

1 pike weighing 2¼–2½ lb (1 kg)
2 oz (50 g) butter
7 fl oz (200 ml) dry white wine
1 small bunch fresh herbs (e.g. thyme, tarragon, parsley, chervil)
1 lime
1–2 cloves
1 oz (30 g) dried mushrooms, soaked
2 tbsp capers

2 tbsp plain flour

salt and pepper

Clean the pike thoroughly, trim, remove the head and tail and gut (see page 9); rinse and cut into pieces. Brown these lightly all over in 1½ oz (40 g) butter in a deep pan; add the wine, the herbs and the lime cut into slices, the cloves, salt and freshly ground pepper. Bring to a gentle boil, then lower the heat and simmer, uncovered, until the liquid has almost completely evaporated (20–25 minutes). Having soaked the mushrooms in hot water to soften, drain, reserving the liquid, rinse and squeeze out excess moisture; chop and fry in a fireproof casserole dish in the remaining butter with the capers; stir in the flour mixed with 3½ fl oz (100 ml) of the strained mushroom water. Cook for 10 minutes, stirring continuously.

Transfer the fish pieces carefully to the mushroom mixture. Cook gently for 5–6 minutes to coat with the sauce, turning once or twice. Serve straight from the casserole dish.

STUFFED ROAST PIKE

1 pike weighing 3¼–3½ lb (1.4 kg)

6 oz fillets of whiting, cod or hake

1 hard-boiled egg

1 raw egg

4 tbsp finely chopped fresh herbs (e.g. parsley, tarragon, chervil)

1 large slice slightly stale bread (crusts removed)

2 oz (50 g) butter

salt and pepper

First make the stuffing: rinse, dry and finely chop the white fish fillets and place in a bowl; stir in the finely chopped hard-boiled egg, the lightly beaten raw egg, 2 tbsp of the chopped herbs, the finely crumbled bread, a generous pinch of salt, and plenty of freshly ground pepper. Stir thoroughly,

blending to a thick paste consistency.

Descale the fish, trim off the fins and tail, and gut through the gill aperture (see page 9). Rinse the fish thoroughly under running cold water; dry well. Lay the fish flat on a working surface or plastic chopping board; use a very sharp pointed knife to cut right down the pike's back, down to the backbone; work the flesh away from the bones which radiate from the backbone on both sides of the fish but do not detach it: the object is to free the backbone and attached bones (you will need to snip through the backbone just behind the head and the extreme end of the tail); the fish is filleted but will look intact when the flesh is folded back in place. Stuff the fish with the prepared herb stuffing, fold the filleted flesh back into place and tie the fish with kitchen string or sew up the opening neatly with a poultry needle and kitchen thread.

Grease a large sheet of greaseproof paper or foil with butter, sprinkle with half the remaining chopped herbs, place the fish on these, sprinkle its surface with the remaining herbs and trickle melted butter all over it. Season with salt and pepper; fold the paper or foil into a secure, well-sealed parcel, leaving an air space inside and transfer to a large baking tray. Bake in a preheated oven at 400°F (200°C) mark 6 for 20 minutes, then reduce the heat to 350°F (180°C) mark 4 and cook for a further 30 minutes or until the fish is cooked. Unwrap the fish, remove the string or thread and transfer carefully to a warmed serving platter. Serve with hollandaise sauce (see page 37) or tartare sauce (see page 38).

PIKE LOMBARDY STYLE

1 pike weighing 2¼–2½ lb (1 kg)

2 onions

2 carrots

1 large celery stalk

1 leek

3 tbsp olive oil

1 oz (25 g) butter

plain flour	
7 fl oz (200 ml) dry red wine	
7 fl oz (200 ml) fish stock (fumet) (see page 39)	
salt and pepper	

Peel the onions and carrots and slice very thinly; wash the leek and celery thoroughly and slice finely. Sweat all these vegetables until tender in the oil and butter in a large pan or fireproof casserole large enough to take the fish. Season with salt and pepper.

Clean and prepare the fish, gutting it as directed for round fish on page 10. Wash and dry, season inside and out with salt and pepper, coat lightly with flour, and add to the pan containing the vegetables. Cook over a fairly high heat for about 10 minutes, turning once. Pour the wine and the hot stock over the fish, lower the heat, cover and simmer for 15 minutes.

Remove the fish, strain the liquid and vegetables, pushing them through a sieve (or process in a blender) and return the fish and liquid to the pan. Place in a preheated oven at 425°F (230°C) mark 8 for 5 minutes, then serve without delay.

PIKE SAVARIN MOULD

1 pike weighing 2¼–2½ lb (1 kg)	
2 eggs	
3½ oz (100 g) butter	
2½ oz (70 g) plain flour	
7 fl oz (200 ml) milk	
olive oil	
7 oz (200 g) button mushrooms	
2 shallots	
3½ fl oz (100 ml) dry white wine	
1 small bunch parsley	
10 fl oz (300 ml) whipping cream	
salt and pepper	

Fillet the fish and remove the skin (see pages 9–12); cut these fillets into small pieces. Separate the eggs. Beat 1½ oz (40 g) butter with a wooden spoon until soft and creamy; beat in the egg yolks one at a time, then stir in the flour. Season with salt and pepper. Gradually mix in the milk. Transfer the batter to a saucepan and cook over a low heat, stirring until the mixture has thickened and comes away cleanly from the sides of the pan. Grease a large plate lightly with oil and turn the mixture out on to it to cool.

Thinly slice the mushrooms and sauté in 1 oz (25 g) butter; remove with a slotted spoon when pale golden brown and set aside; add the wine to the butter and juices left in the pan, stir and cook until the wine has reduced by half. Place the fish in the pan, season with salt and pepper, add the finely chopped parsley and cook for 2 minutes over a fairly high heat; draw aside from the heat.

Stir in the egg whites and the cooled batter; liquidize to blend thoroughly or beat with a balloon whisk. Stir in the lightly beaten cream and the chopped cooked mushrooms. Grease a fluted mould or ring mould with butter and fill with the fish mixture, smoothing the surface level. Cover with a lightly buttered piece of foil or greaseproof paper pressed lightly against the surface of the mixture, and cook in a pan of hot water (which should come half to two thirds of the way up the sides of the mould) in the oven at 325°F (180°C) mark 4 for 1½ hours. Take the paper off the top and turn out on to a plate. Serve warm.

PIKE BELLEVUE

1 pike weighing 2¼–2½ lb (1 kg)	
vinegar	
2¾ pints (1.6 litres) court-bouillon (see page 39)	
1 sachet gelatine (sufficient to set 18 fl oz [500 ml] liquid)	
2 tbsp port	
1 egg white	
1 sprig tarragon	
2 hard-boiled eggs	

259

1 large ripe tomato
1 lemon
mayonnaise

Prepare the pike, gutting, descaling and trimming off its fins (see page 9); sprinkle the ventral cavity with a little vinegar. Have the *court-bouillon* ready in the fish kettle, lukewarm or cold; lower the fish into it on the grid, bring to a gentle boil and immediately lower the heat so that the liquid barely simmers; cook the fish for about 30 minutes from the time the liquid reaches boiling point. Leave to cool in the *court-bouillon*.

Strain 18 fl oz (500 ml) of the *court-bouillon*, stir in the gelatine, and heat gently while stirring until the gelatine has completely dissolved (do not allow to boil); draw aside from the heat, stir in the port, add the egg white, and beat over a very low heat. Again, do not allow to boil. Strain.

Skin the well-drained fish and place on a serving platter. Blanch the tarragon leaves very briefly and press them, separately, in a decorative pattern along the surface of the fish. Use a pastry brush to cover the exposed surface of the fish with a thin layer of gelatine; chill in the refrigerator for 30 minutes. Repeat the glazing process three or four more times to build up a fairly thick layer of gelatine, returning the fish to the refrigerator each time to set each layer.

Garnish with wedges of hard-boiled eggs, tomato rings (or tomato skin cut and shaped into roses) and lemon slices. Serve with home-made mayonnaise (see page 37).

BLANQUETTE OF PIKE

$2^1/_4$–$2^1/_2$ lb (1 kg) middle cut of pike
2 tbsp oil
1 oz (25 g) butter
2 tbsp plain flour
7 fl oz (200 ml) dry white wine
12 baby onions
4 oz (120 g) small button mushrooms

2 egg yolks
$1^1/_2$ pints (900 ml) single cream
salt and pepper

Clean and prepare the fish (see page 9), gutting, trimming and rinsing it thoroughly; dry well. Slice into fairly thick steaks. Sauté these slices in the oil and butter for 3–4 minutes on each side; do not brown.

Sprinkle the fish pieces with the flour; pour in the wine and $3^1/_2$ fl oz (100 ml) water. Add the peeled onions and the quartered mushrooms; season with salt and pepper. Cover and simmer gently for 25–30 minutes. Beat the egg yolks into the cream and add to the pan a few minutes before the fish is done, working the cream gently but thoroughly into the juices. Do not allow to boil.

BAKED PIKE-PERCH

1 pike-perch weighing $3^1/_4$–$3^1/_2$ lb (1.5 kg)
4 oz (120 g) thin rashers smoked streaky bacon
2 tbsp olive oil
$2^1/_2$ oz (70 g) butter
1 pint (600 ml) dry white wine
juice of 1 lemon
8 oysters
2 tbsp plain flour
4 tinned anchovy fillets; drained
2 tbsp capers
$1^1/_2$ tbsp finely chopped parsley
salt and pepper

Descale and gut the fish (see page 9). Wash well, dry, and season inside the ventral cavity with salt and pepper. Wrap the bacon all round the fish and fasten with cocktail sticks or small skewers. Brush all over with oil and 1 oz (25 g) melted butter, place on a rack in a roasting tin, and cook in a preheated oven at 475°F (240°C) mark 9 for 40 minutes, basting frequently with the wine mixed with the lemon juice. Turn the fish half way through this cooking time. Shuck the oysters (see page 22), save their juices and strain into a small saucepan; detach the oysters from their shells and simmer them gently in their juices for 1 minute only. Transfer the cooked fish to a warmed serving plate and keep hot. Remove the oysters from their juice with a slotted spoon. Pour the cooking juices and liquid from the roasting pan into the saucepan containing the oyster juice.

Pound the anchovies to a smooth paste. Melt the remaining butter in a saucepan, stir in the flour, then gradually work in the liquid. Add the anchovy paste, the oysters and the capers; pour this sauce all round the fish, sprinkle with the chopped parsley and serve.

PIKE-PERCH FLORENTINE STYLE

4 fillets of pike-perch weighing approx. 5 oz (150 g) each
plain flour
4 oz (100 g) butter
14 oz (400 g) fresh, crisp spinach leaves
14 oz (400 g) mushrooms
3 tbsp olive oil
1 clove garlic
1 tbsp lemon juice
1 tbsp finely chopped fresh thyme
salt and pepper

Dust the fish fillets very lightly with flour and sauté in a pan in 2 oz (50 g) butter. Season with salt and pepper and cook very gently over a low heat for 15 minutes.

Wash the spinach thoroughly and cook it with just the water left on the leaves. Drain very thoroughly, chop coarsely, and cook for 15 minutes with 1 oz (25 g) butter, stirring and turning to allow any lingering moisture to evaporate.

Meanwhile, thinly slice the mushrooms; fry them in the oil, season with salt and pepper and leave to cook gently for 15–20 minutes. When the spinach is done, spread it out on a warmed serving plate, arrange the fish fillets on top (reserve their cooking juices) and keep hot in the oven.

Quickly stir 1 oz (25 g) butter into the fish cooking juices and add the partially crushed but still whole garlic clove, lemon juice and thyme. Stir over a moderate heat for a few minutes, remove and discard the garlic and pour this sauce all over the fish fillets. Surround the fish with the mushrooms and serve immediately.

FILLETS OF PERCH WITH MUSSELS

1 lb (500 g) fillets of perch
8 mussels
1 tbsp olive oil
1 clove garlic
3¹/₂ oz (100 g) plain flour
2 oz (50 g) butter
2 lemons
1 small bunch parsley
salt and pepper

Soak and scrub the mussels discarding any that do not close when tapped. Place in a large saucepan with the oil and partially crushed peeled garlic clove, cover tightly, and place over a high heat to open. Leave to cool slightly. Take the molluscs off their shells, discarding any mussels that have failed to open. (Use thawed, frozen shucked mussels if preferred: allow a quarter of the weight given above and substitute dry white wine for the mussel juices.)

Strain the cooking liquid. Rinse and dry the perch fillets and check that no bones are left in them. Coat with flour, shaking off excess, and fry in a wide pan in the butter, turning once. Season with salt and freshly ground pepper and sprinkle with 3 tbsp of the mussel liquor and the lemon

261

juice. Simmer for 5–6 minutes, moving gently so that they do not stick to the pan; add the mussels and simmer for 10–15 minutes.

Transfer the fish fillets carefully to a heated serving dish; top each fillet with a lemon slice, surrounded by parsley leaves, and place a mussel in the centre of each lemon ring.

FILLETS OF PERCH WITH PINK PEPPERCORNS

8 fillets of perch (or other freshwater fish) weighing approx. 2¹/₂ oz (70 g) each
plain flour
2 oz (50 g) butter
4 tbsp olive oil
7 fl oz (200 ml) beer
8 oz ceps (boletus edulis) *or 2 packets dried ceps*
1 tbsp cornflour
1 tbsp pink (or green) peppercorns
salt

Rinse the fillets and dry thoroughly. Season with salt and pepper and coat lightly with flour. Heat 1 oz (25 g) of the butter and the oil in a large pan and lightly brown the fillets on both sides. Pour in the beer and simmer for 7–8 minutes. Use a slotted spoon to transfer the fillets to a warmed serving plate. Strain the liquid left in the pan.

Melt the remaining butter; finely slice the mushrooms and sauté in the butter over a high heat, uncovered, for a few minutes. Sprinkle with a pinch of salt and add the peppercorns and the strained liquid; mix the cornflour with 3 tsp water and stir into the pan. Bring to a gentle boil and simmer for 7–8 minutes, stirring.

Pour this sauce all over the fish fillets and serve immediately.

Note: Garnish with watercress sprigs, and serve with lightly steamed mangetouts and braised lettuce.

FILLETS OF PERCH AU GRATIN

1¹/₄ lb (600 g) fillets of perch
1 onion
butter
10 fl oz (300 ml) dry white wine
1 tbsp plain flour
7 fl oz (200 ml) fish stock (fumet) *(see page 39)*
3¹/₂ oz (100 g) Gruyère cheese, grated
7 oz (200 g) long-grain rice
salt and pepper

Peel and finely chop the onion; sprinkle into a wide, shallow gratin dish or casserole dish liberally greased with butter. Place the fillets on top in a single layer, season with salt and pepper and pour in the wine. Cover and cook over a very low heat for 10–15 minutes. Transfer the fillets to a warmed serving dish, using a slotted fish slice or spatula and keep hot. Strain the cooking liquid.

Melt 1 oz (25 g) butter in a small saucepan, stir in the flour then gradually blend in the strained liquid and the *fumet*. Cook, stirring, for 10 minutes. Add salt if necessary. Pour this sauce all over the fish fillets, coating them evenly; sprinkle with the grated cheese. Grill for a few minutes to melt and brown the cheese.

Note: This dish goes well with moulded boiled rice: mix the hot rice with a little butter until the butter has melted and coated the grains. Press into individual moulds, place in a hot oven for a few minutes and unmould on to each plate.

SOUSED FRESHWATER SHAD

2¹/₄–2¹/₂ lb (1 kg) freshwater shad
plain flour
8 fl oz (225 ml) oil
2 eggs

14 fl oz (400 ml) white wine vinegar

2 cloves garlic

1 oz (25 g) butter

1½ tbsp finely chopped parsley

salt and pepper

Gut and descale the fish; trim off their fins (see page 9) and rinse well under running cold water. Sprinkle with a little salt and coat lightly with flour, shaking off excess. Heat all but 1½ tbsp of the oil until very hot and fry the fish until golden brown and crisp on both sides. Drain well and place in a warmed deep serving dish.

Beat the eggs, then gradually beat in the vinegar, adding a little at a time. Fry the peeled and slightly crushed garlic clove and the chopped parsley in the remaining oil and the butter until pale golden brown; remove and discard the garlic clove. Reduce the heat and pour in the egg and vinegar mixture and cook very gently, stirring continuously until the mixture starts to thicken a little. Do not allow to boil. Season with salt and pepper, pour over the fish and leave to stand for 24 hours in a cool place or in the refrigerator.

BURBOT EN PAPILLOTE

4 burbot or freshwater cod weighing 8 oz (250 g) each

4 sprigs dill

1 large mild onion

2 tbsp dry white vermouth

4 tbsp fish stock (fumet) *(see page 39)*

2 tbsp olive oil

1 lemon

salt and pepper

Gut the fish and skin (see directions for eel, page 11). Place a sprig of dill, a pinch of salt and a generous pinch of freshly ground pepper in the ventral cavity of each fish.

Place each fish on a fairly large square of waxed paper or foil; peel and finely chop the onion and sprinkle one quarter of it over each fish; sprinkle each fish with 1 tbsp vermouth, 1 tbsp *fumet*, 1 tbsp oil then season with salt and pepper. Cut the lemon into 8 thin slices, remove the rind and pith, and place two slices on each fish. Fold up the parcels and close securely. Place on a large baking sheet.

Preheat the oven to 425°F (230°C) mark 8 and bake the parcels for 10 minutes. Serve the parcels closed, to be unwrapped at table.

CHUB WITH LEEKS

2 chub weighing approx. 1 lb (500 g) each (or use perch or whitefish)

3½ fl oz (100 ml) oil

2 tbsp white wine vinegar

2 lemons

1 sprig thyme

5 whole coriander seeds

2 bay leaves

4 leeks

3 oz (80 g) butter

3½ fl oz (100 ml) dry white wine

1 tbsp mild French mustard

salt and pepper

Gut and descale the fish (see page 9). Place in a deep, rectangular dish. Mix the oil, vinegar, juice of ½ lemon, the thyme leaves, crushed coriander, crumbled bay leaves, a pinch of salt and plenty of freshly ground pepper in a bowl; beat thoroughly with a balloon whisk and pour over the fish. Cover and leave to marinate for 2 hours, turning a few times. Drain the fish and strain the marinade. Reserve this.

Trim the leeks and wash thoroughly; using the white part only, slice into thin rings and sweat, covered, in 2 oz (50 g) butter for 15 minutes. Add

263

the wine and a little salt and cook, uncovered, until the wine has evaporated. Process in a blender until very smooth.

Grease an oval ovenproof dish with butter, pour in the leek purée and place the fish on top. Stir the mustard into the strained marinade, blending thoroughly, and pour over the fish. Slice the remaining lemon into thin rounds and cover the fish with them. Cover with a lightly buttered sheet of greaseproof paper or foil. Bake in a preheated oven at 350°F (180°C) mark 4 for 25 minutes, removing the paper or foil after 20 minutes. Serve straight from the dish.

FRESHWATER SHAD WITH SHRIMP SAUCE

1 freshwater shad weighing 2¼–2½ lb (1 kg)
4 oz (120 g) unpeeled shrimps or small prawns, raw or cooked
2 small fillets of cod, hake or haddock
2 oz (50 g) button mushrooms
1 small bunch parsley
5 eggs
2 oz (50 g) slightly stale white bread (crusts removed)
6–7 slices salt pork
14 fl oz (400 ml) dry white wine
2 oz (50 g) butter
2 fl oz (50 ml) double cream
2 tbsp sherry
salt and pepper

If the shrimps are raw, rinse thoroughly and boil in water for 4 minutes. Drain, discarding the cooking liquid, and peel, reserving the shells. Chop one third of the shrimps with the cod or hake fillets and place in a bowl. Add the chopped mushrooms and parsley, 1 lightly beaten egg and the finely crumbled bread. Blend thoroughly, seasoning with salt and pepper. Prepare the shad: descale, trim and gut through the gill aperture (see page 9).

Wash and dry. Run a sharp pointed knife down the back of the fish, cutting through to the backbone; work the flesh away from the bones which radiate from the backbone on either side of the fish in order to remove the backbone and the bones attached to it (you will have to snip the backbone behind the head and at the tail end). Sprinkle the inside of the fish with a little salt and pepper and fill with the stuffing. Fold the flesh back into place. Wrap the fish securely with the pieces of fat and tie with string (not too tightly). Bake in the oven, preheated to 350°F (180°C) mark 4, for 30 minutes.

Make the sauce: boil the wine and the shrimp shells for 15 minutes; drain most of the wine off and liquidize the shells in a processor on the highest speed until very smooth; strain through a fine sieve. Return this mixture to the pan used for cooking the shrimps, beat in the butter (in a solid piece) using a balloon whisk, then beat in the egg yolks and cream. Heat the wine drained off from the shrimps to boiling point, strain and gradually beat into the creamy sauce mixture. Stir the remaining, whole, shrimps into this sauce over a low heat; do not allow to boil. Remove the string and fat wrapping and serve the fish on a heated serving plate, handing round the sauce separately.

·International Menus·

CHRISTMAS EVE MENU

LOBSTER IN ASPIC

——— • ———

EEL RISOTTO

——— • ———

SALMON ROULADES
WITH OYSTER SAUCE

——— • ———

PEA AND HAM
SAVARINS

——— • ———

ORANGE CASSATA

——— • ———

*W*ith the rich, often heavy traditional food of Christmas Day to follow, a deliciously light yet elegant dinner on Christmas Eve provides the perfect start to the festivities. Christmas is a time for special treats and our first course is made with lobster, a feather-light mousse with a glistening coating of aspic which can be made in advance.

Eel used to be eaten on fast days in medieval times, and the eel risotto is a traditional reminder that Advent is drawing to a close, with the feasting about to begin.

The main course of this menu is visually impressive, delicate in flavour and elegantly sauced, a suitable choice for a celebration meal.

The refreshing pea moulds served with the salmon set it off to perfection and add complementary colour as well as taste to it.

The orange cassata can be made several days in advance and is extremely easy and quick to prepare, yet provides an impressive finale to the meal.

For this succession of special dishes to be fully appreciated, care should be taken with the table decoration. Choose plates that will complement the colours of the food: all white, for example, or black and white as shown in the illustration, white and gold or white and silver, with a snowy white table cloth and Christmas decorations in gold or silver that will gleam in the candlelight.

As for the wine, keep everything superbly simple and serve a dry champagne throughout the meal.

PEA AND HAM SAVARINS

Preparation and cooking time: 1 hour

Easy

Vegetable accompaniment

10 oz (300 g) frozen peas

1–2 cloves garlic (optional)

2¹/₂ oz (70 g) butter

2 tbsp olive oil

| 1 rasher streaky bacon |
| few sprigs parsley |
| 1 tbsp plain flour |
| 9 fl oz (250 ml) milk (hot) |
| 1 egg |
| 4 tbsp freshly grated Parmesan cheese |
| salt and pepper |

Partially defrost the peas at room temperature; fry them briefly with the peeled garlic cloves, 1 oz (25 g) butter, the oil, and chopped bacon. Sprinkle with 1 tbsp finely chopped parsley, season with a little salt and pepper, cover and cook gently for 25 minutes or until all these ingredients are very tender. Liquidize or process to a very smooth paste. Make a white sauce: melt the remaining butter, stir in the flour, cook for a minute or two then beat in the hot milk off the heat. Return to the heat and cook for 10 minutes, stirring continuously. Draw aside from the heat: stir in the grated cheese, the lightly beaten egg and the purée. Mix thoroughly. Spoon into individual ring moulds or ramekins and place in a roasting tin. Add enough hot water to come half way up the sides of the moulds and cook in a preheated oven at 400°F (200°C) mark 6 for 20 minutes. Unmould. Serve, as shown, with their centres filled with a few extra cooked peas and a cream sauce of your choice, if wished, or just as they are, with a sprig of parsley.

ORANGE CASSATA

| Preparation: 1 hour + freezing time |
| Easy |
| Dessert |

| 1 Italian panettone weighing approx. 1½ lb (750 g) or same weight sponge cake |
| 1 pint (600 ml) whipping cream |
| icing sugar |
| 3½ oz (100 g) candied orange peel |
| orange liqueur (e.g. Grand Marnier or similar) |
| 3 large oranges |

If Italian panettone is unavailable, you can line a bombe mould or pudding bowl with slices of sponge cake dipped in a sugar syrup flavoured with Grand Marnier.

Lay the panettone on its side and, using a sharp knife, carefully cut out the base leaving a 1½-in (4-cm) border all the way round the edge. Cut any soft crumb off this circle and reserve. Hollow out the panettone by scooping out the cake interior, but leave a layer 1¼–1½ in (3-4 cm) thick in place inside the crust.

Beat 16 fl oz (450 ml) of the cream with 2 oz (70 g) icing sugar until stiff; fold in the finely diced candied orange peel, 3 tbsp Grand Marnier and half the crumbled scooped out cake mixture. Fill the panettone case with this, packing it in fairly firmly. Replace the circle of crust cut out of the bottom of the panettone. Use a very sharp, serrated knife to remove just the outer crust of the top of the panettone, leaving the layer of crumb exposed. Wrap the panettone in foil and freeze for several hours, overnight or 1–2 days.

Shortly before serving, beat the remaining, chilled cream stiffly with a little icing sugar, unwrap the panettone and spread the cream all over the surface. Return to the freezer, uncovered, while you peel the oranges right down to the flesh with a very sharp serrated knife. Slice thinly into neat circles, discarding any seeds, and press on to the cream covering before it has completely frozen. Serve immediately.

TROUT, LOBSTER AND SOLE MENU

RAINBOW TROUT
MOUSSE

— • —

LOBSTER BISQUE

— • —

SOLE WITH SHELLFISH
AND CHAMPAGNE

— • —

ARTICHOKE HEARTS
MORNAY

— • —

CHESTNUT PANCAKES

*H*ere is a French menu that could be served as an exquisitely romantic dinner for two (you may wish to reduce the quantities given, although each dish is very light) or for any special occasion. This combination of freshwater fish and seafood offers an interesting variety of flavours and textures.

The subtle delicacy of the rainbow trout mousse is succeeded by the slightly fuller taste of a velvety bisque. Then comes Dover sole, served with an unusual artichoke accompaniment.

You can substitute almost any well-flavoured flatfish if sole is unavailable.

The Mornay sauce used for the artichokes has a well-defined flavour to set the fish off to perfection; it is named after the eldest son of its inventor, Joseph Voiron, a famous nineteenth-century French chef.

Pancakes are a perennial favourite, typically French and, in this version, utterly irresistible.

A Pouilly Fumé, Chablis or a good Chardonnay would go well with all three savoury courses; with the last course you could serve a dessert wine such as Muscat de Beaumes de Venise.

1	RAINBOW TROUT MOUSSE	p. 233
2	LOBSTER BISQUE	p. 160
3	SOLE WITH SHELLFISH AND CHAMPAGNE	p. 69
4	ARTICHOKE HEARTS MORNAY	p. 272

ARTICHOKE HEARTS MORNAY

Preparation and cooking time: 1 hour

Very easy

Vegetable accompaniment

8 frozen artichoke hearts

3 oz (80 g) butter

1–2 cloves garlic (optional)

2 tbsp plain flour

18 fl oz (500 ml) hot milk

3¹/₂ fl oz (100 ml) cream

2 egg yolks

2 oz (50 g) finely grated Gruyère cheese

3 oz (80 g) freshly grated Parmesan cheese

salt

Thaw the frozen artichoke hearts at room temperature. Melt 1 oz (25 g) of the butter and add one whole, peeled garlic clove (if used) and the artichoke hearts. Cook over a very low heat for 10 minutes, turning the artichoke hearts 2 or 3 times. Season with salt and freshly ground pepper and set aside. Melt 1¹/₂ oz (40 g) butter. In another pan, stir in the flour and cook briefly; draw aside from the heat and beat in the hot milk. Cook over a moderate heat for 10 minutes, stirring constantly. Add salt, remove from the heat and stir in all the Gruyère cheese and half the Parmesan. Continue stirring until the cheese has completely melted.

Cut the artichoke hearts in half if they are still whole and place in a buttered gratin dish, cover with the sauce, sprinkle with the remaining grated Parmesan cheese and place in the oven, preheated to 375°F (180°C) mark 4, for 15–20 minutes or until the sauce has browned on the surface.

CHESTNUT PANCAKES

Preparation and cooking time: 1 hour

Fairly easy

Dessert

2 eggs

2 tbsp plain flour

icing sugar

1¹/₂ oz (40 g) butter

7 oz (200 g) tinned sweetened chestnut purée

1 tsp vanilla essence

18 fl oz (500 g) whipping cream

salt

Break the eggs into a mixing bowl, beat with 1 tbsp icing sugar and a small pinch of salt. Gradually work the milk into the flour in a separate bowl, pour into the bowl containing the eggs and beat briefly.

Melt just enough butter to thinly coat the inside of a 6-in (15-cm) non-stick frying pan and when hot but not smoking, pour in about 2 tbsp of the batter; immediately tilt the pan to make the batter cover the bottom of the pan thinly. Cook for about 50 seconds over a moderately high heat, then turn and cook for approximately 30 seconds on the other side. Stack the pancakes as you cook them. Leave to cool.

Beat the cream until stiff and fold into the chestnut purée. Add the vanilla and blend in. Spread 1–2 tbsp of this mixture over the surface of each pancake, fold in half and then in half again (see illustration); sprinkle with sieved icing sugar, place on a heatproof plate under a hot grill briefly to caramelise. Serve at once. A little brandy or rum can be heated, poured over the pancakes and flamed.

Chestnut pancakes

273

OYSTER AND CHAMPAGNE MENU

OYSTERS WITH
CHAMPAGNE

— • —

CRAWFISH AND DILL
VOL-AU-VENTS

— • —

BAKED BREAM
WITH ORANGES

— • —

DEMI-DEUIL SALAD

— • —

FLAMBÉED
STRAWBERRIES WITH
PINK PEPPERCORNS

When it comes to planning a grand dinner party it is sometimes difficult to be original without making the meal too elaborate and fussy. Choosing various types of fish and seafood for the first three courses will provide an interesting variation and talking point and, given the inherent lightness of these dishes, there is less danger of your guests' appetites being blunted before the last course. Obviously this menu is only advisable if you have access to a reliable source of extremely fresh molluscs, crustaceans and fish.

This is a meal to be eaten at a leisurely pace so that all the rich yet subtle flavours and aromas can be savoured to the full. The alliance of the humble potato with black truffles is the gourmet's equivalent of casual chic and something your guests will no doubt want to copy once you have introduced them to the experience. The name of this sophisticated salad, demi-deuil, means 'half-mourning', and is derived from the black and white colour combination.

Pepper with strawberries may seem an unlikely marriage, but it is one of ancient origin. This is an adventurous but delicious dessert.

A good dry champagne will set off each course to perfection; you may choose to substitute an excellent, though less expensive, sparkling dry white wine instead.

DEMI-DEUIL SALAD

Preparation and cooking time: 1 hour

Very easy

Vegetable accompaniment

1 lb 10 oz (875 g) waxy potatoes

1 black truffle

1 tsp mild French mustard

1 tsp white wine vinegar

3 tbsp extra-virgin olive oil

2 tbsp single cream

salt

Wash the potatoes well and boil in their skins until tender. Leave to cool, then peel, dice and place in a salad bowl. Brush the truffle and slice very thinly (small tins of truffle peelings are also available and cost less than whole truffles; drain before use). Cut these slices into slivers and mix with the potato. Mix the mustard thoroughly with the vinegar, then beat in the oil, a pinch of salt and the cream. Pour this dressing over the salad and mix carefully.

FLAMBÉED STRAWBERRIES WITH PINK PEPPERCORNS

Preparation time: 20 minutes

Very easy

Dessert

14 oz (400 g) wild strawberries

good white wine

1 oz (25 g) unsalted butter

2 tbsp sugar

2 juicy oranges

¹/₂ tbsp pink peppercorns

2 fl oz (50 ml) Grand Marnier

2 fl oz (50 ml) brandy

14 oz (400 g) home-made or best-quality commercial vanilla ice cream

Place the strawberries in a bowl, pour about 8 fl oz (225 ml) white wine over them, stir very gently, and then drain off all the wine. This is a good way of cleaning the strawberries and at the same time enhancing their flavour. Heat the butter gently with the sugar in a non-metallic saucepan until the sugar has dissolved. Pour in the juice of the 2 oranges and add the pink peppercorns.

Stir briefly and gently and add the strawberries. Mix just sufficiently to coat all the strawberries with liquid and heat them without cooking at all. Heat the Grand Marnier and the brandy together in a separate, small saucepan, pour over the strawberries and flame. When the flames have died down, transfer to small plates, place a small scoop of ice cream on each plate and spoon the strawberries and liquid over the ice cream. Serve at once.

Flambéed strawberries with pink peppercorns

PAELLA AND SANGRIA MENU

PRAWN TORTILLAS

—— • ——

PAELLA

—— • ——

CATALAN ZARZUELA

—— • ——

LEMON CREAM ROLL

—— • ——

SANGRIA

The regions of Spain have kept their very distinctive culinary traditions largely intact over the centuries. These vary as widely as the Spanish countryside does, from the lush grazing pastures of the Basque country in the north, over high mountainous regions, to the hotter, drier lands in the centre and south.

One thing is certain: wherever you go in Spain you will be able to eat remarkably good, fresh fish and seafood, particularly crustaceans as the Spaniards have a passion for these: refrigerated lorries thunder down the roads towards the capital, Madrid, in an attempt to meet the inhabitants' insatiable demand for prawns, lobster, crab and many other, lesser-known seafoods. The prawn tortillas with which we start our menu reflect this enduring taste.

Such wide knowledge and love of fish has led to the creation of many excellent Spanish fish dishes, among them the various versions of paella, of which the most famous comes from Valencia in eastern Spain and which, for the best results, should be cooked in a very large, two-handled cast iron pan known as a paellera.

Substantial fish soups and casseroles also abound in Spanish cuisine, rich in a variety of complementary ingredients, like the aptly named zarzuela (the word means operetta), a triumphant chorus of flavours from the sea. As with paella, there are many recipes for fish soups and casseroles, each region favouring its own version, for which a selection is made from the large catches of fish made all round Spain's long coastline, washed by the Atlantic ocean and the Mediterranean sea.

In keeping with Spanish custom, you could offer your guests a glass of slightly chilled dry sherry just before the meal which will stimulate the taste buds and the appetite. With the meal serve the typical sangria.

LEMON CREAM ROLL

Preparation and cooking time: 1 hour

Easy

Dessert

5 eggs

4 oz (125 g) caster sugar

1 tbsp finely grated lemon rind

4¹/₂ oz (140 g) plain flour

butter

18 fl oz (500 ml) whipping cream, chilled

2 tbsp icing sugar

Separate the eggs; beat the yolks with the sugar in a bowl until very pale and creamy; a ribbon of mixture should fall from the beater or balloon whisk when it is lifted above the bowl. Stir in the lemon peel. Beat the egg whites very stiffly and, using a mixing spatula, fold gently but thoroughly into the egg mixture. Fold in 4 oz (125 g) of the flour.

Lemon cream roll

Grease a Swiss roll tin with butter and line it with a lightly greased sheet of greaseproof paper dusted with flour. Pour the egg and lemon mixture into the tin, smoothing the surface evenly over the paper. Bake in a preheated oven at 375°F (180°C) mark 4 for 10–15 minutes until golden. Cover with a damp, wrung-out cloth and leave to cool in the tin on a wire rack.

When cold, turn out carefully on to a dry, clean cloth and peel off the greaseproof paper, taking care not to damage the sponge. Beat the cream stiffly with 2 tbsp icing sugar and spread thickly and evenly over the surface of the roll. Using the cloth underneath it to help you, roll up the cream roll. Serve slightly chilled, with a light dusting of sifted icing sugar.

SANGRIA

Preparation time: 20 minutes + 2 hours standing and chilling time

Very easy

Beverage

3 large ripe peaches

2 oz (50 g) sugar

2 fl oz (50 ml) brandy

2³/₄ pints (1.6 litres) light, dry Spanish red wine

1 vanilla pod

nutmeg

1 lemon

sparkling mineral water or soda water

Peel and stone the peaches, slice thinly, and place in a very large punch bowl or decorative non-metallic bowl. Sprinkle in the sugar and brandy and leave to stand for 2 hours.

Pour the wine into a bowl or very large jug, add the vanilla bean, a small pinch of freshly grated nutmeg and the whole rind (without any white pith attached) of 1 lemon, cut in one spiral piece. Leave to stand for 2 hours, then strain into the bowl containing the peaches. Chill for 1 hour, then add chilled sparkling mineral water to taste.

SALT COD MENU

PORTUGUESE
SEAFOOD SALAD

— • —

PORTUGUESE SALT
COD SOUP

— • —

SALT COD FRITTERS

— • —

SALT COD WITH
PEPPERS

— • —

ICED PORT MOUSSE

*W*ith no part of Portugal being very far from the sea, its seafaring people inevitably eat a great deal of fish. They are particularly partial to dishes made with dried salt cod and any Portuguese cook worthy of the name is reputed to know as many different ways of cooking and preparing salt cod as there are days of the year.

Portuguese cooking tends to be at once homely and sophisticated, a marriage of flavours and textures that skilfully sets good basic ingredients off to best advantage.

All three dishes in this menu are fairly substantial so you will probably choose to serve just one or at most two of the salt cod dishes at one meal: starting with the Portuguese seafood salad of squid and sardines, the main course could be the salt cod and red pepper casserole (reflecting the Portuguese fondness for the combination of peppers and fish); the salt cod fritters and salt cod soup would make another hearty Portuguese meal.

You may need to hunt around a little before finding dried salt cod but it is usually available to order from good fishmongers.

For the last course, a delectable dessert made with Portugal's most famous product: port.

ICED PORT MOUSSE

Preparation time: 1¹/₂ hours + 6 hours freezing time

Very easy

Dessert

2 eggs

3 oz (80 g) caster sugar

9 fl oz (250 ml) full-cream milk

few drops pure vanilla essence

12 fl oz (350 ml) whipping cream

1 rectangular 8-oz (250-g) sponge cake

5 fl oz (150 ml) ruby port

3 oz (80 g) sifted cocoa powder

Beat the egg yolks with the sugar in a heatproof mixing bowl until they are pale and frothy; the mixture should form a ribbon as it drops from the whisk when this is lifted over the bowl. Sift in the flour and fold in; stir in the milk and vanilla. Place the bowl over hot water over an extremely low heat and cook the mixture gently, stirring, until it thickens. Place the bowl in a second bowl containing cold or iced water and continue stirring until the mixture has cooled completely.

Beat the chilled cream stiffly and fold into the cold mixture. Slice the sponge cake into three rectangular layers which will neatly fit into a rectangular cake tin. Line the mould with foil, place one layer of sponge in the bottom and sprinkle with one third (just under 2 fl oz [50 ml]) of the port. Cover with one third of the cream mousse mixture, tapping the bottom of the mould on the work surface to release any trapped air and smoothing level. Repeat the layering process with the sponge, port and cream (using one third of the original quantity), then cover with the third and final sponge layer sprinkled with the remaining port. Refrigerate the remaining cream mixture.

Cover with a sheet of foil, place a weight on top and freeze for at least 6 hours.

Just before serving, unmould, and remove the foil. Stir two thirds of the cocoa powder into the reserved cream and spread quickly over the exposed surfaces of the iced mousse. Place the remaining chocolate powder in a very fine mesh sieve and sift all over the surface of the dessert. Serve.

Iced port mousse

285

SALMON MENU

SMOKED SALMON IN
ASPIC

———— • ————

SALMON TARTARE

———— • ————

SALMON COULIBIAC

———— • ————

CRISP WINTER SALAD

———— • ————

ORANGE SORBET

287

*S*ome of the best salmon in the world comes from British rivers, and the wild salmon fished in Scotland are the best of all. These astonishingly acrobatic, saltwater and freshwater fish leap amazingly high to 'climb' upriver from the sea, overcoming obstacles such as small waterfalls and cascades when the time comes to return to their birthplace to spawn.

Scottish smoked salmon is unmistakably delicate in flavour and is paler and more moist and tender than smoked salmon from other parts of the world; another characteristic of the Scottish product is the presence of well defined paler layers or lines of healthy, unsaturated fat which are revealed when the 'side' of smoked salmon is sliced. You may choose to use Pacific or Scandinavian smoked salmon (both very good) for the aspic and save the Scottish product for a simpler treatment, such as sliced and eaten with brown bread and butter, in order to enjoy it at its best.

The tartare of salmon is extremely simple and quick to make; use only the freshest salmon for this recipe. The other, main-course salmon recipe, salmon coulibiac, is rather more time-consuming but well worth the effort: here again fresh wild salmon is best of all but fresh or frozen farmed salmon will also be delicious. The winter salad is delightfully crisp and provides a good contrast for the salmon texture.

The rich colour of the blood orange sorbet echoes the magnificent warm colour of raw salmon and makes a refreshing conclusion to the meal.

CRISP WINTER SALAD

Preparation: 30 minutes

Very easy

Vegetable accompaniment

3 carrots

1 celeriac root

5 fl oz (150 ml) mayonnaise

1 tsp mustard powder

2 tbsp single cream

salt

Peel the carrot and the celeriac root and cut into julienne strips. Mix well with a pinch of salt. Blend the mustard with the cream and stir into the mayonnaise, mix the shredded vegetables with this dressing and transfer to a glass or crystal salad bowl.

ORANGE SORBET

Preparation and cooking time: 40 minutes + standing and freezing time

Very easy

Dessert

6 large blood oranges

9 oz (250 g) caster sugar

3 tbsp Grand Marnier or Curaçao

candied orange peel

Cut the tops off 4 oranges, just sufficiently low down to make it easy to scoop out the flesh. Keep the skins intact if you wish to use them as containers for the sorbet. Use a cannelling knife or potato peeler to cut the rind (leave behind all the white pith as it is bitter) from the 2 remaining oranges; if you have used a potato peeler, cut the rind into short, thin julienne strips. Squeeze juice

Orange sorbet

from these 2 oranges and strain into a bowl. Press all the flesh from the other 4 oranges through a sieve into the same bowl.

Heat the sugar and 8 fl oz (225 ml) water in a small saucepan and cook, stirring, over a moderate heat until distinct bubbles form on the surface of this sugar syrup. Add the orange peel, remove from the heat and leave the syrup to stand for 2 hours.

Stir the orange liqueur into the juice; strain the flavoured sugar syrup into the juice. Stir well and pour into an icecream maker. Freeze and stir following the usual process. If you do not have an icecream maker, pour the sorbet mixture into a shallow bowl and freeze until mushy; beat thoroughly to break up the ice crystals, return to the freezer, removing and beating twice more as the mixture thickens. Fill the empty oranges with the sorbet. Freeze for 2 hours. Decorate with strips of candied orange rind just before serving.

289

TURBOT AND STOCKFISH MENU

SMOKED SALMON
NORWEGIAN STYLE

— • —

TURBOT IN SHRIMP
SAUCE

— • —

STOCKFISH BERGEN
STYLE

— • —

CAULIFLOWER
BELLEVUE

— • —

RASPBERRY MOUSSE

The Atlantic and the North Sea have always teemed with vast shoals of cod, herring and haddock, the cold, plankton-rich waters helping to produce splendid specimens with a wonderful flavour. One can still see cod hanging up to dry, rather like washing, in small fishing ports hidden away in the deep Norwegian fjords. Other superb fish are also landed in good quantities: turbot and sole and, of course, salmon, which the Scandinavians treat with the respect it deserves, preparing it in all sorts of ways, of which gravad lax is perhaps the most internationally famous. In contrast with the plentiful supplies of fish, there is a small choice of vegetables, there being only a comparatively short growing season for all but root vegetables. Scandinavians make the most of the very long days of their short summer, however, and can grow a range of vegetables, increasingly supplemented by imported foreign produce all the year round. We have chosen home-grown produce for the vegetable accompaniment suggested here. In the beautiful woods and countryside grow plentiful wild berries, mushrooms and many other delicacies; we have chosen raspberries for a feather-light dessert, but Scandinavians also enjoy creamy rice or tapioca puddings, stewed dried fruit with pouring cream and other sweet things high in calories to provide plenty of warmth and energy during the long, cold winters.

1	CAULIFLOWER BELLEVUE p.293
2	TURBOT IN SHRIMP SAUCE p.132
3	SMOKED SALMON NORWEGIAN STYLE p.235
4	STOCKFISH BERGEN STYLE p.121

CAULIFLOWER BELLEVUE

Preparation and cooking time: 50 minutes

Very easy

Vegetable accompaniment

1 cauliflower weighing 1³/₄ lb (750 g)

1 lb (500 g) spinach

3 carrots

1 clove garlic

2 oz (50 g) butter

salt

Trim off all the green leaves and most of the stalk from the cauliflower, keeping it whole; make a deep cross-shaped cut into the stalk and steam the cauliflower until tender (about 30 minutes), sprinkling it with a little salt. While the cauliflower is cooking, wash the spinach and cook with only the water left clinging to the leaves and a little salt, for 10 minutes. Drain well and squeeze out all the water; chop coarsely and sauté in 1 oz (25 g) melted butter and the peeled clove of garlic until all the moisture has evaporated. Peel the carrots, chop into thin round slices, and steam until tender (approx. 15–20 minutes); sauté in 1 oz (25 g) butter.

When all the vegetables are cooked, place the cauliflower in the centre of a warmed serving dish and surround with the spinach and the carrots. Serve at once.

RASPBERRY MOUSSE

Preparation time: 30 minutes + 2 hours chilling time

Very easy

Dessert

1¹/₄ lb (600 g) fresh raspberries

3¹/₂ oz (100 g) caster sugar

1 lemon

2 tbsp raspberry-flavoured aquavit or brandy

1 egg white

5 fl oz (150 ml) whipping cream

sponge fingers or langue de chat biscuits

Rinse the raspberries very briefly; reserve one third for decoration and process the rest in a blender with the sugar, lemon juice and aquavit or brandy until very smooth. Pour into a bowl; fold in the very stiffly beaten egg white, followed by the stiffly beaten cream, combining the ingredients gently but thoroughly.

Fill small glass bowls with this mixture and decorate with the reserved raspberries. Chill in the refrigerator for 2 hours and serve with the biscuits.

Raspberry mousse

SPICED FISH MENU

SPICED HAKE INDIAN
STYLE

— • —

SPICED SOLE DELHI
STYLE

— • —

MUSSELS WITH
GINGER

— • —

INDIAN SIDE SALAD

— • —

EXOTIC FRUIT SALAD
ON ICE

*I*n India the ancient art of flavouring and colouring food has been developed to perfection. Fresh spices, chosen with care and used with discretion, enhance rather than overpower really fresh fish. Turmeric and saffron, for example, give fish wonderful warm colours, the former more vivid than the delicate hue of saffron which also adds to the flavour; ginger and various types of pepper also make very frequent appearances in Indian cooking, together with a wide variety of other spices.

India's coastline is 2,500 miles long and coastal communities rely heavily on fishing for their sustenance and income.

The most widely known fish species which we have in common with India (although they are not always identical) are sole, cod, hake, mackerel, mussels, and prawns varying from tiny specimens to enormous ones which look like lobsters. The spectrum of Indian cookery is infinitely varied, from the subtle and delicate flavours of the north to the full, often extremely fiery hot curries of the far south. Fish is often but not always served with Basmati rice; grown in the foothills of the Himalayas, this is the finest rice, with a delicate aroma, which is served plain, boiled or coloured with turmeric and flavoured with bay leaf and cardamom seeds. Vegetables figure prominently on Indian menus (many Indians are vegetarian) and the side salad we have chosen here refreshes the palate and contrasts with the spicy flavours.

Indian desserts are often wickedly sweet: here we have an echo of the wonderful fruits available in India, adapted for more temperate climates and a fitting end to a spicy meal.

INDIAN SIDE SALAD

Preparation time: 10 minutes
Very easy
Vegetable accompaniment
10 oz (300 g) firm ripe tomatoes
1 mild onion
1 lemon
1/2 green chilli pepper (optional)
3 tbsp chopped coriander leaves
salt and pepper

Blanch and peel the tomatoes, and slice. Peel the onions and slice into wafer-thin rings. Arrange these in a bowl or dish and sprinkle with a little lemon juice, the chilli pepper finely sliced into rings (if used), and the coriander leaves. Sprinkle with a little salt and, if you have not used the chilli pepper, a little freshly ground pepper. Serve.

EXOTIC FRUIT SALAD ON ICE

Preparation time: 20 minutes
Very easy
Dessert
3 kiwi fruit
12 tinned lychees, drained
5 oz (150 g) peeled mandarin segments (fresh or tinned)
1/2 ripe melon
7 oz (200 g) fresh or tinned cherries, stoned
7 oz (200 g) small strawberries
sherry
caster sugar
crushed or chopped ice

Slice the kiwi fruit in half and scoop the flesh out with the smaller end of a melon baller (or cut into small pieces). Use the large end of the melon baller to scoop out balls of melon flesh (remove and discard the seeds and threads first). Drain the cherries thoroughly if tinned and hull the strawberries. Place plenty of coarsely crushed or chopped ice in a crystal bowl; arrange the fruit in layers on top of it, contrasting the colours. Place a very small bowl of sherry, a small dish of caster sugar and wooden skewers or a fork by each person's table setting; each piece of fruit is speared, dipped in the sherry and then in the sugar.

Exotic fruit salad on ice

297

PRAWN MENU

PRAWN BEIGNETS

———— • ————

DUMPLINGS WITH PRAWN
FILLING

———— • ————

CURRIED PRAWNS

———— • ————

CANTONESE RICE

———— • ————

EIGHT-TREASURE RICE
PUDDING

*C*hinese cooking, perhaps the oldest of the world's cuisines, is extremely varied and sophisticated. The imaginative refinement and resourcefulness of Chinese cooks led them to turn raw materials that Westerners had never dreamt of eating into imaginative and exquisite dishes.

With so many imported eastern foods now readily available, it is easy to invite friends and family to enjoy a Chinese meal (complete with chopsticks for those who can use them) at home. The four fish dishes we have chosen here highlight how crustaceans can be transformed by different treatments; the contrast between crisp, light and crunchy deep-fried beignets and the tender, delicate steamed dumplings underlines this.

You may choose to add a dish of stir-fried mixed vegetables to the menu, cooked for such a short time at high heat that they are still crisp and full of goodness. In our predominantly Cantonese menu the main course consists of large prawns in a very light curry sauce. But to talk of courses is, to a certain extent, inappropriate when it comes to a Chinese meal: these dishes can all be placed on the table at the same time and you need not wait to try the rice pudding until last. A typical Chinese meal would end with a savoury clear broth or soup, not with something sweet.

CANTONESE RICE

Preparation and cooking time: 30 minutes

Very easy

Side dish

10 oz (280 g) long-grain rice

5 oz (150 g) frozen peas

2 thick slices ham

2 eggs

sunflower oil

salt and pepper

Place the rice in a heavy-bottomed saucepan; pour in sufficient cold water to come approx. ³/₄ in (2 cm) above the level of the rice. Bring to the boil, turn the heat down very low, cover tightly and cook gently for 20 minutes or until the rice has absorbed all the liquid.

Cut the ham into tiny dice. Beat the eggs with a pinch of salt. Heat 1 tbsp sunflower oil in an omelette pan and use half the eggs to make a thin firmly set omelette. Repeat with fresh oil, using the remaining beaten egg mixture. Cut these omelettes into thin strips or small pieces.

Sauté the thawed peas for a few minutes in a little oil in a very large pan; reduce the heat to very low, add the rice and ham, stir for a few minutes, then add the omelette pieces. Mix gently and serve.

Eight-Treasure rice pudding

EIGHT-TREASURE RICE PUDDING

Preparation and cooking time: 1 hour + 2 days soaking time for the rice

Fairly easy

Dessert

1¹/₂ oz (40 g) lard

12 glacé cherries

1 oz (25 g) candied citron peel

12 walnut halves

12 blanched peeled almonds

2 cups pudding rice, soaked in cold water for 2 days

4 tbsp caster sugar

4 oz (125 g) raspberry jam

12 dates, stoned

Grease a ring mould or fluted cake mould very generously with the lard. Cut the cherries in half; finely slice the candied citron. Break each walnut half carefully in two. Arrange the walnuts and cherries on the inside of the mould, well away from the top (i.e. rim) of the mould and make them stick to the lard. Refrigerate for 2 hours.

Drain the presoaked rice well and place in a large saucepan; add sufficient cold water to just cover, bring to the boil, cover tightly and cook very gently until the rice has absorbed all the water and is very tender. Stir in the caster sugar thoroughly and leave to cool.

Press half the rice gently but firmly against the sides of the mould as a lining (do not dislodge the cherries and walnuts). Spoon the jam evenly all the way round the rice and cover with the remaining rice. Press the dates into the rice, positioning them as close as possible to the outside rim. Pack the rice firmly back in place. Place in a roasting tin filled with sufficient hot water to come half way up the sides of the mould. Cook for 1 hour in the oven, preheated to 350°F (180°C) mark 4. Remove from the oven; place a heated plate upside down on top of the mould, and turn the right way up, releasing the rice ring very carefully on to the plate. Serve hot.

RAW FISH MENU

*T*he Japanese are particularly fond of raw fish. It must be extremely fresh and is often bought live at the market and killed at home; it is then cleaned, filleted and prepared with great skill and artistry into a great variety of dishes. It will come as a surprise to those who have not tried raw fish before just how delicious it can be, especially when accompanied by the peppery, salty or piquant sauces at which the Japanese excel.

It is inadvisable to eat certain types of fish raw but those we have recommended here are suitable; all you need do is make sure they are very fresh.

1	TAKIAWASE	p. 304
2	TEMPURA	p. 168
3	SASHIMI	p. 67
4	SUNOMONO	p. 305
5	GOHAN	p. 304
6	USUZUKURI	p. 61
7	EBI SHIOYAKI	p. 179
8	SUSHI	p. 61

GOHAN

Preparation and cooking time: 25 minutes
Very easy
Side dish

2 cups short-grain Japanese rice

Place the rice in a sieve and rinse thoroughly under running cold water, then place in a non-stick saucepan with a tightly fitting lid and using the same cup you used to measure out the rice, add 2½ cups cold water. Bring slowly to the boil over a medium heat and boil gently for 2 minutes. Cover tightly, reduce the heat to very low and cook for 15–20 minutes or until the rice has absorbed all the water. Turn off the heat and leave to stand for 10 minutes, covered. Place in individual bowls and serve with sashimi (see page 67). Do not add any salt at all, during or after cooking.

TAKIAWASE

Preparation and cooking time: 40 minutes
Very easy
Vegetable accompaniment

2 potatoes

2 aubergines

14 oz (400 g) pumpkin flesh

2 large carrots

7 oz (200 g) tofu

sunflower oil

light soy sauce

Trim, peel and prepare all the vegetables. Cut into small pieces, the carrot and pumpkin preferably into decorative shapes.

Heat 2 tbsp sunflower oil in each of 4 separate pans; add one type of vegetable to each pan and fry gently, turning now and then, until the vegetables are tender but still slightly crisp. (Cooking times will vary for the different vegetables and depending on how thin you cut them.)

Cut the tofu into cubes and fry in another pan; add 2 tbsp to each pan and mix gently. Serve all the vegetables and tofu together.

AWAYUKI KAN

Preparation and cooking time: 1 hour + 1 hour chilling time

Very easy

Dessert

¹/₄ oz (5 g) agar agar powder

9 oz (250 g) caster sugar

2 eggs

9 oz (250 g) small strawberries, evenly sized

Stir the agar agar (a seaweed jelling agent available from health food shops) into 10 fl oz (300 ml) cold water in a saucepan and bring to the boil; add the caster sugar and continue cooking and stirring with a wooden spoon until the sugar has completely dissolved. Draw aside from the heat and leave to cool. Agar agar will set at cool room temperature; as soon as it shows signs of thickening and beginning to set, beat the egg

whites until white and fluffy (preferably in an electric beater with a large bowl) and then gradually add the agar agar as you continue beating until the mixture is very stiff. Rinse a fairly shallow rectangular mould or cake tin with cold water, fill almost to the top with the fluffy mixture and then push the hulled strawberries in, making an attractive design. (Stoned cherries or kiwi fruit slices can be used instead.) Serve cool but not chilled.

SUNOMONO

Preparation time: 5 minutes + 1 hour marinating time

Very easy

Vegetable accompaniment

1 cucumber

2 fairly thick slices ham

1 oz (25 g) fresh ginger

2 fl oz (50 ml) sambai zu *sauce*

salt

Rub the cucumber's skin all over with plenty of coarse salt to preserve the green colour which would otherwise alter when marinated. Slice off the two tips of the cucumber and cut it lengthwise in half and then in half again. Scoop the seed-bearing flesh out of each long, thin quarter and discard. Cut the quarters into even-sized matchstick pieces as neatly as possible. Cut the ham into the same shape and size. Mix gently but thoroughly with your fingers. Place in the refrigerator to chill for 1 hour.

Peel and grate the ginger very finely to form a juicy paste; mix this juice and paste with the *sambai zu* sauce and chill for 1 hour.

Just before serving, heap the cucumber and ham salad into mounds on individual plates and place a tiny bowl containing a little of the dressing to one side. Each person dresses their own portion at table.

OYSTER AND SCALLOP MENU

BAKED OYSTERS

— • —

CLAM CHOWDER

— • —

SCALLOPS IN CORAL
SAUCE

— • —

WALDORF SALAD

— • —

·CHERRIES JUBILEE·   307

The American love affair with fast food and high technology cooking has never been a total infatuation: millions of cooks have kept the traditions of excellent home cooking alive and flourishing, using an abundance of superb basic ingredients produced in vast quantities by their efficient farming, fishing and market gardening industries. Americans are able to draw on many national cooking traditions when it comes to fish, with recipes for species both from the sea and from their lakes and rivers.

For our first menu we have chosen traditional, favourite recipes which are easy to prepare.

The clam chowder and the dessert can both be largely prepared in advance and the early stages of preparation for the salad, scallop and oyster recipes can be completed several hours before you intend serving them.

WALDORF SALAD

Preparation and cooking time: 45 minutes

Very easy

Side dish/Vegetable accompaniment

1 crisp lettuce heart

4 oz (120 g) diced red apples

juice of 1 lemon

4 celery stalks

2 oz (50 g) chopped walnuts

4 fl oz (125 ml) mayonnaise

salt and pepper

If using red apples with a tender skin, do not peel, otherwise use any dessert apple and peel if wished. Once diced, sprinkle the apples with some of the lemon juice to prevent discoloration. Dice the celery.

Stir the remaining lemon juice into the mayonnaise. Mix the apple, celery and walnuts with the mayonnaise in a large bowl, adding a little salt and pepper to taste. Chill well. Separate the lettuce leaves and arrange in a salad bowl or platter; transfer the chilled Waldorf salad to this bowl and serve while still very cold.

CHERRIES JUBILEE

Preparation and cooking time: 20 minutes

Very easy

Dessert

1 lb (500 g) net weight tinned cherries

1 tbsp caster sugar

1¹/₂ tbsp cornflour

2 fl oz (50 ml) brandy

1 lb (500 g) vanilla ice cream

Chill ice cream coupes or plates in the freezer. Drain the cherries and pour the syrupy juice into a small saucepan. Stir the sugar and cornflour together (dry), then mix in a little of the cherry liquid and stir into the saucepan containing the rest of the juice. Cook over a moderate heat, stirring, until the juice thickens.

Add the cherries and heat through, stirring continuously. Heat the brandy, pour into the saucepan and flame. Stir well. Place 3 small scoops of ice cream in each of the chilled coupes or plates and spoon the hot cherries and sauce over them. Serve immediately.

Cherries Jubilee

CRAWFISH/ LOBSTER MENU

CRAWFISH COCKTAIL

———— • ————

RICE TIMBALES WITH
CRAWFISH SAUCE

———— • ————

LOBSTER THERMIDOR

———— • ————

CARAMELISED
CARROTS

———— • ————

FRUIT ICE CREAM MOULD

311

*L*obster is fished off the United States coastline from Maritime Provinces of Canada as far north as Belle Isle down to the coast of North Carolina and is most abundant in the waters of Maine, Nova Scotia and Newfoundland. Maine lobsters usually weigh in at anything from 1 to 5 lb (500 g–2.5 kg) but specimens have been known to weigh more than 40 lb (18 kg)! It is a myth that lobsters are more flavoursome when small; larger ones are just as delicious.

Fresh lobster barbecued and eaten in the open air must be one of life's keenest and simplest pleasures; lobster is equally irresistible when prepared in a slightly more elaborate fashion, as in these recipes.

The ice cream recipe we suggest here is delicious, quick to make and will provide a suitable dessert for this seafood meal.

CARAMELISED CARROTS

Preparation and cooking time: 1 hour

Very easy

Vegetable accompaniment

14 oz (400 g) baby carrots or young carrots

1¹/₂ oz (40 g) finely diced streaky bacon

3 tbsp mild clear honey

pinch cinnamon

salt

Cut the carrots into fairly thick rounds. Dissolve the honey in 3¹/₂ fl oz (100 ml) very hot water in a non-stick saucepan.

Add the bacon to the saucepan, followed by the carrots, cinnamon and a generous pinch of salt. Stir, cover tightly and cook over a low heat until the carrots are tender, stirring occasionally, and adding a little more hot water when necessary.

Serve very hot. Carrots prepared in this way are an excellent foil for lobster.

Fruit ice cream mould

FRUIT ICE CREAM MOULD

Preparation time: 35 minutes + freezing time

Very easy

Dessert

9 oz (250 g) cream cheese

9 fl oz (250 ml) soured cream

4 tbsp caster sugar

1 medium-sized tin diced mixed tropical fruit

1 medium-sized tin stoned cherries

2 slices tinned pineapple

2 or 3 fresh kiwi fruit

kirsch

The cream cheese should be at room temperature. Place the cheese in a mixing bowl and work with a fork until soft and fluffy. Add the soured cream and beat with a balloon whisk (or process in the food processor) until well blended, light and considerably increased in volume.

Drain the tinned fruit very thoroughly. Stir the tropical fruit into the cheese and sour cream mixture, followed by one third of the cherries, both pineapple slices cut into small pieces, and the peeled, thickly sliced and diced kiwi fruit. Fold in thoroughly. Rinse a ring mould with cold water or moisten the inside with kirsch or any liqueur of your choice. Fill with the mixture, smooth level and freeze for several hours. About 10 minutes before serving turn out on to a chilled serving plate. Place the remaining cherries in the central well just before serving.

·INDEX·

315